PERSONNEL POLICIES IN LARGE NONUNION COMPANIES

PERSONNEL POLICIES IN LARGE NONUNION COMPANIES

Fred K. Foulkes
Harvard University

Prentice-Hall, Inc., Englewood Cliffs, New Jersey 07632

Library of Congress Cataloging in Publication Data

Foulkes, Fred K
   Personnel policies in large nonunion companies.

   Bibliography: p.
   Includes index.
   1. Personnel management—United States.
1. Title.
Hf5549.2.U5F68   658.3'03   80-10695
ISBN 0-13-660308-4

To E. Robert Livernash

Editorial/production supervision and interior design: Marian Hartstein
Cover design: Edsal Enterprises
Manufacturing buyer: Gordon Osbourne

Printed in the United States of America

10 9 8 7 6 5 4 3

Prentice-Hall International, Inc., *London*
Prentice-Hall of Australia Pty. Limited, *Sydney*
Prentice-Hall of Canada, Ltd., *Toronto*
Prentice-Hall of India Private Limited, *New Delhi*
Prentice-Hall of Japan, Inc., *Tokyo*
Prentice-Hall of Southeast Asia Pte. Ltd., *Singapore*
Whitehall Books Limited, *Wellington, New Zealand*

Contents

PART FIVE   THE CONCLUSION

Preface

The objective of this book is to share with the reader the findings of an exploratory study that compared and contrasted the key personnel policies and practices of a select group of large, entirely or predominantly nonunion companies in the United States. This study has made it possible to construct a model or profile of the values, policies, and climates characterizing the sort of large corporation that will remain nonunion. In addition to providing better understandings and explanations of the policies of the companies studied, this study has suggested the beginnings of a theory of the effective management of human resources, which I believe will assist management in developing more effective employee relations approaches in nonunion as well as unionized companies. The book consists of five parts.

Part One, which includes five chapters, is entitled "Areas of Inquiry and General Characteristics." The purpose and methodology of the study are outlined in Chapter One. In examining the list of companies studied, one can raise a number of questions. For example, where are they located? Are they all rapid growth companies? When were they founded? Who owns them? A number of these environmental factors bear upon the consideration of remaining nonunion. They are discussed in the second chapter, "Environmental Factors in Remaining Nonunion."

While the focus of this study is on the key personnel policies and practices of the companies studied, what quickly becomes apparent, however, is that what is extremely important is the top management's philosophy or motivation behind those policies and practices. Therefore, Chapter Three focuses on "Top Management: Values and Goals." Chapter Four discusses the "perceived Advantages and Disadvantages of Being Nonunion." It is concerned with both the intended and the unintended results of the chosen companies' policies and practices.

The personnel department in each of the companies studied plays a critical role in formulating, implementing, and monitoring its company's personnel policies and practices. Chapter Five, the final chapter of Part One, is on "The Status and the Role of the Personnel Department."

The purpose of this study was not to write a text book, but rather to focus on key policies and practices. Part Two focuses on two critical ones: employment stability and promotion systems. One extremely important concern that emerged, in response to questions about the way layoffs are handled, concerns job security and employment stability. Indeed, several of the companies studied have never had a layoff. Chapter Six, accordingly, concerns "Employment Security." Promotion from within also turned out to be very important; Chapter Seven discusses "Promotion Systems."

One could not do a study such as this without looking at the financial aspect of the employment relationship in these companies. Therefore, Part Three, "Compensation and Benefits," is concerned with economics. Chapters Eight to Twelve discuss "Pay Policies and Their Administration," "Merit Pay Policies and Their Administration," "The Salaried Method of Payment," "Benefit Policies and Their Costs," and "Retirement, Bonus, Savings, and Stock-Purchase Plans."

Part Four focuses on the broad area of feedback mechanisms and formal communications programs. Chapter Thirteen concerns attitude surveys; Chapter Fourteen examines other communications techniques. The fifteenth chapter concerns "Grievance Procedures." Finally, the last chapter is the conclusion.

Fred K. Foulkes

Cambridge, Massachusetts

Acknowledgments

"No man is an island," especially if engaged in a field survey involving many people and organizations. I am the grateful beneficiary of the fine cooperation on the part of twenty-six companies and several hundred executives, managers, supervisors, and employees. In addition to responding to questions in personal interviews, over the telephone, and by mail, one or more representatives at each company reviewed this manuscript in draft form. Although time-consuming, this review process, explained in the introductory chapter, added immeasurably to the development of this study.

But for their number and the fact that they must remain anonymous, I would thank each company person by name for his or her cooperation, patience, understanding and support. I am very appreciative of their willingness to share their knowledge and experience with me. Obviously, without their cooperation, this book would not have been possible.

I am also appreciative of the help and advice I have received from so many of my academic colleagues at Harvard and elsewhere, as well as from several business executives.

Among those at Harvard who have read the manuscript, either in its entirety or several chapters in draft form, and have made helpful comments, are: Professors Kenneth R. Andrews, Chris Argyris, Alfred D. Chandler, John T. Dunlop, James J. Healy, M. Thomas Kennedy, George C. Lodge, George F. F. Lombard, E. Robert Livernash, D. Quinn Mills, Wickham Skinner, and Richard Vancil. I am especially appreciative of the comments and suggestions of Professors Andrews and Healy. I am also particularly grateful for the suggestions and wise counsel of Professor Livernash, the man to whom the book is dedicated: my teacher and good friend for more than a dozen years.

Academic colleagues from other institutions whose comments on the first draft have also been very helpful include Professor W. Clay Hamner of the Graduate School of Business Administration at Duke University, Professor Robert B. McKersie, former dean of the Cornell School of Industrial and Labor Relations, Professor Weldon J. Moffitt of the College of Business at Brigham Young University, Professor Charles A. Myers, Director of the Industrial Relations Center at the Sloan School of Management at the Massachusetts Institute of Technology; and Dr. Henry Morgan of the Boston University School of Management; and Professor James Portwood of Temple University's School of Business Administration. Bert L. Metzger, President and Secretary of the Profit Sharing Research Foundation, made several useful suggestions with regard to Chapter Twelve, as did Professor Jack Stieber, Director of the School of Labor and Industrial Relations at Michigan State University, with respect to Chapter Fifteen.

Many others have also been very helpful. Maddy Pfau and John Fitzgerald, former MBA students, did field research reports from which I have benefited. They each visited one of the cooperating companies. Scott Hutchinson of the *Harvard Business Review* edited the first draft. Gay Quimby Auerbach typed several revised chapters and also made many helpful editorial suggestions; other secretaries who worked on this project, from initial company field notes to revised drafts, include Susan LaMar, Janell Tyson, Sue Kimmins, Cathi O'Hara, and Carmen Vaubel. I am most appreciative of their fine work and cheerful attitudes.

I am also indebted to several authors, and their publishers, whose work I am unable to cite in footnotes in the text. This is because such citations would reveal the identities of the cooperating companies, something I had promised not to do. I am of course also grateful to Harvard Business School and its Division of Research for not only providing the financial support for this study, but for giving me the time to do it. Professor Richard Walton, the Director of Research when this project commenced, was particularly helpful with respect to several design questions and field work procedures. Dean John McArthur, former Dean Lawrence E. Fouraker, and Professor and former Associate Dean Walter Salmon have been sources of support and wise counsel.

I of course take responsibility for the final product, including its shortcomings.

Fred K. Foulkes

Cambridge, Massachusetts

PART ONE

Areas of Inquiry and General Characteristics

CHAPTER ONE

Introduction

In the United States, the growth of the labor movement has not kept pace with the growth of the labor force. While union membership as a percent of employees in nonagricultural establishments increased from 12 percent in 1930 to 35 percent in 1945, between 1955 and 1978 it declined from approximately one-third to 24 percent. (If employee association membership is included, the figure is about 27 percent.)

Despite organized labor's percentage decline, an examination of large U.S. industrial corporations shows that the vast majority are unionized. However, a relatively small but impressive number of large corporations are *entirely non-union*; that is, there is no union representation within the United States, or the amount of union representation is so negligible, with respect to its impact on the personnel policies and practices being studied, that it is of little or no consequence. For example, one company I referred to as an entirely nonunion company has three employees at its main plant who belong to a union. Although some of the other entirely nonunion companies have acquired unionized companies in different industries, the acquired companies are operated independently and are not part of this study.

A much larger number of companies in the United States are predominantly nonunion. By *predominantly nonunion,* I mean a company in which the majority of the production and maintenance employees in the United States are nonunion. The latter category may have come about in one of two different ways. The first way is that the company may have kept all or most of its new plants nonunion for so long that the new plants and their employees outnumber the old plants and their employees. There is also the possibility of decertification elections in the old plants. The second way the predominantly nonunion company comes into being is through the acquisition by nonunion organizations of large companies that either are or have become unionized. Unlike those entirely nonunion companies, which may have a very small number of employees organized without any significant effect on the company's personnel policies and practices, the organized employees of the predominantly nonunion companies do influence the company's personnel policies and practices with respect to the nonunion segment of their businesses.

Examples of the first type—the entirely nonunion large company—are relatively rare. One study found that approximately 5 percent of the *Fortune 500* companies are entirely nonunion.[1] When I informed the administrative vice-president of one of the companies that I was visiting twenty-six nonunion U.S. employers, he said, "Gee, I didn't realize that there were that many of us." Examples of the second type of company—the predominantly nonunion large company—are more common. While there are many companies such as Chrysler and U.S. Steel that are almost entirely organized, there are many large, national companies in the United States that are predominantly nonunion.

There have been numerous studies of labor management relations and collective bargaining in the United States. The impact of collective bargaining on management has been well-researched.[2] The large company nonunion segment, however, represents a significant component of the total picture. The large, entirely or predominantly nonunion companies that are the subject of this study represent a group of important companies that has received little prior attention. It is important to better understand the personnel policies and practices of these companies, as well as the status and influence of their personnel departments. This group of companies represents an important vehicle for gaining a better understanding not only of the modern management of human resources, but also, possibly, the indirect impact of the institution of collective bargaining on the nonunion company.

THE STUDY

In the tradition and spirit of the work of Sumner H. Slichter, James J. Healy, and E. Robert Livernash, this is an exploratory field study of the personnel policies and practices of over two dozen large companies that are either

---

[1]Michael R. Bruce and David W. Hunt, "Communications in Non-Union Companies" (unpublished Master's thesis, Massachusetts Institute of Technology's Sloan School of Management, May 1976), chap. 1.

[2]Sumner H. Slichter, James J. Healy, and E. Robert Livernash, *The Impact of Collective Bargaining on Management* (Washington, D.C.: The Brookings Institution, 1960).

entirely or predominantly nonunion. While my sample primarily contains entirely nonunion companies, it does contain both types. Some predominantly nonunion companies were included in the sample for purposes of contrast and comparison

The principal purpose of the study was to ascertain what the personnel policies and practices of large, nonunion companies have in common. I wanted to identify and analyze the various personnel approaches of these different companies. I also wanted to study the different elements of their personnel–employee relations policies and programs to determine similarities and differences. One way to determine what is critical is to look for important commonalities.

Accordingly, the purpose of this study is not to provide a manual on how to stay nonunion, or a plan on how to win organizational campaigns. Instead, it is to explain and to help one understand the relationship between the personnel policies and practices used by the companies studied and their nonunion status.

I selected large companies for my study because I feel that it is decidedly difficult to maintain effective personnel policies when there are many organizational units and large numbers of employees. Also, large companies are more likely to be targets for union drives. The companies selected have stood the test of union organizational drives, in that when they have occurred the unions did not win.

In the small company too much can depend on the personality of the founder-president and his or her personal relationship with employees. Indeed, a significant finding is the impact the founders had on so many of the large companies studied. Kenneth R. Andrews borrowed from Emerson to say ". . . a corporation is essentially the lengthened shadow of a man."[3] My study contains much evidence to support this idea. What is particularly interesting is the manner and mechanisms by which the philosophy and the values of the company founders became institutionalized in today's large organizations.

Gaining Cooperation

Neither identifying the large nonunion companies to study, nor gaining access to them was particularly easy. I was unable to find any person or reference with the necessary information. At the time the idea for this study came about, there simply was no list of large nonunion companies.

While individual company personnel would cite a few other similar companies (for example, some were known through survey work in the pay and benefits area) they were often surprised to learn that another large company I would name was nonunion. In addition to generally not knowing each other, there is little comprehensive survey work of these companies going on in the area of

---

[3]Kenneth R. Andrews, *The Concept of Corporate Strategy* (Homewood, Ill.: Dow-Jones/ Richard D. Irwin, Inc., 1971).

personnel practices. A few companies, however, do keep track of one another. Executives interviewed from almost all the companies were therefore very interested in my study and in what I was learning.

By talking to people, by reading, and through correspondence, I subsequently developed my own list of large nonunion companies. I made contact with the selected companies in a variety of ways. Sometimes I used the name of the person who suggested contacting the company to gain access. Generally, I wrote a letter to the company's vice-president of personnel to arrange for an appointment. In some cases, however, I first contacted the company's president, chairman, or administrative vice-president, who often turned my request over to the personnel department.

Once I had fully explained the purpose of the study and the ground rules, I visited the chosen twenty-six companies to interview a number of executives in each one. All of the selected companies cooperated in the project. While company representatives were initially quite guarded with respect to the information they gave me, once I had visited the company and established the basis of the relationship, managers were quite open and frank.

A few companies, however, were understandably unwilling to respond to certain questions. For example, one executive would not reveal his company's employee benefits-to-payroll ratio other than to agree with my estimate that it was quite high. The personnel director of another company would only release the number of worldwide employees his organization had because, he said, the number of employees in the United States was considered confidential. Yet another company was unwilling to give me a copy of its personnel policies: An executive said that the company "only cooperates to a degree with other companies," and that it does not share its personnel policies with any outsiders.

I am sorry I can not name the cooperating companies. If I did so, most readers would be astonished. They are important companies. The names of most of them are household words. Each company was assured, however, that all of the information I gathered would be treated on a confidential basis; in fact, this was the basis of their cooperation. The names of each of the companies studied, therefore, must remain anonymous. With so many companies, especially with some disguised, it would be hard to identify particular companies in the different chapters.

I also gave a designated representative from each company the opportunity to review the entire manuscript. This review provision was part of my design for three reasons. First, it would enable the representative to check that my understanding of particular company facts and situations was correct. Second, the reviewer could make sure that the anonymity or disguise of the company, if it were a problem, was adequate. Finally, from previous experience I knew that I would gain additional insights and richer understandings from the comments of these knowledgeable readers; indeed, this turned out to be the case.

Both the anonymity and clearance aspects of this work were critical. A representative of one company, in reviewing some of my field notes, wrote:

*Enclosed is the original and a copy of your "field notes" with certain
revisions, primarily to be certain that [someone's] identity is fully masked.
You may think I'm being overly cautious but it could result in substantial
damage in either our labor or employee relations if we could be identified as
part of the study.*

METHODOLOGY

This field study utilizes the case study–interview approach. In
every case, I interviewed key members of corporate personnel, including the head
of the personnel department as well as members of his or her staff. I also
interviewed line managers, including chairmen and presidents, operating executives, and lower-level management people such as supervisors. I conducted
in-depth supervisory interviews at five companies.

On rare occasions, I likewise interviewed hourly workers. While executives
of two companies encouraged me to talk to many of their employees, most did not.
In addition, I had neither the time nor resources to interview an extensive number
of hourly people.

My purpose of interviewing a variety of people in both line management and
staff, and in upper- and lower management positions in each company, was to
learn about personnel policies and programs from a number of different points of
view. I wanted to have a reasonable personality mix, and to obtain different job
perspectives within each company. A personnel executive, for instance, might talk
of the importance of the company's training efforts, whereas a line manager might
not consider it of equal importance.

In addition, I also interviewed management consultants, trade association
executives, business professors, union leaders, community leaders, and people in
other companies to gain additional perspectives on the companies visited. In total,
I interviewed over 500 people for this study, with approximately 100 of the
interviews with first- and second-line managers.

As has been stated, this field study was exploratory in nature. I was trying to
gain an overview, and to learn what was going on and why. I spent more time with
some companies than with others, and I am not equally knowledgeable about the
approaches of each company. Some companies were revisited several times;
others were not. I contacted some other companies simply to find out about
specific programs and policies. The number of companies I selected was also a
reasonable total to visit in an academic term, although after about fifteen company
visits additional different basic patterns failed to emerge. As is normal in such
work, subsequent company visits revealed that the point of diminishing returns
had been reached. While the additional visits provided more examples and a few
new things, I did not add much to what I had already learned from the first fifteen
companies. At this point, I gained greater insights from the supervisory interviews
than from the additional top management interviews.

Company Profiles

There are a few companies in the United States that have a reputation for being militantly antiunion. Their histories reveal some questionable, if not illegal, practices in their efforts to stay nonunion. I have not included these companies in this study because my concern is with the positive or constructive approaches, even though their policies may in fact be similar to those of the companies that were included.

While I will say more about the cooperating companies in Chapter 2, something more descriptive needs to be said here about the included large companies. To begin with, I use the term *large* in a rather indiscriminate manner. While the size of a company can be viewed in a number of ways, I look at it in terms of sales and the number of employees.

Two nonunion companies were acquired by larger organizations several years ago, and are now divisions of these larger organizations. Consequently, their sales figures are no longer available. Two other nonunion companies are privately owned, and do disclose financial information—if they were publicly owned they would be among the *Fortune 500*. The range in sales for the companies in this study is $100 million to several billion. Half of the companies had 1975 sales of $1 billion or more. With the rapid growth experienced by some of the companies, several that had around a billion in sales in 1975 had around $2 billion by 1979.

In terms of number of employees, the range is from approximately 2,200 employees to 300,000. Almost half of the companies have 25,000 or more employees. The total number of employees, however, has to be qualified for two reasons.

First, many of the companies are multinationals. Some of them have up to 50 percent of their employees located outside the United States. While only some of the companies also operate on a nonunion basis abroad, the focus of this study is on the United States. Accordingly, the number of employees in the United States ranges from approximately 2,200 to 150,000, with 60 percent of the companies having 10,000 or more employees.

Second, some of the companies have a relatively low proportion of production and maintenance employees. This is the group that generally joins unions and thus became the focus of my study. One of the smaller companies, for example, has sales of approximately $350 million and 17,000 employees. Of the 17,000 employees, 12,500 of them are located in the United States. However, if we break down the 12,500 figure and subtract the sales, service, technical, office, and executive group, we are left with the fact that the company has only 2,000 blue-collar workers, all located in three plants in one suburban community. The range with respect to production and maintenance employees is from approximately 2,000 to about 20,000.

All but three of the companies are industrial manufacturers; the other three are service companies. Each of these three exceptions is in a different industry—

industries that are heavily unionized. Neither banks nor insurance companies are included in this study, as these are nonunion industries whose production and maintenance employees are primarily clerical and secretarial and who, until quite recently, have generally not been the target of union organizational drives.

The companies selected are either entirely or predominantly nonunion, and most of them are on the *Fortune 500* list for 1975 of the largest U.S. industrial corporations. Six companies in the sample are not on the *Fortune 500* list. This is because they are not large enough, because they are service corporations as opposed to industrial ones, or because they are privately owned. The economic performances of the companies studied has, by and large, been quite good. A 1973 compilation of *Fortune 500* companies listed on the New York Stock Exchange with five successive years of return on equity exceeding 15 percent showed that thirty-six companies met this criterion. Of those thirty-six, many are nonunion and several of them are included in the group of companies studied.

Another compilation lists twenty-two companies in the *Fortune 500* that consistently achieved net profit/net worth ratios in excess of 18 percent during the seven-year period 1965 to 1971. Of the twenty-two, several are nonunion and are also part of this study.

The shares of many companies studied have also performed very well in the stock market over the years. Several of them sell at price earnings multiples substantially above the price/earnings multiple on *Standard & Poor's* 425-stock industrial index. As of January 5, 1976, when the Dow-Jones multiple was less than twelve, the shares of fourteen of the companies studied sold at a multiple above fifteen, eleven of the fourteen sold above twenty times earnings, and several sold above thirty. Many of the companies studied also share two other distinguishing characteristics, which relate to diversification and ownership.

The first distinguishing characteristic is that, as a group, the companies are relatively undiversified. While some companies in the sample are somewhat more diverse than others, my sample does not contain any company that could be called a conglomerate or even a highly diversified company. Although there are two old-line companies in the sample that have made several acquisitions of unionized firms, my study is focused on the old-line nonunion companies. The significance of this point is that the natures of these companies more easily lend themselves to a more centralized management of the employee-relations function, something that will be discussed in Chapter 5.

The second distinguishing characteristic relates to the relationship between ownership and management in many of the entirely nonunion companies. As has been mentioned, two of the companies are privately owned, with members of the founding families still active in management. The other companies are publicly owned. In several cases, however, a significant percentage of the company's stock is owned by one or more families, members of whom were or still are active in top management. The founder-president and/or his or her children or grandchildren are the top management in some companies, while in other companies a transition has been made to professional management. The ownership–management relationship in some companies, even when publicly owned, may give some of the companies in the sample more degrees of freedom than those enjoyed by some other publicly-owned companies where such a relationship does not exist.

The list of companies studied is an impressive one, but more cannot be revealed as to their profile characteristics, and the significance of these profile characteristics, because of the need to preserve the anonymity of each cooperating company.

Investigative Areas

While my approach was not structured and was quite open ended, there were a number of specific topics I wished to investigate. If these topics were not mentioned by the person interviewed, I would raise them. The topics on my initial list were pay and benefit policies and their administration, existence of a profit-sharing plan, grievance or complaint procedures, use of attitude surveys, job posting, promotion policy, communications, layoff policy, attitudes of top-level management, roles of personnel, the reward system for management, management selection and training, and location of the company. An item I added to the list after some initial visits was the physical condition of the facilities. While I think the reasons one would look at these factors in undertaking such a study are self-explanatory, perhaps it would be useful to say a little about each factor and the reasons why I selected it.

Pay and benefit policies are of interest because many believe that leading nonunion companies may stay nonunion simply by paying more. Obviously, this is an area that needs investigation. Of particular interest is the administration of pay policies, for the essence of policy is administration. In a similar view, it has long been thought that most nonunion firms have a profit-sharing plan. Finding out if this is so and if these plans do indeed exist, then ascertaining their purpose as well as the way in which they actually work would be useful. Investigation in the field revealed many other types of bonus- or equity-oriented plans, such as savings and investment or stock purchase plans, in addition to the traditional profit-sharing plan.

Unionized companies have grievance or complaint procedures that provide for outside arbitration after a number of internal procedural steps. Of particular interest is ascertaining what procedures, if any, might substitute in the nonunion firm for the unionized company's grievance procedures. This, then, would also be an area for investigation.

I knew that two of the companies used attitude surveys extensively, and therefore it was of interest to learn not only how common this management tool was, but also how it was actually used. This is also the case with respect to job posting.

Promotion policy is an area worth examining for a variety of reasons.

Although this matter is complex, many union contracts provide that much weight be given to seniority in promotion decisions. One of the possible advantages of being nonunion is that ability and potential could be the sole criteria. How promotion decisions are handled, then, would be an important topic to investigate.

One often hears of the importance of good communications. This would seem to be particularly so for the nonunion company, for the union-organized company the union establishes a wholly new and independent communications network that builds on all the informal networks. Investigating the communications approaches of the different companies, therefore, was a must.

The unionized company, with its well-established seniority system, has a layoff policy that is time honored: There are seniority districts, and those hired last are the first to be laid off; this is a matter of contract between the parties to the labor agreement. How does the nonunion company handle layoffs? What weight is given to seniority in layoff decisions? Or more importantly, what emphasis does a company attach to employment security?

While hard to assess, it is nevertheless clear that it would be important to make some judgment about the attitudes of top management toward unions and toward people. Related to this issue is the question of the roles of personnel in the nonunion company. What are these roles? What, if any, are their sources of influence? The reward system for managers, and management selection and training are also related issues that need to be considered.

Finally, one frequently hears of companies that move or locate new plants in states that have right-to-work laws* or in parts of the country where organized labor is not strong. It is important, therefore, to note where a company is located and where it locates its new plants. Why and what policies, if any, exist with respect to labor relations considerations and the location of new plants? In my initial visits, I often heard of and observed for myself very attractive working conditions. I noted clean subsidized cafeterias with hot food and well-lighted buildings with nicely landscaped courtyards. As stated, it quickly became clear that I could not ignore the physical condition of the work facilities.

It is not possible, however, to make the study truly comprehensive. Some aspects of the study are probably discussed too briefly. Clearly, what is needed is more general as well as more specialized studies to do justice to such a broad area of inquiry.

Attitudes and Reactions

It should be noted here that many executives in the companies visited emphasized the fact that they were not anti-union. As one put it, "We're not anti-union, we're nonunion." Another said, "We're not anti-union, we're pro-

---

*The Taft-Hartley Act, under right-to-work laws, left to the states the option whether or not to outlaw closed and union shops. About twenty states have right-to-work laws.

employee.'' These statements, of course, could be interpreted as anti-union remarks.

While I will discuss management motivation in Chapter 3, take note none of the managements of the companies studied behave like sleeping dogs when confronted with a union organization drive: They fight, and they fight hard. Executives of the companies studied are not like Irwin Miller, chairman of Cummins Engine, who two decades ago made the following statement about unions:

> *I wouldn't know how to run a big company without a strong union. The unions are management's mirror. They tell you things your own people won't admit.* [4]

The reactions of different people to this study have been interesting. Some trade union officials seemed to view my work with suspicion. Some, understandably, had trouble if the purpose of their institution was questioned, even implicitly. A law school professor, upon learning that I was visiting many large, nonunion companies asked, "Who *are* the devils?" A Department of Labor official admitted having difficulty with the concept of the nonunion company, seeming to think it a natural law or state of affairs that companies should have unions. Some European executives also have trouble understanding the concept. Executives of the cooperating companies, as well as many other American executives, have been quite interested. Academic persons in my field, as well as in related fields such as organizational behavior, have also been interested. These academicians have also been sources of support and encouragement.

Framework for Analysis

As the earlier comments and questions suggest, there are several areas of inquiry that have been pursued. These categories of inquiry, six in number, constitute a framework for analysis that the reader will find useful: They represent clusters of questions that will be asked of the data used in analyzing the phenomena of the large, nonunion company; they provide a basis for choice in certain kinds of management decisions; and they also serve as an initial preview of the principal conclusions of this book. These categories of inquiry help us focus on the determinants of the possibility of a large company, or one or more of its plants, being nonunion. They could also be viewed as the beginnings of a "theory of nonunionization" that, in some ways, is the reverse of a theory of union organization, or, more positively, as a theory of the management of human resources. They will help us construct a model or profile, significant to the field of personnel

---

[4]T. George Harris, "Egghead in the Diesel Industry," *Fortune,* LVI (October 1957), 264.

management, of the values, policies, and climate characterizing the sort of large corporation that will remain nonunion.

Obviously the nonunion status of the large employer cannot be understood or implained by any single factor. As in a kaleidoscope, there are many factors that facilitate understanding and explanation. While there are both external variables (the environmental factors mentioned earlier) and internal variables (the internal climate and policies and practices that constitute the essence of this study), neither one, in my view, is sufficient. Instead, it is some combination of the two—the environmental factors (their broad influence and their specific impact on growth, profits, and occupational mix) and the internal variables—that is capable of producing the nonunion results that are one focus of this study.

The first category of inquiry is an examination of certain environmental factors and company characteristics, in order to determine their degree of favorableness or unfavorableness toward unionization. There are several that can facilitate the employee-relations approaches of the companies studied. While some factors are fortuitous with regard to the company's goals, others are managed so as to help achieve the company's objectives. Examination of the factors and how they should be analyzed may be found in Chapter 2.

The second category of inquiry is the degree to which the motivation of top management is to either "do right" by the employees or to maintain a nonunion company—or, more likely, to do both. The way employees are to be treated can be an important part of the purpose of the organization. It is presumed that the way employees are actually treated is intimately related to the values, goals, and aspirations of top management. The motivation, commitment and concern of top management has to be announced and communicated to the rest of the organization. I found that strong top management motivation is a necessary but not sufficient condition for the development of meaningful personnel policies and practices. This subject will be treated in some depth in Chapter 3.

The third category of inquiry asks about the extent to which the performance of managers in creating a climate of positive employee relations is considered important. It is presumed that the way human resources are managed will receive much top management attention and priority. Evidence and support of this statement will be uncovered in a variety of places, from the ways in which the performance of managers is judged to the steps that are undertaken prior to the discharge of an hourly worker. Management, presumably through a variety of means, will try to create and maintain a climate of trust and confidence where employees will not fear arbitrary and discriminatory treatment. Steps will be taken to not only enhance the security needs of employees, but also to inform employees of the purpose and problems of the organization. Attempts will be made to make each and every employee feel a part of the company.

The fourth category of inquiry concerns the role and status of the personnel department. Consistent with and reinforcing the goals and the climate that top management attempts to achieve, it is presumed that there will be a strong personnel department. The personnel departments of these companies will have and will exercise considerable power and influence. The role and status of the personnel department is a key analytical variable that helps us understand one of the ways the values and goals of top management are institutionalized. All the companies studied have developed the personnel function in depth.

The fifth category of inquiry centers on the relevance of various personnel policies and programs to the attitudes of employees. How important is employment security and promotion from within? How important are better-than-average pay policies and comprehensive benefit programs? Although it is presumed that there will be some differences based on the philosophy of the founder, environmental factors, competitive conditions, and the economics of the business, it was predicted that there would be quite comprehensive personnel packages. While there are some differences, important basic uniformities have been found, which will be developed in later chapters. Equally interesting are some important differences in policy. As we will note, the importance attached to employment security and promotion from within in many companies is an important commonality. There are also many similarities in the policies and practices with respect to wages and benefits.

For the sixth and final category of inquiry, what impact do different forms of feedback mechanisms and communications programs, which one would expect to be quite fully developed in these companies, have on employee attitudes and an organization's climate? Feedback mechanisms and communications programs permit top management to evaluate the climate of the organization, and the content and the manner of administration of the company's personnel policies and practices. These mechanisms not only permit top management to review the behavior of lower-level management but, of course, tend to influence it as well. Moreover, they give the employee an opportunity to be heard at a higher level and demonstrate top management's interest and concern to the employee.

These six categories of inquiry, then, constitute a set of questions that are helpful in analyzing the phenomenon of the large, nonunion company. They constitute a framework of analysis that helps us interpret the principal features of the environment in which the company finds itself, and the internal policies and practices that, taken together, produce a nonunion state. This framework will not only permit us to examine certain variables in a more systematic manner, but will also allow us to look at the relationships between them.

Since so many executives stated that they were not anti-union, the distinction between being *nonunion* and *anti-union* needs to be briefly explained. The executives interviewed seem to honestly believe that their company can perform all of the services a union performs; therefore, in their organization a union is unnecessary. This is why they look upon union organizational drives as indications of inept management and management failures. As the reader will note, the last four categories of inquiry have to do with union service functions. The top managements of these companies, moreover, want to be trusted by the employees.

They want the employees to have confidence in them and to believe in them, and they take many steps to establish and maintain this trust, confidence, and credibility.

After doing this study, I realized that one could look at the six categories of inquiry and the data gathered from two different perspectives. One perspective is that of management performing the functions generally done by a union. A union, for instance, will bargain for higher wages and improved benefits. These nonunion companies, as subsequent chapters will develop, institute wage and benefit policies that are generally superior, or at least comparable, to union settlements. Therefore, an employee of one of the companies studied has no reason to be interested in a union from the point of view of low or inadequate wages and/or benefits. Continuing this example, a union will bargain for grievance procedures so that management decisions affecting workers can be challenged and reviewed with respect to possible contract violations. These nonunion companies, on the other hand, establish comprehensive personnel policies and practices and feedback mechanisms—for example, open-door policies, complaint procedures, and the like—with the hope of accomplishing the same objectives.

The second perspective from which to view the categories of inquiry and the data gathered is from the point of view of top management taking steps to enhance its credibility with the employees. Management, for instance, may have a number of upward-communication programs, but these will mean very little if employees do not believe in or trust top management. To go back to the wage example, one nonunion company studied not only establishes superior or comparable wage and benefit levels, but also communicates its rates and benefits, as well as those of its competitors, to the employees via an annual slide show. Thus, one traditional union role is performed, and employees see the credibility of top management in this particular area. As this book unfolds, one will note many activities whereby management is either performing the union function or is enhancing its credibility with employees. Management, therefore, attempts to create and maintain a climate in which the idea of a union, for at least the majority of the company's employees, is either unnecessary or irrelevant.

CONCLUDING ANALYSIS AND COMMENTS

It should be stated that while it cannot be proven, the personnel policies and practices of the companies studied seem to be, for the most part, quite effective. These companies are a rich laboratory for the student of personnel management. One indicator in support of this presumption is that these companies have stayed nonunion, even granting some of them the assistance and benefits of several strong environmental factors. Effectiveness, however, is a difficult concept. Subjectively speaking, not all the companies are equally effective. Some companies are certainly more effective than others. However, it is hard to prove effectiveness: its detailed proof, therefore, is not a major focus and is beyond the scope of this book. There is a presumption that this group of companies would stand high on anyone's list in terms of effective personnel policies. Certainly, however, this study makes it possible to suggest a model of the basic requirements for effectiveness with respect to personnel management. Another reason for doing the study, then, is that if one wanted to study effective personnel policies and practices in action, there would probably be no better place to start than with this particular group of nonunion companies.

CHAPTER TWO

Environmental Factors
in Remaining Nonunion

Several environmental factors seem to be very important, not only to staying nonunion but also to the facilitation of the personnel policies and programs of the companies studied. This chapter will present an overview of these factors and their significance. Though this is not subject to proof, some factors appear more important to some companies than others. Furthermore, some companies seem to have benefited from some environmental factors that they had nothing or little to do with, while other companies seem to have manipulated and used certain environmental factors to their advantage.

When examining the list of the particular large, nonunion companies studied, one is struck by a number of factors. As mentioned in Chapter 1, these companies are generally successful ones: They are profitable, some extremely so. Many are high-technology growth companies, have dominant market positions, and are industry leaders.

The combination of rapid growth and good profitability facilitates the personnel policies and programs that the high-technology companies offer. For example, the combination of growth and the personnel policy of promotion from within creates many promotional opportunities. Growth aids full-employment practices. It helps make layoffs less necessary. Rapid growth and good profits make profit-sharing and/or other bonus plans worthwhile from the employees' standpoint. Similarly, if the company offers an employee stock-purchase plan, and not only has the stock greatly appreciated but its dividends have continued to rise, the employees have reason to be pleased with the plan. High profits also mean that a company can afford to implement leading policies on pay and benefits, and can also afford to invest the resources necessary for good personnel staffs and programs.

Many company executives stated that the nonunion status of their companies contributes to their success. It may be that the nonunion status of these companies is both a consequence and a partial cause of the success of these companies. Nevertheless, there can be no doubt that the growth and profitability of the companies definitely facilitates their personnel policies and programs.

However, many managements realize that the future will not be like the past. Company growth, at least where employment and promotional opportunities are concerned, has slowed for many of them. Consequently, many company characteristics that were extremely favorable from an employee-relations point of view may be less so in the future for some companies.

In addition to examining data on financial performance, market share, and the level of wages and benefits, one who is interested in personnel relations and in how these companies have remained nonunion can also look at a number of other factors that might be termed "environmental." These, too, have an impact on employees' attitudes toward the company and the union. Consider these six environmental factors:

1. date of founding
2. geographic location
3. size of plants
4. female and/or professional percentage of the work force
5. the handling of sensitive work and employee groups
6. the quality and intensity of union organizational drives

These factors are important because they undoubtedly also contribute in varying degrees to one's understanding of employees' attitudes toward the company and the union, and, consequently, of the nonunion status of the companies in the study.

This chapter will discuss the ways in which the characteristics of the companies and the six environmental factors (as well as the company policies or practices that relate to them) have an impact on employees' attitudes toward the company and toward unions. These are really opposite sides of the same coin.

It is my contention that these company characteristics and environmental factors have important direct and/or indirect effects on employees' attitudes toward the company and its management, and toward unions. These factors influence not only employees' attitudes, but also the personnel policies and programs of the companies. In addition to analyzing these variables and their impact, this chapter will also discuss the ways in which they are changing.

DATE OF FOUNDING

The labor movement in the United States experienced a surge of growth in the 1930s and 1940s. Between 1935 (the year the Wagner Act was passed) and 1945, union membership grew from 3 million people to almost 15 million people, almost 36 percent of the nonagricultural work force. One could say that some of the large nonunion companies of today escaped becoming organized because (1) they did not exist during the 1930s and 1940s, (2) they were very small at that time, or (3) they were not part of the industries that experienced major organizational drives. However, of all the large companies studied that are either entirely or predominantly nonunion, only two were founded after World War II. A number of the others were quite small in terms of the number of employees at the time of World War II and into the 1950s, and therefore were probably not as vulnerable to union organization as larger companies were at the time.

Undoubtedly, time has also had an impact on employee attitudes toward unions. Although difficult to document, there appears to have been a basic change in employees' attitudes: They have become less favorable over the years. National Labor Relations Board election results show a steady decline over the years in the proportion of elections won by unions. The large, nonunion company of today does not face the same pro-union attitudes that the large employer of thirty or forty years ago encountered.

GEOGRAPHIC LOCATION

An environmental factor that cannot be ignored in examining the personnel policies of large, nonunion employers is geographic location. Three-quarters of the management representatives interviewed mentioned it voluntarily, or responded affirmatively when the question was raised. Some examples will illustrate the importance of location.

One company had recently been through an organizational drive, which the union lost by a 2-to-1 margin. A manager of this large company, which has all of its plants in one city (thereby making it easier to implement its full-employment policy), cited "a lot of indifference to unions in this particular part of the United States" as a reason for the company's nonunion status.

In another company, a vice-president also mentioned location as a reason the company was nonunion, saying: "Being in [this area] is certainly a contributing factor, for the climate is nonunion." Located close by were two other large, nonunion employers. This vice-president did admit that there were some unionized employers not too far away, and admitted feeling disturbed that a successful union organization drive had recently taken place at a neighboring university. "The problem at that university is that they are always mopping up and they ought to be turning off the faucet." To this person, "turning off the faucet" meant having supervisory training and management development programs, something this company emphasized.

The unions' share of the southern work force of the United States is approximately half of its share of the nation's work force. Only 14 percent of all employees in the South are unionized. Moreover, according to the National Labor Relations Board's (NLRB) statistics, the unions' success rate in southern representation elections is not only less than in the North, but is declining as well. In their July 1977 report to the Trilateral Commission, George C. Lodge and Karen Henderson discussed this point:

> *Union membership in the U.S. is concentrated geographically. The most highly organized state is New York, with 45.4% of non-farm workers in unions or associations, followed by Michigan, West Virginia, Pennsylvania and Washington. Southern states, on the other hand, have relatively few union members, and the 19 states which retain "right-to-work" laws are mostly in the South. North Carolina, whose textile companies are notorious for their resistance to union organizers, has only 6.9% organized non-farm workers; South Carolina, Mississippi, Florida and Texas all start at 13% or less. Since the long-term shift of the nation's manufacturing base is to the South and Southwest (because of factors including superior transportation, cheaper energy, lower taxes and living costs, and incentives to attract business), it is clear that labor unions face a difficult task in keeping their membership from eroding further. The South historically has a strong anti-union bias, and even highly organized industries such as automobile manufacturing are resisting organization of new southern plants.* [1]

Of the more than two dozen companies studied only three have a significant percentage of their work force located in the South, and two of these companies also operate nonunion plants in highly unionized industrial areas in the North. Furthermore, several of the companies studied have their corporate headquarters, as well as many if not most of their employees, in either New York or Pennsylvania.

Locating New Plants

In several companies much attention is paid to labor relations considerations, among other factors, when the time comes to select a site for a new plant. This is done in different ways and with varying degrees of sophistication. An officer of a major high-technology corporation said that among the several criteria

---

[1]George C. Lodge and Karen Henderson, "Changing Relationships Among Labor, Business and Government in the United States," a working paper prepared for the Trilateral Commission, July 1, 1977, p. 5. It should be added that this paper was written before General Motors Corporation agreed with the United Automobile Workers' Union on a "neutrality letter" with respect to the organization of southern plants. The significance of this change is discussed later in this chapter.

used were the quality of the public schools, the proximity to a university, the area's attitude toward unions, and the size of the minority population. With regard to the application of the last criterion, this officer stated: "We would not build a plant in [one area] because of the lack of blacks, and we would not build a plant in [another area] because [it] is a hotbed of unionism." The minority criterion, a relatively recent one, was adopted because the corporation has nationwide responsibilities for the recruitment and advancement of minorities. Under this policy many of the sites in this corporation's land bank will not be used because they are in areas where there are few minorities.

At another company that tries to keep its new plants nonunion, the person in charge of "union avoidance" activities for the company's "up-country plants" said: "The company looks at the community carefully and it picks locations where it feels it has a better chance to stay union-free."

Some companies have done an extraordinary amount of research work in choosing new plant sites. One company contacted a professor of labor relations at a major university, who analyzed the NLRB's election statistics by state and by geographic regions of each state, and also looked at the locations where the particular unions which would be likely to try to organize the company were winning and where they were losing. Based on this analysis, the professor recommended several areas to consider and several others to avoid. In a memorandum, the professor wrote:

> In . . . [conducting the review] I have given almost exclusive consideration to the matter of potential unionization and have not been concerned with the labor supply, the availability of critical skills, and similar considerations. The conclusions are based upon data re union intensity in certain geographic areas, with special reference to recent trends.
>
> In addition, even though union intensity may be relatively low in a geographic area, the presence of one or more large unionized firms has been considered. The presence of such firms frequently heightens the risk of an organizational drive.
>
> Also relevant is an analysis of the geographic distribution of representation elections held under the auspices of the NLRB and the results thereof.
>
> Finally, I have relied upon personal information concerning prospective union campaign areas.

Based on this analysis, the professor classified eleven states into four categories ("eliminate," "borderline eliminate," "borderline accept," and "accept"), and in the last two categories recommended that the client company avoid proximity to particular cities.

At another company, the vice-president for administration stated that:

> It is the company's philosophy to stay away from urban areas. We always tap agrarian labor. It is our belief that people off the farms are skillful with their hands, independent in spirit, loyal, and self-motivated. This was the

policy when the company was started in 1918—this area [now company headquarters] was all farmland.

Interestingly, the company also applies the same philosophy with equal success abroad:

All plants worldwide are either in small towns or on the edge of large cities. Our large Canadian plant [800 employees] is nonunion, and in Canada our other plants are in small towns. Worldwide, our philosophy is to go into farming areas. In England we are on the outskirts of large cities.

The only union the company has abroad is in Italy. Commenting on this, the vice-president said:

We have good employee and union relations in Italy. When the workers were told they had to strike, they said they would strike on Saturday so that they could come to work on Monday.

At a third company, a vice-president of personnel reported that a little "due diligence" revealed that a certain city would not be a good place to construct a "blue-collar, male, production-type plant":

[This city] is sixth among the top fifty cities within the United States with having more down-time due to strikes, jurisdictional disputes and other related union conflicts. Moreover, there are more EEO [Equal Employment Opportunity] charges in that city than in only two other major cities. It is third in the number of fair employment practice cases and unfair labor practice charges. The city has several militant and aggressive unions and the wage-and-benefit level for even the lowest job in a grocery store represented by a union is about equal to the two highest other cities in the United States. Further, productivity levels seem to be lower among the men than almost any other city in the United States, whereas female productivity is extremely high.

This vice-president also cited an instance where one community well met all the criteria of the site-search team except the personnel ones. Upon reviewing the personnel deficiencies, there was a unanimous decision by the president and the operations committee not to place a plant in this community, but to instead go the second-best choice, which on balance turned out to be an outstanding location for the plant.

In addition to highlighting the importance attached to location decisions, these cases also show the contributions that competent personnel executives can make if they are members of the site-selection team, as opposed to only being people from engineering, marketing, and finance, a point that will be discussed later, in Chapter 5.

Rural Settings

There can be no doubt that the large employer frequently encounters employee and community attitudes in some rural communities, where there may be significant anti-union feelings, that are different from those met in urban areas. Some rural employees may fear the consequences of holding pro-union views. However, a secretary-treasurer of a major union said that the combination of a rural environment with the way the U.S. labor laws are administered gives a decided advantage to the employer who opposes unions:

> *Political elections and union elections are not equivalent. The employer holds economic power over the life and death of the workers. In small towns in agricultural areas there frequently is no other available employment. Moreover, when we were organizing in the South in the 1950s we could not find a lawyer to represent us. They did not want to upset their business clients. And union organizers couldn't sleep in town. The motels refused them, and the issue had nothing to do with civil rights.*

With respect to the way labor laws are administered, this person thought that delays are likely to favor the employer, and pointed out that even though the laws provide protection for the worker from being fired, it may take a year for a case to be processed by the National Labor Relations Board, after which the employer can appeal to the courts:

> *The union does not get quick remedies. Delay is a good employer tactic. The company will fire five workers. Such a move stymies the organizational drive. Three years later the employer will receive a "slap on the wrist." He'll be told not to do it again. Even though the employer will have to take the workers back with back pay, it is a good investment. The employer saves a lot of money.*

At another company, however, it was stated that there can be real risks in building a plant in a rural area. Of the fifty plants built by this company at all sites since World War II, only four have become organized. The director of labor relations said that the company has nonunion plants in highly unionized areas, and it has union plants in cornfields:

> *A community of unionization sometimes is a plus for a company wanting to operate nonunion, for there will be a number of people who are down on unions as a result of the experience. It can be dangerous to build a plant in a cornfield. The risk is that sometimes another company with poor personnel policies will come in. It will be nonunion and pay low rates. Then, if it becomes unionized and the first negotiation results in big increases, it can be an indirect message to your own employees.*

Although it does not involve rural locations, one company president and founder interviewed expressed a similar concern. Having been in Milwaukee in the 1930s and vividly recalling the Allis-Chalmers strike, this person was able to understand the strike, but was bothered by "the passion of the times" and "the emotion which swept the streets. Even the good employers, the people who had been doing well for fifteen years or more, also got organized, just because of the mass psychology." While it may not be related, this person founded this company in a right-to-work Southern state, and has taken many steps in order to remain nonunion.

Unionized Areas

Some of the companies in the study that have nonunion plants in rural areas also have plants in highly unionized areas. Furthermore, some of the companies in this study are located in highly unionized parts of the United States. Both types of situations are illustrated by examples.

One large company that is entirely nonunion, even abroad, after much deliberation and internal management disagreement built a new plant in a highly unionized but depressed area just one and-a-half hours away from company headquarters by car. Land in a southern state had been purchased, and a labor-relations consultant the company had on a retainer basis recommended that the new plant be built in this location. Although many line managers favored this southern location, they also wanted to transfer experienced personnel from company plants in the headquarters city to start the plant. However, top management, in response to a request from the state governor as well as for other reasons, decided to locate the plant in this unionized area and to start the operation with new employees.

Despite the fact that most of the people hired had been union members at other companies, there was no organizational attempt made at the new plant. The production vice-president said: "It was hard to convince the new employees of the way we operated; they just didn't believe it." The plant started with 500 employees, and an extra personnel representative was added for the transition period. However, due to some operating problems, the company finally had to transfer some experienced employees to the new location. When asked about the significance of the presence of the transferred employees, this company's labor-relations consultant said:

> The transferred employees have helped keep the plant nonunion. They represent not only votes against the union, but they are also people whom the new workers can talk to. The idea of workers talking to workers is important.

The plant was being managed by its third plant manager at the time of my visit; this manager had been a plant personnel director. A high-ranking personnel executive said that one of the reasons this manager was put in charge of the plant was because of his sensitivity to employee concerns.

Several other companies visited operated in unionized environments and still remain nonunion. Some have unionized competitors literally next-door and, for a variety of reasons including the nature of the product market, it would be impossible for them to move to another location. Indeed, a senior officer of one company that is located in a highly unionized area estimated that of the company's 24,000 employees, at least half had been union members at other companies, adding that: "Some, in fact, still hold their union cards because they have to maintain membership in their union to qualify for their union pension." This officer emphatically stated that he is not against unions but does believe that if management runs the kind of company in which each employee participates, unions will not be necessary. He said this company has believed in participative management for over forty years, adding that the employees have had a number of opportunities to join unions. Over the years, four international unions have tried to organize the company—only once did the organization drive get to the election stage, and in this case the union lost by a 10-to-1 margin.

In another company, which located one of its major divisions in a right-to-work state and subsequently became one of the largest employers there, twelve of its old plants nevertheless continued to operate on a nonunion basis in and around its headquarters location, which is an urban and highly unionized northern city. A former union organizer, who had tried to unionize this company, said that organizing their employees was an impossible task because the company's management "really works hard at making the employees feel that unions are unnecessary."

Consider the case of a company that is the only nonunion company in its industry. In several cities it operates right next-door to its unionized competitors: A union organizer said that this company's employees did not really need a union because the company maintains an excellent employee-relations and communications program.

In another case, a company in a large metropolis that pays less than its industry's competitors is the only major company that is not unionized in that city. In yet another case, a company maintains its nonunion status despite being in an area in which the Steelworkers Union (the union that has long eyed this company) is quite strong.

Finally, two other companies, both of which pay very well, operate on a nonunion basis in a city where organized labor is strong. Commenting about one of these companies, a union official said, "That company is un-unionable," due to the nature and administration of the company's personnel policies and programs.

One company, with several unionized competitors, is almost exclusively nonunion throughout the United States in unionized areas. This company's vice-president of personnel reported that they had recently "beat" the Machinists Union in one city and the Teamsters Union in another. An 800-worker unit of the Teamsters lost by a 2-to-1 margin at a time when comparable unionized companies were paying $1.00 to $1.25 per hour more. It was alleged that the Teamsters had spent over $250,000 on the campaign. When asked why the union failed to carry a majority in this election, the vice-president of personnel replied, "Hard work on the company's part." In addition to "playing offense" during the campaign, the company tried to maintain a very good set of personnel policies and practices.

The fact that several companies remain nonunion in highly unionized areas obviously suggests that, unless companies are hiring from an anti-union segment of the labor market, there are critical variables other than location for these companies in maintaining their nonunion status. Nevertheless, the factor of location is extremely important to many companies. While not sufficient by any means to explain their nonunion status, it is undoubtedly a contributing factor.

SIZE OF PLANTS

Related to location policies as an environmental factor in remaining nonunion is size of plant. One company builds very small plants in rural or suburban locations, which employ from 25 to 225 employees. They are generally located in out-of-the-way places. Both their size and their location appear to have made them less vulnerable to organization attempts by international unions. Company management believes that organizing such small plants is simply not worth a union's effort. Commenting, the company's personnel director said:

> We like to keep our plants reasonably small. We don't want them to get over 200 employees. After that, both management and personnel lose personal contact with the employee.

With respect to the rural locations of these plants, the company's personnel director reported that this philosophy grew out of government directives during World War II:

> During World War II, the government said that an employer shouldn't build plants on the East coast and that he shouldn't build them too close together.

It should also be pointed out that the small size of the company's plants fits its business strategy. The company produces a diverse product line, the economics of which favor many small specialized plants. This company has also located plants in some suburban communities. There are some plants of sixty people where most of them are able to walk to work. The company's Florida plant is located in a place where the company could take advantage of the highly-developed machine skills possessed by retirees living in this area.

At yet another company, the personnel director said that the company maintains "a low profile and hides from the union." Although he added that he was kidding, investigation revealed that the company's employees, half of whom are women, are scattered throughout the United States in small plants. Each maintains a two-shift operation so that at any given time there is an average of less than seventy-five employees working in a particular plant.

With respect to the appropriate size for a plant, the vice-president of personnel in another company holds a similar view, but believes that, although it is possible to well manage those plant sites consisting of up to 1,000 employees, the optimum size is a plant of 500 employees:

> Top management makes it a policy not to have plants of more than 500 employees. We build self-contained units of 500 employees. Our president thinks that there are many people who can manage a 500-employee plant. There are, however, few who can run a 5,000-man plant.

While it is not decisive, size of plant is another environmental factor over which management can exercise control. It is the judgment and experience of many managers that "small plants," however the word "small" is defined, are easier to manage, can have favorable employee relations, and are less a target for union organizational drives.

However, there are many small companies in the United States which are organized. One could even argue that many small plants located far from head-quarters are more difficult for top management to monitor and control. In any event, control and auditing techniques (discussed in Chapter 5) in the employee-relations area would seem essential. Nevertheless, the number of organizing attempts cannot be independent of location and size of plant.

It must also be recognized that many of the companies in this study do have large manufacturing facilities. Thus 5,000 employees or more at one site is not uncommon. A few companies have more than 20,000 employees at one particular location.

Finally, while "small may be better" from an employee-relations point of view, it also needs to be recognized that plants can be too small. A plant has to be large enough for a company to justify the expenses of good supervision. One executive made this point:

> Where a location can't justify a decent management team, you end up either by staffing it with supervisors who are really over their heads or by overstaffing each position which can also be a problem.

This executive believes that the ideal plant size is somewhere between 250 and 500 people, and that at this level a company can afford to have good managers "who can hardly miss in that size plant." Relating the issue of plant size to organizational drives, this person said:

> Remember, in a 20-man plant you don't need many people to get 30 percent of the cards and get an election. Moreover, the union wins with only eleven votes. One good issue, properly managed by a union organizer, can turn the situation around over night. At 250- to 500-man plants, before things

really get going enough to become serious, you have time to assess the situation, make appropriate corrections and salvage the facility.

A newly acquired division of one of the companies in the sample has many such small units, and there have increasingly been unionization attempts in these units. When they occur, corporate personnel takes charge of the company's campaign. In one case, corporate personnel also unsuccessfully argued before the National Labor Relations Board that the appropriate bargaining unit was not the one small unit but a group of similar units in either the state or the city. Another company has taken steps to make it clear that, should the issues ever be raised, the appropriate bargaining unit would be *all* the company's production and maintenance employees, rather than those in a single plant. The company's seniority system, as well as its job-posting system, are companywide. In this case, the company's large size would be an advantage in its attempts to remain nonunion, if an organization drive should occur, if the manager of one plant permitted a deterioration in employee relations through the mishandling of people.

In testimony to Congress from a study conducted by William L. Kircher, a director of organization for the AFL-CIO, of 495 NLRB elections in which AFL-CIO unions petitioned, and in which the national organizational staff of the AFL-CIO participated during a thirteen-month period ending in April 1967, there is a breakdown of winning percentages by size of units, as seen in Table 2-1.

TABLE 2-1

	Winning Percentages
Overall	53
Units of 0 to 50	64
Units of 51 to 75	52
Units of 76 to 100	57
Units of more than 100	41

In commenting on the results of the study, Kircher wrote:

> *In general, these figures indicate a phenomenon which most union organizers have experienced for years. The winning percentage in NLRB elections generally decreases as the size of the unit increases. The one exception to this general rule is the 76-100 unit size. This unit size is also an exception for other types of analysis in this study, thus tending to indicate that it is best suited for union organization.* [2]

---

[2] *To Amend the National Labor Relations Act, to Increase Effectiveness of Remedies.* Hearings before the Special Subcommittee on Labor of the Committee on Education and Labor, House of Representatives, 90th Congress, First Session, to H.R. 11725. A bill to amend the National Labor Relations Act in order to increase the effectiveness of the remedies. Hearings held in Washington, D.C., August 7, 10, 11, 14, 16, 17, 18, 24, 1967. Published in Washington, D.C.: U.S. Government Printing Office, 1968, p. 41.

The results of Kircher's study were similar to the findings of a Conference Board (formerly known as the National Industrial Conference Board) study regarding unionization among white-collar employees. It also showed a strong correlation between size of the election unit and the outcome of the election, with unions generally winning elections in smaller units and losing them in large groups. Specifically:

> . . . out of 59 election units between 10 and 20 employees, 34 (or 58%) voted for union representation, while out of 36 units with more than 40 employees, 13 (or 36%) voted for unionism. In medium-sized units with between 20 and 40 employees, the win–loss split is more even.[3]

Thus, if there is an organizational drive at a small unit of from zero to fifty employees, the probability of the union winning is higher than if the unit has over 100 employees. A question that of course remains is what percentage of small units have organizational drives compared to larger units. It may be that, although the chances of a union drive are higher at a small unit, if there *is* a drive the probability of becoming unionized may be less, because due to limited union organizational resources, all the small units cannot be contacted.

Size of plants, then, is an important consideration. There can be potential employee-relations disadvantages if a plant is either too large or too small.

FEMALE AND/OR PROFESSIONAL PERCENTAGE OF THE WORK FORCE

During the course of the study, several interviews made it clear that a question that had not been part of the original list did need to be asked: What percentage of the production and maintenance work force is female and/or professional? The percentage of women in the company's production and maintenance work force, as well as the percentage of professionals there, should be considered another environmental factor.

Female Percentage of the Work Force

Two interviews suggested asking about the percentage of women in the work force. One interview was with a foreman at a plant of 400 employees, who had previously been an hourly worker and a union organizer at the plant. (The plant had been owned by a different company at the time of the organizational drives.) This foreman said that the women in the plant were the reason the union had lost the two different elections:

---

[3]Edward R. Curtin, *White Collar Unionization* (a research report), Studies in Personnel Policy No. 220 (New York: The National Industrial Conference Board, Inc., 1970).

> *We got beat twice. What defeated us was the women. They didn't want to pay the dues. We got all the cards signed but the women felt the dues wouldn't pay off. Therefore, they voted against the union.*

The other interview was with the personnel director of another company. In giving his views on the reasons for the company's nonunion status, he said: "It is probably helpful that each plant has a small number of employees and that many of the employees are women."

One official interviewed at an industry trade association said: "A lot of the part-timers in our industry are women. These women are hard to organize because they are housewives first and workers second."

Finally, a personnel director at a very large company admitted that his company's high percentage of women was "probably an advantage" in explaining the company's nonunion status. Commenting, he said, "Women are not career types and they do not want to get involved in the politics of a union."

Analysis of the employee population of the companies studied indicates that at almost half of the companies, 50 percent or more of the production and maintenance employees are female. In addition, at several other companies women comprise more than 25 percent of the work force. Also, at a few of the companies where women comprise a substantial segment of the work force, a good number of the first-line supervisors are female.

Of course, women do comprise more than 40 percent of the national work force. Moreover, this figure has been rising. However, many women are in office and clerical jobs rather than in manufacturing. In two highly unionized industries—automotive and steel—one does not think (at least not historically) of the production and maintenance work force as consisting of females in any significant numbers.

The director of employee relations at a company that has kept all of its new plants (those built since World War II) nonunion, when asked about this subject, said:

> *In one of our divisions, 50 percent of the employees are women. Moreover, all of our plants in this division in the South are nonunion. In this company, there hasn't been a successful organizational drive since 1951. It is also true that since that time the nature of our business has changed and in our new businesses we utilize women heavily. But the plants that employ primarily men have remained nonunion since that time, too.*
>
> *I think it is true that women are antiunion in their outlook. Frequently, in our plants there is a mother–son relationship where the women adopt the plant manager as a son. But things are changing and there are some risks now associated with our approach. Women are getting more militant and there will be some risks associated with aggressive leadership.*

HISTORICAL PATTERN

There is a literature that indicates the difficulty the union movement in this country has had with regard to the organization of women. Women, particularly those who are secondary wage earners, may prefer not to get involved with an outside organization that could call a strike sometime in the future. The company, then, that has a high percentage of a certain kind of women employees would have an advantage in the possibility of staying nonunion.

This observation ties in nicely with the observations and experience of the labor-relations staff at one of the companies visited. This partially-unionized company has been quite successful in keeping its new plants nonunion. However, over the years a few of its plants have become organized. When asked for an explanation of why the employees at these few plants had chosen to be represented by unions, the labor-relations staff stated the importance of recognizing the existence of three different groups of employees in any plant:

This staff considers it a fact that, within any group of employees, there are *union advocates* as a matter of principle. These employees, in the view of the staff, may be excellent performers who have no concerns or gripes about their jobs, levels of pay, working conditions, or attitudes and actions of management; they nevertheless believe that unionization is the right thing for them. To this base load, the staff then adds a number of malcontents who would probably be *antimanagement* wherever they were employed. Then, there are the *balance tippers*, described as employees who will give management a chance to work in the best overall interest of employees. They will vote for third-party representation when they believe management has failed them.

Following this analysis, we could probably assume that there are fewer women than men who join unions on principle, and that there are fewer female than male malcontents. Even if this is not so, women—at least prior to the women's liberation movement—have probably been more tolerant of or more willing to accept poor conditions than men, simply because they had not seen themselves spending a career with the company. In short, female balance tippers are probably easier to work with than male balance tippers.

CHANGING ATTITUDES

It needs to be recognized that a number of women have joined unions, and some observers have noted that, once organized, women become very militant. It also needs to be recognized that although a number of companies having a high percentage of women in their work force are nonunion, this situation is not universally true.

Indeed, sometimes industry competitors, with the same kind of employee profile with respect to sex, are unionized. For example, three companies come to mind where the employees are predominantly women (as are the employees of the competitors in their industries), but these three companies are the only nonunion companies in their respective industries.

Similar to the other environmental factors mentioned, a high percentage of women in the work force may be helpful in staying nonunion, though it is neither necessary nor sufficient to understand the company's nonunion status.

It also must be recognized that the times are changing rapidly. Women's liberation and affirmative action are having their impact. With more women working, with more women pursuing serious careers, and with more women doing work that has been traditionally done by men, attitudes are changing. In fact, one company's division narrowly won in a union organization drive; subsequent analysis revealed that the women had voted as a bloc for the union.

Professional Percentage of the Work Force

HISTORICAL PATTERN

It is also important to know the percentage of professional employees in the work force. In one very large company, less than one-eighth of its entire work force is in blue-collar jobs. Since professional workers have historically not been as interested in unionization as production and maintenance employees, the company with a significant professional population would not be as likely to experience unionization for two reasons: (1) professionals are less interested in finding, and/or are less likely to find, unions to join that they find attractive, and (2) with a high percentage of professionals, the employer has fewer production and maintenance employees to worry about. Also, presumably for the reasons previously discussed, it is easier to keep a small group nonunion than it is to keep a large group nonunion.

The nature of the work force is related to the type of work and the technology. To the extent that the company's work does not include any or much heavy, dirty, or assembly-line work, it attracts a different type of work force, one perhaps that is, or at least traditionally has been, less interested in joining unions.

CHANGING ATTITUDES

Like the attitudes of female employees, the attitudes of professional employees are also changing. Many of them are more interested in collective bargaining than they were a few years ago. In fact, some of the companies studied were more concerned about the possibility of their white-collar, technical, and professional employees joining unions than they were their blue-collar employees.

THE HANDLING OF SENSITIVE WORK AND EMPLOYEE GROUPS

The practice of some employers is to subcontract so-called "sensitive" or strategic work. *Sensitive* work is defined as work frequently done by unionized personnel. One company, for example, subcontracts its printing work. Many of its unionized competitors do their own printing. This practice obviously makes a union drive less likely. In addition to farming out work, sometimes the sensitive work is done in-house by the unionized employees of a subcontractor.

One company studied responded to an organizational drive by abandoning a certain business. What had happened was that the company had purchased a truck and hired two drivers, the purpose of this being to try to save money by assuming the responsibility for local deliveries. When the Teamsters Union tried to organize the drivers, the company sold the truck. Ironically, four of this company's employees are members of the Operating Engineers Union. With this group the company has agreed to the wage pattern of the city where it is located.

If the sensitive work is not farmed out or done on the employer's premises by employees of a subcontractor, management pays close attention to the working conditions and wages of the sensitive employee groups. Steps are taken to ensure that their wages and benefits are comparable to or better than those earned by unionized personnel.

One company's management has a monthly luncheon for its truck drivers, as well as other programs for them. One manager, however, was worried that with CB radios there could be risks of their drivers talking too much to unionized drivers. Significantly, the trucking work of this company that is subcontracted is given only to nonunion concerns.

The Influence of Nepotism

Perhaps the opposite of the way some companies handle sensitive employee groups and sensitive work is the way some companies handle employment of more than one person from the same family. For some companies, at least in the past, familial relationships to present employees have been an important hiring screening device. Perhaps as another way of highlighting the family spirit of the companies, other companies have given positive emphasis to familial relationships in employment decisions.

Although obviously related to the size of plants and to location decisions, some companies will allow several members of the same families to work for them. In fact, nepotism had been a practice of several companies, with special job preference given to the sons and daughters of employees. A division personnel manager of a large company said:

> Summer hiring used to be the sons and daughters of employees. They were given preference. There used to be, in fact, two files for permanent employees—those with relatives in the company, and those without. But now with equal employment opportunity all that has changed.

However, another company recently allocated all of its summer jobs to the sons and daughters of its employees. Because so many applied, considerably more than the number of jobs available, and not wanting to disappoint any of the summer students or their parents, the company converted its full-time summer jobs to part-time summer jobs so that everyone who applied would have at least a part-time job for the summer.

This practice was similar to that of one large company in which a recent survey showed that more than four out of ten employees have members of their immediate family working at the company. Indeed, the manager of benefits, who had been with the company for seventeen years, said that his grandfather had served the company for forty-seven years:

> The pride of this company is unparalleled. I remember being six or seven years old and talking about the company. It is a family-type company with a lot of grandfathers, fathers, and sons. It started with built-in loyalty. It really means something to say you are an employee of this company when you go to cash a check at the hardware store. But the attitude is changing some with the younger employees.

Although nepotism may have fit the style of some companies in the past and may have had certain favorable employee-relations consequences, it is a practice that does not fit well with the principles of equal employment opportunity. Consequently, it is on the decline.

It should also be pointed out that other companies in the sample make it a practice to employ only one member of a family. Moreover, in some companies if one employee marries another one, then one of them must resign from the company. Management of the companies that have such policies consider them superior to nepotism policies. While they may lose out on the opportunity to employ some good people, they nevertheless think an anti-nepotism policy is best, given the potential problems they avoid. It may be noted that such policies may be less practical in small communities where a single company or plant is the town's principal employer. Moreover, if two employees marry and it is the woman who generally resigns, this practice may also not fit well with good affirmative action principles.

In discussing the problems associated with employing members of the same family, one personnel executive made the following points:

> If you are going to run a "tight ship," eventually you find yourself in a position of disciplining and maybe even discharging an employee who is an immediate member of the family of another one of your employees. It is my observation that no matter how well you handle the situation, the remaining members of the family react negatively, maybe even negatively motivated to the point of it affecting their performance, which subsequently requires discipline or maybe even discharge for them, too. Why not have your cake and eat it too? If you create the kind of pride in the community and it's real, if you don't employ immediate members of the family, you can have the positive results which that pride generates without running the risk of problems that can be associated with that.

This executive even tied in the company's policy of employing relatives with the company's union-avoidance program:

> *If you have an organizing all are all the union has to do is to work at one member of the family, and three or four borderline people come along too. Not that they really want the union, but they don't not want it badly enough to conflict with the other members of the family.*

This executive also felt that this way of thinking applies to groups or subgroups of employees, such as blacks or Indians. While this may be logical and is based on this person's experience, one wonders if this is so, and if it is, to what extent: Members of families as well as members of a minority group have been known to disagree among themselves.

THE QUALITY AND INTENSITY OF UNION ORGANIZATION DRIVES

Despite their growth and profitability, date of founding, geographic location, size of plants, percentage of female and/or professional work force, and the ways in which the sensitive work and employee groups are handled, each of the companies studied has experienced union organizational efforts among its employees in at least one of its plants. Some companies have only had one or two organizational drives in their entire history, but others have experienced periodic organizational drives. Also, although the union organizational efforts have not always resulted in an election, in many cases elections have been held, and in those that have been, a majority of the employees have (sometimes repeatedly) voted against being represented by a third party.

Supervisory Practices

Union-organizational drives are generally attributed to poor supervision. Most managers interviewed subscribed to the view that unions are a result of poor management. When asked about the reasons for the union drives, managers generally blamed themselves. Direct comments from different executives on this subject include:

> *Union drives are viewed as a management failure.*

> *A union campaign tests the consistent application of your policies and practices.*

> *Our chief executive officer always considers it a management failure if we have a union organizational drive.*

The executives also cited instances in which they felt either that particular supervisors were neglectful or that supervisory practices were responsible for the union drive. Assessing the only real union-organizing effort in one company's history, a personnel director said:

> [*The union-organizational drive*] *occurred in the late 1950s at the time of the layoff. But the layoff was not the issue. The issue was bad supervisory behavior and it really all boiled down to a single supervisor. This supervisor told employees they were going to get a wage increase. He told them he would process the increases but he did not do it. Later on we found out that he was holding up the increases. We found fifteen forms in his desk which he never sent through.*

Other managers related similar stories of authoritarian supervisors who had acted in a unilateral way. Union-organization drives suggest to management that they are not performing the traditional union service role effectively, and/or that they have lost credibility with the employees. This affects their pride and disturbs them very much.

Other Explanations

While supervisors and supervisory practices were the predominant explanations offered by many managers, some managers cited two other reasons for union drives. One had to do with acquisitions, and the other with chance and with geography.

Several managers told of union-organizational drives at the time of an acquisition. One experienced employee-relations director, of a company where the union has won only seven out of seventy-eight certification elections during the past three decades, said:

> *Characteristic of each union success was that the election took place within a year or two after a company was acquired. This period is a very uncertain time for most companies, especially the employees who feel threatened by the larger acquiring company. The fear of being swallowed up by the bigger company and an apparent lessening role to play in their own future results in the employees turning to the union for apparent security and protection.*

Given this experience, it is now the practice of this company to refrain from replacing any of the first-line supervisors of the acquired company until it has had a chance to put its personnel policies in place and to reassure the assimilated employees.

Another company that experienced a union-organizing effort immediately after an acquisition asked the employees to give management a chance. In the words of the parent company's vice-president of personnel:

> *After the acquisition, there was a flurry of union-organizing activity [in the newly acquired section]. We were quite concerned and we talked to the people. We went over their problems. We found plenty of them—the working conditions were poor, the plant was hot, there were flies, and the toilets didn't work. There were many compensation inequities.*
>
> *We told the employees that we had just acquired the company and that we should be given a chance. We said that in no other facilities of ours in the United States was there a union and that our approach was to treat people in a fair and honest manner. We won the election and the union-organizing efforts fizzled out there.*

The vice-president of personnel in another company said that the only time the company had experienced a union drive was when management had not known that one had been taking place in the new company at the time they acquired it. Responding to the problem, the company had gotten the election delayed by appealing to the National Labor Relations Board regarding the composition of the bargaining unit. During this period of time, the company had flown eleven hourly workers over 2,000 miles to its corporate headquarters, so that they could meet with their fellow employees and find out from them how the company operated. The union lost the election by one vote, and the next day top management not only granted everyone a large pay increase, but also advised employees of a number of benefit improvements. According to the company's vice-president:

> *The union criticized us for flying the employees out, but they did it in such a way that they questioned the intelligence of the employees. The union did not make any ground by the way they made this particular charge.*

Some managers felt that their companies are singled out for union drives by reason of chance or geography. As discussed earlier, a number of companies, given their size or location, feel they are natural targets for international unions seeking to expand their membership. Some managers also thought that their companies' nonunion status is somewhat of an embarrassment to these unions.

At one of these companies, a personnel manager reported that employees at a southern plant had beaten up some union organizers at the plant site, because these employees had been angry that anyone would think they wanted to join a union. It is also this personnel manager's experience that, if an employee wants to join a union and discusses unionism, the rest of the employees will ostracize him or her.

The company in which the unions lost almost all of the elections had a similar experience with its pro-union employees. Concerning this, the director of employee relations said:

> *Most plants are not continual targets of organization attempts. One reason is that after an unsuccessful attempt the employees who have organized and lobbied for the union frequently depart within a year, because they are disgruntled to begin with, and partly because they have lost face among fellow employees and want to remove themselves from an embarrassing situation.*

Corporate Response

Companies meet organizational attempts in a variety of ways. If the drive is viewed as a serious threat, it is not uncommon for a corporate personnel team, with the backing of top management, to come to the site and direct the company's campaign against the union.

While top management's involvement is common, at one company the president became very personally involved. In 1946 there was an organizational drive, and the employees voted 60 percent to 40 percent against the union. The president, remembered by a personnel manager as "big, soft-spoken" and "a very good speaker," held meetings in the company's courtyards with the employees, and invited the union officials to attend these meetings. Describing what the president had done, the personnel manager said:

> He cooperated to death with the unions. He thought that the employees
> should decide—either we deserve to have a union or we do not. He stressed
> that the company was not antiunion. It was simply nonunion.

This president was later invited to be a guest speaker at the state AFL-CIO convention, being the first president of a nonunion company to be invited to address this group.

It could probably also be argued that some of the companies that have experienced organizational drives have not faced the most sophisticated union organizers. To the extent that this is true, the companies have of course benefited. Both the frequency and the quality of union-organizing attempts are important. One company vice-president told of a situation in which one-hundred employees in one company plant turned out for a meeting with the union organizers. The company considered this an alarmingly large number of employees, although after the meeting, to the company's surprise and delight, the international union decided not to finance the organizational drive. "While I would like to take credit for this," said the vice-president, "I'm not sure I can. We simply benefited from the union's mistake."

It could probably also be argued that the unions that have tried to organize these companies have generally faced strong employer opposition. The top managements of these companies are not neutral with respect to union-organizational drives.

In addition, it should be recognized that certain industries lack unions whose primary focus and experience is their industry. For example, there is no United Drug or United Pharmaceutical Workers Union. To the extent that this is true and remains so, the companies in these sorts of industries will benefit, because the probability of their being unionized is reduced. Moreover, some industries have weak unions. For instance, the United Automobile Workers of America is (to say the least) a strong union interested in the automobile industry. It is hard to imagine a nonunion automobile company of any significant size in the United States. But for many of the companies in this study, there *is* no large, identifiable, industry union.

It is important to understand the industry in which a company operates. For example, there is not an automobile company or a steel company in this study; and because this is so, some of the large nonunion companies studied are simply in a different position from other U.S. companies that are in union-dominated industries. However, this factor is now also changing as unions develop more expertise in organizing. The Teamsters Union, for one, is becoming increasingly interested in organizing in a wide variety of fields. This is also true for the Steelworkers and the Autoworkers Unions. Although the Teamsters Union conducts many organization drives, it does not win a high proportion of the elections.

CONCLUDING ANALYSIS AND COMMENTS

Although the focus of this study is on the personnel policies and practices of selected, large, entirely or predominantly nonunion companies in the United States, it is nevertheless important to be aware of certain company attributes, environmental factors, and related policies that are in varying degrees associated with these companies.

To put it simply, it is my hypothesis that if a company has been founded subsequent to World War II, is located in a right-to-work state in the South, operates small plants in rural communities, subcontracts its sensitive work, employs a large percentage of women and/or professionals in its work force, competes in any industry not clearly identified with a large and successful union, and has been characterized by rapid growth and high profitability, the chances of its being successfully organized by a union are significantly reduced.

Conversely, if the company was founded prior to World War II, is located in a northern industrial city, has large plants, employs a high percentage of semiskilled males, competes in an industry clearly associated with a large union, has had a weak profitability record, and has had such slow growth that frequent layoffs were necessary, the odds of its being successfully organized by a union are greatly increased.

Although the date of founding cannot be affected, the geographic location, the size of plants, and the subcontracting of sensitive work are key management variables. But there is no evidence to suggest that the same is true with respect to the sex of the employees. For example, in many cases over the years, it has been a management practice to employ women for light assembly work because women were thought to be dexterous. Thus the work was at the time considered to be "women's work." Unlike location decisions, however, there is not any evidence to suggest that the practice was adopted because it was thought women would be less likely to be pro-union. As has been indicated, this inadvertent employer "advantage" may boomerang as the women's movement grows and as discrimination laws and affirmative action take hold.

Although a number of the companies studied have one or more of the company characteristics and environmental factors cited, it is nevertheless significant that none of the companies is so isolated that it has not experienced some form of organizational activity, though not necessarily by a dominant industry union, in at least one or more plants.

It must be recognized that some environmental factors are more important than others, and that some companies have benefited more from favorable environmental factors than other companies have.

In 1955 Professor John T. Dunlop was asked to predict what the industrial-relations system in the United States would look like in 1975. Dunlop examined a number of factors that he believed would either retard or accelerate the growth of the American labor movement. In 1955 the labor movement constituted approximately one-third of the total nonagricultural employees. Looking toward 1975, Professor Dunlop wrote:

> *The net effect of these two lists of factors, the first retarding and the second stimulating the rate of union growth, in my judgment suggests that labor unions will be doing well, in the absence of a climactic period, to maintain their present relative proportion of nonagricultural employees in the period until 1975.*[4]

Dunlop also thought that "considerable changes in organizing methods may be required simply to expand union membership as fast as the work force." The two lists that Dunlop developed are particularly interesting. The first list cited seven types of changes that were taking place in the community, in the characteristics of the work force, and in the business organizations he believed would retard the growth of unions. Briefly stated, they were:

1. "The size of individual plants or establishments tends to be smaller . . ."
2. "The location of new plants . . . a shift of new plants to smaller communities and to regions of the country where organization has been difficult; even where plants are located in greater metropolitan areas, they are more frequently in the suburbs and smaller surrounding communities"
3. "The growth of suburbs, and the shift of workers and their families increasingly to these communities . . . where the employer–employee relationship becomes less pointed"
4. The rise in educational levels which pose new problems and opportunities for

---

[4]*See* John T. Dunlop, "The American Industrial Relations System in 1975," in *U.S. Industrial Relations: The Next Twenty Years,* ed. Jack Stieber (East Lansing, Michigan: Michigan State University Press, 1958), pp. 27–54.

union organizational activities—although Dunlop did not consider formal education necessarily hostile to unionism, he thought it might create employees who were more questioning of both managements and unions and who would challenge traditional organizing approaches

5. The changing composition of the work force, specifically, more women in the work force, continued relative expansion in the professional, technical, and administrative occupations, and the further relative expansion in managerial and supervisory personnel, which would reduce the proportion of total employees within bargaining units, as customarily defined

6. High income levels, changing income distribution, stability of employment, and the prospect of steadily rising incomes are economic facts affecting the rate of growth of labor unions

7. Modern managements, which have developed a variety of policies that scarcely make the unions' task of organization any easier

The second list cited four factors that he thought would make the organization of unions in the work place less difficult, which were: (1) better public-opinion acceptance of unions, (2) the growth of second- and third-generation union members, (3) the prospect of gradual inflation, and (4) the merged AFL-CIO and the no-raiding agreements. Unlike most articles on long-range changes, Dunlop's prediction that labor would be doing well to hold its own has stood the test of time remarkably well.

It also needs to be recognized, however, that both the company characteristics and the environmental factors discussed may still be in the process of considerable change. To the extent that growth slows down and profitability declines, it becomes more difficult for a company to offer the job security and/or the promotional opportunities that it once did, or to be the leader it once was in pay and benefits. Large unionized companies have caught up, narrowed the gap, or gone ahead. The benefit packages of some large, nonunion employers do not stand out as much as they once did. Similarly, with mandatory retirement at 65 years of age illegal, this becomes another challenge to companies trying to maintain full-employment practices.

While profit sharing, for example, might have once been a unique and distinguishing feature of a company's personnel program, it must now be likened to a union-negotiated defined-benefit pension plan that is probably quite comparable, if not superior. The advantages of the benefit packages of some nonunion companies, with their "cradle-to-grave" protection, used to stand out much more than they currently do.

Despite the fact that geographic location is and will continue to be important, it will probably be less so in the future, because major unions are becoming more sophisticated and are developing "southern strategies." Also, the South is becoming more industrialized.

In the 1976 automobile negotiations, the General Motors Corporation (GMC) abandoned its alleged "southern strategy" by agreeing to a "neutrality clause" with respect to organization of its southern plants by the United Automobile Workers (UAW). GMC agreed to "observe a posture of neutrality" toward UAW organizing drives among its production and maintenance employees. Significantly, the company has lost two elections held after the signing of the agreement. The subsequent Steel and Rubber agreements also contained a neutrality clause with respect to production and maintenance employees. The steel companies have agreed "that they will not actively oppose the Union's attempts to organize production and maintenance employees at any basic steel-producing operations which they may hereafter construct." Agreed to by all the major rubber companies except Goodyear, the 1979 rubber "Organizing Neutrality Letter" included, in the case of B.F. Goodrich, the following paragraph:

> *In situations where the URW [United Rubber Workers] seeks to organize production and maintenance employees in a plant in which a major product is tires and which is not represented by a union, B.F. Goodrich management or its agent will neither discourage nor encourage the Union efforts to organize these employees, but will observe a posture of strict neutrality in these matters.*

If other companies agree to such neutrality clauses, and if unions consequently become more successful in the South, this will also have an important effect. The advantages that certain locations offered will thus be sharply reduced. Even if other companies do not agree to such neutrality clauses, the presence of unionized auto, steel, or rubber plants in nonunion areas of the South would have an impact on neighboring companies. Furthermore, the 1979 General Motors–United Auto Workers agreement guarantees automatic certification for workers in most new General Motors plants by replacing the neutrality letter with an "accretion clause." Commenting on the significance of this change, veteran labor observer A. H. Raskin wrote:

> *A spread of this pattern to other major industries could drop into the union basket, without struggle or election, hundreds of new factories in the Sun Belt. Such a concession would nullify the "Southern strategy" many companies have adopted, by which they confine their expansion to areas where unions are weak and organization efforts easy to repel.[5]*

In 1978 the Carter administration and organized labor supported a series of revisions in the nation's labor laws designed to facilitate union-organizing efforts, especially in the South and the West. The proposals were supposed to strengthen the unions' chances by expediting representation elections. In addition to limiting the time that managements have in which to argue against union-organizing

---

[5]A. H. Raskin, "Lane Kirkland: New Style for Labor," *New York Times Magazine*, October 28, 1979, p. 92.

efforts, there was also an equal-access proposal. That is to say, if company personnel spoke to employees on company time, then the union would have to be afforded the same privilege. The proposed legislation also provided for quicker National Labor Relations Board decisions on disputed matters and for higher penalties on companies found to have engaged in unfair labor practices. The frequently effective management tactic of delaying an election would therefore be much less likely. The likely consequences of these changes, organized labor believed, would be a higher percentage of union victories. Although Congress did not pass this labor law reform legislation in 1978, Professor D. Quinn Mills has argued that the triumph of "employers and their organizations" casts a long shadow over the future. In fact, he sees the contest over the labor law reform bill as "a public defeat for moderate leadership" within the AFL-CIO. . . ."[6] Certainly similar "reform" proposals can be expected from organized labor in the near future. Although there are several public-policy aspects to this study, this book is not concerned with these subjects.

It is also becoming commonplace for school teachers, public employees, and professional employees to join unions. As this continues to happen, it will undoubtedly have a softening impact on employees' attitudes toward unions.

Finally, as has already been mentioned, a high percentage of women and/or professional employees in the work force may not be the "anti-union" advantage it once was. Also, a more active and full participation by minorities in the work force may benefit the growth of the labor movement, as the civil rights movement has shown them the advantages of collective efforts. Some companies have reported that minorities do not seem to respond as positively to the traditional personnel programs that have worked effectively with white employees. Moreover, to the extent that the enforcement of civil rights legislation and executive orders forces companies to abandon their philosophies and practices of individual treatment in favor of equal treatment, employees may see advantages in unionization that they did not see before.

As a counter to these trends, personnel management is increasingly becoming more professional.[7] Personnel policies and practices are improving. Personnel staffs are gaining additional expertise, and for a variety of reasons they are playing an increasingly larger role in the affairs of many companies. Human-resources management becomes all the more important if company characteristics and environmental factors will not be as favorable in the future for some companies as they were in the past.

Also, one often hears of the indifference and sometimes outright disdain toward unions of many of the newer entrants to the work force—namely, the youth workers. In fact, these workers have been a problem for organized labor, for

---

[6]D. Quinn Mills, "Flawed Victory in Labor Law Reform," *Harvard Business Review*, May/June 1979, pp. 92–102.

[7]*See* Allen R. Janger, *The Personnel Function: Changing Objectives and Organization* (New York: The National Industrial Conference Board, 1977).

although they become union members under a union shop and dues-checkoff arrangement, they are not like the union's past traditional members. To the extent that this phenomenon is not transitory, large, nonunion companies become the beneficiaries of the anti-union attitudes of these employees. Also, to date, unions have, in general, failed to develop imaginative organizing approaches and programs that appeal to the young, the minorities, the white collar, and the professional employees.

Given Chapter 1, and this chapter on company characteristics and environmental factors and how they are changing, it is now time to turn to the essence of this study—namely, an analysis of the personnel policies and practices of large nonunion employers. However, one should bear in mind that many company characteristics and environmental factors not only influence employees' attitudes toward companies and unions; they also facilitate the personnel policies, practices, and programs of the companies studied in important ways.

CHAPTER THREE

Top Management:
Values and Goals

Interview data from this study suggest that historically there have been two primary types of top management motivation in large companies that are either entirely or predominantly nonunion. The evidence also suggests that all the companies in the sample have strong people-management concerns and objectives at the top of the organization, and as a logical consequence of these concerns devote substantial time, effort, and money to the management of human resources.

One primary type of motivation appears to stem from a set of values or from a philosophy on employees and how they are to be treated. The other primary type of motivation appears to stem from a fundamental purpose of remaining nonunion.

Companies with the first primary motivation may be described as *philosophy-laden*. They have well thought out beliefs concerning the treatment of employees; their philosophy is usually in writing, and was generally first articulated by the company's founder. Their nonunion status seems, at least initially, to not be a goal but rather a result of the successful implementation of that philosophy. However, inherent in their thinking is the view that if management does its job well, the employees will feel that a union is not necessary—the nonunion status of these companies is then an essential by-product.

Companies with the second primary motivation may be described as *doctrinaire*. For certain reasons, top management has decided that the company, or perhaps just its new plants, are to be kept nonunion. In such companies, "union-avoidance programs" are implemented. The resumé of a vice-president of personnel in a company that is primarily doctrinaire included, under "employment history":

> Maintained a union-free status in those locations that did not have prior unionization. Won a major NLRB [National Labor Relations Board] election in the company's distribution facility. Kept numerous union-organizing efforts from reaching petition state.

Although it makes sense historically, the distinction today between the two types of management motivations is not clear-cut. The philosophy-laden companies are aware of unions and of union concerns. In fact, over time some have taken on the characteristics of doctrinaire companies. In addition, doctrinaire companies are not devoid of management values, philosophy, or policy statements about the treatment of their employees.

This chapter will examine both the philosophy-laden and the doctrinaire companies. While separate examples of each type will be offered, the motivation of most companies is mixed. The real question is one of relative emphasis. In examining the personnel programs and policies of these different companies, the distinction between motivational frameworks becomes less meaningful, because in certain fundamental respects the approaches of all the companies are very similar.

PHILOSOPHY-LADEN COMPANIES

As indicated, there is a certain group of companies whose primary concern has not been to remain nonunion, but rather to implement a philosophy about people. When top managements were asked the reasons for their companies' nonunion status, many statements like this were given in reply:

> The men who started the company believed in fair treatment for employees and getting individuals involved in the business, listening to them, and being concerned with them.

Company A

In commenting on company A's approach, the personnel director there said:

> The matter of trust or integrity of intention is fundamental. This means believing we are all equal as human beings in the sight of God and nature. A feeling of respect for the other fellow's dignity and an interest in listening to him because you want to know what he thinks and feels is part of this. An interest in an individual's potential capacities, and a concern and sympathy for his troubles and problems follow. He wants to be treated as a human

*being, especially by his supervisors. He will give and support increased
productivity when he has faith in the worthiness of the common purpose, the
honesty and competency of his leaders, and when he believes they care about
him and other people and sincerely want to do the right thing.*

*The kind of situation I have suggested as a way of living means there
will be a more wholesome atmosphere at the work place. There will be less
social distance during the working day. Innovations which are needed will be
seen as confirmations of a feeling of mutual trust and good intent. The
company receives the benefit of increased productivity, low turnover, flexibility in employee assignment, and employee responsiveness in time of production crisis or in other situations which require special efforts by all concerned.*

*Of course, if management has not built this kind of atmosphere (which I
think people hunger for), then naturally employees will not trust the administrative judgment because they don't feel that management really cares about
them as human individuals—and they are probably right.*

According to a retired personnel director of this company, ''If the day comes
when we do things only to keep unions out, then we will be in trouble.''

Company *B*

In company *B,* a basic principle is respect for and fairness to every individual. This principle was firmly laid down by the founder, who did not think or
worry about unions, but was very concerned that it was too easy for people without
power (that is, employees) to be controlled. Thus, it is said that the founder was
sympathetic with employees, but autocratic with managers; he wanted employees
to have opportunities to be heard and had a great concern for justice in the work
place.

A person who had worked for the founder for three years said that only once
did he hear him speak about unions, saying:

*I don't think we will ever have to worry about our company becoming
unionized. Our people are treated well. We have what the unions want. That
is our goal. Let them look to us.*

The founder's son, later a chairman of the company, said that his father's
philosophy was mainly a simple one:

*What I think is the most important is our respect for the individual. This
is a simple concept, but in [our company] it occupies a major portion of
management time. We devote more effort to it than anything else.*

*This belief was bone-deep in my father. Some people who start out in
modest circumstances have a certain contempt for the average man when they
are able to rise above him. Others, by the time they become leaders have built
up a unique respect and understanding for the average man and a sympathy*

for his problems. They recognize that in a modern industrial nation the less fortunate often are victims of forces not wholly within their own control. This attitude forms the basis for many of the decisions they make having to do with people. [our company] was in the latter category.

Company C

In a special issue of a company magazine, which had been developed primarily for new employees, the president of company *C* wrote:

> *Any group of people who have worked together for some time, any organization of long standing, indeed, any state or national body over a period of time develops a philosophy, a series of traditions, a set of norms. These, in total, are unique and they fully define the organization, setting it aside for better or worse from similar organizations. [Here], all this goes under the general heading of "the [company] way." I want to emphasize that the [company C] way" cannot be demonstrated to be unique, and that although based on sound principles, it is not necessarily transplantable to other organizations. But what can be said about it is that it has worked successfully in the past . . . and there is every reason to believe that being a dynamic "way," it will work in the future. If this is true, and if it differs from more conventional practices, then it is important that whatever this "way" is that it be conveyed to, and understood by, this very large body of [company C] people.*
>
> *What is the [company C] way? I feel that in general terms it is the policies and actions that flow from the belief that men and women want to do a good job, a creative job, and that if they are provided the proper environment they will do so. But that's only part of it. Closely coupled with this is the tradition of treating each individual with consideration and respect, and recognizing personal achievements. This sounds almost trite, but [the co-founder] and I honestly believe in this philosophy and have tried to operate the company along these lines since it first started.*
>
> *. . . I could cite examples, but the problem is that none by themselves really catch the essence of what [company C] is all about. You can't describe it in numbers and statistics. In the last analysis, it is a spirit, a point of view. It is a feeling that everyone is part of a team. . . . As I said at the beginning, it is an idea that is based on the individual. It exists because people have seen that it works, and they believe in it and support it. I believe that this makes [company C] what it is, and that is worth perpetuating.*

Some quotations from managers indicate the success with which company *C* has implemented its philosophy. Consider:

> *Actually, the "people philosophy" shows up in just about everything that goes on . . . The open floor plan—the lack of walled offices and status symbols—and the coffee breaks are part of it. The idea is that if you can see or*

meet people easily, then you can communicate with them better. You'll be more informal about it, and that's good, because it means one less barrier to overcome.

corporate officer

In the shops, of course, you meet a lot of guys who have come in from other jobs. Maybe they've had four or five other jobs, and they're kind of disillusioned about industry. They're not ready to believe what we say about the company. They think it's another "line," which they've heard before, and that sooner or later they're going to get pushed around or fired if they don't "toe the line" or business falls off. They've never heard the philosophy that: "We want you as a permanent employee. We want you to succeed and we will help you."

equal employment opportunity manager

If I were back in Milwaukee I'd probably be just like a lot of my old buddies—stuck in a job shop. Believe me, being a supervisor at the shop level in [company C] is a lot more challenging than in a job shop. Here we don't solve problems by firing and hiring. If we notice a fellow isn't producing, we will try to find out what is bugging him—not by threatening him but by listening to him, gaining his confidence, and directing him to the proper place for help.

section manager

How the philosophy is implemented is critical, of course. While some companies go further than others, in many there is either an absence or at least a minimum of double standards. Traditional status symbols between management and nonmanagement people, and between blue- and white-collar workers, are either eliminated or minimized. For example, parking spaces may not be reserved and there may be a common cafeteria for everyone to use; whether an employee is a chairman or a janitor, he or she is covered by the same medical plan. As will be discussed in subsequent chapters, salary and profit-sharing or other savings and investment plans for everyone are quite common in the large, nonunion company.

Growing Pains

It is important to remember that companies and their environments change over time, which can complicate the implementation of a company philosophy. In one of the philosophy-laden, entirely nonunion companies studied, the vice-president of personnel, a former director of labor relations at a unionized company, in looking at the current situation, said:

Change is coming so rapidly that it would drive a bulldog off a meat truck. The problem now is that the company is so big, the work force has changed, profit sharing is no longer a tonic, and the sophistication of the industry has changed.

This vice-president said that when he arrived on the scene, the company did not know the difference between an exempt and a nonexempt employee, which (although dysfunctional for salary administration purposes and for bargaining unit determination questions during an organizational campaign) may have been one of the company's strengths from an employee-relations point of view. Several unsuccessful union-organizational drives led this company to adopt a more sophisticated and defensive position with respect to employees. A statement addressed to its supervisors read:

> *[This] corporation wants to maintain a relationship with its employees which will permit fair treatment and encourage employees to use their talents in contributing to the success of the company. Both the company and its employees derive the greatest benefit from this type of relationship.*
>
> *However, if employees unionize, it will be virtually impossible to maintain such a relationship with them. Therefore, we are opposed to the creation of a union on the basis that a union would not be in the best interest of either employees or the company and is not needed.*
>
> *This position is not intended to be critical of all aspects of the union movement. The only question we should be involved with is whether a union is appropriate here today. The answer to that question is "No." We must advise our employees of what is at stake so they strongly support our position that a union is not in their best interests or the company's and is not needed.*

Another primarily philosophy-laden company, though it has never had a union election, nevertheless maintains a staff person at each plant to monitor "sensitive" employees. (Sensitive employees, as defined in Chapter 2, are those who, either by the nature of the work they do or by virtue of outsiders they come in contact with, are thought to be potentially interested in unionization.) In describing the special attention that is paid to such workers, one personnel person said:

> *The company is not engaged in any invasion of privacy. When we say that someone monitors sensitive employees, we simply mean that you watch the back dock.*

It is at the back dock that company employees may converse with unionized truck drivers. Group activity, such as a multiply-signed grievance, is also monitored, for obvious reasons. Contracts with outside vendors are reviewed carefully because the company does not want to risk the possibility of being forced into a collective-bargaining structure as a joint employer.

The way in which the philosophy or the values of the founder become institutionalized as the company grows in size is critical. Over time, management frequently develops a real pride in the fact that the company is nonunion. This in turn seems to increase the motivation of management to stay nonunion. Having discussed the companies that either are or were philosophy-laden in their primary motivation, let us turn to the group of companies whose primary motivation appeared to be a strong desire to stay nonunion.

DOCTRINAIRE COMPANIES

Of those companies put into the doctrinaire classification, there are two types. One type has had direct experience with unions, and based on that experience, decided to avoid unions in the future. The other type has not had any direct experience, although key individuals may have had some in other companies. Top-level managements of doctrinaire companies are opposed to third-party interference. As one top official and member of the founding family put it:

> *This company has virtually no unions; in other words, we have never been interested in having [an outsider] . . . telling us how to run our business.*

Direct Experience

One company's doctrinaire nonunion stance stems from an experience it suffered over thirty years ago, when several local unions coordinated their actions for a concerted strike against the company. At the time, the company had twelve operating sites, of which ten were unionized. In all, over 90 percent of the company employees were union members. As a result of this strike, the president established a new policy toward unions. Briefly stated, it was to treat the present unions fairly, but to follow a policy of starting and keeping plants nonunion. The policy was to be pro-employee and pro-company, not anti-union.

The current situation is that out of 146 operating units, 115 are nonunion, and only 43 percent of the company's wage employees are union members. The increase in the number of union plants is predominantly due to acquisitions of already-unionized companies. Since 1946, the union has won only seven out of seventy-eight certification elections. This company considers its approach successful, and demonstrates it by citing higher productivity and morale and lower absenteeism in its nonunion plants. Management carefully selects and trains personnel administrators and foremen for the nonunion facilities, gives them a copy of a booklet entitled *The Supervisors Handbook on Maintaining Nonunion Status*, issues plant personnel superintendents a copy of *Confidential Guide to Nonunion Status*, and prescribes a rigorous role for corporate personnel in approving changes at the plant level and in auditing personnel activities.

In another large doctrinaire company, the percent of employees organized has decreased from 90 percent to 45 percent during the past thirty years. The history of this trend began long ago when management recognized the importance of employees' views and involvement, and therefore established work councils at several locations. When the National Labor Relations Act was enacted, such arrangements became of questionable legality because the employer had fostered their formation. Accordingly, company recognition of such councils was withdrawn. Thereafter, the employees formed independent unions at many locations. Upon proof of majority representation, the company recognized these unions according to law. However, during World War II experiences in expanded operations indicated to management that many new employees did not want unionization. At the time, the company's few nonunion plants were running well. Management then concluded that unions were not needed. Of the fifty plants built since World War II, only four are unionized.

One doctrinaire company arrived at its objective of being nonunion in a somewhat unusual manner. At this company, which had been unionized in the 1930s and 1940s, the union was decertified after World War II. Commenting on this, the director of personnel stated:

> The company's experience with the union brought a reappraisal of our climate and our management methods. We'd been to hell and back. Having gotten out, we decided it was not good for anyone. The long strike without pay, even most employees agreed, was no good. So, basically, we got the house in order, and we have determined to keep it so.

Putting the house in order, this person said, meant making substantial improvements in pay and benefits—but, more importantly, it meant "treating people as people." Since the institution of these and other significant personnel policy changes, there have been two union-organizational attempts, with the vote each time 2-to-1 against the union. The personnel director thinks that management can always depend on 25 percent of the employees being against the company. His view on union organizational drives is interesting: "No union organizes a company. You give it away. If an election is lost, it was lost prior to the campaign." This person's view appears to support the findings of Getman, Goldberg, and Herman, whose empirical study showed that neither the company nor the union is particularly successful in changing employees' minds during an election campaign.[1]

No Direct Experience

There is another group of doctrinaire companies that, for a variety of reasons, desire to remain nonunion even though they have not had any direct

---

[1]*See* Julius G. Getman, Stephen B. Goldberg, and Jeanne B. Herman, *Union Representation Elections: Law and Reality* (New York: Russell Sage Foundation, 1976).

experience with unionization. The vice-president of personnel in a West Coast company who feels that unions are the result of "inept management" admits that management has done all it can to avoid unionization. When asked why the company opposed unionization, this person gave these two reasons:

> *A union complicates matters. Without a union you are able to deal directly and quickly with the work force. With a union, this is not the case.*
> *A union creates a bad atmosphere. It creates an adversary kind of relationship. Where a union exists it pits people against the manager and this is not healthy for the company, for the manager, or for the people.*

The employee handbook of another company, which is entirely nonunion clearly states the company's position with respect to unions:

> *[The company's] personnel programs are designed to assist [workers] in satisfying their personal objectives in their work readily and without the need or cost of a labor union. [The company] does not say that unionism is either "bad" or "good." There are instances where employees have been helped by unions; but, on the other hand, there are many instances where unions have hurt employees. [Our company's] position is that unionism . . . would not help [our workers] in terms of pay and benefits or job challenge and satisfaction, and that unionism definitely would cost [our workers]—perhaps a great deal.*
>
> *During your employment with [us], you may be approached by a union organizer or another [company employee] trying to get you to sign a union card. You should be aware that no one can force you to sign such a card. If this does occur, we encourage you to, as a large majority of [our workers] all over the United States have done, reject the union's attempts to organize.*

In another company, which was originally family-oriented but is now managed by "professionals," an internal memorandum that was written by the vice-president of personnel on raises and benefits stated the nonunion policy well:

> *It is [our] policy to take all lawful steps necessary or desirable to operate on a nonunion basis. In effect, we have an implied, unwritten contract with our employees which says . . . that we will voluntarily take those steps which are necessary to ensure that . . . they will receive compensation and benefits which in their totality are competitive with the unionized companies in our field in this area.*

In this company, the approach was recently questioned by a new president, who was brought in from the outside. There was a union-organizational drive going on at the time, and at a top management meeting at which the company's strategy was being reviewed, the new president asked:

> *What's wrong if our employees want to join a union? It is their right under the law and I've managed in unionized companies before.*

Needless to say, this statement "upset the apple cart," and the situation calmed down only after the vice-presidents for administration and personnel were able to talk privately with the new president about the advantages of continuing the company's nonunion approach. The vice-president of personnel was somewhat uncomfortable with the company's nonunion position: Earlier in his career, he had been a union organizer; now he was being paid to keep the union out. He could do it, he told the new president, because he had worked out the conflicts.

Top management at another company has a very explicit goal of staying nonunion for two reasons: (1) no outside third-party interference is desired, and (2) the president wants to have something more innovative than a union. The "something" in this case is an employee committee, whose functions and responsibilities go far beyond the responsibilities of the employee committees of the 1920s. The company also has a profit-sharing plan and a pension plan, job posting, a formal grievance procedure with outside arbitration, much training and education, and a career-counseling system.

When this company experienced its first and only union-organizational drive, the president drew up a handwritten letter on personal stationery, which was reproduced and sent to each employee. The letter revealed much about the president, and about the president's philosophy and the nature of the company. A powerful document, the letter helped kill employee interest in the union.

In yet another case, the chairman of a large company said:

> We're not anti-union, but we're pro-company. Unionization is divisive, and for that reason we are opposed to it. For example, the United Auto Workers people are first auto workers, rather than Chrysler people or GM people or Ford people.
>
> Unions advance individual goals in a massive, monolithic way and they make it more difficult for the company. I believe that unions are generally restrictive—sheet-metal workers do sheet-metal work. This leads to jurisdictional issues, something our company does not have.
>
> Given that our company is nonunion, it is easier to mix exempt and nonexempt employees in programs and projects and have them all working and thinking that they are at least part of the same team. When we do it well, when we don't take advantage of the nonexempt employee, things go well.
>
> Poor supervision is associated with union drives. In most cases the company can predict where it might have a problem. When we do have a problem, we find that the company rules have not been obeyed, that there have been wage differentials which shouldn't have existed, that people who should have been promoted haven't been promoted, that there have been complaints for a year which haven't been followed up. Really, they are all quite simple things.

The vice-president of personnel in a company that is the target of an increasing number of union-organizational drives agreed that management's neglect is a major cause of such activity: "In six-out-of-ten campaigns the problem is ourselves. In the others, it seems to be based on geographic circumstances.'' Another executive interviewed made the same point another way: ''In the voting booth, the employee is never voting for the union. He is voting for or against management.''

In its effort to stay nonunion, one company adopted a harsh attitude toward an acquired plant that is unionized, located less than an hour away by car from one of the company's large nonunion plants. A close observer of this company stated that the unionized plant is used in a strategic and highly effective way as a scapegoat, to make it clear to the nonunion employees that they would not benefit from being unionized. Examination showed that wages and benefits *are* lower in the unionized plant. When asked why this was so, the vice-president of personnel defended the company's practices:

> *The plants are in different communities and our philosophy is to pay in relation to community averages. Also, we're willing to take a strike there. We'd rather have 250 employees on strike than have 3,000 join a union. We don't, in any sense of the word, let the union plant dictate what we will do for our nonunion employees.*

However, management maintains that it applies the same philosophy to all employees. For example, another vice-president said:

> *We give merit increases to everyone twice a year, even in the unionized plant. Even in the unionized plant we approach things the same way—the philosophy is the same. We believe in sitting down and talking to our employees.*

When asked how layoffs are handled at the unionized plant, the vice-president of personnel said:

> *We don't have layoffs at the unionized plant. They are sharing the work, too, because people are still human beings and we try to treat them the same way.*

CONCLUDING ANALYSIS AND COMMENTS

In this chapter, I have concentrated on the values and goals of predominantly and entirely nonunion companies. One group of companies was primarily philosophy-laden in which the nonunion state seems to be a by-product of the successful diffusion of the management values or philosophy. For a variety of reasons, top managements in the other group, the doctrinaire companies, have remaining nonunion as an explicit goal. It needs to be recognized, however, that the sources of motivation, even to a psychologist, are complicated. As suggested by the work of the late Raymond A. Bauer, the sources of motivation are so complicated that in more instances than not the individual may not well understand his or her own motives.[2] To the extent that the motives are understood it is possible for the individual to rationalize his behavior in almost any terms he chooses.

Perhaps it is useful to think of top management motivation as being on a continuum, as shown below:

$$\longleftarrow \hspace{6cm} \longrightarrow$$

Militantly   Anti-union   Doctrinaire   Semiphilosophy-Laden   Philosophy-Laden
anti-union

At one extreme would be those companies which are militantly anti-union; at the other would be the companies described as philosophy-laden. The continuum notion implies various shades or degrees of motivation with the word *reactive* associated with the left side and the word *proactive* attached to the right side of the spectrum. In addition to this notion of various degrees of motivation, it is also necessary to recognize that there is much fluidity as to where an organization lies on the continuum. For instance, the semi-sainthood status that could be implied by the categorization of the term "philosophy-laden" may cease if individual employees show an interest in joining a union. If a vigorous union drive began, the company's position on the continuum might shift to the left, toward the militantly anti-union side of the spectrum.

The top managements of many of the companies studied take pride in the fact that their organizations are nonunion. It seems to give them a certain status and prestige in the management community. Maintaining this source of self-respect also appears to be a powerful management motivation.

All this is to say that the distinction between philosophy-laden and doctrinaire companies may be somewhat academic. Motivation is always complex, explanations can be rationalizations, and the values of managements may change over time. In fact, the motivation for most companies comes from a combination of sources, and is a question of relative emphasis. The reality is that the companies studied are very much motivated by a desire to stay nonunion because of efficiency, philosophy, pride, and anti-union bias, or all of these or some combination of these reasons. The motivation to stay nonunion is perhaps more clear-cut in those predominantly nonunion companies that have had experience with unions, and based on that experience, have decided to keep all of their new plants nonunion. Their goals are generally more explicit.

The basic finding is that, in all the companies in the study, there is a strong concern at the top about people management and the climate of the organization. Although the character of it varies, there is also strong top management motivation to remain nonunion. Consistent with this objective, all of the companies in the study devote substantial time, effort, and money to the management of human

---

[2]*See* Raymond A. Bauer, "An Agenda for Research and Development on Corporate Responsiveness," in *Soziale Daten Und Politische Planung,* ed. Meinoff Dierkes (Frankfort/New York: Campus Publishers, 1975), pp. 69, 70.

resources. An essential point, then, is that strong motivation is necessary, but is not a sufficient condition to stay nonunion—it is crucial; it is the basis for everything that follows.

As has been hinted several times in this chapter, what is important is the way in which the values and goals of top management are expressed or are made manifest in these organizations. Obviously, effective policies are a critical must. The importance and difficulty of the institutionalization process cannot be overestimated. One key to it is the role of the personnel department. Another key is a comprehensive set of personnel policies and programs. However, before turning to the role of the personnel department and of the key personnel policies and practices of the companies studied let us first examine the consequences of remaining nonunion.

CHAPTER FOUR

Perceived Advantages
and Disadvantages
of Being Nonunion

I have been asked if it could be said that any of the companies I studied are nonunion by chance or by luck. Frankly, no company in this study was nonunion by chance or by luck; in fact, each had been working hard to implement its philosophy or to achieve its goals. Since this is the case, it is important to understand *why* these companies work so hard to remain nonunion, and why it is so important to them to do so. In this chapter, we will take a look at the advantages and disadvantages of a nonunion operation, as perceived by the senior management and, in some cases, by the supervisors who must put company policy into practice.

PERCEIVED ADVANTAGES

The overwhelming majority of executives interviewed maintained that a nonunion operation is a more efficient one. They primarily attributed the greater efficiency to the flexibility that exists in the absence of the work rule restrictions that govern unionized plants.

The freedom to make changes in work assignments and shifts was probably most frequently cited to be the result of this greater flexibility. "People here do two jobs," said one executive, "and they can be asked to do three or four." Without work rule restrictions, cross-utilization of personnel is possible. According to many managers, the greater efficiency results in substantial savings. One executive said, ''if we could not change peoples' jobs and shifts as easily as we do now, the company would be in great trouble.'' Some managers also felt that movement between work assignments reduces job boredom for employees.

Another major advantage of nonunion status, according to many executives, is low turnover rates. One company figured its turnover rate to be only about 40 percent of the industry average. Another company had such a low rate that it had not even kept records of turnover for the past two years. Still another company showed a turnover of 5.5 percent annually (only 3.5 percent when retirement losses are omitted). The combination of low turnover with a policy of promoting from within can, however, create a personnel problem, according to the senior vice-president of a company with a turnover rate of 0.5 percent per month. At this company, its low turnover rate and its promotion policy led to difficulty in implementing affirmative action plans for women and minorities, particularly in higher-level jobs.

Some managers felt that they employ fewer people than union plants do in order to achieve the same levels of productivity. One company chairman, for instance, boasted of the superior productivity in his company compared to competitors. He cited a number of ratios in support of this point; for example, the company ''mans lean'' in the shipping department, with a volume comparable to the unionized competitors.

In some cases, managers felt that their approach to employee relations as a nonunion company gives them a distinct competitive advantage in hiring. Several statistics support this claim: One company, located in a city and known as the best employer in the area, receives an average of 8,000 to 10,000 applications for the 500 job openings it has in a normal year. Another company, which has been leading its industry in pay and benefits, had 23,000 applications on file for only 375 job openings. (This company also had fewer employees per sale dollar than any other company in its industry.) Many personnel officers were convinced that their employees are more loyal or hard-working and have higher morale than average workers. One vice-president, although skeptical of others' claims of superior productivity in a nonunion plant, did believe that ''being nonunion assures a fair day's work for a fair day's pay,'' something he seemed to imply does not occur in a unionized plant. Another executive reported that: ''Our employees really put out in times of crisis; they'll work hard and won't even want to collect overtime.''

Another advantage of nonunion status perceived by some members of management was that resistance to technological change is lower in a nonunion environment. Therefore, nonunion companies can make operational changes more easily than unionized companies can.

Due to the more efficient operation of the enterprise, then, the majority of executives believed a nonunion operation to be less costly. However, if it costs the companies in this sample less to operate on a nonunion basis, it is not because of lower wages. In general, wages and benefits are likely to be higher in the nonunion firms of an industry, with the exception of plants in southern and lower-wage communities. One executive did comment that the percentage of the sales dollar going to payroll was less at his company than at any unionized competitor, adding that "the company has saved millions of dollars over the years because our hiring wage rates are considerably lower than those offered by our unionized competitors." This company's management apparently believes it can attract enough capable people, in spite of its lower starting pay, by quickly advancing good performers to rates that are actually higher than those paid by its unionized competitors. Although a low starting wage is rare among the companies studied, it should be observed that the use of merit increases is widespread.

Another reason some managers thought that operating on a nonunion basis is less costly is that the expenses associated with strikes are avoided. One management official noted that his company had not lost one hour due to a labor problem in forty-seven years. He observed that this is undoubtedly a good selling point to customers. Another manager stated that his company "picked up business from a struck competitor that they never regained." Some managers felt that the reduced threat of employee unrest not only made them more attractive to customers, they expressed the belief that employees who have never paid union dues are also beneficiaries of the company's nonunion status.

Less managerial time spent on grievances and contract negotiations was another frequently cited cost-saving benefit of nonunion status. Several people, however, denied that there are any cost advantages at all associated with remaining nonunion. According to one official in a company with both union and nonunion plants, "it certainly doesn't cost less. It's about the same as a unionized organization, because we spend on training and communications instead of on negotiations, grievance administration, or arbitration." He felt that since pay scales are higher at the company's nonunion plants than the unionized ones, the nonunion ones probably cost slightly more. As a final word in the costs debate, the corporate director of employee relations at a different company with both union and nonunion plants said:

> The costs are hard to measure because many are intangible. One definite cost is the higher wages and better benefits package [at our nonunion plants]. However, the premium paid is not large and is more than offset by the productivity gain. The costs of specialized training of supervisors, attitude surveys, etc., are not relevant because they are used in both our union and nonunion plants.

Whether or not a nonunion plant is more economical, many of the managers interviewed maintained that time spent positively on human relations programs, rather than negatively on grievances, has a distinct effect on employee and management morale. Managers preferred to handle human relationships on a direct, individual basis rather than through an organization or a group characteristic of a union. In this way, they felt, employees' loyalty will then go to the company rather than to the union. Managers mentioned positive attitudes, high morale, and loyalty. The chairman of a company that spends much time on wage and salary administration put it this way:

> *The pay policy isn't really the reason the company remains nonunion. When the company is successful it is because it involves the employees. If you get your whole story across to the whole company, and we do this frequently through profit-sharing meetings, you are successful.*
>
> *I believe that in a nonunion environment it is easier to obtain the objective at the same cost, and when it is obtained all the employees get more, particularly through profit sharing.*

In the view of many of those I interviewed, the freedom to experiment with employee-relations plans, the opportunity to deal directly with workers, and the avoidance of an adverse relationship between management and employees lead to improved company morale. In the course of our conversations, it also became clear that a further advantage of a nonunion status is the satisfaction of certain emotional needs of top management. Many managers took obvious pride in their personnel philosophies and accomplishments, and felt that their efforts had a direct and visible effect on the life of the company. With such belief in the perceived advantages of a nonunion environment, it is not surprising that some looked upon a union as a personal affront.

PERCEIVED DISADVANTAGES

The senior managers interviewed were almost unanimous in agreeing that there are no disadvantages associated with being nonunion. However, one possible disadvantage began to emerge by implication rather than by outright declaration: the apparent freedom to experiment claimed by so many personnel managers may be illusory. As will be shown in subsequent chapters, many managers deny themselves some of the flexibility advantages that their company's nonunion status gives them. Some companies, for example, have full-employment practices. Some companies give considerable weight to seniority even in promotion decisions. The practices of many companies are such that they refrain from using much of their cherished flexibility.

Occasionally—although examples are rare—employees who knew well that management wished to remain nonunion would exercise their power to unionize to their advantage. At one plant, for instance, there had been an election drive to unionize each year for thirteen years, and each year the employees invited one of three unions to come in and organize the plant. Part of management's response had been to give a formal dinner dance for the employees. After this had gotten to be an annual affair, the three unions finally realized they were being used, and declined further invitations from the employees to organize the plant. (It should be noted, by the way, that this company's other nonunion plants were infrequently targets of organization attempts.)

At another company, the employees of one small, isolated unit threatened to unionize in order to obtain more recognition from its large parent company. According to the firm's vice-president of personnel, these employees had argued that they had to say they wanted a union in order to get a management of their own. In yet another company, personnel managers felt that their annual attitude survey,* which top management assessed very seriously, was abused by employees. The managers objected in particular to one question on the survey that asked the respondent to agree or disagree with the statement: "Most employees I know would like to see the union get in," their objection being that employees who did not actually want a union would agree with the statement simply to keep management on its toes and sensitive to employees.

Judging from these cases, it appears that the doctrinaire nonunion company can become the victim of what it perceives to be a blackmail routine. However, from the standpoint of workers, in the absence of union organization the *threat* of unionization is their only source of collective power. Whether this power is wielded frivolously or is reserved for serious complaints remains an unanswered question. The cases cited above appeared to be uncommon; they tended, moreover, to be associated with companies that were predominantly nonunion, and with those committed to avoiding unionization at almost any cost as a matter of doctrine rather than philosophy (see Chapter 3). For our purposes, we simply note that some members of management did feel that employees can exploit the knowledge that their company desires to remain nonunion.

The second disadvantage of a union operation was expressed most strongly by the supervisors and managers who actually implemented the policies of top management. The only person, among all the top management people I interviewed, who directly expressed any doubt at all about the advantages of being nonunion, was a vice-president of personnel who said:

> I frankly feel that there are substantial disadvantages to being nonunion if you have weak managers, especially at the first and second level, because it takes good judgment, honesty, integrity, and much hard work by each and every member of management to maintain a positive employee-relations climate. If you don't have strong supervision, a well-written, tightly managed union contract might be the best way to go. I believe some of the low-paying companies with poor supervision are a good example of this.

Many other executives did agree that the management job at a nonunion plant is more difficult than at a unionized one. One officer, who had held a variety of jobs

---

*I will examine the use of attitude surveys as an important feedback mechanism in Chapter 13.

in unionized plants, thought that the personnel manager's job is easier in a unionized plant because the decisions are not as far reaching there: "You have a contract to help you interpret various things." On the same issue, the vice-president of personnel of another company elaborated:

> *Some say that the advantage of being unionized is that things are spelled out. I do believe that being union means that policies are clear. In my view, being union works well if you have a lot of autocratic supervisors around.*

As an example of this:

> *The [company's sick-pay] policy is that the employee—on the day he joins the company—has 180 sick days if he needs them, and none if he does not. The supervisors, however, keep asking for guidance with respect to the administration of the policy. We [in personnel] say to them, "Make tough decisions—it's your job."*

Finally, with respect to the management job in a nonunion plant versus one in a unionized plant, a company chairman made this point:

> *If the union were to come to our company, in some ways it would make things easier, for certain things would then be clearly left to the union. Some of our supervisors, in fact, think that it would be easier to manage with a union.*

There was not complete consensus on this matter, however; one vice-president of personnel said that any supervisor who says that working in a nonunion plant makes his job more difficult has probably never worked in a union plant. In his view, the supervisor in such a situation is always in the middle between the employee, the union steward, and management.

Many supervisors, however, agreed with the opinion that their function would be more difficult in a nonunion company. Indeed, it was not clear to me whether the top managements of some of the companies studied had given adequate consideration to the concerns of their supervisors. I uncovered some cases that were not only difficult from the supervisory point of view, but also appeared disadvantageous for the company, at least in the short run. Those supervisors who did agree had three general complaints. First, they believed that decisions were more difficult because of the flexibility of their companies' policies. Second, they felt that some employees abused certain policies, and that the risk of excessive tolerance was high. In addition to finding it difficult to discipline employees for poor attendance records, many supervisors found it virtually impossible to discipline for poor performance. Finally, some supervisors found the work environment to be too loose for high productivity. It should be observed before we explore these concerns that supervisors in unionized companies will voice the same or similar complaints, and that most of these problems may arise whether or not a company is nonunion.

The threat of employees abusing what is perceived to be the greater freedom of a nonunion plant particularly worries some supervisors. One, who formerly worked for a highly unionized firm, commented:

> *This company is more ambiguous than any other company I am used to. One of its strengths is the fact that we treat people as individuals, but it is also a weakness. For example, the company has an extremely liberal short-term disability plan, and, as a result, the company suffers much absenteeism. Supervisors, moreover, have a lot of discretion. Instead of having a hard and fast rule, there is a lot of flexibility. The supervisor has to consider the reasons for the absence, and he can still recommend raises. You don't just look at the numbers.*

A personnel administrator at the same company told of some of the frustrations of dealing with employee problems in a company that prides itself on individual treatment. She said that when difficult problems are taken to top management for solutions, guidance or direction, the answer frequently received from the top is "do what is right."

A manager of another company also talked about the lack of specific direction, saying:

> *There is a problem because we are nonunion. The line manager's job is more difficult. There is a lack of specific direction under policies and practices. The policy manual is loosely interpreted and there is no consistency in how we operate even in our division. There is a night-and-day difference in terms of the way some policies are administered.*

In particular, some supervisors found discipline onerous in their companies. According to one manager:

> *Discharge and discipline are almost impossible. If you become a permanent employee, your job is very secure. Dismissal is almost unheard of at this company. The company stresses attendance, and besides stealing, about the only way for a person to be discharged is for having a very bad attendance record. But it is extremely difficult to discharge an employee. You have to put an ironclad case together.*

At another company, a supervisor made the highly dubious statement that:

> *It is easier to fire an employee in a union shop. Here, it doesn't pay to rock the boat. Senior employees feel a lot of security. Unless you are a complete alcoholic, a rapist, or absent an awful lot, you are not going to get*

fired. After a person has been with the company fifteen years, he cannot be
fired without the president's approval.

One wonders if this supervisor has ever tried to fire anyone in a union shop!

Another supervisor spoke of the absenteeism encouraged by his company's salary plan. Years ago the company did not pay an employee for the first three days of absence. Today the company does, and according to this manager, there is some short-term abuse. Other supervisors felt that certain employees learn the attendance guidelines and, with this knowledge, take advantage of the company.

In addition to the difficulties associated with disciplining employees for poor performance and attendance, supervisors also complained of other employee behavior that can make the supervisor's job more difficult. One company, for example, maintains a recreation room for employees. Equipped with pool tables, card tables, current magazines and fresh coffee, this lounge is very attractive by any standard. Commenting on it, a supervisor of skilled maintenance people said:

The company offers so many things for the employee to play with that it
makes the supervisor's job harder. I'll have some employees shooting pool
fifteen to twenty minutes after their break time. I went up to one employee and
he said, "Well, what are you going to do, fire me?" He knows I can't do that.
It makes it bad for the supervisor. Nothing is said about half-hour breaks,
two-hour lunches, or coming in late. Our hands are tied.

Illustrating the difference between a line view and a staff view concerning these problems, the personnel director at this company had this to say about the lounges:

Some of this company's nicest facilities are the employee lounges.
While some outsiders see this as a waste of money, it is this way because we
think good working conditions and good resting conditions go hand in hand.

In one company, which had dispensed with time clocks as part of its decision to put all workers on salary, some supervisors felt that workers were taking excessively long lunch breaks and were working less overtime than they had been assigned. One supervisor said: "No one has the guts to address this problem. I don't either. The employees take turns on the machines, and without time clocks, they lie when they fill out their time cards." This supervisor would prefer an individual incentive system and a return of the time clocks. Another supervisor at this company, who also complained about the loss of the time clocks, mentioned that when the clocks were removed many of the supervisors were up in arms. However, a vice-president had argued that if the supervisors pushed the issue, he would know that more time clocks were needed, and fewer supervisors. This supervisor also said that the removal of time clocks was consistent with the liberal philosophy of the company: In his view, the company is run for people rather than for profits.

One additional complaint came from a supervisor who said that his company takes better care of its nonexempt employees than its exempt ones. In his view, the company overlooks and overworks its first-line managers; he supervises 90 employees, and some supervisors have as many as 120 people.

In sum, lower management may be the casualty in a nonunion firm. Some of their views of upper management and the personnel department sounded to me like the negative views supervisors generally take of unions. They felt that they were constrained by management philosophy, that those on-high sided with the employee, that they were persistently being examined and judged by the upper echelons, and that they themselves could not take action. In many companies there appeared to be definite penalties for a supervisor known to have difficulty dealing with employees. In the words of several supervisors: ''The manager here will not be promoted unless he is good in employee relations''; ''it does not pay to make waves, and be labeled as someone who has people problems''; and ''in this company it will stifle your career to get a reputation that you cannot get along with people.''

CONCLUDING ANALYSIS AND COMMENTS

The most difficult question to answer is whether or not a nonunion operation is more efficient, and therefore more economical. The absence of hard data is the greatest obstacle to discovering the truth. Moreover, few companies in the sample had comparable competitors. During the course of my study, in fact, two persons asked if I could supply any evidence for them, as both wanted data with which to convince their top managements that the effort to remain nonunion was worthwhile. There is by no means any consensus on this issue among executives that is based on hard data.

Some consultants estimate that a union will raise labor costs 20 percent to 35 percent. One has broken it down to first-year and ongoing costs, and has included such items as legal and arbitration expenses. Also, the initial costs for a company wishing to remain nonunion may be high, but if a union comes in it would be easy for the costs to increase, as the experience of the consultants suggests. In his book, *Making Unions Unnecessary*, Charles L. Hughes wrote:

> *Unions are expensive. A privately-conducted study of eighty-three companies shows that the payroll and benefits costs of unionized companies average 25% more than those of nonunion companies or the nonunion facilities of companies that have both labor organizations and union-free operations. This cost is not primarily in individual wages and benefits, but results from redundant employees, narrowly defined jobs, restrictive production, strikes, and slowdowns. The costs are the price of inefficiency and*

ineffectiveness. The tragedy is that the money does not go to people. With few exceptions, employees within a given industry earn about the same rates of pay whether they are union members or not. Many nonunion companies keep their wages in line with unionized companies, and most particularly unionized companies match nonunion wages to their labor contracts. The additional costs that result from the presence of labor unions is mostly in lower productivity: union members lose, company management loses, and the consumer loses.[1]

Dr. Hughes informed me that his sample included about 300 companies with both union and nonunion operations. His statements were based on payroll and benefits as a percentage of billings. According to Hughes, it takes fewer people to run a nonunion company due to the absence of restrictive work practices.[2] However, the fact that the nonunion plants of many companies are the newer, more modern facilities that have younger work forces may help explain the ratio; indeed, unless the data is corrected for these variables as well as for many others, it is difficult to get a handle on the precise costs of operating a union company versus the costs of operating a nonunion one.

Although there is a remarkable absence of hard data for very understandable reasons, most senior executives did *think* that it costs less to operate on a nonunion basis. However, for a variety of reasons, there are major comparability problems even among companies in the same industry with respect to any independent analysis of this issue. Some of the companies in the sample, moreover, have relatively unique product–market situations. While this is changing, a few of the companies have, or at least have had, little effective competition. Of course, there are also difficult productivity measurement problems. If it does cost the companies in my sample less to operate on a nonunion basis, except for a few very unusual cases the savings for these companies are clearly not due to lower individual wage and benefit costs. The savings come from higher productivity, which in turn results from greater flexibility in the use of people, less resistance to technological change, a more favorable employee relations climate, and the savings associated with lower absenteeism and turnover.

Unless there are opportunities for the study of nonunion plants versus comparable union plants, companies should be very skeptical of the statements made about the costs and benefits of operating nonunion. Such statements need to be examined with caution. While costly and inefficient union plants may exist, this is not necessarily a result of their unionized status only. By the same token, the perceived lower costs of apparently efficient nonunion plants may be the motivation for, rather than the result of, their nonunion status. What seems particularly clear, in any case, is that investigation into the precise costs and benefits of being nonunion is needed.

---

[1]Charles L. Hughes, *Making Unions Unnecessary* (New York: Executive Exterprises Publications Co., Inc., 1976), p. 2.

[2]Private correspondence.

In the absence of hard data, people are left to their subjective perceptions. In sum, the testimony of top management is that the productivity of the nonunion company is higher. The views of some supervisors, however, raise questions about the testimony regarding high productivity of some of the senior managers interviewed. Even if the perceptions of top management are faulty (and I am not prepared to say that they are), they do count: Myths can be significant.

The assertions of higher productivity of some of the predominantly non-union companies would seem to have more merit, since some of these companies have comparable facilities that are unionized. Here too, however, the data is vague. For example, is productivity higher in a nonunion plant *because* it is nonunion, or is it due to a younger, more rural work force associated with the plant's location? Moreover, in some cases productivity in a unionized facility is below management's desires due to concessions erroneously made to the union over the years in order to avoid strikes.

Management at one large company not in the sample became increasingly frustrated by the work rule restrictions agreed to over the years. Under a new chairman, this company began to bargain more toughly (allowing several strikes) and to regain, via work rule changes, the money spent in wage and benefit increases. In fact, some people have said that some plants are managed in such a way as to encourage decertifications. Also, this company's management has actively worked to keep its new plants nonunion through the introduction of a merit-salary concept resulting in premium pay and job enrichment, and by (in the words of an executive of a competitor) "running its plants fairly." The motivation for the behavior of this management, to emphasize, springs from the unsatisfactory work rules and inefficiencies existing in its unionized plants. This being the case, and for other reasons as well, the productivity of its newer, nonunion plants is higher than at its unionized plants.

Viewed broadly, the economic motivation for staying nonunion seems stronger in the predominantly nonunion company and in some doctrinaire companies than in the companies I have termed philosophy-laden. In the latter, lower costs seem more of a by-product of the successful implementation of the philosophy rather than its goal. But what is rationalization or myth, and what is fact or fiction, is not always clear.

Again, as noted in Chapter 3, the distinction between philosophy-laden and doctrinaire companies is not clear. The philosophy or values of managements may change over time. Companies do become unionized, even though their primary goal was to remain nonunion. Given the motivation of top management, the skill with which the management philosophy is applied is crucial if the desired consequences are to be realized and the undesirable consequences minimized.

Discussion and analysis of this larger task will occupy major parts of the subsequent chapters of this book. In addition to top management's commitment, the role of the personnel department is important, as is a number of basic personnel policies and practices including employment security, promotion from within, pay and benefits, and formal communications programs. However, as discussed in Chapter 2, geographic location, the company's technology, the size of plant, and the nature of the work force are also important.

The role of the personnel department, however, is basic, and it is to this topic that we now turn.

CHAPTER FIVE

The Status and Role
of the Personnel Department

In its relationship to the values and goals of top management, the personnel department is the structural home of many influential activities. As a rule, the chairmen and presidents of the companies studied are committed to and support their personnel organizations. With such support, the personnel department has and exercises much power. This power generally comes about as a result of delegation by the founder or by successors of the founder, often through the traditions of the organization, and through the individual ability and initiative of the personnel officers.

This chapter will focus on both the status and the role of the personnel department, its sources of influence, as well as on how personnel interacts with line management at different levels within the company. It will also examine reporting relationships and their functions, the ways in which personnel departments are structured, the relationships of corporate personnel to division and plant personnel, how personnel departments are viewed by supervisors and line managers, and the nature of the people who manage them.

SOURCES OF PERSONNEL'S INFLUENCE

There is much evidence that suggests the high status, power, and influence of the personnel function in the companies studied. Some of the evidence consists of the content of casual conversations; some of it is derived from an examination of organization charts, committee memberships within the company, reporting relationships, and actual responsibilities and behavior.

Toward the end of a lengthy interview about personnel's role with the vice-president of personnel of a company whose two founders have a goal of remaining nonunion, the vice-president casually remarked: "When the president is away, I run the company." He modified this statement somewhat by adding that all the top people are peers, but that they nevertheless come to him when they have problems.

This is an amazing statement for a vice-president of personnel to be able to make. This executive had been recruited to the personnel vice-presidency ten years earlier. When he arrived as vice-president of personnel, there was much conflict at the top, and he had to do a lot of organizational development work as well as pull a fragmented personnel department together. Today, unlike the case in many companies where personnel is merely told about the company's plans and is asked to keep the organization out of trouble, his personnel group is very much involved in all front-end planning. As a member of the top-level operating committee, this personnel executive has a voice in such corporate policy-setting matters as strategy, pricing, sales, facilities planning, and acquisitions.

Position in the Management Hierarchy

Indicative of their status and influence, more than half of the human resource or personnel vice-presidents of the companies studied report directly to the chief executive officer. Most of the others report to an administrative vice-president or to a staff vice-president. Several of the administrative vice-presidents had formerly been their company's director of personnel: Thus, while they now have broader responsibilities and no longer carry the personnel title, in many cases they seem to be their company's real personnel head.

The reporting relationships say much about the status and influence of the personnel officer in the companies studied. These people are at a high level, in a position which allows their views and recommendations (as are those of the financial, marketing, manufacturing people) to be directly heard by top management. If the chief personnel executive is truly a member of top management, this better ensures that the personnel viewpoint is adequately represented in all broad policy decisions.

At one company, the vice-president of personnel, who was recruited from a labor-relations post in another industry, wears several hats, reporting to three different executives: the chairman (who is a grandson of the founder), the president, and the manufacturing vice-president. Given this unusual reporting relationship, the manufacturing vice-president must regard the vice-president of personnel as an equal at least.

Illustrative of personnel's involvement in broad policy matters, the vice-president of personnel at four of the companies studied is a member of his or her company's board of directors. When insiders are on a board of directors, it is common that the chief financial officer is one of them. However, it is rare indeed for one of the inside members to be a vice-president of personnel. When asked about this, the "Number Two" person in personnel at one of these four companies said: "The key point is that you have to balance the financial people." At another company, the senior vice-president of personnel, also a member of the company's board of directors, is viewed as a possible heir-apparent to the presidency. In fact, the present chairman used to be the company's vice-president of personnel. Although not on their company's board of directors, many of the other vice-presidents of personnel are members of a management committee or executive committee.

Since the personnel department has traditionally lacked status and influence, it is possible that some of the personnel officers interviewed have somewhat exaggerated their power and clout to an outside investigator. However, much evidence was gathered in support of the contention that they do have and exercise considerable authority. Several of those interviewed certainly do not view themselves as traditional staff advisors—rather, they see themselves as having a key responsibility for the management of the human resources of their company. For example, consider the views of two different vice-presidents of personnel:

> The staff advisory notion is fine conceptually, but if we didn't have some muscle we wouldn't be where we are today. We try to be reasonable and practical, but we are the experts in personnel and employee relations and we do that job. Managers and employees in other company functions are knowledgeable and expert in their respective fields, and we expect them to present and discuss their point of view. Therefore, we believe disagreement is healthy, and we don't bring top management into the picture very often. Naturally, since we are nonunion, we are particularly sensitive to employee concerns. There are letters from employees and responses to them. We don't always contradict line management but it happens frequently enough so that the employee knows the whole procedure does work.

> Although we will bend over backward to save an employee, we are not an advocate for the employee. Our job is to run the people part of the business. This job has been delegated to us by the CEO [chief executive officer]. We in personnel are management. I am, for example, the final decision maker on salary. We try to be in on the front end of policy setting and do a minimum amount of monitoring and policing. In a number of our plants, the personnel manager is the "Number Two" man.

We can better understand personnel's role in one organization by examining the nature of the hiring-and-firing process. In this 34,000-employee company, the large central personnel group interviews and hires job applicants. Local management simply screens applicants and refers those it considers qualified to corporate headquarters for testing and additional interviews. This is so despite the fact that only 30 percent of the company's employees are located at corporate headquarters; the rest are in various facilities throughout the United States. While the investment this company makes in employment must be very large indeed, its turnover is extremely low. Moreover, the company hires people for a career rather than for a job.

At this company, corporate personnel also must approve all discharges. To illustrate the way the discharge procedure works, if a manager is having problems with an employee, he or she is to counsel with the employee and document it in writing. If these counseling efforts fail, the employee will receive a "last-chance letter," which the employee must sign. The purpose of the letter is to inform the employee that he or she is on probation, and that any subsequent infraction may result in dismissal.

If the employee is "bad" again, the manager may suspend him or her. The manager will then submit a written report, requesting certain disciplinary action, to the department head. This request, in turn, must be approved by a division senior vice-president. If the division vice-president concurs, the request will go to corporate personnel and to the company's equal employment opportunity coordinator. If approved at this step, the request goes to the senior vice-president of personnel for final approval. These checks and appraisals are to minimize the chance of an action being taken on the basis of poor judgment.

An employee who has been disciplined can appeal his or her case to anyone in the review process, including the company's president. Some decisions are reversed, such as when an employee presents new information or evidence of extenuating circumstances of which the line managers in the decision process were unaware.

Policy Making and Involvement with Top Management

The involvement in broad policy decisions not only lends status to the personnel function but also ties into personnel's policy-making function. Many of the personnel vice-presidents interviewed said that they were deeply involved with senior management. Describing the function, one vice-president said:

> The personnel function here has more responsibility than at most companies. For example, we are involved in all the hiring, including the hiring of executive vice-presidents. We are involved in all the training and development, including sales training and organizational design and strategy.

That is a very unusual role for personnel, for many personnel directors have had nothing to say about the selection of supervisors, let alone the selection of vice-presidents!

Commenting on his sources of influence, another vice-president of personnel said:

> I report to the CEO. I am a king maker but that is a negative way to put
> it. I have been involved in organization analysis. I participate in every
> upgrading, promotion, or transfer. I have taught the president and the
> chairman not to make key personnel decisions without talking to me.

In examining the nature of personnel's involvement with top-level management as well as the question of power, one instance came up in which a plant manager had refused to bring his employees all the way up to the pay rates recommended by corporate personnel. This situation escalated into a confrontation between the vice-president of personnel and the plant manager, in the office of the chairman. The plant manager lost. The vice-president of personnel commented:

> The confrontation had to do with the principles of nonexempt reviews.
> This is clearly part of the management system of this company and the
> confrontation was really quite embarrassing. But it is personnel's job to make
> sure that the legitimate needs of employees are taken into account in the
> decision-making processes. Things that make good sense have to be done,
> otherwise you are vulnerable to unionization.

Essential to the strength of the personnel department are the rights to elevate decisions to a higher level of management and to establish rules of conflict resolution.

To illustrate the relationship of the personnel department to line management, and the power of the personnel department with respect to discharge, here is a statement written in the early 1950s by the vice-president of personnel in one of the companies:

> The only individuals who can separate a person from the company are
> those in the personnel department. This, I think, is a fundamentally sound
> philosophy, because if it is understood by the employees, then they know their
> cases will have proper and complete consideration and they will receive fair
> treatment.
>
> This philosophy on discharges also helps the line supervision, because
> they know they must have a just and reasonable cause for recommending the
> separation of an individual and, just because they don't like Bill Jones or
> Sadie Smith, they can't have that particular person separated from the
> company.

Similar to other enterprises started as a family business, this company was molded by the personality and philosophy of its founders and their descendants. The personnel function continues as a strong one indeed. The chairman, the president of a major division, and an executive vice-president have each held the post of vice-president of personnel. Several former directors of personnel are on the company's board of directors, and young personnel representatives feel they are on a good track to advance in the company.

The current vice-president of personnel said that sometimes the personnel department is criticized for being too powerful, and that snide remarks are heard from time to time about "personnel running the business": "The line managers like to pay well, give raises, and they don't like being told what they can't do." It is also said that in this company it is hard to fire people because of personnel. However, the vice-president of personnel insisted this is not the case, saying that the line managers are reluctant to fire people and that personnel really has to push to get the managers to be objective. Yet, as the statement makes clear, personnel does have veto power.

The head of personnel for another company, a member of the board, was described by a senior member of the employee-relations staff:

> *He has been with the company for forty years. He is known as "Mr. Equity." Employees know that they can call him and if they do they will get a fair shake. He is a senior officer and he executes the philosophy of the family. He even strengthens or enhances it.*

A younger member of the employee relations staff described him and the situation more bluntly:

> *Until five years ago, the company was extremely paternalistic. People were congratulated on their anniversary. They received a birthday card from the company. Personnel was looked upon as the gestapo. You were the enforcer of the policy. You came around when there was trouble. You represented top management. The source of power was "Mr. Equity." He helped form the company. He knows everyone and he is very close to top management. He is on the board.*

Within the past five years, the founder's son has become president; a professional personnel director, with much labor-relations experience, has been recruited from the outside and reports to "Mr. Equity," who is now close to retirement.

At another company the industrial relations vice-president felt that the important point to understand about this company, unlike some other organizations, was that industrial relations is on a par with manufacturing. At the time of one visit to this company, the manufacturing vice-president was trying to transfer several senior employees for reasons not within accepted policy. The industrial relations vice-president had to force abandonment of these plans. Although admitting that the transfers made short-run sense from a manufacturing viewpoint, the industrial relations vice-president knew they violated policy, and could have a long-run detrimental impact on employee relations.

Indicative of the power of personnel, a vice-president of personnel in another company said: ". . . we would not build a plant in [a certain area] because [it] is a hot bed of unionism." A member of this staff, in response to a question, said that corporate personnel would not permit one plant to move to a four-day workweek or to a flexible working-hours program. This is due to top-level management's desire for consistency and uniformity throughout the corporation with respect to key personnel policies and practices.

This personnel department, with top-level management's help, has directed considerable effort to defining its role in the organization, and the ways in which it can intervene in the line organization are carefully spelled out. However, some line managers talked about personnel people being police. "They tell us what we cannot do," is the way several line managers put it.

In some companies there was talk of employee-relations "czars" who used to run the personnel function. They were always close to the company's founder, and it was reported that they exercised their power in a manner that could be described as ruthless. They got compliance with their wishes by saying that if something was not done the way they recommended, the company would have a union. While these charges may be exaggerated, their successors—people who view themselves as personnel professionals—claim they operate in a different manner.

Power that is wisely exercised is a key to effectiveness. Although many more illustrations of personnel power in the companies studied could be cited, there is no need to overstress the point. Often this power is simply the delegated right to say "no." This veto power gives enormous significance to the advise-and-counsel function of personnel staff members. Their audit-and-control function, discussed in a later chapter, is also an important source of power and influence.

Another way of saying this is that personnel departments are either an integral part of or very close to top management. Illustrative of this relationship to top management are the size, decor, and location of their offices. The effective vice-president mentioned at the very beginning of this chapter had recently been promoted to vice-president for administration. Commenting on the staging of officers and how the company's vice-presidents are purposely commingled, this person said:

> [The new personnel vice-president] could have stayed with the personnel people or joined the other vice-presidents. He joined the vice-presidents because it is important that people be able to communicate by only having to walk across the hall.
>
> In one plant, personnel was on the lower level. It is now three floors up with the other offices. It is very good to have the personnel person a member of his peer group—that is, with the other top people.

Access to and use of company airplanes is another indication of status in large organizations. The vice-president of personnel in one company who is a member of a national personnel advisory council arrives by company airplane. One vice-president of personnel uses a company jet to visit universities, and another regularly uses the company plane to visit plants and attend meetings in distant cities. These personnel executives, like their counterparts in marketing, finance, and manufacturing, use the company plane for business purposes.

Although personnel's status and its relationship to top management has been discussed at some length, one should recognize that these characteristics do not always exist. Not all personnel departments are headed by someone who wields such extreme power. In some cases, the chief executive officer retains the power that a strong personnel department would have in other cases. With respect to one company, a university administrator who knows the company well asked this very probing question: "Is it possible to have a strong personnel function without having an effective personnel department?" This administrator was impressed with the line managers, particularly with their motivation, commitment, and loyalty to their organization, at this particular company, though not particularly impressed with the personnel department. Thus it was this person's tentative conclusion that it is possible to have a strong personnel function without having a strong personnel department. It may be accurate to say that this company has an extremely strong personnel function because it is really headed by the company's founders, and because the line managers are their own personnel managers.

In general, if the people-oriented founders still influence the business there is less need for formalization and institutionalization. Discussing these issues, a vice-president of personnel who has worked for two large, nonunion companies said:

> When I was with [the other company], I could still see [the founder's] philosophies having a significant impact on our employee relations strategies and tactics. Now that I am at [this company], I can see it even more clearly. I believe the philosophies which [were] initiated in founding the company will be with us for a long time.
>
> It is an interesting challenge for a vice-president of personnel to come into a company where you have a founder and president who is such a good personnel man. It is a tough act to follow. Some would not like it but I find it very rewarding because you can take his basic intuitive style and extend even further his intent with appropriate policies, strategies, and tactics to assure that his basic philosophy continues through time, regardless of how fast and dramatic corporate change may be.

It is probably a rather good generalization to say that the strength of any personnel department is in a direct relationship with the strength of the people-orientation of the president, how much power is delegated to the department, the size of the organization, and the ability and personality of the vice-president of personnel and his or her staff. In addition, the amount of power delegated to the personnel department has increased in some companies as a result of threats of or actual union-organizational drives. If such a founder is still active in the business, and is by inclination a "good" personnel person, or if the tradition and culture of the company are strong, the personnel department may not be very strong unless it has been delegated some specific powers, such as the right to approve discharges or to audit certain personnel practices. In these cases, since the line management is very good with respect to personnel management, there is no need for as strong a personnel department.

However, if the founder and/or the descendants of the founder are no longer active in the business, and if the current professional managers lack some of the founding values or charisma or if there are frequent union-organizational drives, the personnel function is probably strong or at least gaining strength. One of the personnel department's tasks is to help institutionalize the founder's philosophy and/or the company's union-avoidance programs. As the founder passes from the scene, his or her philosophies become institutionalized in a package of personnel policies and programs that, together with the ways in which they are administered, try to maintain a climate of openness and trust. Personnel's audit-and-control role is critical to this institutionalization process.

Independent of a company's interest in implementing a philosophy or in achieving a goal of remaining nonunion, new government regulations and environmental factors are also forcing the further development of personnel's role, including the growth and development of its auditing function.[1] Also, although a strong and effective personnel department can play a crucial role in employee relations, a company's approach will only work if its line managers are committed to it. Effectiveness in the area of personnel management must be a part of the reward-and-punishment system for line managers, whether they are divisional presidents, plant managers, or supervisors. This means that skill in managing people needs to be part of the evaluation criteria for the selection, performance appraisal, salary administration, and promotion of line managers.

In many organizations, deliberate structures had been created for the purpose of approving and evaluating major personnel policies and for keeping line management involved in personnel issues. These structures, in combination with the company's reward system for managers, tend to integrate line and staff and create an environment that encourages line managers to be sensitive to personnel problems as well as to personnel's advice and counsel.

The chief vehicle for communication and interaction between personnel and line management is a committee composed of members of both functions. To take one example, a member of the founding family of one company established a senior board of executives in the 1920s, its purpose being to capture the experience of different specialists and of those with different backgrounds. Each executive had an equal voice and one vote, and all decisions had to be unanimous. In the

---

[1]*See, for example,* Allen R. Janger, *The Personnel Function: Changing Objectives and Organization* (New York: The National Industrial Conference Board, 1977).

early 1930s, the son of the former president and grandson of the founder became chairman and coordinator of this board. Shortly thereafter, the company also established a junior board, which consisted of middle-level managers. Although it had no decision-making responsibilities, it suggested for itself general problems to be studied. In addition, the chairman gave the junior board specific problems on which to work. According to the current vice-president of personnel, the company's personnel policies and practices came out of these executive boards. The management processes, which have long been a part of this organization, helped to develop manager awareness and commitment to personnel issues. From the junior and senior executive boards have come a sick-pay plan, a disability plan, a profit-sharing plan, an employee-savings plan, and this industry's first retirement plan to include early vesting.

Two companies have personnel-policy committees. At one company, this committee is composed of vice-presidents and is chaired by a senior vice-president, with the personnel department serving as staff to the committee. This committee, as its name designates, is responsible for approving all personnel policies, and also hears final-step grievances.

The other company's personnel-policy committee is chaired by the personnel director. This committee's members include the chairman, president, the treasurer, a secretary, a legal counsel, and the engineering vice-president. This personnel director is in turn a member of the company's executive, manufacturing, and planning committees.

At yet another company, the vice-president of personnel is chairman of a works-manager committee that meets regularly to discuss management problems. The membership of this committee includes the division managers, the controller, and the treasurer. Agenda topics at one meeting included the wage-and-fringe package, cost-of-living changes, and improvement of physical security (because a new highway was being built near the plant).

To accomplish similar objectives, another company initiated an organizational change a few years ago, whereby different members of the executive committee are periodically appointed liaison vice-president or vice-presidential advisor for employee relations. The company does this for other staff departments as well. Describing this change, a key member of the personnel staff said:

> [One person] is the vice-presidential advisor and liaison vice-president for employee relations. He is a member of the executive committee as well as being a member of the board of directors. Our president used to be the employee-relations advisor. The company moves this assignment around so that all of the executive committee members have exposure to employee relations.

In addition to the many formal ways in which personnel interacts with line management on key personnel issues and employee problems, there are also many informal and behind-the-scenes ways in which personnel is involved with line management.

For example, the reward-and-punishment systems of many companies encourage managers to give much attention to personnel management. No manager wants to be the first victim of a successful union-organizational drive. Supervisors in many of the companies feel they will not be promoted if they have too many employee problems. Thus they are more responsive to the various formal communications programs and grievance procedures that give employees a way of bypassing their jurisdiction. The managers, in turn, have many incentives that encourage them to remain sensitive to human problems and to the personnel department.

The top management of one large company thinks that personnel's basic job is to train managers to handle people more effectively, as each manager is viewed as his or her own personnel manager. Although it has one professional personnel person for every 100 employees, the supervisor to employee ratio is 1-to-10. In addition, the company has guidelines that state that personnel may contact an employee only under the following circumstances: pre-employment, exit interview, morale assessment, employee complaint situations, and areas requiring specialization or line direction. While these guidelines are not always rigidly followed, top-level management feels strongly that personnel exists to help its managers do a better job of managing.

It is possible to identify different organizational structures and policies in companies that serve to define line and staff roles with respect to employee-relations issues and to better integrate line and staff people with regard to common objectives. These structures and policies not only make line managers more aware of and sensitive to personnel issues, but also make them more receptive to expert advice and counsel.

CENTRALIZATION—CORPORATE POWER VERSUS LOCAL PLANTS

While the personnel job is a complex mixture of coach, cop, employee advocate, neutral third party, and human-resources functionary, it is clear that, in the companies studied, corporate personnel staff people have much power relative to division or plant personnel people where personnel policies and practices at the local level are concerned. Corporate personnel conducts audits or reviews, and is capable of "blowing the whistle" on certain local plant decisions if it thinks it necessary to do so.

For example, despite the fact that wage increases at one company are determined at the plant level, before any increases can be implemented they are subject to corporate approval for two reasons: (1) to ensure that proposals are not out of line among plants with similar characteristics, and (2) to prevent individual plants from giving larger-than-necessary increases.

In one unusual case, after the local pay-practices survey and much discussion at the plant level, local management recommended a 9 percent increase. However, corporate personnel approved a 10 percent increase instead, because it wanted to ensure that this plant's wages were higher than the expected wage level at a unionized plant in the area.

In another organization, corporate personnel monitors all written performance appraisals. The company's performance-appraisal form contains space for employees to state any comments they might care to make. Commenting on this, a member of corporate employee relations said:

> We monitor the performance-appraisal reports and this helps us determine the kind of job the supervisor is doing. If the supervisor always writes the same comments, we know he isn't doing the kind of job in performance appraisal that we want him to do. We'll then visit him when we're in the area or we might select him for a training program.
>
> The forms are also employee safety valves. As an example, there was one employee who wrote on her form that she didn't like the fact that her desk was located in a draft. When we noticed that we sent someone from corporate to talk to her. She said that she didn't believe that anyone read the forms, and she was extremely pleased.

This study uncovered several such instances of direct corporate involvement with employee problems at the plant level. For example, these include the investigation of formal employee grievances or the review of the responses to grievances by local management.

REPORTING RELATIONSHIPS

As the reader might infer from the foregoing discussion, various policies and practices make cases of corporate involvement at the local plant level legitimate in the companies cited. However, in two divisionalized companies the formal organization structure and reporting relationships are designed to ensure that personnel matters receive an appropriate amount of attention. Specifically, personnel directors at the plant and division levels do not report to their respective line managers but directly to corporate personnel.

The comment of the vice-president of human resources of one of these companies illustrates the ambiguity and delicateness of the role of the plant or division personnel director:

> While they all report to me, I always tell them that the quickest way for them to get fired is for them to stop pleasing the line managers.

This reporting relationship is not viewed as especially attractive by line managers. At one division the manager was frustrated because he had not been allowed to change the corporate job evaluation and pay system for a group of employees involved in a job-enrichment experiment, because the division director of personnel did not report to him. This decision may have been dysfunctional for the organization.

The organizational combination of personnel being at a high level and having direct reporting relationships means that personnel has a great deal of power relative to the line organization. For example, personnel in this company can say "no" to a high production run, and shut down an unsafe plant. When asked to give some examples of where this unusual organizational arrangement had benefited employees or the company, this company's second vice-president of personnel listed six illustrations:

> *(1) During a time of business recession, managers must make decisions on who is to be laid off. During such periods, an employee may use the direct reporting channel to appeal the decision of lower-level management.*
>
> *(2) Same situation, when an employee is "bumped down" to a lower-level position and sometimes at a lower rate of pay. Here again, the ability to find someone who is capable of objectively viewing the proposed decision works to everyone's advantage.*
>
> *(3) Because of the ability of an employee to command high-level interest in his or her particular grievance, it makes experienced managers go through a rational choice process before the fact. They know that if they "goof the job," they run the risk of calling attention to their decisions.*
>
> *(4) When times become difficult, the workload of the personnel function increases. This increase occurs at a time when the operating groups are trying desperately to reduce their costs. On some occasions, we have had to "blow the whistle" on proposed personnel department cost reductions on the basis of short-term expediency but long-term increased cost.*
>
> *(5) By having personnel at a somewhat arm's-length relationship, they are viewed more as impartial consultants and do not run the risk of personal loss of stature when, say, they buck a proposed decision of a divisional general manager.*
>
> *(6) Personnel can become involved in management development because they are not necessarily part of the management team involved when a decision goes one way or another. They are free to comment on a candidate's promotability, assets, strengths or weaknesses, and organizational changes where they don't become entangled with their own careers.*

While the advantages cited are interesting, it would seem that the same results could also have been accomplished with a more traditional reporting relationship. However, there can be little doubt that this unusual reporting relationship does serve as a check on the behavior of plant and division management in this company.

This unusual organizational arrangement exists in another company, where personnel is also a separate organization that does not report to the line organization. The only personnel person reporting to a line manager is the head of personnel, who reports directly to the president. Commenting, the personnel director said:

> *We don't want a personnel person to get into a hassle where he has to worry about being fired because he didn't please a particular line manager.*

The personnel people are in the plants on a daily basis and they have an override on hiring and firing decisions.

When asked about the rationale for such reporting relationships, one experienced vice-president of personnel said:

> *If a manufacturing manager makes a bad decision on a batch and has to flush it down the drain, you can calculate the cost almost immediately. If a personnel manager, on the other hand, makes a bad decision which ruins the positive employee relations climate at that location, trying to earn it back is a long, tedious, and expensive proposition if you are ever really able to attain it as well again.*
>
> *In my judgment, that is the reason why you need not only corporate resources, advice, and counsel, but also review and audit over the actions of your division or plant personnel managers. That is a delicate posture but a good personnel executive knows how to do that without taking the initiative away from line management.*

Different organizational arrangements were used for a similar purpose in other multidivision companies studied. In two companies, the personnel managers operate in a matrix organization. Thus a plant personnel manager reports directly to both his or her division manager and to the corporate director of personnel. The relationship to corporate personnel seems to be the stronger of the two, according to one personnel director: "I am really the one who controls things. I have the records, and I administer the pay increases." Given that career development is by and large in the personnel field at this company, it is easy to understand the reality of the reporting relationship situation. In a third company it is designed in a similar manner: The plant personnel director has a dual reporting relationship. That is to say, he or she reports both to the plant manager and to the corporate director.

Needless to say, in functionally organized companies the personnel department is not only at a high level but is also quite centralized with respect to policy and administrative decisions. In one company of 25,000 employees, a centralized personnel unit serves the entire corporation. While there are personnel people in the plants, the central group develops all personnel policies.

At another company, in talking about the personnel organization, the vice-president of personnel said:

> *The personnel organization is a unique one, with no true staff specialist people. This is because each staff person also represents an area. Each staff*

guy has a group to represent because this way he will realize how hard it is to
sell ideas rather than simply proposing ideas that can't be sold.

To illustrate this point, at this company the director of compensation and benefits
is also director of personnel for engineering services, and the director of corporate
recruiting is also director of personnel for the financial area.

More than one organization is using a multifunctional organizational approach. For example, at one company one person is not only the retirement plans
expert for the entire corporation, but is also responsible for administering benefits
for an entire division. Another person is responsible for another division and also
has expertise in group life insurance. The effects of this arrangement are twofold:
first, people are not narrow; and second, it is easier for the company to operate
during vacation periods. The structure itself demands that there will be a lot of
training, education, and professional development.

Although the usual relationship is for division and plant personnel directors
to report on a "dotted-line" basis to corporate personnel and on a "solid-line"
basis to a line manager, as the earlier comments suggest, the "dotted-line"
reporting relationship is generally very strong; the "dots" are very close together
(that is, almost a solid line) and the reality often seems to not conform to what is on
the organization chart.

Although one company's reporting relationships are traditional, the combination of its contention system—whereby it is possible to elevate decision making
to the next higher organizational level—and its career development system seem to
accomplish the same purpose as some of the less traditional organization structures. In this organizational arrangement, division personnel directors report on a
"straight-line" basis to line general managers and on a "dotted-line" basis to
corporate personnel.

However, if the division personnel directors do not agree with a certain
decision, under the company's contention system they may state their reservations
and elevate the decision to the next higher level of management. This means that
on occasion a division personnel director may have to elevate a disagreement he or
she is having with his or her general manager. When asked about the possibility of
alienating the boss, a division personnel director replied:

> *That really doesn't matter. What happens to me in this company*
> *depends on what the corporate vice-president of personnel thinks of me.*
> *Therefore, I do not mind getting my line boss mad because he doesn't*
> *determine my career even though he holds my card.*

When asked for an example of this procedure, this director described a discharge
decision he had overturned. Discharge in this company requires concurrence
between line management and personnel. In this particular instance, the investigation revealed that the personnel department had not been given the whole story by
line management in its investigation prior to the discharge. On learning this,

personnel asked that the decision be reversed. When local management would not go along, personnel elevated the case. The outcome was that the general manager was reversed and the employee reinstated.

In commenting on the consequences of this decision on his relationship with the general manager, the division personnel director said:

> *This case ended up building and cementing my relationship with the general manager. Personnel now has tremendous influence. We are involved in all sorts of decisions, even nonpersonnel decisions. I think that because the general manager's decision was overturned he now feels he has to consult me in advance. I think he feels he has to make sure he gets in bed with the personnel director.*

It could also be noted that this company's career development program for personnel professionals seems consistent with its contention system. It is conceivable that if this personnel person viewed the next job in line management as opposed to in personnel, perhaps he would have been more reluctant to challenge his line manager boss. The fact that his next job, if he is to be promoted, will definitely be in personnel may make him more willing to utilize the company's contention system.

Whether the reporting relationship is officially direct, dual, or represented by a ''dotted-line'' relationship, in general local plant personnel has much influence relative to line managers and, as has been disclosed, corporate personnel has much power relative to division and plant personnel. What the precise reporting relationship is may not be all that important. Rather, what is more important is that top management has created a situation wherein personnel and line managers can be equal members on the same team. Specific line and staff responsibilities need to be delineated. Decisions need to be based on balanced inputs between line management and corporate staff management postures. There should be shared objectives, and a partnership between personnel managers and line managers; they need to be equal members of the same team. If it takes structural arrangements and different reporting relationships to facilitate this, then these should be used.

Personnel's Other Functions

As discussed, personnel has three primary functions. The first function relates to the development of personnel policies. The companies studied seem to have much line manager input and involvement with respect to this function. The second function relates to personnel's traditional advice and counsel and service role. Personnel departments advise line managers as well as employees. The third function, one which seems to be growing in importance, relates to personnel's auditing role. Audits are a feedback mechanism undertaken to assure top management that the company's policies and practices are being carried out as they are supposed to be. If this is not the case, questions will be asked and corrective action will be undertaken.

In considering personnel's role in the light of these different functions, it is helpful to think about it from three different perspectives. One perspective is from the corporate or top management point of view. (That is, the way in which personnel policy relates to business policy or corporate strategy, and also the way in which the personnel officer relates to senior management.) The second perspective is from the vantage point of the plant and the first level of supervision. The third perspective is from the viewpoint of the employees. While personnel's functional role is obviously not the same in all of the organizations studied, there are a number of similar threads. Let us now consider personnel's service and audit functions.

Personnel's Service Functions

In all of the companies studied, part of personnel's role, to some extent, is to advocate the employees. For the employees, the personnel department can represent a way around their immediate supervisor. Personnel represents the employees' point of view within management, especially at the top level of management. Personnel audits management's practices, and may "blow the whistle" in individual cases when basic personnel policies are violated or compromised. Personnel also sometimes views itself as serving employee needs in a very personal sense. This is different from and in addition to personnel's broader service role as an adviser and counselor to line management.

For example, within the centralized personnel department of one large company there is a group called "employee services." The members of this unit operate a blood-donor service. They visit the sick and arrange for immediate transportation home in the event an employee is taken ill at the plant. They are available any time of the day or night upon a death in the family, volunteering to assist the bereaved. They attend the services, send flowers, and if the head of the family is deceased they offer to assist with funeral arrangements, straighten out financial difficulties, and attend to other problems.

In addition, so that employees may not lose time from work or be inconvenienced standing in line at state Motor Vehicle Bureaus, the employee services people obtain license plates and renewals for driver's licenses. They obtain theater and baseball tickets, check food and beverage vending machines, and make all the arrangements for the company's extremely successful and well-attended annual picnic. They also administer an active job-posting, career-counseling, and development program.

At another company, personnel maintains the employee athletic facilities, runs subsidized employee travel programs, operates a store, and arranges for the showing of major movies during the lunch hour. (Every film is divided into five daily segments shown three times during the lunch period. In this way, an employee can see a major film each week.) An unexpected benefit of the movie program is that absenteeism has dropped in the clerical work force. When employees start viewing a new film on Monday, they usually want to see it through to the end on Friday.

Companies frequently employ "personnel representatives" to keep in direct contact with employees' needs. Such representatives are sometimes used as a neutral third party. Commenting on this role, one corporate manager said:

> *They are personnel specialists with relatively little direct-line experi- ence. In general, their task is to advise objectively both managers and employees in different areas. Frequently they are not directly involved in the grievance procedure. They remain objective and advise the involved mana- gers and employees on possible solutions to the grievance.*

For example, in one company there is a group of over fifty "personnel representatives" who seem to perform as "shop stewards." They play a role in salary increases, promotions, and transfers. Each one generally represents 200 employees, though that figure can be as high as 400, depending on a variety of factors. One of the creators of the program, which began in the 1940s, said that the group's title was purposely ambiguous; "We don't know who the PRs represent: the company or the employee," and that the company wants intelligent action and fairness; and ensuring that this happens is part of the personnel representative's job.

However, two of the PRs interviewed referred to themselves as shop stewards, and felt that they represented the employees. One personnel representative said:

> *I see my job as a liaison between employees and supervisors. Attend- ance and performance problems constitute the bulk of my work, and I like to get the employee and the supervisor together.*

The other representative, who has a BS degree in finance and an MBA degree in personnel, commented:

> *The PR has to define the fine line and he has to know the supervisor well. Some supervisors hold bad feelings from the past. They feel that if one of their people goes to see a PR he must be complaining about them. Some think that the PR always sides with the employee.*
>
> *PRs are deeply involved in hiring and the PR sees the employee a lot during the probationary period. PRs are told there are no doors in the company which are closed to them.*

Both of these representatives also said that 90 percent of the time they have to do the firing because the department head shrugs off his or her responsibility on the

PR. An experienced personnel executive at this company offered this comment about the role of the personnel representatives:

> *Most line managers bitch about the PRs. The line sees them as getting in the way. The PR is an integral part of any disciplinary process and the PR is a check on management.*

However, in discussing the representative's role, the company's production vice-president said:

> *The PR can make sure the message gets to the people. The PR also gets involved in community affairs, for we want to be a good neighbor. The PR is a third party if there is a misunderstanding. He is tuned into what is going on.*

One department manager said that he views the personnel representative as someone who makes sure that company policies are carried out in a consistent manner. In a real sense then, the PR is an auditor as well as a steward; but a skilled trades supervisor said that many of his employees will not go to see the personnel representative because they feel little can be done:

> *A lot of our problems are personality clashes. Our personnel representative comes through once a week. I would say that he is no gain or no loss. He'll ask questions and say that he has heard rumors. But in my opinion there is no need for a personnel representative.*

At many companies, the personnel representatives render "cradle-to-grave services" to the employees. Employees can go to them with their problems and/or questions. Similarly, the representatives are available to counsel and advise supervisors. Effectiveness in their work requires them to walk a very fine line between management and the employee. (Further discussion of the performance of these counseling functions is found in Chapter 14.)

Personnel departments can directly help the organization meet some employee needs. They can also help managers to be sensitive to employee problems and concerns. Their advice and counsel will be taken seriously by line managers if it is useful and/or if they speak from a position of organizational strength. What seems to make a personnel department's counsel and advise role take hold is its status and clout in the organization, as well as the company's reward-and-punishment system. Moreover, some of its authority is derived from its auditing function. Managers may be fearful of being caught because of possible detrimental effects to their careers. Myths in the organization about the removal or demotion of managers may actually reinforce this type of thinking. While the top management in one company insisted it was no longer so, some managers at lower levels believed that they would be fired if their operation had a successful union-organizing drive.

As stated earlier, the personnel department also performs an auditing function, which is one source of personnel's power. The purpose of such checking is to make sure that personnel policies and practices are being carried out as they should.

In describing personnel's role, an executive who has served as both a personnel administrator and a line manager stated:

> *Unfortunately, personnel is frequently not a resource to the manager, but an auditor on him. As a result, managers do not go to personnel asking for help. Employees, on the other hand, do go to personnel when they are unhappy with their jobs and want a transfer.*

If the auditing function is not done well, personnel diminishes the likelihood of its being able to perform its more traditional advise and counsel function effectively. In one organization, some line managers said that they viewed the personnel people as police. At another company they are referred to as auditors.

One skilled trades supervisor talked of an encounter with an unskilled personnel administrator. The supervisor had given one of his workers an outstanding performance-appraisal rating, had showed it to the worker and had had him sign it. Company policy is that unapproved ratings are not to be discussed. In describing his telephone conversation with the personnel administrator, the supervisor said:

> *He didn't even introduce himself. He just said, "Who do you think you are?" He never even asked me why I did what I did. I was guilty and I was wrong. I told him to see my boss and that started my downhill trend in the company.*

How the audit and control function is exercised is critical. If personnel second-guesses line managers too often, it runs the risk of alienating them. While the auditing function may be easier to state than to do, it should be performed as often as possible in a coaching, advising, and training mode.

Illustrative of this is the way one company administers its pay-for-performance program. While there are guidelines to be used, in this company the line managers are responsible for deciding both the timing and the size of pay increases. For example, an outstanding performer might receive a 12 percent increase in eight months, whereas an average performer might receive a 6 percent increase in eighteen months. Once the decision has been made, it must be approved by two levels of management.

Subsequent to that, the personnel people do a postaudit on the administration of the pay program. If they find discrepancies that cannot be explained, they coach and counsel the line managers. Personnel has also developed a short education program for line managers on the philosophy and administration of merit pay.

One company dealt with some of the complexities and ambiguities of personnel's role with a unique organizational change. After much experience and thought, top-level management came to the conclusion that personnel's service and control roles had to be separated. The executives thought that it was an impossible situation for the personnel people at one moment to tell line managers what they could or could not do, and at the next moment act as a helpful resource to them.

Consequently, this company established two vice-presidents of personnel. One has the control role, and his or her responsibilities include labor and employee relations, compensation and benefits, and employment and affirmative action. The other has the help-service role, and his or her responsibilities include organizational development, executive recruiting, manpower development, organization planning, and executive compensation.

Supervisory Reactions

As might be anticipated, supervisors have mixed feelings about the personnel department and its role. Some supervisors said that personnel was the protector of the employee. This is particularly so with respect to the administration of discipline. It is also true, but to a lesser extent, with respect to the ways in which promotions are handled. At one company, a manufacturing superintendent said:

> *The personnel department is an objective observer of a problem. The personnel people usually do not take sides, but if they do they side with the employee. The supervisor has to prove his case. The supervisor fails when he has nothing documented.*

A line manager at another company said:

> *Personnel is not very supportive. With respect to discipline, the managers feel that no matter what they do the company's paternalistic approach will prevail. Personnel does not stand behind the policies as they are written.*

A general supervisor said:

> *Personnel people sometimes makes things difficult. They stand behind the employee. It is hard to get rid of a person after three months. They make sure there is very good documentation. Personnel always takes the view of what is fair and just for the employee.*

At another company, a supervisor articulated the same idea:

> *It is tough to discipline here. If you do everything you should, three-fourths of the employees would be on warning. But then the employees would*

complain to personnel and personnel would tell us to back off. I say boot the bad employees out. I don't have the time to document as personnel wants. It is almost like a court case.

If an employee has been here fifteen years, the chairman has to approve his discharge. Therefore, you have a guy who was good in 1962 but is not now. It raises such a stink to go to corporate. You might win but you will probably lose. It takes a lot of time so you don't do it. Therefore, the employees feel very secure.

However, some supervisors did speak positively of the help they and their employees received from personnel. For example, one supervisor of quality control viewed personnel as a resource, and seeks policy clarification and interpretation when seeing her personnel representative. This supervisor said that she receives much help from her personnel representative because he attends the meetings that the vice-president of quality control conducts. A press department manager at one company described the role of the personnel representative in his plant:

Tom is a good middleman between the managers and the employees. He irons out a lot of problems. The employee has a right to see him. In most cases, we win. If we are wrong, we give in and learn something. But we're right 90 percent of the time. Sometimes I go to see Tom before I take action.

A manufacturing manager, who had spent several years in personnel in one company, discussed some reasons why line managers view personnel with some disdain there:

They really don't understand the personnel function or its uses. The front-line guy sees personnel as the rear echelon who never gets his hands dirty and who really does not appreciate the problems of manufacturing.

This manager also said the line managers feel that personnel people have nicer offices and desks, that they do not have to work overtime, that they work one-on-one or in small groups, and that they have time to engage in many nonbusiness-related discussions:

Personnel really is a big mystery to them. People say to me, "Have you begun to refer to personnel people as they yet?" It is very much we–they.

Reflecting on personnel's image in his division, this manager explained one reason why personnel is criticized:

The managers place the best employees before personnel knows there is an opening. Therefore, personnel is left with a group of employees who are not the good guys. Some will have medical restrictions. In our company, there is a saying that we grow our own handicapped. Employees become physically

> *obsolete. When a manager tries to peddle them, he comes to personnel and says, "Find him a job."*

Therefore, although one manager may feel well-served when he gets the personnel department to place a difficult employee, another manager who is asked to take that employee may understandably not react too positively to the efforts of personnel.

This manager also thought that many managers attribute a lot of imaginary things to personnel:

> *Some line managers have mistakenly assumed that the personnel people are high level, involved, and know the secrets of the business.*

There are other reasons why personnel may not enjoy a good reputation with line managers. For example, consider one company's policy for the communication of good and bad news. The policy, written many years ago, is:

> *Whenever anything advantageous to the employees has been put into effect, we have always felt that this information should be given to the employee over the signature of the president, because it furthers the belief in the minds of the employees that he is a fine fellow and is interested in their welfare.*
>
> *Conversely, if anything of a difficult nature is necessary, then this must be sent out to the employees over the signature of the top personnel individual. If that individual has enough contacts throughout the organization and has the proper acceptance by the employees, they will accept the decision, feeling that if it were not right and fair the individual at the head of the personnel activity would not have signed it.*

This is an unusual policy. When followed, it is certainly conceivable that the messenger of the bad news could be blamed for the bad news. If so, personnel's image could be tarnished.

Thus, for many reasons, it is frequently the case that personnel people, and especially plant personnel people, do not always command the respect of line managers and supervisors. As employees need to know what they can and cannot expect from the personnel department, managers and supervisors need to be trained with respect to the personnel department's appropriate role and functions. Also, top management needs to understand and recognize the complexities and difficulties inherent in personnel's role.

Types of Personnel People

One cannot do justice to personnel's role without discussing the nature or caliber of the top people found in these personnel departments, for they obviously make a difference. In addition, one should note something about their diverse work and educational backgrounds.

Findings of this study reveal two types of people holding the top jobs in personnel. One type can be called a "personnel professional": Such a person has spent a number of years in personnel work, has risen from the bottom, and may hold a professional degree in psychology or a related field. The other type can be labeled a "converted line manager": Such an individual has served as a line manager and has moved to personnel, either for a relatively short development experience and/or to solve some problems, or for the remainder of his or her career.

Three of the companies studied currently have, or have had, people with Ph.D. degrees in psychology heading their personnel functions. Most of the others currently have experienced personnel professionals leading their functions rather than former line managers, though early in their careers these people may have had some line-management experience. These are people who have advanced through the personnel hierarchy, and who frequently have much background experience in employment, employee relations, training, labor relations, and compensation.

There were only two cases in which the personnel function was headed by a lawyer (and one of them had formerly been a union organizer). In some companies it is not uncommon to find lawyers on the corporate personnel staff, some of whom have had National Labor Relations Board experience.

If there is a common thread, it is that at several of the more doctrinaire companies the top person is one with labor-relations experience acquired at another company. This is the case for approximately one-third of the companies studied. It seems to be particularly true for those companies that have experienced a great number of union-organizational drives. For example, when a union organizer was questioned about what he viewed as the secret of a company that has remained nonunion in a highly unionized part of the country, he pointed out that one of the reasons was that management hired labor-oriented people from other companies to staff its personnel department.

One company that has both union and nonunion plants uses a well thought out career development program for its personnel–labor-relations people. Commenting on it, the corporate director of employee relations said:

> Personnel people frequently begin their training in areas not involved in employee relations. Once acclimated to the company's policies, they are rotated into employee relations. They are also rotated through union plants to see what disadvantages exist in unionization. Additionally, by handling union problems they learn what is politically acceptable to large groups of people. This exposure to unionization reinforces to personnel people the benefits of a nonunion plant. To be successful at the company, personnel has to demonstrate the ability to be successful in employee relations.

Direct experience with unions and contract negotiation and administration seems to be viewed as excellent training for human-resource management jobs in many nonunion companies.

The vice-president of personnel at one company with one union operation (purchased in an acquisition) started a career with the company as personnel manager in that unionized plant. Prior to this, he had been manager of labor relations at a unionized company. After a stint at the plant, he moved into corporate personnel, and after attending a university's thirteen-week management-development program, became general manager of the unionized facility. His next job was a promotion to personnel vice-president at corporate headquarters. This person's job changes and career development indicate the time, the resources, and the attitude that are devoted to the development of personnel managers in this company and in many of the companies studied.

In the philosophy-laden companies, the personnel function is generally staffed with professionals and former line managers promoted from within. As I heard in more than one company, "We like to train and grow our own personnel people." Two companies, with outstanding reputations in their respective fields and well-known for their good personnel work, have been a resource for many other companies that copy or adapt the personnel programs they develop. In fact, some companies staff their personnel departments with people recruited from these companies.

As has been indicated, the caliber of people one finds in the key personnel jobs in these companies is very high. One company that uses personnel representatives recently hired an outstanding person with a doctorate in labor relations to be one of its representatives. During the course of this study, this person was moved from a personnel representative job to assignments in executive compensation and sales training.

Another company assigned an assistant to the vice-president of personnel to be company coordinator for this study. Assisting the vice-president is viewed as a good development job for young managers. Illustrating how rapidly people move, during the course of the study I had four different coordinators. This company thinks that the growth and development of personnel people is so important, another assistant to the vice-president spends all of his time on the development of personnel people in the company on a worldwide basis.

In another company, the assistant vice-president of personnel, a person with an MBA degree, started a career in the organization as assistant to the president, prior to moving into personnel. Before my study was completed this person (at the age of 35) was made vice-president of personnel reporting to the company's senior vice-president of personnel.

When asked about the company's vice-president of personnel, one company president said:

> We consider Sam one of our key executives here. He has added so much to the company not only in the area of personnel, but also in the overall administrative assistance and counseling for our executives.

The successful interaction with other key executives in the organization no doubt contributes much to his effectiveness. At the time this study was completed, that fast-moving executive had been named the company's administrative vice-president.

One person at a trade association talked about the changes she had noted in the number of people going into personnel work in an industry that is increasingly a center of union interest:

> *Top management has finally realized that the people costs are as important as other costs. Of late, I've noted more forceful people in the personnel and labor relations field. They are now a voice in top management. You just can't talk it. You have to do it. The person entering the field today is not the has-been who used to hang around in this field. If the guy is weak and doesn't clean up the trouble spots, unions walk in. Weak personnel departments can cause unionization.*

The point is that, in general, the people in the personnel field in these companies are good, and those at the top are strong. They are effective in terms of their relationships with others in top management, and they have power.

While many lower-level personnel administrators are not highly regarded by line managers, part of this undoubtedly stems from their police role. It may be that personnel can never have a good image with line managers, not only because so much of the effectiveness in personnel work is invisible and therefore hard to receive credit for, but also because personnel, like a union, "attracts lightning."

To some line managers, personnel—like a union—keeps interfering in the way they want to run their operation; and even though the chief executive officers' commitments to personnel makes its policy enforcement legitimate, that role does not make personnel people popular with many line managers.

CONCLUDING ANALYSIS AND COMMENTS

In this chapter, four general points have been made. Consider:

(1) Personnel departments of nonunion companies have and exercise great power. Frequently the power they have is simply the power to say "no." Much of their clout comes through their close relationship to top management and their delegated audit-and-control role. Furthermore, corporate personnel has considerable influence over its division and plant counterparts. Personnel's security and the long-run usefulness of its power extends to good judgment as to when and how to use that power.

(2) Structures such as committees and reporting relationships have been developed that reinforce personnel's status and role. Such organization arrangements also facilitate personnel's interaction with line management.

(3) Personnel people have well-defined policy and administrative roles, whether it be as cop, coach, employee advocate, neutral, or some combination of these roles at different times and with different issues. Generally, it is some

combination of these roles, with the balance varying from company to company.

(4) For the most part, the top people in the personnel positions are very capable. They are well-trained by both education and experience, they have credibility, and they command respect. They are very conscious of wanting to build departments of able people rather than of cast-offs from other parts of the company.

Much of the literature in the personnel field dwells on the staff role of personnel. Personnel's role is said to be advisory, and it is suggested that line managers should be free to reject the advice they receive from personnel. However, this study suggests that such conventional wisdom does not hold up well in many large nonunion companies.

Few of the top personnel managers visited were simply staff advisors. Line managers are not free to ignore their advice—if they do, they do so at their peril. Perhaps because there is no union, personnel sometimes has a higher loyalty to the employees and to the long-run interests of the corporation than they do to the immediate problems of local management. This sometimes makes them unpopular with managers and supervisors. In short, many of the personnel organizations studied are not "typical" staff departments.

Personnel's role in these companies seems similar to the role of a labor-relations staff group in highly unionized companies. In such companies, labor relations is frequently a very powerful department and "calls the shots," while the personnel department (which may be responsible for only the office employees) is weak. It is in the large, nonunion companies where personnel, for many reasons, is a powerful group.

Perhaps it is accurate to say that the personnel departments in the great majority of the companies studied are analogous to those found in Japanese companies. In a paper entitled "Toward Convergence of Japanese and American Management Practices," Yoshi Tsurumi wrote:

> *Traditionally, in any Japanese firm, the personnel department is very close to the president who is, in turn, expected to maintain a personal interest in individual employees. The personnel department (and the personnel manager) is indeed a power center within the Japanese firm. Therefore, there is very little chance that the initiative and authority of the personnel department might be undermined or over-ridden by other departments.[2]*

This quotation captures much of the essence of my findings.

---

[2]Yoshi Tsurumi, *Multinational Management: Business Strategy and Government Policy* (Cambridge, Mass.: Ballinger Publishing Co., 1977), p. 213.

PART TWO

Employment Security and Promotion Systems

CHAPTER SIX

Employment Security

Though some companies go further than others, employment stability was found to be an important goal of the companies studied. Nine of the entirely nonunion companies reported that they have never had a layoff. Indeed, six of these nine reported that they have never even had a reduction in hours. In fact, if this study had been conducted five years earlier, even more of the companies in the sample would have been full employment companies.

A remarkable number of techniques to provide full or nearly full employment or to delay layoffs were used by different companies. Among the techniques noted were: hiring freezes, reliance on attrition to reduce the work force, use of temporary and/or former employees for specified periods of time, inventory buildups, use and disuse of subcontractors, voluntary leaves of absence, vacation banking, special early-retirement programs, moving work to people, moving people to work, training, and work sharing. Certain environmental factors and company characteristics greatly facilitate the employment security practices of the companies studied. These include rapid company growth, good profitability, and the percentage of women in the work force.

In this chapter, the focus will be on these employment stability goals, as well as on the reasons behind them. Next we will consider the companies' full employment, work sharing, and layoff practices, and the ways in which these practices are carried out. Finally, there will be the concluding analysis and comments.

FULL EMPLOYMENT AND WORK-SHARING PRACTICES

In discussing his company's confidence in and concern for people, and in elaborating on management's philosophy, the president of an industry-leading corporation with approximately 30,000 employees wrote, in a company publication for new employees, of a significant decision:

> *What are some examples of this application of a confidence in and concern for people? One was a very early decision that has had a profound effect on the company. That decision was that we did not want to be a "hire and fire" operation—a company that would seek large contracts, employ a great many people for the duration of a contract, and at its completion let those people go. Now there is nothing that is fundamentally wrong with this method of operation—much work can only be performed using this technique—it's just that [the other founder] and I did not want to operate in this mode. This one early decision greatly limited our freedom of choice and was one of the factors that led us into the business in which we are now engaged.*

Upon reflecting about this approach, an officer of the company said:

> *. . . when we were small, we were given an opportunity to take on a $7 million contract. Now this was completely out of our bracket. To accomplish that sort of thing meant hiring a lot of people, and later firing them at the end of the contract. In thinking about this, it was clear that it would affect not only the temporary people but also those who were permanent. They would know that anytime we saw an opportunity to make money we would grab it regardless of the results on people.*
>
> *Instead, the philosophy has been that when you come to work at [company name] we hope we are offering you a permanent job: You do your work well and we will provide the employment. So we turned the contract down, even though it probably would have made a lot of money.*

While the reader might consider this "the tail wagging the dog," this approach demonstrates the importance the company's founders attached to the decision not to be a "hire and fire" company. Job security is an essential part of this company's strategy.

In another company, although business is quite seasonal in nature, the founder was committed to employment security from the beginning. In order to maintain employment security year-round, he built large and expensive warehouses that were quite well-known in their time. In addition, he encouraged employees to take their vacations in the winter by offering them an extra vacation week if they did so. In this company's handbook, under a section on employment stability, is the following:

Stability of Employment

There are wide seasonal variations in the demand for many company products. In order to avoid, so far as possible, the effects of these variations upon stability of employment, the company gives continual attention to planning its production schedules. The result has been a marked stability of employment.

Such planning cannot, of course, prevent reduced employment when business conditions are generally unfavorable or when the demand for company products is greatly reduced.

Personnel Reduction and Reemployment

In the event that business conditions require reduction in the number of persons employed, consideration will be given to such factors as length of service, individual ability, workmanship, and general record. The same factors will be used to determine the recall of individuals who have been laid off.

Improvement in Operations

Continual development and introduction of new and improved methods and processes are necessary for the successful conduct of the business. Only by utilizing such improvements can the company continue to operate successfully and provide opportunities for employment. Nevertheless, before such improvements are made, careful attention is given to any possible effect upon the individuals concerned. Through this policy, the company adopts improved methods essential to its growth and at the same time endeavors to avoid any considerable hardship to the individual.

Statements concerning job security found in the employee handbooks of three other companies read as follows:

[Our company], through modern planning and manpower utilization programs, makes every effort to provide employment security for each individual based on seniority and job performance—the only real job security that any company can provide.

[Our company] realizes the importance of rewarding the dedicated service of employees. Therefore, the length of service you have with the company will be one of the criteria used in determining eligibility for promotions, job placement, and other privileges and benefits. Also, if abnormal circumstances necessitate the demotion or layoff of employees, they will be demoted or laid off according to their length of company service and qualifications.

[Our company] has a long history of providing job security. The greatest contribution employees can make is to give full attention to the job and perform high quality work.

Given the job security statements, let us now look at the full employment companies.

FULL-EMPLOYMENT COMPANIES

As has been stated, six of the companies studied are truly full employment companies, for they reported they have never had a layoff or a reduced work week. The president of one company cited this as one of the reasons why his company is nonunion: "We have a history of stability. There has never been a layoff. One-sixth of the work force has been here over twenty-five years and there are a lot of fathers and sons in the labor force."

This company produces very basic consumer products and it has a large share of the growing markets in which it competes. The company has done extremely well in introducing new products. However, demand for its products does fluctuate. To illustrate how human resources planning and business planning relate in light of this employment stability goal, when a new product is launched, or when for other reasons there is to be a temporary buildup of employees, temporary employees are hired. Although the company's policy provides that a temporary employee is hired for a specific job of a temporary nature, or for a limited period of time—usually less than ninety days—the practice is to extend the period to six months and to then make the employees with good work and attendance records permanent if openings are available. While temporary employees are denied some benefits, they can use the company's job-posting system. They also receive holiday pay and vacation credit, and can participate as permanent employees in the company's Christmas bonus program. When asked about the fate of temporary employees, a personnel official said:

> We have many temporary employees for promotional work. While the official period is ninety days, we extend it to six months. If they are here after six months, they generally become permanent employees. I would guess that 40 percent to 50 percent of the temporary employees eventually become permanent employees. After all, they are entitled to bid in our posting system and we have promotion from within. The only way unskilled people come into the company today is through the temporary employee route. Skilled people, such as repair mechanics, on the other hand, start off in a permanent status.

The combination of temporary employees, hiring freezes, and attrition are therefore important cushions for this company.

At another large company, known for its high productivity and excellent employee relations, full employment is one of the most treasured traditions in the business. The company's assistant vice-president of personnel said:

> *Security is a great concern and although other companies might refer*
> *to this as extreme, we try to instill confidence that the company will do its best,*
> *and that the employee is protected from factors beyond his control.*

In discussing the same topic, a division manufacturing manager of the company wrote:

> *Full employment—indeed job security—is the very foundation of in-*
> *creased productivity. If there ever came a time when we had to lay off people*
> *for lack of work, how could we ever convince them that we have a common*
> *interest in trying to put out more goods in fewer man hours?*

With respect to the operation of a full employment practice from his point of view, this manager also wrote:

> *. . . What we're concerned with here is the "people" part of the*
> *question: how to insure the job security of the people we assign, despite the*
> *uncertainties of our future production demand.*
>
> *Two main elements go into these calculations: (1) keeping the initial*
> *labor force as lean as possible until product acceptance is assured, and (2) a*
> *system of buffers to soften the impact of the unexpected. Actually, these two*
> *elements somewhat overlap, and are the same elements that are built into the*
> *annual operating plan to ensure job security.*
>
> *Finally, we have a major buffer that is reserved for extreme and*
> *prolonged cases of demand dip, one that is available only to sizable com-*
> *panies that have diversified products. Even in times of general business*
> *recession, a company like [ours] has one or more products, usually new ones,*
> *for which the demand is expanding. What we have done on occasion is to move*
> *some of the manufacturing of those high-demand products to a plant whose*
> *regular products are in temporary trouble. Such a transfer, of course, is*
> *expensive and can seldom be justified purely on a cost basis. But we consider*
> *it imperative on a people basis. Having hired a work force for a particular*
> *plant, the company is obligated to provide work for that force. This is one of*
> *the costs that may sometimes be incurred to keep full employment a practice,*
> *not a theory. To have the benefits of a full employment practice, it is simply*
> *necessary to pay certain costs.*

The buffers this manager uses are: (1) overtime (which he describes as a buffer against the unexpected and, at the same time, a way to keep the labor force lean); (2) lengthening the delivery schedule (". . . this may be inconvenient to the customer or may even endanger a sale . . . but we accept that risk for the sake of full employment, to which we attach a higher priority"); (3) a large warehouse for consigning inventory; and (4) subcontracting.

The manager also uses some minor buffers, such as the scheduling of company (as opposed to customer) work to level off dips, and the temporary transfer of some people to the work of reconditioning salespeople's demonstrators and trade-ins during slack periods.

This manager and staff estimated that these buffers, used with foresight and planning, permit the company to absorb the shock of as much as a twenty-five percent decrease in demand without involving the extreme step of moving a product from one plant to another for employment reasons. In considering the question of whether the cost is really worth it should the extreme step become necessary, this manager wrote:

> *I will answer in the affirmative but will not argue my case on the basis of social responsibility (though I have strong feelings on this subject). I'll just point to the statistics . . . Our people, by using their minds as well as their hands, have cut two-thirds of the hours that go into manufacturing our product. The cost of the product went down 45 percent during a ten-year period when wages vastly increased. That achievement would have been impossible without productive and committed employees. And much of their commitment stems from the security they know is theirs through [the company's] practice of full employment.*

Many managers of this company think the full-employment practice is critically important to understanding why the company is nonunion. Moreover, they think that should the company ever abandon this practice it would quickly become unionized.

At another of this company's plants, a superintendent of manufacturing went to a blackboard to explain how the company "solutions the workload" so that full employment is a reality. The company projects five years ahead, and on top of what it calls "permanent employment" it adds the possibility of five percent overtime. In addition, the company adds temporary employees and outside vendors.

Temporary employees may be hired for up to ninety days. While their term of employment may be extended beyond ninety days, this requires high-level approval and such an extension is extremely rare. Temporary employees are generally hired for work of a short duration and/or for peak workload periods. While in some communities there have been rumors that the only way to get a job at this company is to be a temporary employee, the rumors, a personnel officer told me, are simply not true. It *is* true, however, that some temporary employees do become permanent employees. The company's policy is to select the best qualified people, and because many good people are not available for temporary work, many temporary people do not meet the company's very competitive high standards for permanent employees.

Each location, the superintendent explained, "must solve its full employment problems." These proposed solutions are then sent to division and then to corporate headquarters. Depending on circumstances, it might be that the work would be done in another company plant rather than by an outside vendor. The outside vendor must perform at the company's cost or better. It is the company's practice to prevent vendors from becoming overly dependent on the company's business. This is accomplished by limiting the percentage of the vendor's business that is derived from the company. To a degree, however, the company's full employment practice becomes the vendor's fluctuating employment practice.

This commitment to full employment, not surprisingly, began with the beliefs of the company's founder. During a lecture at a major university in the early 1960s, the company's recent chairman, son of the founder, discussed his father and his beliefs:

> . . . He [my father] had known hard times, hard work, and unemployment himself, and he always had understanding for the problems of the working man. Moreover, he recognized that the greatest of these problems was job security.
>
> . . . having been fired as [a] sales manager . . . following a series of clashes . . . , my father was brought in to run . . . a loose alliance of three small companies. It was the organization that was to become [company name] ten years later.
>
> [It] was a demoralized organization. Many of the people there resented the newcomer and quarreled among themselves. It was a situation that presented him with an early test of his belief in job security.
>
> Despite the questionable condition of the company, no one was fired. [Father] didn't move in and shake up the organization. Instead, he set out to buff and polish the people who were already there and to make a success of what he had.
>
> That decision . . . led to the . . . policy on job security which has meant a great deal to our employees. From it has come our policy to build from within. We go to great lengths to develop our people, to retrain them when job requirements change, and to give them another chance if we find them experiencing difficulties in the jobs they are in.
>
> This does not mean that a job at [company name] is a lifetime ticket or that we do not occasionally let people go—we do, but only after we have made a genuine effort to help them improve. Nor does it mean that people do not leave us—they do. But policies like these, we have found, help us to win the good will of most of our people.
>
> Among plant people, when job security is ordinarily a matter of major concern, _____'s ability to avoid layoffs and work interruptions has encouraged our people to respond with loyalty and with diligence on the job. Over the years, we have been willing to take chances and strain our resources rather than resort to layoffs. For almost a quarter of a century now, no one has lost an hour's time in layoffs at _____, in spite of recessions and major product shifts.
>
> Fortunately, we have had a relatively steady market, which has helped make this record possible. But there have been times when we might have taken the easy way out to save payroll. During the Great Depression, for example, when nearly one-quarter of the civilian labor force was un-

employed, [our company] embarked on a program of expansion. Rather than resort to mass factory layoffs, [company name] produced parts for inventory and stored them. It was a gamble that took nerve, especially for a company doing less than $17 million worth of business a year. Happily, the risk paid off in 1935, when Congress passed the Social Security Act and _____, in competitive bidding, was selected to undertake one of the greatest bookkeeping operations of all time. Thanks to our stockpiling of parts, we were able to build the machines and begin delivery almost at once.

Today, our frequent attitude surveys show that the importance we attach to job security is one of the principal reasons why people like to work for _____.

The recession of 1974 to 1975 challenged the company's policy. At the time of my visit in early 1975, the vice-president of personnel said that maintaining the full employment policy was one of their biggest problems. But the company has maintained the policy and it has done so by:

severely restricting hiring

taking stock inventory

"remissions" (that is, moving work to people)

transferring personnel (including much retraining)

permitting employees to carry over or bank vacations, and encouraging them to take them during difficult times

buffering the work force (some "dirty work" and low-level work being contracted out)

instituting a special voluntary early-retirement program for any employee with twenty-five or more years of service

This company's "banking vacations" policy is an example of a personnel policy that well fits the needs of the business. In many companies, unlike in this one, if an employee does not take all of his or her vacation by a certain date, it is forfeited. As this company's vice-president of personnel said: "During the recession we told employees that there was nothing they could do that would help their company more than taking their extended vacation weeks which they had banked." One top-level personnel officer said that all these activities are very expensive in the short run, and one just has to accept on faith that full employment pays in the long run. Remissions, for example, are extremely expensive, and financial analysts noted that the special early-retirement program greatly penalized company earnings.

The term "rebalancing the work force" is used frequently at high levels of this company. Moreover, there is a special resources-control group that reviews manufacturing situations and backlogs. The fact that a personnel representative is a member of this group indicates how closely business planning and personnel planning are related in this company. As a direct outgrowth of the group, hiring in growth situations is being controlled, people are being retrained, and in some cases people are being moved.

At another company committed to full employment, the vice-president of personnel said:

> *There has never been a layoff, even during the depression. "Voluntary" early retirements would even go against the grain here. Though we have a good early-retirement program, we value experienced, senior people and we wouldn't want to go out and say we want all you old-timers to leave.*

What the company does during difficult times is to put a freeze on hiring, and to utilize people in different ways while letting them retain their pay rates. When supervisors were asked about the strengths of the company's personnel policies and practices, several mentioned the full employment policies. A group leader, who had been with the company for twenty-seven years, said:

> *If there is no work, they do not lay you off. You may be dusting or sweeping the floors. Twenty years ago, I painted for one whole summer. The company never lets you go and you never lose your pay rate.*

On the same subject, a department head said:

> *You try to get the people promoted to other jobs so as not to declare them surplus. You have lateral moves and promotional moves. It takes much planning ahead. People are declared surplus, by seniority, by job classification. Their pay is not affected when they are declared surplus, but they will cut grass, wash windows, and paint. Some people have been surplus for three or four years. But they have confidence that the company will find them a compatible job.*

A group leader at the company, recalling having been placed on another job at one time, said:

> *I was once placed for three weeks on an easy job. There was quite a bit of resentment over the fact that I got the job. The resentment was based on the fact that I got the job on the basis of the amount of time I had with the company. They are mad if some guy gets ahead of you.*

A labor-relations consultant the company has on retainer related that during the depression one of the founders toured the plants and told the employees not to worry about being laid off. He told them this was so because they had "made" both the company and his family, and that he wasn't going to let them down by laying them off.

On his ninetieth birthday, a member of the founding family still partly active in the business visited the company and told the financial vice-president, "My brother and I ran this company during the depression without a layoff. Don't you have one now."

The company's intention of providing job security is not unknown to the employees. It was undoubtedly a factor in an unsuccessful union-organizing campaign after World War II. In the employee handbook, a copy of which is given to each employee, under the heading "Steady Employment," appears the following:

> It is the company's intent to provide the opportunity for continuous employment for all employees who work on permanent jobs full time.
>
> There are times when the need for people in a particular area may decrease because of a change in production requirements, the discontinuance of a service, or some other reason. Layoffs are avoided at such times by placement of employees on productive work in other areas.
>
> When such a work situation develops in a department, employees having the fewest years of service are designated for transfer to other assignments. If the result of this policy will seriously limit a department's effectiveness, exceptions to the policy may be made with approvals of the director concerned and the personnel director.
>
> Employees are transferred to comparable job levels whenever possible. If it should be necessary, because of the work situation, to reassign an employee to a lower-rated position, the personnel department will continue to search for a job opening more comparable to that formerly held by the individual.
>
> In any event, when such an employee is placed on a new assignment, his or her salary is protected.

Two other steps also aid the company in implementing its full employment policy. First, during slack times employees will be given the option of taking a two- to four-week leave of absence. This particular method of reducing the work force relates to the environmental factor regarding a high percentage of women in the work force. Many women at this company volunteer for these leaves because they like to use the time for work around their homes. Second, during times of expansion the company will hire temporary employees. Explaining this policy, a department head said:

> The company sometimes hires temporary employees. These are sometimes former employees who come back to work part time. There will be well-qualified people who have quit to raise a family. This is better than hiring permanent people and then making them surplus.

In still another large service organization, which is considered a "people" business and is the only nonunion company in a highly competitive industry where layoffs are common, the senior vice-president of personnel reported that there has never been a layoff. The company's "no layoff" policy is adhered to strictly.

Even when there are declines in demand, as there were during the 1974 fuel crisis and the recession of 1974 to 1975, the company works out reassignments whereby the employee is guaranteed an income close to the one earned in his or her regular job. In addition, employees are offered an option of taking a voluntary leave of absence.

This company, in which 43 percent of every revenue dollar goes for salaries and benefits, is quite public about its policy. Its 1971 annual report to shareholders stated that:

> All adjustments to staffing levels have been accomplished through normal attrition, in keeping with commitment to maintain stable employment for all employees.

Regarding the same subject, the company's 1974 annual report includes this statement:

> During the March quarter of this year, when fuel crisis related . . . reductions were at their peak levels, . . . [employees] were temporarily reassigned to other duties in the company. This was in keeping with [company] tradition and policy to provide stable employment and the need for additional temporary staffing to meet the added work load caused by increased . . . demand.

The company has extremely low turnover and high productivity. Moreover, independent evidence indicates great company loyalty and high employee morale. During seasonal peaks in the company's business, temporary employees are hired. A number of the employees hired for the busy winter season are either former employees or former temporary employees.

While employees sometimes complain about their reassignments, especially when they involve a change of hours, there can be no doubt about the positive impact this policy makes. This is because the layoffs of competitors are very visible to the employees of this company. Company experience is that employee reclassification to lower jobs is a good long-term strategy that fits well with various company practices, for two reasons. First, the company is extremely selective in employment, and, accordingly, invests considerable sums of money in hiring and training. A person at this company is hired to do many jobs and is selected for a career rather than for a job. Training is considerable, and promotions—based on ability—are rapid. Promotion from within is a policy rarely violated, and there is a great deal of job rotation. The rotation program gives the company a lot of job flexibility. From the company's point of view, this investment in people makes layoffs very expensive. Second, the company runs a "lean shop," preferring to hire temporary help in rush seasons and to invest a small amount in their training in order to avoid possible layoffs in slow seasons. Employees interviewed during the recession of 1974 to 1975 were 100 percent confident that there would not be a layoff.

Finally, at yet another large nonunion company, where top management holds "jobholders meetings" at which employee questions are answered, an employee asked, "What about our layoff policy? Will the company extend early retirement to older employees?" The corporate vice-president who responded to this question was brief and to the point: "We're working on a policy, but we really hope there won't be a need for one." The company, used to low turnover, has never had a layoff.

As the above discussion makes clear, these companies attach a great deal of importance to the maintenance of full employment. They use a variety of techniques to avoid the necessity for layoff of those employees deemed permanent. While favorable environmental factors facilitate their practices, what these companies do is expensive. However, these companies believe that the benefits of their practices are worth the associated costs.

WORK-SHARING PRACTICES

On rare occasions, other companies have had to include the temporary practice of work sharing as an additional technique to avoid layoffs. This practice can visibly demonstrate top management's confidence in and concern for people.

One company's employment security policy was severely tested in 1970. Writing about it in 1973, the president stated:

> During that time, orders were coming in at a rate less than our production capability. We were faced with the prospect of a 10 percent layoff—something we had never done before. Rather than a layoff, we tried a different tack. We went to a schedule of working nine days out of every two weeks—a 10 percent cut in work schedule with a corresponding 10 percent cut in pay for all employees involved in this schedule. At the end of a six-month period, orders and employment were once again in balance and the company returned to a full work week. The net result of this program was that effectively all shared the burden of the recession, good people were not turned out on a very tough job market, and, I might observe, the company benefited by having in place a highly qualified work force when business improved.

Visibly demonstrating the principle of equity, the pay cut applied to everyone, including the chief executive officer. This step no doubt enhanced management's credibility and gave added meaning and reality to management's philosophy for the employees, as do the company's profit-sharing plan, counselor system, coffee-break system, and flexible working hours program.

At another company built on a philosophical principle of sharing ("we share the good times and we share the bad times" is the way the personnel manager described the founder's philosophy), work during the 1974 to 1975 recession was shared by reducing schedules rather than by having layoffs. The good times at this company are shared through a profit-sharing plan, a cash-bonus plan, and an employee stock-purchase plan in which fifty percent of the current employees are shareholders.

At another company, which has been characterized by rapid growth and employment stability, management in 1974 went to all employees, plant by plant, and told them about the inventory problems and the economic situation. All merit increases had been frozen and all exempt personnel had their pay cut by 12 percent. Management said, in essence: "We can lay off 25 percent of the work force, or we can have a few weeks off without pay for everyone." Group meetings were held at every location and the employees preferred the option of weeks off without pay.

One employee, who was being interviewed at one of the company's southern plants by a TV reporter for the local evening news program, said, "It's simple. We're sharing what we've got with each other."

Thus the company adopted staggered work weeks to meet its needs as well as the needs of most employees. The vice-president of personnel commented on that approach:

> Stability is our goal, though there have been some reductions. We ride the storm out by extending people, reassigning them, building inventories, and staggering the work week. But if there is a need for layoffs, and there have been some minor ones, we rigidly follow seniority.

At a different company, which has also long been characterized by employment stability, the following words appeared in its anniversary booklet:

> . . . [the founder] himself was always well aware of the importance of the employees' and the company's well-being. He thought twice about entering a factory because someone would usually stop him and ask him for a raise, which he found hard to turn down. Once, when there was a surplus of . . . [the company's product], instead of laying off workers, he went on a selling trip that created an immediate market for the extra product. [The company] introduced the stock participation plan in the early 1900s. It enabled all— workers as well as president—to share in the profits. Many modestly paid employees were able to accumulate rather impressive sums over the years.

This company has still not had a layoff as such. The only possible exception involved a large engineering operation in which a number of employees were hired in a permanent–temporary category to build the power system in a new plant. Once the job was finished, those employees were offered plant jobs (a number of them accepted). Consequently, this should not really count as a layoff.

However, in the early 1970s a certain environmental problem caused a significant decline in the demand for the company's products—in response to this the company redistributed the work and went on a four-day workweek. The company had twelve four-day weeks before it was able to resume normal operations.

The sharing of work in bad times is nothing new. In fact, this practice may have been one factor responsible for the bringing about of unions. The significant point about the work-sharing experiences of the companies studied is that the work was not shared too deeply or too long. In no company, for example, were work schedules reduced by as much as one-third or one-half. Moreover, the reductions were not for very long periods of time. Instead, these companies were able to reduce work schedules by a relatively small amount for a relatively short period of time. These adjustments were temporary and short-lived—under these conditions work sharing can certainly be preferable to a layoff. Under less favorable conditions, workers might prefer the security of a supplemental unemployment benefits plan, a program that is part of the benefits package in some highly unionized, cyclical industries. Like the truly full employment companies, the behavior of companies that have had to use work sharing not only shows the "people" commitment of top management—it also shows the influence of favorable environmental factors as well.

QUALIFIERS OR SPECIAL CONDITIONS

Three of the companies in this study have made a partial rather than a total commitment to a no-layoffs policy.

In one large company that has had only two small layoffs in its long history, no employees with more than a year's seniority were let go.

In another company, a policy was adopted in the mid-1950s for the purpose of minimizing the threat of improved technology and encouraging cooperation between management and employees. When there was a major methods change, a guarantee was given that no one would lose his or her job for at least six months. At the end of the six months, if no "reasonable" job existed (and there were policy guidelines defining the word "reasonable"), the employee was then paid at a gradually reduced scale, received separation pay (one week per year of service), and could take the vested part of his or her pension. If a branch closed, the employee received two years' notice, separation pay, and moving expenses. The company's vice-president of personnel said that these policies "cost piles of money" but that the company did many "far reaching things." When asked about the benefits of this policy, he said:

*We could make operational changes that others couldn't make. Our
objective was to minimize resistance to technological change. The benefits
which resulted from the changes we introduced greatly exceeded the costs
involved.*

The policy of the 1950s was subsequently modified in important ways. Now
the company will never close a plant without placing all of the employees with at
least two years of service in another plant or another subsidiary. Moving expenses
for relocation are covered by the company.

While admitting that this policy can be expensive, a personnel administrator
insisted that it is important to provide the work force with a sense of job security.
As an extreme example, he mentioned that one worker went through twelve
replacement interviews to find a suitable (by the employee's definition) job during
a plant closing a few years ago.

Recent layoffs at this company have been handled in two ways. First, only
people with less than two years of service can be furloughed. Then, if the
remaining work force is still too large, the company relies on normal attrition and
voluntary layoffs. Management has gone to groups of employees and asked for
volunteers to leave with separation pay. This latter option has been successful, as it
has given a number of older employees the opportunity to retire early.

The recession of 1974 to 1975 forced a different company to change its
traditional policy, in such a way as to minimize the consequences to employee
relations. The new policy was also used as a plus factor during a recent organizational drive. In a document prepared to help supervisors explain the pros of the
company's policies and all the problems that would be caused if a union came in,
there appears under the heading "Job Security at [company name]":

*Throughout its history, [our company] has established a record of
security unparalleled in the . . . industry. . . . Even during the depths of the
depression in the 1930s, [we] never laid off a single permanent employee. It is
our intention and our commitment to continue this tradition. As a matter of
fact, it is [our] . . . policy to permit staff members when they reach retirement
age to continue working as long as they want with the consent of their
department managers and the medical director. Large numbers of employees
have taken advantage of this privilege. The best current examples of the . . .
job security commitment to our employees has been during the past several
months. During the second half of 1973 levels of business fell below expectations. Most companies in our industry, confronted with our business situation
and faced with limitations in the assignment of personnel implicit in the
unionized company, would have resorted to layoffs. [We] laid off no employee
with more than one year of service who was under retirement age and who was
performing at a better than marginal level. Furthermore, many persons in
excess positions with more than one year of service were relocated . . .
without loss of pay. Some employees were asked if they wanted to take reduced
hours schedules. Some volunteered, others didn't. It was strictly voluntary.*

Upon inquiring how this modest layoff was actually carried out, I could not help but be impressed with the care and thought devoted to the process. The vice-president and the senior vice-president of personnel met with every plant manager, assistant manager, and personnel manager. They listened to the budget goals, and made either suggestions or modifications with respect to the layoff or reduced schedule plans. Personnel officers monitored the process carefully, and it can be said that management invested an enormous amount of effort and attention to a layoff that affected less than 1 percent of the work force.

While different from the commitment to full employment for permanent employees, the commitment to nearly full employment for employees who have been with this same company one or two years provides much job security. The combination of management philosophy and the traditional stability of the business makes this practical commitment to full employment offered by these companies the same as a full commitment for most of the employees—namely, for all those employees with over a year or two of service. Although they work in the company for a much longer period of time, these employees are similar to the temporary employees of the full employment companies.

SOME LAYOFF EXPERIENCES

As indicated, a sizable number of the companies studied are characterized by a high degree of employment stability or full-employment goals. Others have instituted work-sharing arrangements as a way to satisfy their employment goals and the realities of the business. However, even in the companies that have layoffs, special attention is devoted to the process. It is the policies and practices of some of these companies that we now briefly examine.

One company, which has been almost totally successful in achieving its goal of keeping its new plants nonunion, does not have a full-employment policy. Its layoff policy, not unlike the one found in the unionized part of its business, is based on seniority and qualifications. Recently, however, the company did two different things prior to the layoff. First, it eliminated all subcontract personnel. Then, it instituted a system of voluntary and forced vacations for the current year and the year following. Finally, the layoffs began.

In the judgment of the corporate employee-relations director, the reaction to this process was favorable because it accomplished two things: It postponed the layoff for six months, and it was progressive rather than sudden, so that people could prepare for it.

A visit to one of the plants of this company confirmed the judgment of the corporate employee-relations director. At this plant, which had once employed 480 people and had not had a layoff in 13 years, 125 hourly and 5 salaried people had been furloughed. Although 40 percent of them had been called back at the time of the visit, the superintendent of personnel said:

The layoff was viewed as a last-ditch effort and seniority was used. The plant has a history of stability and it was one of the last plants in the area to experience a layoff and one of the first to begin recalling people.

A foreman who had tried to organize the plant when an hourly worker at the time it was owned by another company, commented:

They held the layoffs back here. In a union shop, the people would have been let go a month earlier. Seniority and security are very big here.

During this crisis there was also a mass meeting in the cafeteria to explain the layoffs to all crews. These mass meetings are a communications device the plant holds on a monthly basis for all its crews. The plant manager who runs the meetings uses them to explain the state of the business, to discuss changes in benefits, and to discuss good and bad news. According to the foreman:

People like to see him. He'll give a short speech. He'll talk about the state of the business or safety or hours. We're very proud of our safety record here. The plant manager always says, "You people are the ones who do the work." The previous plant manager didn't do this as well. It seems like you get a new plant manager every two or three years and they all have their good qualities.

The plant manager is on the floor and says good morning to you. He knows everyone on a first-name basis and people like him. He is young, tall, and good-looking and people on the floor like to see the white-collar guys. It is a policy to stop and talk and people really like it.

Thus the way in which a layoff is handled seems important. It is critical to note that in this case the company has regular meetings with its employees. Such formal communications programs, found in many of the companies studied, will be discussed in Chapter 14.

Yet another company, also one that has been almost totally successful in keeping its new plants unorganized since World War II, tries to exhaust all other means before having a layoff. This is done in both union and nonunion plants, but in the union plants the company considers a real plus the flexibility associated with the fact that it has retained its right to subcontract. Commenting on this, the company's director of labor relations said:

If services are contracted out, we will discontinue this practice, be the job taking care of the lawn, painting, or whatever. There is always a backlog of minor construction projects and we will divert people if need be. We have some advantages, particularly in the union plants, because we can get rid of subcontractors and provide jobs for our own people.

One company that has recently had large-scale layoffs had not been very cyclical, but for two exceptions, until the past six years. The administrative vice-president thought this fact was one of the reasons behind the company's nonunion status. When an old-time employee was asked what he liked about the company, he listed a number of reasons, and job security was first on his list.

This company, which at one time employed 38,000 people, had its first major layoff in 1945, and another in 1957 when 300 employees were let go. When a vice-president was asked how the recent layoffs were handled (employment is now 24,500), the reply was: "With a great deal of difficulty."

Review boards, consisting of managers and hourly people, play a major part in the administration of the layoff policy. In commenting on the procedure, the vice-president said:

> *Every person is handled individually. A list of names comes before the review board and everything is taken into account. Layoffs have not been based exclusively on seniority. If everything else is equal, then seniority is followed. Our guidelines (rather than ground rules) are designed to give the supervisors flexibility.*

The review boards serve as a check on management. Employees who think they have been unfairly laid off have the right to appeal their cases to the board. Some employees have done this, and some of them have been subsequently reinstated.

At a different company, which until recently had offered a high degree of job security, in the 1973 annual report the president stated that:

> *During the past four months, economic and market conditions have necessitated the furloughing of approximately 12,000 . . . people, worldwide. Additionally, about 4,000 are currently working less than full schedules. These staff reductions were not easy actions to take, and careful effort was taken to ensure that the separations were determined with a high degree of fairness. Eliminating the job or reducing the paycheck of even one [employee] is difficult, and we earnestly look forward to the day on which we can begin calling these people back to work and, even more so, to the day when all of them will have been offered reemployment on a full-time basis.*

As illustration not only of top management's concern about job security, but also of its interest in innovation in the personnel area, in 1977 this company's personnel department was investigating, with state unemployment insurance officials, the economics of work sharing. For instance, one idea was that rather than to have a layoff when demand slackened, the entire work force would be retained but on a reduced workweek, with the loss of company pay made up from the state. The impact, on the state unemployment compensation fund and on the company's own tax rate, of paying benefits for part-time idleness under work sharing was being studied. While wanting to know the bottom-line effects, a company official thought such a plan had appeal, not only due to the attractiveness of maintaining a stable work force, but also because reduced training and recruiting costs would be associated with such a plan.

Another growth company with an explicit goal of remaining nonunion for many years considered itself a full-employment company. A former director of personnel at the company had even considered the adoption of a tenure policy for employees at one time. But the recession of 1974 and a less than successful introduction of a new product made it necessary to cut the work force by approximately ten percent. The company developed a written layoff policy in 1970, but 1974 was its first layoff experience.

In addition to largely doing layoffs by straight seniority, with some special protection given to minorities and women, the company had a generous severance pay plan, as well as a liberal voluntary special early-retirement program. Due to the management's concern for its laid-off employees, it also established an active job-placement service. This activity consumed much space in the personnel office. Telephones, copy machines, and office space were made available to employees. A bulletin board listed job openings in other companies. And career counselors helped employees write résumés as well as to think through their career objectives. The company's outplacement effort was considered quite successful in helping those who had been laid off to find other jobs.

Due to the management's continuing concern, an internal organizational development consultant was designated to interview those severed employees in order to ascertain their feelings about the company and the way in which they had been treated. In discussing this, the consultant said:

> *The surprising finding was that people were not mad at the company. People seemed to say, "How can you be mad at someone when you're treated as well as we have been treated?"*

In fact, it was my impression that some people thought the company a little too generous in the amount of severance pay it gave out to those who were leaving permanently.

An interesting aside to this story, and one that illustrates the important interrelatedness of the various elements of a company's approach to staying nonunion, is that prior to the layoffs in the company discussed above, management had considered reducing seniority units to a plantwide basis. The company, on the advice of outside labor counsel, had always operated a single companywide seniority system, although all of its plants are in one state, with some as far apart as fifty miles from each other.

The reason for the large companywide system, from a labor relations viewpoint, was to minimize the chances of collective bargaining occurring. The rationale was that it would be much harder for a union to organize the entire company than a single plant or location, which under different conditions might be viewed by the National Labor Relations Board as an appropriate bargaining unit. For a variety of reasons, at the time of the layoff management had considered making the seniority unit plantwide, but because top management felt that the company would then be more vulnerable to union organization, it retained its established companywide system.

At none of the companies where layoffs became necessary were they done in a hurried or arbitrary manner. Seniority was generally respected. As with the other companies discussed earlier, these companies utilized hiring freezes, inventory buildups, and in some cases the transfer of work normally done by subcontractors to their full-time employees.

CONCLUDING ANALYSIS AND COMMENTS

In this chapter we have discussed a remarkable number of techniques different companies have used to provide job security. From routine hiring freezes and the elimination of subcontractors, to retraining and relocation, the variety of approaches used and the steps taken to ensure that these techniques work have been impressive.

While those companies that take extraordinary measures to provide their permanent employees with job security boast of the flexibility advantages derived from their nonunion status, one freedom that they have denied to themselves is the ability to lay off workers as a response to changed business conditions. While their nonunion status gives them the freedom and flexibility to reassign and even move employees, the costs associated with these practices are substantial. Some of the costs and benefits of these full employment practices are listed in Table 6-1.

TABLE 6-1

Costs	*Benefits*

Extra payroll and payroll related expenses:
   training costs
   possible temporary red circle rates
   extra overtime because of reluctance to hire
   extra costs of any special early retirement
     plans
 Moving expenses
 Possible slower delivery schedule
 Productivity losses associated with people assigned to different jobs
 Extra financial charges because of larger-than-necessary inventory
 Extra employment costs associated with extreme selectivity in hiring
 Possible slower rate of methods or technological change due to need to avoid displacing any permanent employees
	Better employee morale because of lack of insecurity
	 Productivity advantages associated with less employee resistance to methods or to technological changes due to fear of job loss (greater acceptance of methods and technological changes)
	 Lower unemployment insurance costs
	 Savings of subsequent employment and training costs if there had been a layoff
	 Favorable image in the community

For a variety of reasons, it is not possible to say whether the benefits actually exceed the costs for any particular company. Workers, in their turn, have to be willing to do different jobs, to be trained, and to be moved, if necessary, in exchange for job security.

There can be no doubt about the importance of job security. For some companies, full or nearly-full employment is an important cornerstone of their employee-relations and business philosophies. Without layoffs, these companies do not have to decide whom to let go, which is always a difficult decision. Examining the concept of full employment and realizing its significance, one can better understand the reasons why banks, insurance companies, and universities have remained unorganized for the most part: These organizations have offered their employees an unusually high degree of job security. As discussed in Chapter 2, it is probably also the case due to certain environmental factors, including long-term growth, adequate profits, and a high percentage of female employees in the clerical work force.

Richard M. Pfeffer, a professor of political science at The Johns Hopkins University, took a job in a piston ring factory while on a sabbatical. In a subsequent article in the *New York Times,* he had some strong comments to make that gave some insight into what is happening "between the lines" when layoffs occur:

> *Profound economic crises expose how socio-economic systems oper-ate. Layoffs strip away whatever niceties and human concerns appear to be part of the normal operations of inhuman societies. . . . In such institutions as factories, where even under the best of conditions the system of hierarchi-cal domination hardly appears humane, the impact of the present economic crisis has been immediate, the dehumanization total.*
>
> *Layoffs, as a particular kind of crisis, dramatize issues embedded in normal work relations. Subordinates feel a one-sided dependency upon hierarchical powerholders and a concomitant sense of individual helpless-ness that at times approaches terror.*
>
> *That subjective appreciation accurately reflects the objective treatment of workers as commodities in every sphere of production in the United States. They are human commodities whose entire value lies in their capacity to produce whatever is defined as "productive" by the manipulated, interlock-ing markets.*
>
> *In the factory, where individualism and meaningful specialization on the job are repressed, it is almost impossible not to see oneself as a commodity—a commodity that is replaceable on the labor market, a commod-ity whose human qualities are irrelevant to its disposition.*[1]

A study, conducted by the Conference Board, concerned with white-collar unionization gave another insight into the importance of job security. Eighty

[1]Richard M. Pfeffer, "When the Niceties Go," *New York Times,* April 30, 1975, p. 41.

employers, who indicated that their employees had initiated union drives, were asked what they saw as the reasons for the initial interest in unionization among their white-collar people. The report stated their replies:

> *Next to dissatisfaction with salaries, the most frequently cited cause of union interest among employees is concern with job security—mentioned by 22 companies. (Pay was mentioned by 35 of the 80 companies.) In most of these companies, proposed or actual changes in staffing, location, supervision, or production methods apparently gave rise to employee unrest and subsequent union interest. For example, the general manager of a school-supplies manufacturer cites as a major factor "considerable upheaval and confusion, with an abrupt change in branch management structure, with two managers and six salesmen dropped. These changes in procedures and personnel caused a feeling of insecurity in the office." (Subsequently, the office employees voted the union in—and according to the manager, one of the union's key selling points was "protection against arbitrary management action.")*[2]

The ability to maintain steady employment relates to certain environmental factors as well as to management's ability to plan and forecast and to consequently make full employment possible. Forecasting and coordinating production to the market have many advantages, including job security.[3]

Some of the employment security practices of the companies studied go way beyond those that could not be achieved in a relationship that horrifies them. Many of the companies have embraced ideas that are startling in relationship to the achievements of union contracts. These companies have extremely broad seniority units, incur huge training costs, and even have interplant transfers. Ironically, some of the layoff practices of the past that have given rise to unions become frozen, and employment stability becomes worse in a unionized company than in a nonunion one.

The practices of some of the companies studied are similar to the unemployment practices of Germany and Switzerland. Like these countries, these companies export their unemployment: Germany and Switzerland export their unemployment by denying work permits to guest workers; some of these companies export their unemployment to their subcontractors. The position of the temporary worker at many of these companies is similar to temporary workers in Japan. Japan is known for its life-time employment for all of its people who are not temporary workers!

---

[2]Edward R. Curtin, *White Collar Unionization* (a research report), Studies in Personnel Policy No. 220 (New York: The National Industrial Conference Board, Inc., 1970).

[3]*See* Albert Bradley, "Setting Up a Forecasting Problem," reprinted in *Giant Enterprise: Ford, General Motors, and the Automobile Industry*, ed. Alfred D. Chandler (New York: Harcourt Brace Jovanovich, Inc., 1964). Bradley discusses forecasting in relation to fundamental policies and mentions steadier employment for the work force as a result of the more even rate of operations.

Needless to say, the extent to which the companies studied are in growth industries, rather than in seasonal or cyclical industries, facilitates their practices of full employment. Even so, growth companies have had their policies and practices challenged by the recent economic contraction. When asked about the significance of rapid growth and its relationship to full-employment practices, a senior personnel executive replied:

> There is a great deal more to full employment than growth. For example, major automobile manufacturers have had tremendous long-term growth over the last fifty years. They have also had numerous layoffs. Perhaps the layoffs were necessary. But almost certainly something else was lacking. You have to have the desire to avoid layoffs, careful planning of work, the willingness and financial ability to spend money to avoid layoffs, and you need a willingness on the part of the employees to accept various work assignments as long as their pay and benefits are protected. The auto industry, as well as many others, must have missed out on some of these points. I think all of this is a real, though intangible, part of the environment in which employees work.

While it may be too easy for other companies to dismiss full-employment practices as being wholly attributable to environmental factors, how could a major automobile company offer full employment unless it has designated everyone with less than several years of service a temporary employee? The automobile industry is simply too cyclical for full employment to be manageable. The companies would not know what to do with the surplus employees when they were not building cars. The realities and economics of the automobile business make the union-negotiated short workweek benefits and the guaranteed annual salary plan (which consists of unemployment compensation and supplemental unemployment benefits) preferable to either full-employment practices or work-sharing arrangements. A vice-president of personnel was very interested in the significance of the job-security concept. In a letter, with respect to job security, he wrote:

> Of all the union organizing drives that I have ever participated in, one way or another the manner in which management created this feeling of job insecurity seemed to be basic to every one of them. I'm amazed at how obvious it is, how much is written about it and yet how unresponsive many of us are to this fact. I'm absolutely convinced that, if the president of almost any company in any industry made a policy decision that they were not going to have any layoffs and that it was the responsibility of his key management staff to plan to keep the cost to a minimum, we could have continued employment without layoffs at virtually no cost to the company except for very rare and unique circumstances, e.g., 1 percent to 5 percent of the time we now have layoffs. The rest of the 95 percent of the time there would be no layoffs.

While this person may have also exaggerated what it is possible to do with respect to maintaining full employment, clearly the importance of full employment, as well as what it takes to make it a reality, cannot be overemphasized.

While there are favorable environmental factors that contribute to the realization of full employment practices, the depth of the conviction on the part of top management in addition to the necessary planning to make it happen cannot be ignored. It is an expensive policy: Its costs in terms of money, planning and training are substantial.

The advantages a company can realize by offering full employment are, though not measurable, very real. While removing the effects of fear and job insecurity cannot be quantified, it is nevertheless a significant benefit. Greater loyalty to the organization, less resistance to technological change, greater cooperation with respect to new methods and processes, and better employee relations are certainly advantages that contribute to higher productivity.

Interestingly, many of the full-employment companies doubted they could maintain their practices if they were unionized. They thought that with unionization they would lose their flexibility and their right to move and reassign people as they now do. However, one might well wonder if these companies would agree to full employment by contract even if the union were to grant them the flexibility desired.

The special adjustments made at the time of a layoff, especially the work-sharing arrangements described, can also visibly represent the management's approach or philosophy. Steps taken, such as the ones described above, are a few of the ways in which the philosophy can become real and credible to the employee.

However, as this study suggests, a guarantee of job security is not a necessary or a sufficient condition for the maintenance of a nonunion status, since there are large companies that have not provided such job security and have still remained nonunion. They have done this, it seems, not only through the way they have historically treated their employees (including during times of layoff), but also through other important policies such as pay, benefits, and communications.

In contrast, there have been cases of successful union drives among organizations that do provide job security. Tenured college professors, for example, have voted to join unions, as have government employees with a great deal of job security. Nevertheless, there is no doubt that job security is extremely important. Furthermore, it is an important foundation on which to build a successful employee-relations and business philosophy. It can be a major component within a comprehensive package of personnel policies and practices.

CHAPTER SEVEN

Promotion Systems

The practice of promoting from within the company is as important to the companies (if not more so) as employment security. While promotion policies and methods may differ from company to company, promotion from within is a fundamental principle among all the companies studied. It is a principle, moreover, enhanced in part by the rapid growth experienced by the majority of the companies in the sample. Such growth provides a significant number of promotional opportunities each year.

This chapter discusses the practice of promotion from within. Because it is increasingly the dominant method, this chapter examines the pros and cons of job posting and its various forms, the administrative problems that inevitably seem to be associated with the process, and some of the alternative methods of promoting from within. Finally, we will discuss the important issue of seniority versus ability in selection decisions.

PROMOTION FROM WITHIN

One financial vice-president stated emphatically that theirs is a promotion-from-within company. The president of the company had started many years ago as an hourly worker, and all but a handful of top managers had started at the bottom and worked their way up. With regard to management's deep commitment to individual development and promotion from within, the financial vice-president said:

> *For example, our company doesn't hire computer programmers from the outside. When I need programmers, we post the jobs. Hourly people are given aptitude tests and we train those who do well enough on the tests to be programmers.*

A location manager identified some of the advantages from his point of view of the promotion-from-within policy:

> *I started with the company fourteen years ago in the loading department. I have worked every job that every employee is working in this location, so I can identify with each of them and with their problems. If they want to talk about the cold weather and a wet midnight shift, I can talk about that because I used to work at those times.*
>
> *Except for a few specialists, the entire field managers' group are people who have come up through the ranks.*

This person's comments shed light not only on the importance of promotion from within, but also on his and on what seems to be the company's style of management. A number of employees said that the company's system means that an individual can advance at his or her own pace. They were convinced that this was not the case with their unionized competitors.

The company's chairman, a career personnel officer and former president of the company, associates promotion from within with high employee morale. Employees know that they are competing for promotions only with insiders and that management will not bring in outsiders to fill supervisory openings. Illustrating the scope of an internal promotions policy, another company will train existing employees to be plant guards rather than hiring ex-policemen, as is often done.

Office and laboratory jobs at some companies are filled by people who started in production assembly lines in the factory. Career counseling, training, and educational opportunities can facilitate job upgrading. For example, in one company factory workers are encouraged to upgrade to the office by successful completion of clerical tests and training programs. The personnel representative interviewed had started her career at the company as an inspector in the factory. Subsequently, she became a clerk, then an administrative clerk; more recently she moved into her present position, where she is responsible for about 500 employees located in four different plants.

The companies that have implemented promotion-from-within policies to the greatest degree are those that have primarily selected their managerial and supervisory personnel from the ranks of hourly employees, have provided opportunities for factory people to move into research or to the office, have offered much in the way of training and education, and have had a restricted number of entry jobs.

JOB POSTING

At many nonunion companies, promotion from within is institutionalized through job posting. Although several of the more diversified companies do not have posting in all of their plants or divisions, about 65 percent of all the companies studied do use job posting. All 35 percent of the other companies have considered job posting at one time or another, but have adopted an alternative method, which they consider a superior means of accomplishing the basic objectives of a job posting system.

Before discussing why some companies reject job posting, and the methods they use in its place, let us consider the reasons for job posting, the nature of different job-posting systems, and the administrative problems that may arise under this system.

Reasons for Having Job Posting

Most of the companies that post jobs have done so for a considerable number of years. As the former personnel director of one multiplant company that has had companywide job posting for many years said: "Every company has its thing, and with us it is job posting." Executives of companies with job posting gave six reasons in support of their practices.

JOB POSTING IS BENEFICIAL TO INDIVIDUAL CAREER DEVELOPMENT

First, posting was viewed both as a benefit to individual career development and as a constructive way to alleviate morale problems. Posting was generally considered consistent with the commitment to promotion from within and with the philosophy of upward mobility. As one personnel director put it: "With job posting the employees feel they have an opportunity." For many employees, getting promoted is the principal way to improve income. Company attitude surveys and other feedback mechanisms frequently reveal that employees want more knowledge of job opportunities. A bidding procedure, accordingly, can be one of the most important benefits a company provides, because it makes promotional opportunities better known.

Although still viewed as a plus, the posting system did draw criticism from one manager for its competitive nature, and for encouraging employees to feel that they must move up in order to survive in the company. "Here," this manager said, "everyone bids, and employees feel that they *have* to do so if they have been in a job too long."

JOB POSTING KEEPS SUPERVISORS HONEST

Second, posting was seen as a way of preventing supervisors from suppressing talent or from picking only their favorites for promotions. Supervisors, for very understandable reasons, are often reluctant to let their good workers go. Because posting directly tells employees about advancement opportunities, the employees (rather than their supervisors) can decide if they want to bid for a job. Some executives said that favoritism, with respect to the administration of either merit pay or promotions, can encourage unionization, and that with posting the company had a better chance of combating favoritism. With posting, job opportunities are out in the open. Employees not only know of opportunities, but also may know who else has applied. With posting and bidding, foremen must justify their decisions to interested employees. As one director of employee relations said: "Posting helps keep management honest." Some executives also view an open-posting system as more democratic than other systems.

As will be pointed out later, some executives favored job posting because they thought it can combat a practice that might give rise to unionization, while other managers opposed job posting because they felt it too closely resembles what goes on in a union shop.

Job Posting Discovers Hidden Talent

Third, some managers noted that job posting is a mechanism that can enable a company to discover talent within the organization that was not known to exist. "There is really no other way for a supervisor to know the resources that exist in the division other than through job posting," said one vice-president. One hears many stories of an executive's surprise at finding a well-qualified company employee, surfacing through the company's bidding system, who had acquired certain experience in another company or at night school. If the company would otherwise go to the outside to recruit such an individual, job posting can also be a cost-effective policy for the company. From a different perspective, some employees interviewed felt that the major success of the job-posting system is not with respect to promotion opportunity—rather that the system allows dissatisfied workers the chance to get out of unhappy situations.

While job posting is certainly a valid mechanism for discovering hidden talent, one needs to recognize that a good personnel information system, with accurate employee input, can also provide management with this same information.

Job Posting Is a Communications Device

Fourth, some managers considered a job-posting system a communications device. To the extent that employees review the postings, this is so, for the job opportunities can reveal areas of company expansion and growth. While other communications devices can accomplish the same objective, the job-posting system does so in a very real way for the ambitious and upwardly-mobile employee. Even if not selected, the employee has an opportunity to talk with supervisors in other parts of the company, and to learn more about the company as well as what is needed in order to qualify for the job in the future. It not only helps the employee; it also assists him or her to talk knowledgeably to outsiders about the opportunities the company offers. This can make an employee feel more a part of the company, and can thereby enhance his or her morale and status.

JOB POSTING REDUCES COMPANY TURNOVER

Fifth, if a company's posting system prevents a bored but competent employee from quitting, the company benefits because the costs associated with turnover are reduced. Also, the costs associated with hiring from inside the company are generally much less than those associated with hiring from the outside. Thus, while it was seldom discussed this way, economics may favor posting.

JOB POSTING FACILITATES AFFIRMATIVE ACTION

Finally, some companies have adopted job-posting and bidding systems quite recently for affirmative-action purposes due to pressure or legal advice, or as a result of direct negotiations with government-compliance officers. One company, which was implementing a job-posting system patterned after the system used in one of the largest companies in my sample, justified it in these words:

> *The company is moving to job posting for two reasons. First, on the advice of counsel, we are moving from a department- to a plantwide-seniority concept. We are doing this because of the threat of a class action suit. Second, the opinion survey shows that employees want more knowledge of job opportunities. In the past the company has had a weak system: one bulletin board in the personnel office where we listed jobs.*

Many consent decrees in affirmative-action suits require a company to develop a job-posting system. Judges may direct companies to post notices stating the name and shift of every job vacancy, including the training pay rate, usual length of training, and the full pay rate.

If it is true that women and minorities have not been part of the promotion grapevine or have not expressed as much interest in promotions as white males have done, then job posting can be beneficial for affirmative-action purposes. Job posting, unlike a closed system, makes job opportunities generally known.

As has been noted, affirmative action is the most recent reason for posting jobs. Other reasons for job posting have been used at some companies for a very long time. As the above discussion suggests, however, posting at company X may not be the same as posting at company Y. Before examining some of the more common administrative problems associated with job posting, let us first note some of the variations in job-posting systems.

Variations in Job-Posting and Bidding Systems

While there are many differences among various job-posting and bidding systems, comments will be limited to the major ones, which are differences in: scope, unit, exceptions, lateral moves, time, and other various administrative rules or guidelines.

SCOPE

While this study was focused on personnel policies as applied to production and maintenance employees, it should be noted that in some companies the job-posting systems apply to office, clerical, technical, and even some managerial jobs, as well as to blue-collar jobs. In other companies the job-posting systems apply only to blue-collar workers. Although the trend is toward the expansion of job posting, at present only a minority of the companies studied include senior-manager jobs in their job-posting and bidding systems.

UNIT

Unlike job posting in many unionized companies, among the companies studied there is a great diversity in promotion units. In most cases the unit is extremely broad. For example, in one multiplant company with plants located in more than one state, job posting is companywide. This is also true of a multiplant company with all of its plants located within one state. In other words, workers who are ten, one-hundred, or three-thousand miles away can know of job opportunities for which they may bid. In some companies, the unit may be the region, the locale, or the plant. However, even where there are broad units the company probably does not ignore normal career ladders and lines of progression. For example, in one company with companywide job posting, all mechanics jobs are bid separately because of the special skills required. A nonmechanic, however, could bid for an entry-level junior mechanic's job. As this company's system is companywide and does include lateral moves, an experienced mechanic in Chicago could bid for the same job in Florida because he or she wants to live in a warmer climate. This mechanic would get the job if he or she competed with a junior mechanic based in Florida. This is because in this company, where selections are based on qualifications and length of service, a lateral move takes precedence over a promotion. The person applying for the transfer is clearly better qualified, by virtue of the fact that he or she has *been* doing the job. In some other multiplant companies where the plant is the promotion unit, employees are told that the personnel department will try to help them if they are interested in transferring to another plant. With new plants open, present employees are often invited to apply and are given job preferences.

The units used by most of the companies studied are broad. The policies and practices of these companies appear more liberal than those found in the typical unionized company.

EXCEPTIONS

Company policies vary with respect to job posting exceptions. In one case, all jobs except the lowest two job classifications must be posted unless there is a qualified person interested and available within a specific local department. For example, if there is an opening within the shipping dock and one member of the shipping crew is qualified, then the job will not be posted. Another company has the policy that jobs that can be filled within the department need not be posted, resulting in the fact that many of the posted jobs are entry positions.

Another company that uses job posting for entry-level as well as senior-manager jobs spells out the situation for which job posting is not necessary. For example, one case is when "persons who are continually adding to their skills and increasing their contribution in the same field of work prove themselves eligible for promotion on the basis of personal competence." Such *in-line* promotions may take place only when all the following criteria are met:

1. The jobs are in the same department, and one job genuinely prepares the incumbent for the next.
2. There is no limit set by the department to the number of incumbents in the higher job.
3. The incumbent has already demonstrated the ability to perform the higher job.
4. Steady work exists in the higher job.
5. The incumbent continues to perform the same field of work for the same supervisor.
6. The incumbent has met any special requirements, such as a course or a skill.
7. No replacement is required.
8. Publicity is given the promotion
9. There is no intention to protect the member from being bumped.

The corporate administrator of this company's job-posting program said that over 90 percent of the jobs posted are filled from within, and that nearly all the company's jobs are posted. While very few exceptions take place, at the higher-level jobs it is most likely that the obvious candidate (the boss' selection) will get the job. One reason that so few exceptions occur is that this company's job-posting system also includes lateral moves: that is, there may be a candidate for the position with the same or more experience in another plant.

When a company has a job-posting system, it is important to ask about the exception policies and, if these are different from the stated policies, to ask about the actual practices.

Lateral Moves

As mentioned earlier, it is also important to investigate whether or not a company's posting system permits lateral moves. Although it is the practice of some companies to try to informally accommodate individual desires for lateral moves, the job-posting systems of these companies only handle promotions. This policy cuts down on the number of bids, and on the time that personnel representatives and supervisors must take to interview candidates to fill positions. At one company, which prohibits an employee from bidding for a job that will not represent a promotion, the only time a lateral bid is considered is when there is clear change in career paths (for instance, a factory-grade worker bidding for an office-grade job) and when all other bidders have been disqualified. Management in this company maintains that if lateral bids were permitted, the motives for job bids might include getting a different manager, being with friends, or receiving more overtime, thereby unnecessarily disrupting the organization and diluting the opportunities of employees for whom the job would be a bona fide promotion. Yet, in many companies employees favor a job-posting system—not only to get promotions, but also to be able to remove themselves from an uncomfortable situation.

However, the job-posting systems of other companies in the study do include and even encourage lateral moves. In one multiplant company in a recent year, 27 percent of the people who were selected for posted jobs filled them on a lateral basis. When asked what motivated this large number of lateral bids, an administrator said that employees were "chasing overtime," or were "getting closer to home or to an opportunity to get to a better shift." While many line managers at this company allegedly objected to allowing lateral moves, this administrator felt that in the long run "the company ends up with happier employees, with a greater degree of freedom. They don't feel that they are being leaned on and they don't feel that they are being regimented."

Allowing lateral moves can also add to the number of bids for job openings. In one extreme case, a company reported that for one job opening there were 300 bidders. Of these 300 bidders, the personnel department screened out 250 people and referred the remaining 50 people to the hiring supervisor to be interviewed. Judging by company experience, many of the bids represented lateral shifts.

Time, and Other Various Administrative Rules and Guidelines

There are many timing and other various administrative rules of job posting that differ from the four other types discussed. One company, for example, requires that a job be posted for twenty-four hours; other companies require a longer period of time, such as three, seven, ten, or fourteen days. While supervisors prefer the shortest time possible, employees generally prefer that jobs be listed for a longer period of time, giving them adequate time to notice the posting, to inquire about the job, to consider applying, and to apply. A longer period of time also accommodates absent employees. However, additional time is costly from the supervisors' and company's points of view.

There is also variation in the amount of time an employee must have been in his or her present job before being eligible to bid for another position. One company, for example, requires a minimum of six months' service in the current position, with satisfactory performance. Another company requires only a three-month minimum. Companies' policies also vary with respect to the bidding rights of those who turn down jobs for which they have bid. For example, one company's policy provides that employees may not reject more than two jobs within any 180-calendar-day period. The amount of screening of bidders done by the personnel department also varies; some personnel departments do much more screening than others. The manner and timing of supervisory notification can differ as well. Generally, employees are encouraged, but not required, to inform their supervisor that they have decided to apply for a posted job. There is also great variation in the way the successful and unsuccessful bidders are notified: sometimes it is the responsibility of the hiring supervisor, other times this work is handled by the personnel department. All companies appear to be requiring more written documentation and feedback to unsuccessful candidates. One company's policy states:

> If you are not the successful applicant, the hiring supervisor must notify you and explain to you why you are not selected. After the selected candidate has been informed of his/her selection, non-selected candidates may, at their request, have the opportunity to discuss with the Personnel Administrator or the hiring supervisor, the name and seniority date of the selected member, and basis for selection. If you wish, the Administrator or supervisor may also advise you as to what you could do to better prepare yourself for such a position in the future.

This company's policy, which is atypical, also provides for the filing of job-selection grievances. Jobs for which the selection is in dispute are kept open. When asked about the company's experience with promotion grievances, a personnel manager said that "less than one percent of all jobs get to the final stage of the company's grievance procedure." The explanation given for this was that grievances are resolved before they reach the final stage, either by the department manager stage or by the division manager stage of the procedure. Another reason was that supervisors will give much attention to the seniority date and to the attendance record of job applicants, and in cases that are likely to be controversial they will take the advice of an experienced personnel representative. While such behavior may tend to avoid grievances, it can also result in an abandonment of the merit principle.

Finally, there are different rules relating to the way in which successful bidders are released from their present assignments. Generally, a department is allowed to hold a successful bidder for a very short period of time, such as two weeks, unless there are some well-documented extraordinary circumstances.

So that the reader will better understand the differences among job-posting systems, and the way these systems actually work, let us briefly discuss some different systems, and what appear to be the common administrative problems in following them.

Problems in Administration

While the most senior personnel people and top management talked enthusiastically about job posting, supervisors had mixed reactions. From a supervisor's point of view, the job-posting system can be undermined by pre-posting selection. It can also be time-consuming, and a source of disappointment to employees. Consider the remarks of some supervisors who were critical of the system:

> There are a lot of bagged jobs* that should never be posted. They just raise expectations. There will be fifty bids, and you have to interview them all, even when it's a bagged job or it's politics.

> Most employees feel it is a farce. I think it's necessary so the people will know what is happening. But sometimes I see a job posted which looks like it's designated for a particular person. The manager will say a job is wide open, but picks a guy with little experience—a bagged job from the beginning.

> I'll generally have to interview ten or twelve people for a particular job.

> Although the system is fair, it is a little cumbersome. It can take over four weeks. Then there is the problem of the people who want to get out of your department. They may throw in seven bids. If they have seniority, you have to wait for them to decide.

> Once selected it can take three weeks before the employee goes to the new job. This is because it takes a week to get his [or her] job on the board and another week to interview all the candidates. You may have as many as forty to fifty.

> The job-posting program is one of the biggest sources of dissatisfaction in the company. There are a lot of disappointed people. Only as long as the rules are applied fairly can you stand behind the decisions and honestly discuss with an employee why he [or she] didn't get a job.

Some managers also criticized the personnel department's administration of job posting:

---

*A job is "bagged" if it is felt the supervisor has picked someone he or she wants before the job is posted. This was mentioned as a problem of job posting at every company with this system.

*For example, the job description will say the person needs a license.
Yet, Personnel will send people to you who don't have a license. Personnel
could do more homework.*

While this kind of comment reflects a desire on the part of line managers for the
personnel department to do a greater amount of screening, this personnel department believes the line manager should be the one who says "no" to the internal
applicant. This personnel department also believes it is educational for the
employee and the supervisor to go through this exercise, no matter how time-
consuming it may be.

There are several principal problems that these comments bring to light.
First, there is the amount of time the job-posting system takes to interview
applicants and to fill a job. Second, there is the problem of the so-called "bagged"
job, where it is alleged that the person chosen had been selected prior to the job
posting. This seems particularly associated with the higher-skill jobs, and especially with respect to exempt jobs. Finally, there is the morale problem of
disappointed applicants.

Obviously, some problems of this kind are inevitable and have to be weighed
against the advantages of job posting versus the disadvantages of *not* having a
job-posting system. As one chairman noted:

*The supervisor who loses people hates it, and the supervisor who gains
people likes it. If there is an even flow, it's okay. If there are uneven flows,
however, you can predict problems. Because of rapid growth in certain areas,
there may be a lot of flows toward the existing place. And then you can count
on supervisors not liking it.*

Some problems could be alleviated through more supervisory education and
training programs. Supervisors need to understand, from the point of view of top
management, the long-run advantages to the company of this time-consuming
system. Various administrative changes can also alleviate some of the problems
that bother supervisors. For example, a company can tighten up its bidding
requirements by increasing the minimum period of time that an employee must
have been in his or her present position before applying for a new job.

The posting of very precise job descriptions and necessary qualifications is
another way to reduce the number of bids from employees who are clearly not
qualified. However, when one company went from the listing of very general
qualifications to more specific ones, many employees wanted a return to the more
general system. Apparently, employees did not want to be limited, either in
applying for or in simply finding out about other jobs (and what it takes to obtain
them) in the company.

Other administrative devices can be used to alleviate some of the problems
associated with job posting about which line managers complain. For instance,
there is certainly an incentive for companies to save time by posting job oppor-

tunities frequently: Weekly postings may prevent a delay in the publication of new jobs. One company limits the number of applications by excluding employees who are on probation or who have a performance rating of below average. Also, in this company supervisors have the prerogative of filling jobs from within their cost center or branch without posting them.

Finally, where there is a strong internal candidate, especially for higher-level jobs, this could be noted in the job posting. This would in turn alert bidders of their reduced chances for this particular job, and would also reduce the level of frustration associated with this frequently encountered problem. On the other hand, it could pervert the system by discouraging employees from applying, thereby undercutting a company's affirmative-action commitments.

Of course, one must recognize that if too many administrative modifications and/or qualifications are permitted, an organization and its employees will lose many of the advantages of a more open job-posting and bidding system. A wise manager must simply weigh all the advantages and disadvantages of a job-posting and bidding system for his or her company, considering its particular types of jobs and kinds of people, and decide if job posting seems to fit; if so, what style of job posting must then be decided. The manager who selects job posting will also have to agree to live with its dilemmas and difficulties. For more data with which a manager could better make this decision, let us now turn to companies that do not have job posting.

Reasons for Not Having a Job-Posting and Bidding System

As has been stated, job posting is a controversial subject. Managers from companies *without* job posting stated many reasons why they opposed it. While they advocated promotion from within, they felt that their companies facilitate internal promotion and career development in ways superior to job posting. Before considering these alternative methods, let us discuss the eight principal reasons that managers cited in their opposition to job posting.

JOB POSTING WILL DRIVE A COMPANY TOWARD SELECTION DECISIONS BASED ON SENIORITY

First, the major reason executives opposed job posting was that they felt it would force them to compromise the merit principle by having to give more weight to seniority in selection decisions. An assistant vice-president of personnel for one large company that does not have job posting said: "We feel that job posting would drive us toward seniority in promotions, something we do not favor. Because performance is hard to measure, seniority would inevitably be given more weight."

An advantage of a nonunion environment is that management does not have the seniority restrictions generally found in collective bargaining agreements.

There are sound business reasons to promote on the basis of merit. Management does not want to give up these advantages, and sees job posting as a force that will drive it to do so. Based on the experiences of a number of the companies studied, these concerns are valid. As will be discussed later, some companies that do have job posting explicitly state that the *senior* qualified person, rather than the *best* qualified person, will be selected. In fact, many companies have declined to promote employees on the basis of merit alone, and have considered seniority very heavily.

Job Posting May Diminish a Manager's or Personnel Representative's Management Development Responsibilities

Second, some executives felt that job posting would dull or lessen a manager's responsibility for the development of his or her people, an important part of every manager's job in these companies. An executive at one company said that job posting makes a personnel system employee-centered rather than manager-centered, and therefore violates the employee–manager relationship the company encourages: "Posting would relieve the manager of some development responsibility, something the company would not want to see happen." This company, with a low supervisor-to-employee ratio, invests very heavily in employee training and development, and job posting could be viewed as inconsistent with the other personnel and development systems it has in place.

Though also committed to promotion from within, another company does not have job posting for a slightly different reason. Rather than worrying that job posting would undermine the role of the line manager, this company's top management fears that it would undermine the role of the company's personnel representatives instead. Personnel representatives work closely with employees and have a responsibility to help those interested in promotion. Top management felt that their power and influence would be reduced if the company had a job-posting system.

This company's executive vice-president said that job posting had been considered but not adopted because "the personnel people who would have to push it are not that keen on it," adding that the company may have to adopt it in the future for equal-employment-opportunity and affirmative-action reasons.

Job Posting Is Inconsistent With Full Employment

Third, in at least one company, posting was considered inconsistent with its full-employment practices. In order to realize its full-employment goals, this company frequently finds it necessary to either move people laterally or to train then transfer people to areas of the business that are growing rapidly. In order to insure stability the company needs the flexibility to reserve jobs, when necessary, for people who have been declared surplus from other parts of the business.

Nevertheless, some full-employment companies do have posting. In these companies, when it is necessary to transfer employees to maintain full employment, the jobs to which they are transferred are exempted from the job-posting system. Employees might agree that transfers made in order to implement a full-employment practice should take precedence over the career development opportunities that the posting of these jobs would represent. However, at very large companies there may be some special situations in which administration of a job-posting system within a full-employment framework could be damaging to employee morale.

JOB POSTING REDUCES MORALE

Fourth, some executives think that job posting has a potential to reduce morale in three ways: (1) by creating an adversary relationship between management and the employees, (2) by introducing and creating competition between and among individual employees, and (3) by disappointing the expectations of the unsuccessful bidders.

At a relatively small company, the vice-president of personnel had this to say:

> We don't have job posting because I am against it. I haven't wanted to open up a lot of issues. Now, an employee wishing to transfer can see the personnel representative. I do not want to get us in the position where we have to defend each ability decision. With posting, there would be a lot of general gossip and friction.

Executives spoke about the disadvantages of pitting one employee against another, since employees may know who else has bid for a particular job. This *can*, of course, result in gossip and friction.

While employee unhappiness can be a real problem, these concerns partly depend on the nature of a company's job-posting system, as well as on how it is administered. In a multiplant company with a broad unit, the employee's competitor may be an employee he or she does not know, who is based in one of the company's other plants. While rejected employees are undoubtedly unhappy, their attitudes are probably influenced by a variety of factors, including who was selected, the basis for the selection, and the counseling they received. Some methods for awarding jobs and handling rejections are clearly more effective than others. For instance, it is a wise policy to counsel those turned down as to what they can do to be better prepared for such a position in the future.

JOB POSTING RESEMBLES UNIONISM

Fifth, some executives were opposed to job posting because they felt it too closely resembles what some unionized companies have, and they preferred to avoid anything resembling unionism. Moreover, in considering the way it works in unionized operations, they did not think it effective.

For example, the vice-president of personnel at one company commented:

> The worst strategy for us would be to act like we have a union. What you have to do is create a different philosophy for dealing with issues. It has to be totally foreign. You should not have something which is similar to what union shops have.

According to a director of employee relations, "Posting has a union orientation and it would get you into a bidding system. Under job posting some people are professional bidders." Instead of job posting, this company has an employee application system, which will be discussed later.

As earlier discussion of job posting made clear, however, job posting as practiced in many of the nonunion companies does not closely resemble what happens in the typical union shop. These companies have adopted policies that are often much more extensive, although several do have some of the same problems that unionized employers experience with job posting.

JOB POSTING AFFECTS CAREER PLANNING, INDIVIDUAL TREATMENT, AND DEVELOPMENT

Sixth, some executives felt that job posting precludes many opportunities for career planning and individual treatment, which are desirable not only from the individual's viewpoint but from that of the company as well. One person interviewed, a vice-president of personnel at a relatively small company, was opposed to job posting, considering it a passive system. Believing that management-initiated decisions are frequently better than employee-initiated decisions, not only for the company but for the employee as well, this person said:

> Job posting is a cold system. You wait for the system. Here, we move people. We have people who wouldn't have considered themselves as candidates for particular jobs. In our company if you want to be considered for a particular job you apply for it. We have career consulting and development planning.
>
> Our system is harder for the personnel department for we have to reach for the highest quality people. Job posting would not have selected the guys we have picked. With job posting, you have what the employee perceives. Under our system, management may think boldly. Here, employees are talking about career goals.

The relatively small size of this company undoubtedly facilitates these processes.

While other promotion methods will be discussed shortly, to the extent that both management-initiated promotions and transfers and an employee-application system work effectively, they would seem to have real advantages over job posting.

JOB POSTING AND TIME

Seventh, many executives consider job posting a time-consuming, and therefore inefficient, method of filling open jobs. The amount of time consumed includes the number of days a job must be listed, as well as the management-hours it will take to interview applicants, make a selection, communicate with the rejected applicants, and then get the successful candidate released from his or her present job. The whole process can take several weeks.

JOB POSTING AND UNRESPONSIVE EMPLOYEES

Finally, in one company's experience many of its employees were not interested in a job-posting system. While this company's management was not really sure why its job-posting system failed, it believed the failure was related to the nature of its employees. Thus while some companies worry about too many bidders for posted jobs, this atypical company had the opposite experience. Its system did not produce enough bidders. Before adopting a job-posting system a company also needs to take into account the needs and aspirations of the present work force.

As all these objections suggest, the executives who oppose job posting felt that their companies had superior systems. Let us now examine two: the management-selection system and the employee-application (or prior-request) system.

MANAGEMENT-SELECTION SYSTEM

The majority of companies that do not use job posting use what may be termed the management-selection system, under which there are neither bids nor prior applications for specific jobs. Some companies' methods are so informal that they can scarcely be called a "system," while other managements are quite sophisticated: They may use computerized personal information to check employee career desires.

When the vice-president of personnel of one company was asked how they handled promotions, the answer was:

> Openings are filled in the following ways: word of mouth, the personnel department encourages employees to make their wishes known, and sometimes large groups are canvassed. There is also a manual retrieval system for personnel information.

Informally done, a different company's feedback mechanisms help ensure that promotions are not handled unfairly. "If a manager handles promotions

poorly, he always runs the risk of the employee filing a grievance on him,''
commented a personnel officer. The company's attitude survey asked questions
about promotion policies and opportunities. While this officer felt that the informal methods generally worked well, he admitted that some employees, particularly minorities, did not do as well as they might under these methods. As a
consequence, in 1975 a companywide experiment was begun whereby lists of job
openings were circulated to all managers. "In the past," the personnel officer
said, "it has been informal—that is, you called around when you had an opening." It was felt that, with the lists, promotions would be handled even more
systematically. In promotion decisions this company also makes extensive use of
its performance-planning and evaluation system.

A third company has made a practice of issuing personnel information sheets
on which employees are requested to list their job interests. When a job opening
occurs, management obtains a computer run with the names of employees who
have expressed interest in such a job. Because of Equal Employment Opportunity
Commission (EEOC) pressures to post jobs and because the system was not
working as well as it was supposed to, management planned to modify its system
by including specific jobs on the personnel information sheets, which an employee
could investigate if interested.

Companies using the management-selection system believe their approaches can more easily accommodate the employee who wants to transfer out of
his or her present job. A personnel representative, responsible for approximately
1,000 employees at one such company (a firm that is relatively small) showed me a
list with the names of 220 employees he had helped to get transferred during the
past three years. When asked why employees seek transfers and what would
happen if the company had job posting, this person said:

> Why does a person want to transfer? Because the boss is on his back for
> efficiency or for attendance.
> If I posted jobs, I'd make one [person] happy and several unhappy.
> Can I give a satisfactory answer to the [ones] who didn't get the job? They
> would feel you gave the job to your pet. The company is now moving towards a
> skills inventory system, and that will be very good.

When personnel executives were asked about the risks or disadvantages of
the management-selection system, they generally listed EEOC and favoritism.
However, as discussed, various steps have been taken to reduce these risks.

EMPLOYEE-APPLICATION (OR PRIOR-REQUEST) SYSTEM

The companies that operate formal employee-application (or
prior-request) systems think they are far superior to job posting. A manager at one
of these companies cited four ways in which the company makes it easy for an

employee to change jobs, which the company encourages: (1) the employee may complete a transfer-request form, a procedure described in the employee handbook; (2) the employee may request a transfer, using the merit-review form; (3) the employee can ask his or her supervisor; and (4) the employee can talk to a personnel representative about it. The company's policy is to consider requests for transfers *before* interviewing from the outside. The personnel department staff believe this system has all the advantages of job posting without any of its disadvantages.

According to one executive, with a prior-request system employees do not necessarily know who else has expressed interest in the job. Without public job posting, communications with respect to awarding of jobs can be more effective. The issue of seniority will not become an issue, as it does with job posting. The only problem this executive saw with a prior-request system was that it can either conflict, or be viewed by government officials as conflicting, with the company's affirmative-action goals. For instance, for a variety of reasons minority employees may not come forward to complete a request form for particular jobs. If they do not do so, there is of course no way they can be selected for promotions under this system. In today's environment, statistics for hiring and promotion rates are being watched carefully. When some will presume discrimination if these numbers are not right, it is clear why a company might consider abandoning, supplementing, or at least modifying its traditional promotion and transfer mechanisms. A company's employee-application system could also be dysfunctional if administered in such a way as to produce complaints of favoritism from employees.

Having discussed the different promotion methods, as well as their strengths and weaknesses, let us now consider promotion decisions, especially the issue of seniority versus ability.

SENIORITY VERSUS ABILITY IN PROMOTION DECISIONS

Although it varies by company and by job, in general much weight is given to seniority in promotion decisions. Some companies have imposed requirements on themselves that seem as strict or stricter than those found in the typical union contract.

When one employee-relations vice-president of a company with job posting was asked how much weight was given to seniority in promotion decisions, the reply was: "Probably too much." Elaborating, this person said that the company first looked at seniority, *then* at job performance.

In another company, which also used job posting, the stated policy of the basis for employee selection reads as follows:

> *Job openings are filled by the persons considered to be among the most qualified. Qualifications include such factors as job knowledge, experience,*

quantity, quality, interest, personal qualifications, work habits, attendance, and skills as applicable to the job. Seniority should always be considered.

A personnel administrator at this company said that supervisors too often do not select the best qualified person, "but make the decision on the basis of the person's seniority and attendance record." To improve this system, management was considering a change in the selection criteria: to specify that only in the case when "two or more applicants are judged to be essentially equal will seniority be the determining factor." Whether this proposal change will result in different people being selected remains to be seen. However, it does appear to introduce additional flexibility and responsibility on the part of the supervisors.

In one of the companies where the personnel representatives have much influence in promotion decisions, the policy is that for nonexempt jobs where many equally well-qualified people apply, the decision may turn to consideration of the employee's attendance record and seniority. The personnel representatives screen candidates and send those they believe to be qualified to the line manager. After the line manager has conducted interviews, he or she confers with the personnel representatives.

Several companies claimed that they give little weight to seniority in promotion decisions, citing this fact as an advantage of the nonunion company. Yet at one company where merit allegedly determined position, a senior personnel administrator remarked: "We're very sure of the reasons, however, if we don't promote the most senior person." One wonders if the policy and the practice are substantially different at companies who claim that seniority is given very little weight in promotion decisions. This is an area where an empirical investigation would be worthwhile.

At only two companies, which do not have job posting, is seniority always given precedence. In these two companies, a promotion is first offered to the most-senior qualified employee, who must sign a "promotion refused" form if he or she declines the promotion. Moreover, if the senior employee is turned down, he or she is told why, and is also told what should be done in order to be ready for the promotion the next time. Sometimes the company will offer some training. While such an employee may be asked to "sit it out" one time, he or she may get the job the next time.

When asked if this practice discouraged younger workers, a personnel director at the first company said:

In practice the good ones move up fairly rapidly. We may have six good jobs in a job grade. The combination of a broad base and wide consideration results in a lot of movement. Employees are not locked in here and the combination of our growth pattern, normal attrition and surprising number of people who don't want additional responsibility and who are content, for example, to be inspectors, results in enough job movement to keep the young ambitious employee relatively happy.

Affirmative action brought about an elaborate seniority system of promotion at the second company. According to one personnel representative:

> *Here employees are placed in training according to seniority. If you pass the training, you are promoted into the next higher grade as soon as there is an opening. We have progressive steps for each labor grade.*
>
> *If an employee refuses training he has to sign a promotion refusal form. He is then not selected again unless he asks, in writing, to be considered.*

The important point to note is that only these two companies deliberately weigh seniority heavily, something many of the other nonunion companies said they go to great lengths to avoid.

As mentioned earlier, the practice of job posting tends to drive a company toward giving considerable weight to seniority in promotion decisions. With job openings and bidders known, good reasons have to be given to unsuccessful applicants. While a manager can, and perhaps should, turn down an applicant for reasons of quality, quantity, interest, and the like, this can be difficult to do, especially if there is a risk of a grievance. Turning down an applicant for reasons of seniority or attendance is easier. Sometimes companies will give preference to seniority in nonexempt jobs, and to merit in exempt jobs, on the following principle, stated by one supervisor: "The company wants to make seniority work for what it will do. What it will do is allow for promotion with respect to lower level jobs, shift selection, and vacation scheduling."

The obvious advantage of the seniority system is that subjective decisions and other different kinds of decisions are made more objective. On one hand, the merit principle is generally sacrificed when length of employment is given sole consideration, especially merit among women and minorities, who usually do not have the seniority that white males have. On the other hand, it has been argued that exclusive use of the merit principle may have the same effect, since in some cases women and minority candidates have performance ratings that are lower, in general, than those of white males. Whether this is because the women and minorities are actually not performing as well as the white males or because the evaluation system is biased, is not known. Presumably, emphasis on seniority will also dampen the morale of high-potential, high-performing young people— however, if *no* weight is given to seniority, it would seem unfair, especially for jobs that require little in the way of ability and where it is extremely difficult to measure performance.

These seniority versus ability questions and dilemmas are encountered in unionized companies as well. While the majority of union agreements provide that seniority be just one of the official criteria, unionized companies have also moved toward seniority decisions due to the difficulty of exercising judgment with respect to ability and performance only. Indeed, perhaps the real significance of this issue lies in the fact that many nonunion companies are moving toward methods that so many unionized companies have already adopted.

While generalizations are difficult, it is clear that whatever promotion system and criteria are adopted, they should meet four tests: (1) the system and the criteria must seem fair, and must be understandable to most of the employees and supervisors; (2) the system adopted must be as responsive as possible to management's needs for efficiency and effectiveness in both the short run *and* the long run; (3) the system has to be responsive to the concept of affirmative action; and (4) whatever is done needs to be consistent with top management's philosophy and values.

A mixed system that blends seniority and ability is probably preferable to a nonmixed system. How much actual weight to be given to seniority must be determined by the needs and nature of the business, the philosophy of management, the technology, the nature of the work force, the status of the company's affirmative-action plans, and the nature of the job (including the skill and ability the job requires), as well as by the degree of difficulty in evaluating performance levels and the nature of the performance appraisal process. If the work is machine paced and the supervisor is responsible for forty employees, seniority and attendance may be the best criteria that are possible; however, merit may be the best criterion for other jobs. In any case, time must be devoted to devising ways of measuring performance, assessing qualifications and job requirements, and conducting effective performance appraisals.

CONCLUDING ANALYSIS AND COMMENTS

Promotion from within is an important cornerstone of the personnel policies and practices of all the companies studied, although the methods and the selection criteria by which the companies implement promotion from within vary.

With respect to managerial jobs, the practices range from, at one extreme, few entry positions and only a handful of managers who have *not* come up from the ranks, to, at the other extreme, little more than lip service paid to this concept. These practices seem to be functions of management philosophy and of the nature of the business and the industry. Perhaps it would be unrealistic for a company to follow a promotion-from-within philosophy if it enters a new and unrelated business.

Concerning these particular policies, it appears that the practice of promotion from within may become more and more difficult to follow in the future, due to the increasing importance of specialized knowledge, advanced education, and equal employment opportunity requirements. Will the company that relies on promotion from within as its exclusive source of talent be able to remain competitive? One frequently hears of the "tunnel vision" that can result if everyone comes up from inside the company. For promotion from within to remain viable, it will require high-entry standards and solid management development programs. Promotion from within may also work best for the company that chooses not to diversify from its basic or traditional business. Then, even though the company will be truly hiring people for a career rather than for a particular job, will strict career-oriented hiring standards hold up before a judge if such a hiring pattern has an adverse impact on the hiring rate of women and minorities? The risk is that what has been considered a strength by many companies in the past may be a legal vulnerability in the future. If so, the practice of promotion from within, which has been associated with high morale and business effectiveness, may be severely challenged.

The majority of companies not only have promotion from within, they also have job posting for hourly employees. As we have seen, however, there is considerable variation among such systems. Job posting, which has many advantages, also has many problems, some of which can be alleviated by more sensible job-posting policies and better administration. If a company has a job-posting system, it is important for it to educate supervisors in the reasons for the system, its benefits and costs, and their responsibilities for implementing it. Many problems will remain with a job-posting system, and will need to be viewed as the costs that are presumably outweighed by the advantages. In particular, job posting does seem to tend to drive a company toward giving considerable weight to seniority in promotion decisions.

Changing government regulations have had a significant impact on the manner in which management handles hiring and promotion decisions. These regulations, like job posting, have the potential to create adversary relationships between management and the employee. Management must now do a better job of documenting and defending its hiring and promotion decisions. Today an employee who is not promoted and feels that he or she was discriminated against because of race, sex, or age is free to take his or her charge to a government agency for review.

A well-administered management-selection or employee-application system may have some of the advantages of a job-posting system without its associated problems. Such systems take much less time than job posting, and do not have the employee and supervisor morale problems discussed. Such systems may also be more consistent with the idea of merit, and may favor the young, able, and ambitious employee, whom it was traditionally thought would have an advantage in a nonunion company (rather than in a unionized company that was very seniority-oriented with respect to promotions). Also, performance appraisal, career development and training programs seem to tie in more naturally in management-selection or employee-application systems than they do in job-posting systems. However, if grievances, attitude surveys, and/or comments from old-timers, women, or minorities reveal problems with the way the promotion system actually works (or with the way employees *perceive* that it works), or if the government insists on change because of EEOC problems, then the system and the selection criteria may have to be changed, or a job-posting system must be put in its place.

The question of whether or not to have job posting may become academic, since government equal employment opportunity compliance officers seem to not only look with favor on job-posting systems; they also often demand job posting as part of consent decrees and affirmative-action plans. The question may then become one of how to make job-posting systems work as effectively as possible. Job posting also seems more consistent with employee demands for openness. While it is fine for managers to be responsible for the development of their people, some will give this a higher priority than others. Moreover, in a growth company managers are promoted and transferred quite rapidly, and this lack of continuity could interfere with a manager's ability to counsel and train. Also, if real development is self-development, job posting may help put the burden of advancement where it belongs, on the individual. Furthermore, job posting can be supplemented with career counselors, and with managers still having key information and career development responsibilities.

Both promotion systems and the weight given to seniority in promotion decisions need to fit management's philosophy and the realities of the business. For sound business reasons, some companies claimed they give very little weight to seniority in their promotion decisions, saying this is one of the advantages of being nonunion. Many other companies will give considerable weight to seniority, thereby ignoring this alleged advantage of being nonunion. The practices of the latter group may help them increase the probability of their remaining nonunion, for they will not have favoritism complaints, nor will they have to defend ability decisions in promotion complaints. Furthermore, within the production and maintenance work force, the concept of promotion based on merit seems to have been partially eroded in some companies by job posting and affirmative action. Given the nature of the work and the reality that many people are overqualified for the jobs they actually do, production and maintenance operations may not suffer perceptibly if *senior* qualified people, rather than the *best* qualified people, are promoted within the ranks of hourly workers.

PART THREE

Compensation and Benefits

CHAPTER EIGHT

Pay Policies and
Their Administration

One could not do a study of the personnel policies and practices of large, nonunion companies with respect to production and maintenance employees without examining their pay and benefit policies. Many casual observers think these companies remain nonunion by simply paying more. While the companies studied generally reported that they do pay more, this study indicated that this is only a small part of the story. There are many other factors—including environmental considerations, employment security, promotion from within, and formal communication programs—that are extremely important in understanding the approaches of these companies. Nevertheless, it is a fair statement to say that the companies studied do work hard to ensure that they are not vulnerable to a union organizational drive on the basis of pay or benefit issues. Labor relations considerations were found to play a key role in the setting of pay and benefit policies.

This chapter contains findings with respect to pay objectives, the local labor market orientation of the companies studied, the corresponding importance of survey work, and the way in which compensation information is communicated to employees. While some policy and administrative differences were noted, the findings reveal many similarities with respect to the pay policies and practices of the companies studied.

However, when one analyzes the companies' pay and benefit policies, one immediately finds that it is also important to look at a whole array of some closely related issues that seem to be distinguishing characteristics of the large, nonunion company. For example, one issue consistent with the principle or philosophy of individual treatment is the subject of merit pay. In addition, in examining pay and pay rates one discovers that at many of the nonunion companies the hourly people are salaried. Consequently, one has to examine the salaried method of payment and the various approaches to an all-salaried work force. Similarly, when one delves into benefits, one discovers a broad array of bonus plans and savings plans. There are different types of bonus plans, from traditional profit-sharing plans (which depend on the level of profits), to Christmas bonus plans (which do not), and many types of savings plans. These topics, closely related to pay policies, constitute the following four Chapters of this book.

For the purpose of this chapter, however, I will focus on the pay policies of the companies studied. In Chapter 9, I will examine merit pay plans. Salary plans, or, more precisely, the salaried method of payment, will constitute Chapter 10. While some of the discussion will inevitably also make reference to the subject of benefits, Chapter 11 will concentrate specifically on benefit plans. Then in Chapter 12, I will consider profit sharing, cash bonus, and employee savings/investment plans.

MANAGEMENT PHILOSOPHIES AND OBJECTIVES

Before discussing the issue of pay, perhaps it would be well to cite, in the words of company officials, the pay policies, philosophies, and objectives of most of the companies studied. In knowing these, the reader may better understand the approaches of the various managements. Each speaker is from a different company, and his or her position in the company is identified at the end of each quotation:

The desired position in compensation is to be above the market—equal to or better than.

director of employee relations

We are the top paying company in this area—we spend a lot of time tracking pay and benefits.

personnel director

We lead in pay and benefits as a total package; benefits amount to forty-four percent of the payroll.

benefits administrator

Our pay philosophy is to be, on the average, better than the average of other major companies. We survey fifteen leading companies.

personnel representative

We lead in all areas, not including our bonus.

compensation specialist

The policy for pay and benefits is to be in the top ten percent. We're "Number One" in pay in the industry and the state. Sometimes we worry that we pay too much.

vice-president of personnel

The company pays a slight premium in its nonunion plants over the wages paid in the general geographic area for similar work at union plants. There is also a better benefits package at the nonunion plants.

corporate director of employee relations

The pay policy is to be in the top third of the local labor market. Given what else we offer, there is no need to be "Number One." Benefits amount to approximately 40 percent of payroll.

president

We try to be equal to or higher than for most jobs.

vice-president of administration

The policy is to be among the highest competitors in pay and benefits. We believe that salaries should rank among the leaders of competition. The pay program should be based on merit, with pay administered on a consistent and equitable basis throughout the company. Including the bonus, benefits account for 37 percent of the payroll.

vice-president of personnel

The policy is to be equal to or better than. There are merit ranges. We think it is a mistake to say you are 10 percent above the community because then the community moves up and you have to go 10 percent above it.

vice-president of personnel

The pay policy, an unwritten one, is to be competitive with the area. We use our own surveys. We check midpoints and while the policy is to pay slightly above in practice we pay at the midpoint. The salaried employees are below the midpoint and the hourly people are at the midpoint.

salary administrator

Our pay is considerably better than other companies. Profit sharing adds in 10 percent and there is a thrift plan with one out of five dollars matched by the company.

personnel administrator

The first principle is that a union can't get anything from a company that it couldn't give if it wanted to, whatever it is. The second principle is that it is our philosophy to give what the company can afford. In the unionized company, the employees always have to ask for it and there is a fight. This company takes special effort to know what the employees are thinking. There is good feedback. Because of good employee relationships and high productivity, the company can afford to do more than unionized companies could.

personnel director

We survey our industry. We compare ourselves on all benefits. Our goal is to be in the sixty-fifth percentile nationally. We also look carefully at major employers in the areas where we operate. It is most critical in terms of compensation to be in the sixty-fifth percentile.

benefits administrator

Our pay has always been the best in the industry.

vice-president of personnel

The total package is to be competitive. Note that I used the term "competitive" rather than "equal."

vice-president of personnel

As between pay and benefits, our policy is to lead in pay and lag in benefits. This is because benefits are less visible than pay. With respect to pay, we want to be in the top quarter or the top 10 percent and be clearly a leader in our industry. While we are a leader with respect to long-term disability and travel insurance for employees, we are not quite up to where others are in terms of vacations or holidays.

vice-president of administration

The company tries to keep total compensation equal to or better than the industry, although this is not done on a daily basis.

senior vice-president of personnel

Our policy is to be in the upper bracket of the labor supply area in terms of pay and to have a package of benefits that compares favorably with large, progressive companies.

director of labor relations

It is our policy to pay rates which equal or exceed wages paid by other companies in the area for comparable work. But we have not bought our way out of being unionized. There is concern for people. We keep the lines of communications open. When we have a layoff, we apply the rules as if we had a union.

personnel officer

The pay objective is to be at least average or slightly above average with respect to major employers in our industry and in our local area.

ｉＡｉｉｊｉｉ ｉＮＩＥ ｉｉｉ ｉｙ' ｊＩＩＩｉ ＩＯＩ ｊＩＵｉ

The quotations indicate that, in relation to the level of pay in the local labor markets, these nonunion companies generally pay well. By and large, they do provide their employees with excellent benefits. Moreover, these companies really work at communicating their pay and benefits policies to their employees. Significantly, these communications programs predate the Employee Retirement Income Security Act of 1974 (ERISA), a law which requires greater employer communication to employees. Unlike many unionized companies, which have systems of single job rates, most of the companies studied have rate ranges with movement within these ranges allegedly based on merit. Furthermore, unlike some unionized employers who have national pay rates for particular jobs, most of the geographically dispersed nonunion organizations in the sample have decentralized pay policies—in the sense that pay for production and maintenance employees is in relation to local labor market conditions.

The pay policies of the companies studied are designed to provide and demonstrate equity. They are also designed to attract, retain, and (especially with their merit and bonus features) motivate good people. Though perhaps more fortuitous than planned, they also, because they are derived from the characteristics of today's wage environment, tend to provide the individual with income security in the sense that his or her real wages increase each and every year.

What needs to be examined carefully here is the influence of labor relations considerations as well as the way in which these policies and practices are administered and communicated. Before turning to these issues, however, something should be said about the pay and benefit policies of the full employment companies. One would think that their wages and benefits might be somewhat lower than the upper quartile because the employee would have to recognize the trade-off between job security and high income. Presumably, an employee would be willing to accept slightly less in wages and benefits, knowing that he or she was not going to be laid off. However, this is not the case. These particular companies are also among the leaders in pay and benefits. With excellent pay and benefits and full employment, these companies would seem to constitute a poor target for the union organizer.

LABOR RELATIONS CONSIDERATIONS

In many environments, providing and demonstrating equity generally means that a company's pay rates favorably compare with those of unionized companies. It would be acceptable to say that the activities of many unions in the United States are benefiting many nonmembers; in other words, unions are doing much good for many people who do not pay them any dues.

A vice-president of industrial relations in an entirely nonunion company that is frequently the target of union organizational drives explained this company's pay system, and the influence of unions:

> *Because we are such a union target, we find that we have to get our start rate at or almost at the union rate. If we set our start rate below the union rate, given our automatic range progression, in three months our employee will be fifteen or twenty cents above the union rate. We give yearly increases which are loosely referred to as merit increases.*

It is a safe generalization to say that in all the companies studied union settlements, particularly those of competitors, are closely monitored. A manager at one company—the only nonunion company in its industry and one that views itself as staying as good as or slightly better in pay and benefits than its competitors—said that because of the nature of the industry's three-year union contracts his company sometimes lags a bit during the first year of its competitor's agreements. This is due to the fact that the three-year contracts are frequently front-end loaded, which means that much of what the union negotiates may be granted in the first year of the contract. Concerning this, the manager said:

> *With a front-end loaded union contract, we'll be behind the first year, catch up in the second year, and be ahead in the third.*

The vice-president of another entirely nonunion company, also the only nonunion one in its industry, qualified his statement that his company's total compensation is equal to or better than the industry by stating that this is not so "on a daily basis." In other words, when a union settlement with a competitor makes this company's total package not as good by comparison, the company makes an adjustment though it does not do so immediately. In presentations to employees, this company is extremely open about its pay and benefits in relation to the industry and to specific competitors.

A third company, a regional company that is one of the few nonunion ones in its industry, also watches union settlements closely. A specific illustration of the application of this approach may be found in an internal memorandum written by the vice-president of personnel in July 1974:

> *As a result of collective bargaining in spring 1974, between the other companies and the unions representing their employees, the gap in hourly rates of pay between ourselves and our competitors among employees doing*

essentially the same work has been widened well beyond the justifiable or defensible differential.

Average weekly compensation for us and for our three main com-
petitors, derived from information by our trade association and adjusted to take
into account the results of collective bargaining in our competitor companies
in spring 1974 and our reviews, show the following:

[Company Name]	$150
X	$170
Y	$161
Z	$165

Our competitors granted a $15 per week across the board increase to most employees, with larger increases to others, effective this past spring. The average increase here was about $9. Each of our competitors is scheduled to grant $11 per week next spring.

Management acted as a result of this memorandum, and granted sizable pay increases. In reviewing the company's experience, the vice-president's assistant wrote in a memorandum to the vice-president:

. . . The problem that was brought up by three of our location personnel managers concerned the discussion of reviews. Prior to any review conferences at a headquarters Mutual Benefit Association directors meeting, it seems that some employee directors reported back to the employees at their own locations that everyone would be receiving a cost of living increase plus a merit increase.

In one location the personnel manager estimated that thirty-five percent of the employees thought their increases would be larger than they were. It seems because of this some of the impact of the larger-than-usual increases was lost. Again, we lost some impact due to the fact that the maximum increase an early career employee could receive was $14, which was more than the amount a long-service employee who was rated outstanding could receive—namely, $10 or $15.

In light of these problems, it would seem wise, if when the hiring rate is increased in the future, that it become effective at a time other than the effective date of the personnel review, so that one does not detract from the other.

Continuing, in another part of the memorandum, the assistant referred to the union organizational drive at the company:

All those involved with the administration of the early career and merit increases were extremely pleased with the department manager's notice explaining the reasoning behind the increases for the fall review. There seemed to be little discussion between employees and their supervisors in all locations considering the possibilities the larger increases were based on

> *union organizing efforts in some of our facilities. At headquarters, even with the use of the memo explaining the reasons for the increases, the feedback shows that the employees did relate the increases to the organizational drive. The department manager's notice would be an additional tool ensuring the consistency of personnel reviews from plant to plant if we were to continue its use in the future.*

Concluding the memorandum:

> *Overall, the effect of the fall review was a positive one. The employees as a whole seem to be more than satisfied with the increases they received. The personnel managers felt that the review was successful and raised the morale of the employees in their locations. The review also proved that in the future we can continue to have our reviews conducted during a shorter period of time from start to finish without damaging the review process.*

In general, predominantly nonunion companies report that they pay slight premiums in their nonunion plants. However, they respond to union settlements in different ways. As an industrial relations manager had to say about one company's pay policies in its nonunion facilities:

> *Our wage rates are largely tied to local wages paid for comparable types of activity. Generally, we anticipate [International Union] general increases by moving a month or two earlier with our nonrepresented people, and then make any further adjustments that may be necessary subsequent to the union settlement. So, in effect, our nonunion people receive pretty much the same wages with, however, somewhat earlier general increases.*

A comparable company has adopted a similar approach, though it does not make any adjustments until after the results of collective bargaining are known. "We'll pay a few cents per hour more and have a few improved benefits in our nonunion plants and our sister union plants in the same region in recognition of the greater flexibility we say we have in those plants," said a director of employee relations. The personnel superintendent at one of this company's nonunion plants elaborated on how the policy works there:

> *We're at least competitive at the entry level and the total package of wages, benefits, and working conditions are as attractive as can be found in the area.*

Entirely nonunion companies that operate in industries not heavily unionized also pay close attention to union settlements. This is particularly so for certain groups of employees. For example, it was said more than once that the salaries of warehouse workers and drivers are monitored closely. As one personnel representative put it: "The salaries of these people are kept above those paid to the Teamsters."

Managements are also concerned when their employees work closely with unionized employees of other companies. The president of one company commented:

> *The Teamsters are always around at the loading docks. Recently, one of our troubled employees began to talk union to a small group of employees. The supervisor of these employees was almost immediately given a presentation by personnel. Personnel helped him rehearse the presentation for his employees. Once this dollars and cents presentation was given to the employees by their supervisor, the air was cleared.*

Needless to say, managements are especially alert when there is any sign of union activity in one of its own plants. Managements are also sensitive to union organizational activity in the general area where their plants are located.

At one company, while the survey on pay is done annually, the survey on benefits is done every two years. But this timing changes when there are any signs of union activity in the geographic area. Commenting, this company's vice-president of personnel said: "If there were union activity in an area, we'd do the survey more often."

Another company, which is proud of its high productivity, communicates informally to its employees not only the fact that it pays about 5 percent more than its unionized competitors, but also the news whenever one of its unionized competitors goes out of business. Employees get the word that a union offers no real job security, something the company has been able to provide. It is interesting to note that over time almost all of this company's regional unionized competitors have gone bankrupt.

Thus, whether the company is either entirely or predominantly nonunion, labor relations considerations are significant in the areas of pay and of benefits. Companies monitor union activities and settlements carefully, as an important input to pay-policy formulation. Companies also pay particular attention to so-called sensitive employee groups, such as truck drivers and certain skilled trades. This would seem to be an understandable practice, for the history of union organization in the United States is replete with examples of plants being unionized on the basis of the organization of small groups of high-status employees.

The strong desire of some of the companies studied to stay nonunion may result in some distortion in the legitimate pay policies that they follow, and consequently create some inequities. This would be the case if one group of employees, because of its possible vulnerability to union organization, received more than it deserved relative to another group of employees, who are less vulnerable to union organization due to the nature of their jobs.

However, it is a fair assessment to say that the companies studied work hard to make sure that they are not vulnerable to a union organizational drive on the basis of pay issues. In fact, during a union organizational drive in the early 1970s at one large company, which is the only nonunion firm in its industry, the state director of the AFL-CIO was quoted in a local newspaper article as saying that he wanted to make it clear that pay was not the issue behind the union's organizational drive. He went on to state what was well-known—namely, that the pay was very good at this company. The union drive stemmed from other issues.

POLICY ADMINISTRATION

It is important to examine the administration of pay and benefit policies, for the best-written policies do not mean anything unless they are carried out as intended. Thus it is useful to not only examine the role of the corporate, division, and plant personnel staffs, but to also look at the ways in which the policies are administered by line management with respect to the individual employee.

Pay Surveys

As has already been indicated, survey work is an extremely important staff job in the companies studied. In general, extensive pay surveys are done annually. In commenting on this, a corporate director of compensation said:

> *The desired position is above the market. The policy is to be equal to or better than. We present to the chairman and president each year where we stand in all labor markets. We want to be in the third quartile but we are not in all labor markets because in some we do not have to be. Good surveys are done yearly, though in many areas we are the market. We are the largest employer in one state and the pay is fair, above average, and competitive. If we are not "Number One" we are darn sure we know who "Number One" is.*

Survey work is done with much care and thought. Efforts are expended to make sure comparable jobs are being measured. If a company with no bonus plan surveys a company that does have a bonus plan, that will generally be taken into account, whereas bonus-plan companies will generally compare their wage rates with the wage rates of nonbonus companies, excluding the bonus. That is to say, bonus-plan companies will typically consider their bonus to be a benefit rather than a part of wages. However, companies without bonus plans will generally consider a bonus as part of compensation rather than as a benefit in their surveys.

In a division of one company whose pay policy is to be "among the highest," the personnel manager said that he makes contact with the eight leading companies in the area annually. He then recommends that hourly rates for his plant be set in the middle of the range of the other eight companies.

Another company conducts its surveys in local communities, and rather than surveying many jobs, it uses three bench marks: hiring rate, manufacturing rate, and top mechanical rate. Commenting on this, a corporate official said:

> *Internally we look at the office, technical, manufacturing, and mechanical families and we'll make our judgments based on the bench mark jobs. With respect to neighboring companies, local managements check movements regarding both amount and timing.*

When asked if it were correct to assume that the company lags the leaders, the official said, "At times, although the leaders keep changing."

This company does not take company earnings into account when making its pay decisions for hourly people. In the words of the corporate official: "If we are not smart enough to make a profit paying the local rates, then we need some new products or we need to shut the plant down."

When asked about the impact of the recent recession, this official stated that some employees asked, "How could you give us fifty cents an hour increase when the company just announced a tremendous drop in earnings and cut the dividend?" The philosophy, he explained, is that: "We don't underpay in a bad year and we don't over pay in a good year—we don't take it out of our employees' hides." When pushed on this point, however, he said that in a bad year the managers tended to be somewhat conservative and that in a good year there may be a drift to the higher side.

A compensation analyst at a different company said that there is much joking among personnel people about the fact that the company is in the "125th percentile." While this figure includes the annual bonus, it is widely recognized that this company is the highest-paying company in its industry and in its community. A vice-president of a unionized competitor said that in his judgment this company's approach is "a clear purchase of nonunionism."

The company, extremely profitable, has only had problems with its approach as it has been applied to some related businesses it has entered. Its high wages result in the company being a poor competitor in these other businesses. While the company has considered withdrawing from these other businesses, such a move would threaten the company's full employment practices.

The chairman of another company explained how the system worked in his organization:

> *Personnel does much survey work. They try to identify similar jobs and do the salary surveys. We also have a point system and we have to be very careful.*
>
> *For example, there was a time when the company was paying $3.70 per hour for draftsmen and the market rate was indicating that they should be making $4.50. Yet, the company's point system put the draftsman's job around $3.70. Similarly, the point system puts our secretaries much higher than they would generally be making in the community.*

If you abandon your point system, you get internal inequities in the
company which I think are harmful. In the draftsmen example, I would move
ahead somewhat but I wouldn't go right to the $4.50.

In addition to illustrating the administration of this company's policy, this example
also shows the involvement of the chairman, a co-founder of the company, in the
wage and salary area.

In these companies, not only are good surveys done, but they are also
respected. It is one thing to do a survey. It is another matter to follow the
implications of its findings. Thus it is important that corporate management act on
the basis of the survey work. These points, of course, relate back to top-level
management commitment and the role of personnel within the organization.

Individual Communications

While this subject, especially with respect to benefits, will be more formally
taken up in the benefits communications section of Chapter 11, let us briefly deal
here with the way an individual employee is informed of his or her pay increase.
Individual pay communications are handled with much planning and thought in a
number of the companies studied.

While they are generally the responsibility of the supervisor, in one company pay increases are handled through a letter (sent to the employee's home),
listing the amount of the increase. In addition, a personnel change notice is
prepared for the individual. This is given to the employee by his or her supervisor.

In another company, the chairman writes personal letters at salary increase
time. The letter is read to the employee by his or her supervisor—or perhaps the
supervisor may read a letter to a group of employees. To illustrate how this process
worked in 1974, on November 21 of that year the president and the chairman sent a
memorandum to all managers and supervisors. It informed them that a general
increase would be granted to all of the company's U.S. production and maintenance employees effective November 25. Part of the memo said:

> . . . *The range of increases and the actual amounts by location and*
> *grade vary by facility and reflect the emphasis given to local survey results in*
> *each community where we have plants.*
>
> *Each supervisor who has production and maintenance employees*
> *working for her or him will be furnished a general increase schedule for his*
> *facility. It is the responsibility of each supervisor to determine from this*
> *schedule the exact amount of increase which each of his employees will*
> *receive and then to personally communicate this amount to each employee.*
>
> *This year, the general increase surveys, analysis, and recommenda-*
> *tions were accomplished by facility line management and personnel*
> *specialists. The results were carefully reviewed by division and corporate*
> *management and generally approved as submitted. This method of ac-*

complishing the general increase at the local level of our operations has proven to be quite effective and more reflective of local considerations and realities.

You are the most important individual in the process of implementing the General Increase for the employees who work for you. This is because you are the key communicator and a source to answer questions. You will therefore want to familiarize yourself with the contents of both the "Message to be Read to All Production & Maintenance Employees," as well as the "General Increase Announcement Schedule." The manner and timing of the message to employees is covered in the Announcement Schedule.

We are confident that your participation in the implementation of the 1974 General Salary Increase will contribute to its overall successful reception by the production & maintenance employees.

The announcement schedule detailed the timing of the general increase message to employees. At 9 A.M. on November 21, each division or plant manager was to call a staff meeting in which he or she was to read the statement of the president and the chairman. The instructions stated:

> *. . . The division or plant manager conducting the meeting will be prepared to answer any questions raised by their staff members pertaining to this general increase. The division or plant managers will furnish staff members an adequate supply of these memoranda for meetings to be conducted by foremen, department heads, and supervisors as outlined in succeeding steps. Representatives from personnel will be available to answer questions relative to this announcement.*

At 11 A.M., there was to be an announcement to foremen and department heads by staff members, and at 2:30 P.M. there was to be an announcement to supervisors by foremen and department heads. At 9 A.M. on Friday, November 22, there was to be an announcement to day-shift employees by supervisors; the announcement to night-shift employees was to be made immediately after the start of the shift. With regard to this announcement, the instructions stated:

> *Supervisors will manage to cut off running machinery or equipment where practicable before their meeting in order to reduce the noise level so they can be heard. Supervisors will read the [president's and the chairman's] statement to employees attached to this memo and be prepared to answer any questions. These meetings will probably require about fifteen or twenty minutes, although the supervisor should exercise . . . discretion if the situation seems to require a longer time.* After the meeting, supervisors are to talk to each of their employees individually to advise them of the amount of the increase. These individual meetings should be held as soon as possible after the [president's and the chairman's] statement has been read in the group meeting.

The letter to each employee, signed by the president and the chairman and dated November 22, announced several new employee benefit improvements which would be significant additions to the total benefit program. These included increased coverage of basic life insurance, accidental death and dismemberment insurance, and improved maternity benefits. In addition, the letter announced that a revised and improved supplemental life insurance plan would be offered to all employees, as well as a new stock purchase plan, which would enable full-time U.S. employees to purchase the company's common stock through payroll deductions at the market price. After detailing the benefit improvements, the announcement letter continued:

> *The company is also announcing a general salary increase to apply only to production & maintenance employees effective November 25, 1974. Salary increases for Office and Technical and Managerial employees will continue to be administered under the existing merit increase programs.*
>
> *You are all aware of the current general economic downturn in the national economy. We are all concerned about inflation, its effect on the cost of living and on the cost of doing business which continues to go up faster than ever before. [The company] . . . has been affected by the current economic slowdown. We have also had to cut back on the money we planned and wanted to spend for new equipment and improvements.*
>
> *[The company] is providing these benefit improvements despite these conditions because it is [the company's] policy to assure that each of you receives fair and proper treatment when related to prevailing salary and benefit conditions. These benefit improvements plus those announced last July represent the largest combined benefit improvement in the history of [the company] for any one single year. But there are other reasons why you are receiving improved benefits—*
>
> *You have done your part in making 1974 a successful year for [the company] and for all of us even though there is a slowing of demand in the latter part of the year.*
>
> *We are confident that you will continue to do a good job because you know that the better we do, the more secure our jobs and future will be.*
>
> *The ability to raise prices to cover increasing costs is limited; and, in addition, your management does not want to do so if at all possible in order to help win the fight against inflation. The only way we can continue to be successful is to find creative ways of increasing the utilization and productivity of all our resources at all levels in the company, whether they be people, machines, material, or money.*
>
> *Only in this way can we continue to provide increasing salaries and benefits to all employees. It is a result of the knowledge that we can count on each of you to do this, that we have confidence in our ability to overcome today's problems and accept tomorrow's challenges.*

As we can readily see, much time and attention is devoted to salary and benefit administration at this company, at staff and at plant levels. One cannot ignore how much time and care these carefully scheduled announcement procedures take. Consider how much it asks of the lower-level supervisor, how much it implies about their status, how difficult it is to follow up and how much the whole thing constitutes behavioral evidence of easily verbalized intentions. While the data are limited with respect to supervisors, employee, and community perceptions of company pay policies, they suggest that company policies are understood.

Regarding the large company—the only nonunion one in its industry, discussed earlier—whose policy is to keep total compensation equal to or better than the industry, a union official who knows the company well and respects it, had this to say:

> *[The company] pays slightly more than the rest of the industry. The employees know it. But the company expects and gets more work out of the employees. It promotes from within and it has excellent employee relations.*

A long-service employee at another company, in commenting about the pay policy said:

> *The company pays well. [Our competition], which is nearby, goes on strike and we get the increases and have no strike.*

Those companies that administer attitude surveys certainly receive systematic information on the perceptions of their employees with respect to the pay policies. At one company, it was reported that while some of the exempt technical people frequently said in surveys that the pay was "terrible" just to keep management on its toes, it was felt that the hourly employees were quite honest in stating their views about pay in the attitude questionnaires. From these surveys management can not only ascertain employee feelings about the policies themselves, but it can also find out the way in which the policies are communicated, administered, and understood by employees.

Needless to say, good understanding of a company's pay policy does not happen by chance. Supervisory orientation, continuing education, and training programs frequently include a section on the company's pay policy. Changes are communicated through memorandums and meetings. Slide films and video tapes are frequently used as training aids. Employee perceptions, at least in part, are presumably the result of effective employer communications programs. As previously mentioned, much more on the communications aspects of benefits policies will be considered in Chapter 11.

DIFFERENCES AMONG PAY POLICIES

Although there are great similarities among the companies studied with respect to pay levels, to reliance on regular pay and benefit surveys, and to pay and benefit communications programs, there are significant policy differences in the ways in which companies administer their pay plans with respect to production and maintenance employees. These differences relate to the nature of merit pay plans, the presence or absence of a general increase policy, and the frequency or timing of pay increases. Consider how "Terry," a production worker on the job for one year whose performance is satisfactory would have fared with respect to pay increases in 1977 at six different companies in the sample.

Company A

This company reviews an employee's performance twelve months from the time he or she comes into the job and, thereafter, annually. This company also makes pay scale adjustments (which used to be called general increases) twice a year. Hence, in this company, Terry would receive a 5 percent merit increase on the anniversary date, a 3 percent pay-scale adjustment in January, and another 3 percent pay-scale adjustment in June.

Company B

This company gives a general increase each fall and merit increases two times a year until the employee reaches the premium rate for his or her job. The merit increase is given in relationship to the anniversary date or the time of the last increase. In this company in 1977 Terry would receive a general increase of 7.5 percent in September, and two merit increases six months apart, each amounting to 3.4 percent.

Company C

This company's only increases are for merit. The size and timing of the increase relate to Terry's performance. Since this is satisfactory, Terry would probably receive an 8 or 9 percent increase a year after the last increase.

Company D

This company's pay rates are single job rates rather than rate ranges. The published scale relates to time in the job and satisfactory (or better) performance. All increases are given at the same time each year. In this company Terry would get a general increase of 9 percent in June.

Company E

This company has an uncapped cost-of-living change which is payable monthly. Merit increases are generally given once per year. In this company Terry would receive higher pay each month, based on changes in the CPI (Consumer Price Index), as well as a merit increase of $30 per month. (In this salary company everyone is paid monthly, though production workers may request to be paid twice a month.)

Company F

> *This company's only pay increases are termed merit increases. They*
> are, however, given twice a year. The size of the increase depends on many
> *factors, including competitor pay rates, the rate of inflation, and potential*
> *union organizational drives. Here Terry would probably receive an addi-*
> *tional $15 per week in September and an additional $20 per week in April.*

As the above examples make clear, the majority of the companies studied reported that they have rate ranges and are merit-pay or pay-for-performance companies. The other companies have general increases with either single job rates, perhaps related to time in a grade, or job rates with automatic progression from the hiring rate to the job rate.

Of significance, unlike many unionized companies, just one of the entirely nonunion companies studied has a cost-of-living arrangement. This company, which has had this plan for many years, makes its cost-of-living adjustments monthly. The cost-of-living allowance is expressed in dollars per month, and is included in the employee's regular paycheck. The cost-of-living plan is uncapped and uses the Bureau of Labor Statistics' Consumer Price Index. A change of two-tenths of one point in the index results in a one dollar change a month in the cost-of-living allowance. The amount of the allowance is posted on company bulletin boards during the last week of each month. It was said that there is great employee interest in and attention to these bulletin boards at the end of each month. When asked about the reason behind this company's automatic cost-of-living monthly adjustments, a company personnel officer said:

> *Cost-of-living clauses are not uncommon in our industry, though the*
> *uncapped nature of ours does distinguish us. But you also have to remember*
> *that in our area the United Auto Workers, which have cost-of-living, are*
> *strong.*

This plan has been very expensive in recent years and the company considered dropping it. Top management asked a labor consultant for a view of the consequences of abandoning this plan. The consultant thought it would be unwise, from an employee-relations viewpoint, to drop the plan during a period of rapid inflation. Consequently, the company retained the plan.

However, one wonders why the consultant did not suggest that the company consider substituting a discretionary general-increase plan for its rather rigid cost-of-living approach. It could accomplish the same employee-relations objectives, and give management more flexibility at the same time.

While the concept and practice of merit pay will be discussed in the next chapter, there is, as the examples above demonstrated, some variation in the design and in the administration of merit pay plans. The examples also confirmed the earlier statements about the pay treatment of production and maintenance employees within the cooperating companies. The pay increases appear to be generous. In Company *A* in 1977, for example, pay administrators would point out, Terry would receive pay scale adjustments of 6 percent in addition to a merit increase of 5 percent or a total increase of 11 percent. Employees, however, would view the total increase as 9.5 percent, for the second pay-scale increase did not begin until June. Similarly, in Company *B* the total annual increase amounts to 14.3 percent, or 12.6 percent, adjusted for the fact that the second merit increase comes in the last half of the year. In Companies *C* and *D*, Terry would receive 8 or 9 percent; in Company *E* Terry's total increase would depend on the rate of inflation, with merit increase related to performance; and in Company *F* Terry's increase would depend on performance as well as on competitive and inflationary pressures.

It should be added that in many companies there is much openness about pay. Employees know the pay range for their jobs, and the ways in which they may progress through the range. Employees also know the pay ranges of other jobs. The practice of job posting certainly seems to increase employee knowledge and discussion of pay. It is the policy of some companies, however, to regard pay as secret. For example, in these companies, employees are not (at least not officially) informed of the maximum or top pay for their job. Nevertheless, the trend does appear to be toward more openness about pay.

CONCLUDING ANALYSIS AND COMMENTS

This chapter has attempted to demonstrate that it is generally the policy of the companies in my sample (a group of leading employers) to pay well by industry and community standards. These high pay levels are part of a comprehensive package of personnel policies and programs. The achievement of their pay-policy objectives is facilitated by administering regular surveys that are respected by top-level management. Union settlements, particularly those of direct competitors, are watched very carefully. The pay levels of "sensitive groups" of employees are closely monitored. Moreover, careful and thoroughly considered attempts are made to communicate to employees, individually and in groups, about their pay increases and benefit improvements.

While a few of the companies have national pay rates for nonexempt jobs, most of them relate their pay levels to community averages. The decentralized nature of the wage policies of the companies studied is striking. The environmental factor of location, as well as the nature of the local market pay survey, then become extremely important. Moreover, the companies studied, to a degree, take on the characteristics of the U.S. industrial relations system in that there are never any pay decreases, and in that there is much stability in wages paid over the business cycle. The policies, so closely following union settlements and community averages, have an inflationary bias. Nevertheless, without a commitment to escalation or to cost-of-living clauses, they piggyback on the consequences of union settlements, cost-of-living clauses, and annual improvement factors. In one sense, the companies studied do operate at a disadvantage in relation to unionized competitors that may bargain a certain amount for a fixed duration, such as three years; however, the unionized company (without a cost-of-living clause in the contract, or with a cost-of-living adjustment that has a cap) knows what its labor costs will be for three years. In another sense, the nonunion company can move more quickly and has flexibility, in that it is free to make adjustments in wages and benefits annually (or more or less frequently), depending on its policies as well as on circumstances. While the nonunion company does have flexibility with respect to the size of the increase as well as its timing, it does not have the same certainty about labor costs that is associated with the specified pay rates of a three-year contract.

This chapter has shown that, while there are many similarities in pay levels, in reliance on regular pay and benefit surveys, and in pay and benefits communications programs among the companies, there are some significant policy differences as to how various companies administer their pay plans. These differences relate to the design and administration of merit pay policies, to the presence or absence of general increase policies, and to the frequency or time of pay increases. The next chapter is concerned with the concept and practice of merit pay with respect to production and maintenance employees.

While it is not certain what impact superior pay has on employee motivation, it does appear to aid the companies studied in the areas of recruiting and retention. The policies of the companies studied also tend to make it extremely unlikely that any of them will be vulnerable to a union organizational drive on the basis of compensation issues.

CHAPTER NINE

Merit Pay Policies
and Their Administration

Although a pay system should not be examined independently from the nature of the work, one particular interesting finding of this study (one related to my interest in pay policies and their administration) concerns the issue of merit pay. As the reader will recall, two different groups of large companies were studied. The first and much larger group is those companies which are *entirely* nonunion; the second group consists of companies that are *predominantly* nonunion.

What was discovered was that those companies in the smaller second group, the ones that are partially unionized, do not have merit pay systems for their hourly employees. In contrast, the great majority of the entirely nonunion companies stated that they have pay policies based on merit, usually to the exclusion of general wage increases. The only exceptions to these categorizations are those few companies that have piece-rate incentive systems for many or for most of their hourly employees.

The concept of merit pay fits the philosophy or principle of individual treatment, so fundamental to the approaches of many of the companies studied. Furthermore, the top managements of some of the entirely nonunion companies maintained that their merit pay system was one of the real advantages of being nonunion. This is the case because for them a merit pay policy is an incentive, and thus encourages greater work effort and better employee performance than the system of single rates with general increases typically found in the unionized company.

However, analysis suggests that in most of the companies the administration of these merit pay policies is such that there is a substantial difference between the theoretical concept of merit pay and its practice. Consequently, it is important to examine the nature of different merit pay plans, the manner in which such plans are administered, and the problems that they present, particularly in times of rapid inflation.

That only four companies have a piece-rate-incentive pay system is in itself an interesting finding. Several of the other companies have abandoned piece-rate systems in favor of day work over the years. Day work appears desirable to these companies for several reasons: It seems consistent with less resistance to technological change, fewer grievances or complaints over standards, individual treatment, better supervision and a better employee-relations climate. While management may try to use a piece-rate-incentive plan to manage their operations due to the inadequacies of supervision, incentive systems are often a constant source of conflict, irritation, and grievances. While the trend seems to be away from incentives, two companies in the sample are experimenting with them. One company is experimenting with individual incentives, which top management views as consistent with the companywide adoption of a management-by-objectives (MBO) program, while the other company is trying group incentives (with some success, it reported). Not to seem cynical, I must point out a comment made by one labor relations professional interviewed, who said: "I can demonstrate that in my plant you can make money by adopting incentives if they do not exist there and by getting rid of them if they do."

PAY APPROACHES OF PREDOMINANTLY NONUNION COMPANIES

While the number of predominantly nonunion companies is not large enough so as to generalize about the pay practices of large, predominantly nonunion companies, the few of them that are in the sample do display many commonalities. Except for experimental "all-salary" plants, their pay approaches are remarkably similar to those used in the unionized part of their companies. Describing one company's pay approach, one of its corporate compensation administrators said:

> In general, the treatment is the same whether the plant is union or nonunion. There are no merit increases once the employee reaches the job rate.

Reaching the job rate is simply a function of time. In this company it takes four months for an employee to reach the job rate. All employees receive general increases that, depending on their category, might amount to $10 per week, $0.25 per hour, or 4 percent. In addition, this company gives cost-of-living increases each November.

Why is it that the predominantly nonunion companies do not have merit pay? One company's official summed up its reasons succinctly: "This way the union can't say to our nonunion employees that they [the union] have anything they [the nonunion employees] don't." Consistency, then, avoids claims of inequities. The corporate director of employee relations at another large, predominantly nonunion company summed up the thinking of management:

> *We have learned from our union experience that employees do not want merit pay. This is so for three reasons. First, it is difficult to obtain objective criteria to measure performance. Second, employees do not want a foreman deciding who gets more or less. Finally, our type of production process does not lend itself to merit pay.*

When asked to elaborate with respect to the difficulties of performance evaluation, this person said:

> *We've learned that you have to be damned careful in the performance rating of production people. If twenty people are involved in running a big machine, it is hard to document differences in performance. And because favoritism gets you unionism the quickest, we won't take the risk of fine lining the differentials.*

Herbert H. Meyer has written that "most unionized employees have not accepted the validity of supervisor judgments, and rarely does a union agree to a merit pay plan."[1] In describing the approach at another partially unionized company, the compensation manager said:

> *With respect to our production and maintenance hourly people in both our union and nonunion plants, there is, really, no merit. We say a person gets the increase if he is doing a satisfactory job. We make no attempt to distinguish among satisfactory, good, very good, excellent, and so on. If a person, however, is unsatisfactory, he [or she] is talked to or counseled. But less than 1 percent of the work force is unsatisfactory. Thus in our company, there is really no merit.*

Though not given as such, a merit increase at this company is then really a general increase.

It should be added that a few of the entirely nonunion companies reported that they, in essence, have also abandoned merit pay for production and maintenance employees. The vice-president of personnel at one such company said:

> *We moved away from merit ten years ago. The only vestige of merit which remains is that the company can withhold an increase. But, if an employee's performance is adequate or better, increases are automatic.*

---

[1] Herbert H. Meyer, "The Pay-for-Performance Dilemma," *Organizational Dynamics,* (Winter 1975), 41.

Three other companies reported general increases at the same time for everyone based on time in grade and on satisfactory performance. The vice-president of personnel at one of these companies said:

> We give our increases once a year at the same time for everyone. We publish pay scales. While there are rate ranges with maximums for each job, our scales are such that an employee in a job for two years is paid more than a person in the job for one year. At the low levels, everyone with the same seniority will get the same increase if his [or her] performance is acceptable.

The pay practices toward the production and maintenance employees of the above companies are interesting. These companies deny themselves one of the alleged benefits of operating nonunion, which is to pay for performance. Their general rather than individual approaches, however, do avoid feelings of favoritism and/or racial or sexual discrimination, which might give rise to unionization or to discrimination charges. The supervisor does not have to deny step increases or to justify differential increases, based on performance; nor will there be the possibility of destructive competition among employees for top merit increases. However, whether these systems make the supervisor's job more difficult, and are associated with a significant decline in employee motivation and performance are the interesting questions that only more data can answer. It may be that the way some of the merit companies administer their pay plans is not all that different from what happens in the companies above. It may also be that the relationship between merit pay and performance is not as direct as is sometimes thought. Before returning to these questions, let us consider the different approaches of the merit pay companies.

MERIT PAY POLICIES

Before considering the ways in which the great majority of the entirely nonunion companies administer their merit pay plans, let us first examine the policies themselves. As will be noted later, some of the policies have a seniority emphasis. However, many companies give considerable weight to seniority rather than to merit factors in the administration of their policies. As for the stated policies, to quote from personnel manuals and employee handbooks of eight companies:

Company A

Your Performance and Pay: *Rate ranges have been established for all positions within the company. Starting salaries are normally assigned between the minimum and the midpoint of the range. Related work experience will be considered in determining whether a starting salary above the range minimum will be offered. Questions relating to compensation should be directed to your supervisor.*

Exempt employees receive formal performance and salary reviews at least once each year. Nonexempt employees are reviewed semiannually. Salary increases, under our merit system, are based upon job performance.

Performance evaluation considers factors such as attendance and attitude (to the extent they affect the performance of you or others) as well as the quality and quantity of work produced.

Company supervisors are responsible to inform employees if performance is less than satisfactory and to detail areas in which performance must improve.

Company B

Salary Determination: *Company policy is to pay salaries which reflect the employee's value to the company and the importance, responsibility, and difficulty of the job. It is also company policy to pay salaries which compare favorably with those paid by competitive employers.*

The merit principle is followed in granting salary increases. That is, the amount and the frequency of an employee's increases are based primarily upon his job performance. Continued good performance will merit continued increase within broad guidelines. This allows the company unusual flexibility in rewarding employees and eliminating artificial barriers to salary progression.

An employee's job performance is reviewed continually during the year. In this way, his foreman or supervisor can carefully consider his progress and recommend a raise when he believes it is warranted.

It is your foreman or supervisor's responsibility to answer any questions you may have regarding your salary or your progress on the job.

Company C

Pay Policy: *All employees at the company are paid on a salary basis. It is the policy of the company to pay salaries that compare favorably with pay for similar work performed in other companies in the same industry and community. Our compensation administration program assures (1) a high standard of salary rates, and (2) that the salary rate of each job is equitable in relation to all other jobs.*

Our people are given raises based on performance and length of service.

Company D

Pay for Individual Performance—Base Salary: *Every company job is reviewed and given a classification and salary range or scale. In the review process, jobs are compared with other positions both inside and outside the company. Your monthly base salary within your salary scale depends on your job performance and contributions resulting from experience.*

Your monthly base salary is also reviewed at regular intervals by your supervisor. Monthly base salary increases are based on merit and are not automatic.

Salary scales are continually reviewed and changes are made when appropriate.

Company E

Merit Pay System: *Pay based on performance is a fundamental principle of our compensation policies. With the company's Merit Pay System, you, as an individual, can directly influence your earnings through your performance on the job. Your manager is responsible for frequently reviewing your salary relative to the skill requirements of your job and your performance in it. Increases are granted as they are earned through sustained or improved performance.*

Company F

Merit Increases: *Merit increases are the means by which you will progress through your rate range as your effort and job knowledge increase your value to the company. They are normally given annually, and are governed by your performance rating. The rating determines the size of your increase and, if your job is exempt from overtime pay, the extent of your progress toward your position level (the salary established for fully competent performance of each exempt position).*

Full details about compensation policy are available from your manager.

Company G

Wage Protection: *The company seeks to maintain wages which are in line with those paid for similar work in comparable companies in your area. Periodic surveys are made to see that this policy is observed. These are taken into consideration by management in periodic reviews of wage levels. Your earnings are based upon two factors: the value of your job to the company, and the manner in which you perform that job.*

Company H

Merit Increases: *A merit increase is based on an individual's performance. The amount of the increase is determined by the supervisor. Merit increases are granted to reward sustained improved performance at the next higher level. Five percent is the guideline amount; however, it is acceptable under unusual circumstances of sustained excellent performance to submit a merit increase for over 5 percent. An alternative to a larger increase at one time is to give smaller ones more frequently.*

There is no policy covering the timing of increases. Generally, people learn faster and improve more rapidly early in their careers on the job. Later, this rate of learning tends to slow down. Consequently, their performance and pay may change more rapidly at the start of their careers than in later years.

As the different policy statements make clear, there is some variation among pay for performance or merit companies. For example, some merit companies (a minority) have not only merit pay, but also yearly or even semiannual general increases. While some other merit pay companies have made occasional or intermittent special across-the-board increases, the majority give only merit increases. All companies, of course, adjust their pay structures regularly to reflect changed market conditions, these adjustments being built into the size of merit raises in those companies that do not give general increases.

While the pay approaches of some companies represent more of a blend of automatic progression with merit than do others, the timing of merit increases also varies by company. In some companies, merit increases are given yearly; in others, semiannually; and in still other companies, the timing relates to the level of an employee's performance, with employees whose performance is outstanding being eligible for larger increases earlier. In some companies, all raises are given at the same time, while in others they are given at different times of the year.

The administration of merit pay is also quite different with respect to rate ranges. While all the companies have job evaluation, job classifications, and rate ranges, in some of them there will be five or seven steps of equal cents or percentages within the range. In other companies, the size of an employee's increase will depend primarily on his or her performance, but also on where he or she is in relation to the midpoint of the range.

Although at the great majority of companies the employee who reaches the top of his or her range only receives general increases (if the company utilizes them) or schedule-change increases, at two companies it was the policy to grant seniority increases. At one of these companies, an employee who has been at his or her range maximum for three years, and whose performance and attendance are satisfactory, may receive a seniority increase of 4 percent. This increase, according to the company's policy statement, "recognizes the fact that, although . . . being paid the maximum value of the job to the company, the employee is continuing to exert his [or her] best efforts." At this company, three years after receiving the first seniority increase, and employee may receive a second and final seniority increase. The seniority increases at the other company with this policy are 5 percent after five and ten years.

MERIT PAY ADMINISTRATION

To begin our discussion of merit pay administration, let us examine the practices of those companies which use step increases. Company *H*'s policy statement is clearly set forth in print. Yet the personnel director of this company said that the policy is not administered as written. When asked about it, this person stated:

> *We say we have a merit system but we do not. Increases are called merit increases but they are really seniority increases. If we did not do it this way, the system could be administered in a way to produce complaints of favoritism.*

A personnel administrator at the same company had this to say about the merit pay system:

> *Within our seven steps for each job, Steps 1 and 2 are automatic. It happens after three months on the job. After Step 2, allegedly, everything is merit. But people, especially nonexempts, always receive their five percent merit increase. Most of the merit increase relates to time on the job, attendance, and keeping one's nose clean. I've in fact heard people ask, "doesn't merit count for something?"*

While Steps 1 and 2 are referred to as the learning positions, Steps 3, 4, and 5 are the range positions for the experienced employee. Positions of Steps 6 and 7 are supposed to be for the employee whose performance is exceptional. An industrial engineer at this company echoed similar sentiment about the company's merit system:

> *We have a five-step merit system in theory. But anyone with experience knows that when it is hard to measure performance, and even if it isn't, these systems become very political. Thus, that is why we really don't have a merit system.*

When a supervisor at this company was questioned about the administration of the pay plan, he said:

> *The system is a synthesis of merit and time in grade. I get the feeling that a lot of the supervisors respect the amount of time in the job and correlate the increase with it as opposed to the man's contributions. There are a few cases of fast movement but normally people obtain merit increases because of longevity.*
>
> *The merit system is really not a merit system. For example, you have high expectations for a Level 7 contributor. But the problem comes with the Level 6 guy who is exceptional. He sees a [Level] 7 who is not as good as he is. It is too difficult to administer the system. If you stir up the pot, you'll have a grievance. So, therefore, you become complacent.*

It was said that 65 percent of the employees within the trades were at Level 7. A supervisor spoke of the problem of everyone advancing to Level 7, saying: "For the supervisor to survive he [or she] has to document. The effect of this is that some people get increases who shouldn't." This is because supervisors find it difficult to document poor performance. This company added Categories 6 and 7, for "exceptional performance," to its performance appraisal plan when a large percentage of the employees were rated either "4" or "5." In 1976 there was some lower-level management pressure to add a Category 8, so that their employees could receive pay increases larger than those given through the semiannual pay scale adjustments. Given the company's definition of a Level 7 performer this might be difficult. The following describes a Level 7 performer:

> *This is the occasional man or woman who is an outstanding and exceptional performer whose personal qualifications, cooperation, enthusiasm, and attitude are the mark of a recognized leader type . . . Examples of such outstanding performance might include: quantity that is proportionally more than those in the step below; quality without sacrificing quantity that is characterized by a touch of finesse, distinction, or even individuality that no one else can match; creativity in the form of new ideas and suggestions, skillfully developed and presented.*

A Level 8 performer would no doubt have to be a true superperson who really did walk on water!

The experience of another company was similar. This company also has several steps in its pay range for each job, but all the steps are automatic (in the sense that they are dependent upon time in the job) except the last one, which depends on merit. However, when a personnel administrator was asked about the administration of this policy, and in particular about the merit step, he said: "While the last step is merit, 99 percent of the people get the merit increase. The merit increase is really quite automatic."

At a company that has a five-step merit system (with the last two steps being the true merit steps) there is also a general-increase program. This company gives merit increases twice a year, with the timing of an individual's review related to his or her anniversary date with the company, or to the date of his or her previous increase. When asked how the merit system works, the vice-president said:

> *It is really not a merit system, though we say we have one. The increases are pretty much automatic and 80 percent of the employees are at the maximum. You really can't have a merit system when the nature of the technology is such that the work paces the man and you have a standard— either the person meets it or he doesn't.*

The essential point with step systems is that the employee either does or does not receive the merit increase. The step increases for one low-level job, for example, are twelve cents per hour; It is not a matter of one worker getting 2 percent and another receiving 4 percent, a system which might be more difficult for the average supervisor to administer. By having every worker be eligible for the same increase, even if only a very small percentage of employees do not receive it, it would seem that this system does encourage or motivate good performance—at least until the worker gets to the premium rate. Even if the increases are essentially automatic, the employee cannot feel certain he or she will receive it. Management always has the power to withhold the increase.

In addition, the merit increases, especially because they are all not given at the same time, provide an opportunity for a counseling, communications, planning and/or a goal-setting session between the supervisor and the employee. Commenting on the way one company's step plan works, a supervisor who supports the practice said:

> *I think the plan should work this way. Otherwise you would create the feeling that the employee is being treated specially, either favorably or unfavorably, and this is something you would not want to do.*

Interestingly, this supervisor favors both merit pay and equal treatment, not seeing them as inconsistent.

Employees under the performance-appraisal system that goes with this plan are rated in four different categories: quantity, quality, alertness, and citizenship. One of four ratings must be given in each category: unsatisfactory, fair, good, or excellent. This company's pay system consists of a hire rate, a three-months rate, and a nine-months rate which are truly automatic because they are related to time in the job. Then there is the base or regular rate, which is followed by the premium rate, the maximum for the job. Three "goods" and one "fair" get a person to the base rate; to advance to the premium rate requires at least four "goods." When employees are eligible for either the base or the premium rates, they seem to receive the appropriate appraisal.

The way this system is administered has undoubtedly contributed to a decline in differentiated appraisals. In commenting about the system, four supervisors described difficulties, especially with regard to the employee who has advanced to the premium rate. They said:

> *The system is ineffective. Ninety-nine percent go from the hiring rate to the premium rate in an automatic fashion. We have little leverage with the employees. You can't motivate with money. Everyone is on salary and everyone receives premium wages. Dismissal is almost unheard of at this company. The company stresses attendance and other than stealing the only way to be fired is for a very bad attendance record. Discharge is extremely difficult. You have to put together a real ironclad case.*

Once the employee gets to the premium rate you are dead in the water. The employee knows that promotions are based on seniority and attendance. Therefore, how do you motivate? Merit is meaningful only going to the maximum rate.

The system is good but it would be nice to be able to take money away from the premium operator. But the company won't let you. Advancement is automatic in effect. Sometimes you deny the premium rate but you hardly ever deny the regular rate.

The problem is once people get to the premium rate. You have no way to deal with them. You can't take money away from them. You can't discharge them, and you can't reduce their pay. We have people who go like crazy to get to the last step, then they goof off.

These comments also say something about the problem of motivation, and the apparent decline in the use of financial incentives. Under a system of rate ranges with automatic or nearly automatic wage progression to the maximum rate, once the employee reaches the top rate the supervisor has the same problem with respect to motivation as the supervisor in a unionized company has with a system of single job rates.

A manager of a company whose top management speaks highly of its merit system admitted that the company has had much trouble administering it. This company's merit range also has seven steps, with the increment between steps being 5 percent. While increases are automatic up to the midpoint—the fully proficient rate—they are supposed to be based on merit to and throughout the next three levels, which are the highly proficient rate, the outstanding rate, and the exceptional rate. The policy is to set the going rate for a particular job at the union scale, and then to make it possible for the employee to earn considerably more than the going rate through merit increases. Discussing this problem, the manager said:

The real question is: How much discretion do you give the foreman? We used to give him a lot, but it is our experience that the foreman can't handle it. He wants precise guidelines. A worker gets mad if he finds out that a fellow worker who started with him a year ago is now making three cents more per hour than he is.

Consequently, we have been giving the foreman less discretion and raises pretty much go according to standard steps. I think the biggest problem is that we lack confidence in our performance appraisal system.

In another company, which gives annual general increases and merit increases on the employee's anniversary date that are separate from the performance appraisal, it was reported that "half of our people are at the top of the range, and in the shop 85 percent of the people are at the top." It was also said that in this company it generally takes employees four or five years to get to the top of their range. One company executive pointed out that the merit plan made it difficult to compare its pay levels with those of its unionized competitors. Commenting on the administration of this policy, the administrative vice-president said, "About 85 percent of our people receive merit increases in a year, though not all on the same date."

In conclusion, it is probably fair to say that the merit principle, as associated with step increases and as it operates in the companies studied, results in nearly everyone moving in an automatic or in a nearly automatic manner to the top step. Rather than having a bell-shaped distribution of employees around the middle step, the distribution is skewed toward the last step, with nearly all the employees reaching the top step in time.

Let us now examine those merit systems that are not associated with fixed-percentage step increases. The division manufacturing manager at one such company, one that states that its merit system works, said:

> Merit pay fits well with the high expectations regarding performance which exist in this company. Given that we use maturity curves in salary administration here, in actual fact these are average raises. But there are people who do not get them. We have differences in pay according to performance in this company. The supervisor ranks all his people. The biggest problem is not in measuring performance, but when a new supervisor takes over a group. He may change the rankings.

When a supervisor, who with several lead workers is responsible for fifty-eight people, was asked about the company's system, he said:

> The key is recognition of the individual—his wants, desires, and needs. Some want to advance; some want to do an eight-hour job. We try to give the individuals the opportunities they want.
>
> As for salary administration, we have maturity curves. There are four levels of performance. The distribution of my people is like a bell-shaped curve. While I am not sure that every individual knows his [or her] rating, the vast majority do. The lead [worker] does the yearly performance appraisal on each individual. We tell people that under our wage curve policy they can advance through their efforts. We have people with two years of service who make more than those with ten years of service.
>
> There are claims of favoritism. There is not utopia. But such claims are investigated and there are explanations.

When a worker in this division was interviewed, he said:

> The merit pay plan can be quite controversial. Merit and cost of living seem to go together here and this is where people, especially the women, get sore. A woman gets a raise of $8 a week and she wants to know how much is merit and how much is cost of living. The wage curves are done one or two times per year.

Any merit system certainly has its demotivating elements. Moreover, high inflation, which will be discussed later, compounds these problems in companies that
do not have general-increase policies as well as merit-increase programs.

At another company which rates all employees' performance by a score from
"2" to "10," with "10" outstanding, it was said that there is a blend of
progression and merit with respect to members of the nonexempt payroll. When a
salary administrator at this company was asked how the system works he said it
was important to understand both the rate schedule and the nature of the perform-
ance-review process. Elaborating, he stated:

> Non-exempts are guaranteed a certain amount of movement for satis-
> factory performance. But to move fast you have to do merit work. Cost of
> living changes are handled through the rate schedules which are adjusted
> yearly.
> An hourly employee can get to the midpoint in two to four years and to
> the third quartile with satisfactory performance. For example, recently there
> was a schedule change and satisfactory performers below the midpoint
> received an increase of six cents per hour in addition to the schedule change.
> The review last November, however, was just merit. The merit budget
> was 2.3 percent, with employees getting either 1 percent, 2 percent, or 3
> percent. A person rated "6," for example, received an increase of six cents
> per hour. Those above the midpoint, however, did not receive anything.

However, when a foreman at this company was asked for his views about the
effectiveness of the performance review system with respect to motivation, he
said:

> The differences are not a motivator at all. If the person is rated "2" to
> "4," he gets no increase. But the differences between a "6," "8," and "10"
> is almost insignificant. The difference is 2.3 cents per hour. It is hard for the
> girls to understand. It is easy to go from the minimum to the midpoint, but
> from the midpoint to the maximum is done through merit. It takes an "8" or
> "10." I would say the real rewards here are promotions.

While more information is needed, one can certainly question the effectiveness of this system. When promotion becomes the important motivator, if the
company promotes the senior qualified person rather than the best qualified
person, promotion will not be such a motivator for some young people. It would
seem that the nature of the work, the relationship with fellow workers, and the
employee–supervisor relationship become all the more important in such environments.

While admitting that many line managers had told him there were problems
with the merit pay policy, one vice-president of personnel cited personnel department research studies, which showed that there was still much of value in the
company's merit pay plan. The company's salary ranges are extremely wide, and

top management believes that the possibility of a good merit increase better motivates employee performance than would a single rate system with general increases. Furthermore, his assistant talked at length about the philosophy of the company as it relates to the operation of a merit pay system, saying:

> *Merit pay is consistent with the way we want to treat people. If we had general increases, the employee might lose contact with the manager. I admit, however, that weak managers would prefer a general-increase program over our merit-increase program.*
>
> *While it is true that many employees reach the pay for performance category, in fact, job for job, in our company the better performer is making more money. The better achievers earn more. Differentials are maintained. We do careful audits on pay and the distribution of appraisal ratings and I can say with confidence that some element of merit is maintained. We spend lots of time training managers on merit pay. The manager is responsible for the timing and the size of the increase. Our system is good.*

In this company, the performance of employees is rated by their manager. Different ratings result in differential increases. For example, if in 1976 an employee was rated "4," then he or she would be eligible for a 6- to 7-percent increase. If, on the other hand, the employee received a "2" rating, he or she would receive an 8- to 9-percent increase. A "1" will receive the top increase. A "1" and a "2," it was said, will also do better with respect to promotional opportunities. Several managers and supervisors interviewed at one plant of this high-paying company discussed the merit pay plan:

> *Pay for performance is necessary in our business because we are nonunion. I personally would like a little more latitude. I realize, however, that some people would take advantage of it. Sometimes the system requires you to do strange things. I'll have words with an employee, telling him he is not performing properly. But a month later, I'll give him an increase. Some employees have trouble accepting it. Employees will get a 6-percent increase. With inflation and the company's profitability, the employees don't understand. They don't understand the costs associated with full employment and new product development.*
>
> *Merit pay makes the manager's job easier. Usually a manager has some latitude in treating individuals. Some managers, however, think the plan inhibits them. Most employees do not feel there is a merit pay plan. They think it is hogwash. Employees exchange salary information. There will be a person making $163 per week and another making $175 per week. They will say they have both been there the same amount of time and they'll feel it is not equitable. Employees think it is a pure function of what the manager thinks of you. They don't believe there are guidelines. They think it is favoritism. Employees discuss the differences even though raises are given at different times in this company. The managers have some latitude but there are guidelines. It takes creativity. Some managers can do it and some cannot.*

The average guy feels there is no merit system any more. He is barely keeping up with the cost of living. Pay for performance—some guys believe it and some do not. The guys in the sheet metal shop do not believe they get paid for performance because you can't really measure their work. In the machine shop, they are measured on quantity, quality, and attendance.

Some employees have been appraised by me over the last four years. It's getting a little repetitious. Appraisal is great for the new employee but the guy with twenty-five years in the business will say, "Give it to me and I'll sign it." There is a popularity contest and I haven't won one yet. How do you breathe new life into the appraisal program? That is my question. I'll give the employee the form and say, "Read it, sign it, and then if you have any questions we'll discuss it." Only one out of five will discuss it.

As has been noted, this company does not have a general-increase program. Its merit pay plan obviously suffered because of the rapid inflation of the 1974 to 1976 period. But the fact that this company pays its employees extremely well and also provides them with excellent benefits probably makes its employees more tolerant of what they may perceive as inadequate merit increases than employees of some other companies might be. It should also be added that these interviews were with supervisors at one of this company's older plants. It may be that the company's merit pay system was more effective at this plant in the past. The combination of a maturing employee population who tend to be in the top of their pay grades and inflation undoubtedly count for some of the negatives voiced. However, a personnel supervisor at this company said that there, it was not appropriate to challenge the concept of merit pay, adding: "On this issue it is better to salute the flag. If you challenge merit pay here, it is seen as a challenge to the entire philosophy. So, you salute the flag on this issue."

At another company, the merit system is used to raise people beyond the fixed job rates of unionized competitors. In this organization, there is a four-part rating system based on overall performance. The ratings are A, B, C, and D, and the company tries to weed out marginal performers. Two-thirds of the people are rated "A" or "B," and there are guidelines for "A" and "B" people. Thus, an "A" might receive a $5 to $8 per week increase while a "B" might receive a $4 to $6 per week increase. A "C" would not receive any increase unless he or she was below the company's early career minimums of 6, 12, and 18 months, which varied by plant and by type of labor market.

While everyone will agree that recognition is an important motivator, one wonders if the opportunity to get a $7 raise instead of a $5 raise really does motivate. Perhaps, however, the way that the increase is handled is even more important than the raise itself.

At yet another company there are ranges for each job classification by years of service. Most jobs have more than one salary classification and employees are placed in a certain classification depending on their experience and ability. The salary scales are changed periodically (so that they are kept up-to-date) and there are yearly guidelines on the amount of dollars-per-month that are available for merit increases for each job classification. When asked about the system, a vice president said.

> *People should be in their right salary class for them and pay should be different based on performance, documented by the written appraisals. But supervisors like to promote everyone to the top level.*

The experience seems to be that if a company has a system that allows for little discretion by the supervisors, the supervisors want a system with greater discretion. However, if a company has a system that gives the supervisors considerable discretion, the supervisors do not use it. They instead tend to treat everyone the same, getting as much money as they can for their employees, especially during periods of rapid inflation. Supervisors also ask for precise guidelines. Under one system of advancement they move their employees to the next step; under another system they give an average increase. This behavior of supervisors is understandable, for they have to live with the employees every day. To explain different levels of performance, even if they are measurable, may be difficult, and to try to do so may result in arguments, grievances, hard feelings, divisiveness, or dysfunctional competition among employees. A supervisor's behavior may also result in the personnel department doing pay audits and conducting training programs on the theory and practice of pay for performance.

As the experience of the companies makes clear, no matter what the system, merit pay has its special problems and dilemmas.

THE SPECIAL DILEMMAS CONFRONTING MERIT COMPANIES DURING A HIGH INFLATION PERIOD

Although there is disagreement over the effectiveness of merit pay systems, and over the problems of measuring performance and being able to explain or justify decisions regarding performance to an employee, there is no disagreement over the fact that inflation plays havoc with merit pay systems. It is an understatement to say that merit pay systems are under great pressure in times of rapid inflation. If a company does not have a general-increase program, employees question how much merit is in the increase they receive. If a company does have a general-increase program but some employees have reached the top of their range, these employees look at the size of the general increase in relation to the rate of inflation.

At the only entirely nonunion company that has a cost-of-living clause (this company is also a leader in pay, has a generous bonus plan, excellent benefits, and an employee-savings plan whereby the company has matched 75 percent of what each employee contributes in recent years) the old saying that it is impossible to please everyone and that all things are relative is proven again: A personnel representative there stated that many of the employees were upset with the company's merit pay plan. This representative reported that employees felt the amount of money they received for good work these days was so small in relation to what they obtained from cost-of-living increases and bonuses, that it hardly paid to work hard. Significantly, once this feedback became known, management increased somewhat the sizes of its merit increases.

Companies are coping with this problem in a variety of ways. As one vice-president, at a company facing a union organizational drive, put it:

> *If you lay on an active organizational campaign and double-digit inflation, it means you have to give substantial increases. We have done this, and our merit increases were double those of last year. By doing this, in my view, most of our employees will not sign cards.*
>
> *In our warehouses, where the organizing pressure is the greatest, we've given four increases in the past year. Our pay is now similar to the union structure, and we're not at all embarrassed about saying we're doing this because of the organizational drive.*
>
> *In terms of the warehouses, we and [one] unionized [competitor] have lower rates but high overtime. [Another] unionized [competitor] has no overtime but very high base rates. Therefore, people working for us actually take home more. But now our rates are up but overtime is down. This is causing us a lot of grief.*

In response to inflationary pressures, some merit pay companies have granted one or more special across-the-board increases in recent years. For example, one company gave a five-percent catch-up increase in November 1973, a five-percent increase in May 1974, and a 5-percent increase in December 1974. Similarly, some merit pay companies gave special across-the-board increases after the ending of wage controls in the early 1970s. Other companies have increased the size of their merit increases, their frequency, or both. Companies that give general increases have responded to rapid inflation by simply increasing the amount of the increase, the frequency of the increase, or both. One company, for example, broke precedent by giving two general increases in one year. Another company, breaking with its past practices, abandoned its annual general increase policy in favor of semiannual pay-scale adjustments. Yet another company moved its pay structure sooner. "The earliest we have ever moved our pay structure is nine months, the longest sixteen months," said this company's personnel director. As to how these policies are carried out: At one company, if management is giving, for instance, a six-percent general or structure increase, and an employee is at the midpoint of his or her old range, this employee will be moved to the midpoint of his or her new range and will thereby receive a six-percent increase. He or she may then also receive a merit increase on top of that increase. In another company's overall budget, 8 percent was budgeted for a general increase, 1 percent for progression, 1 percent for merits and 1 percent for promotional increases.

Most companies are reluctant to call either special or general increases cost-of-living adjustments, because they do not want their employees to come to expect them, or to expect that they will be related precisely to the rate of inflation. This is because managements worry about being able to afford becoming locked into such practices. Managements also worry that such practices contribute to national inflationary pressures.

CONCLUDING ANALYSIS AND COMMENTS

Twenty years ago, in their classic study *The Impact of Collective Bargaining on Management*, Professors Sumner H. Slichter, James J. Healy, and E. Robert Livernash wrote about individual employee compensation:

> *The influence of unions has clearly been one of minimizing and eliminating judgment-based differences in pay for individuals employed on the same job. One avenue of influence has been toward the establishment of systems of single job rates rather than rate ranges. A second influence has been toward automatic or nearly automatic wage progressions to the maximum within rate-range systems.*[2]
> *. . . defending a merit system against grievances has not, it seems, appeared to be worthwhile. The path of least resistance has been to develop automatic or nearly automatic increases.*[3]

While the first influence is not at all widespread in the large, entirely nonunion company, the second influence (namely, automatic or nearly automatic wage progression to the maximum within rate-range systems) seems to well-describe the reality today in most large, entirely nonunion companies.

While merit pay plans are common in the entirely nonunion companies studied, for a variety of reasons they are frequently not administered as the stated policies would have one believe. Instead, the principles of seniority, automatic progression, and equal treatment seem to be given much weight. While this phenomenon seems true, independent of the effects of inflation pressures, the problem of rapid inflation greatly complicates the merit pay system, especially for those companies that operate without an accompanying general increase policy.

Whether some merit plans actually are administered as they are intended to be, and whether they are effective, are open questions at this point. If these questions are to be answered, more data are needed. The distributions of merit

---

[2]Sumner H. Slichter, James J. Healy, and E. Robert Livernash, *The Impact of Collective Bargaining on Management* (Washington, D.C.: The Brookings Institution, 1960), p. 602.

[3]Slichter, Healy, and Livernash, *The Impact of Collective Bargaining on Management*, p. 606.

increases over time need to be analyzed. However, it appears that there has been considerable erosion of the merit concept. The rate ranges associated with the large, entirely nonunion company seem preferable to the single-rate and general-increase systems typical of the unionized employer. Merit increases, even if automatic or almost automatic, represent an opportunity for counseling, coaching, and two-way discussion. For companies with step increases, they also appear to have motivation value—at least until the employee reaches the maximum rate for his or her job.

The findings of this study with respect to the actual practices of most companies are consistent with the views of Professor Herbert H. Meyer. He cited research findings related to the concept of self-esteem, which also raise more serious questions about the effectiveness of a merit pay plan.[4] He wrote that a merit pay salary plan is likely to have the effect of threatening the self-esteem of the great majority of employees, because most employees consider their work above average, and will therefore not receive the rewards they feel their performance justifies. There would then be employee relations disadvantages to administering merit pay plans as theoretically intended. In fact, Meyer recommended giving "all employees judged to be performing at a satisfactory level the same percentage increase whenever salaries are adjusted upward."[5] Concerning the advantages of this recommendation, Meyer wrote:

> *A predictable salary progress schedule not only should help to reduce uncertainty about future pay but also should prevent the development of false expectations. In addition, it should minimize dysfunctional competition between individuals for favored treatment.*
>
> *Yet another major advantage of a fairly stable and predictable salary progress schedule is that it would not permit managers to rely on pay as an important motivator. It would force managers instead to acquire skills in more effective ways of motivating individuals, such as giving them added responsibilities or allowing them to participate in decision-making.[6]*

This system, Meyer felt, would focus employee attention on the work itself rather than on the pay.

This study has indicated that many of the companies in it are doing what Meyer recommended. Therefore, they do not have the employee relations disadvantages of a "properly administered" merit pay plan. They are also freed from the risk of employee feelings or perceptions of favoritism or of discrimination. The fact that so many of the companies studied are administering their merit pay plans for their production and maintenance employees as they do is undoubtedly an employee relations advantage, or at least not a disadvantage for them.

---

[4]Meyer, "The Pay-for-Performance Dilemma," 42.
[5]Meyer, "The Pay-for-Performance Dilemma," 46.
[6]Meyer, "The Pay-for-Performance Dilemma," 46.

If there are to be effective merit systems, they would certainly seem to make more sense for jobs where the worker has control over the output, as opposed to jobs that are machine paced. As one vice-president of personnel said: "Automatic increases rather than merit increases are a procedure better suited to paced production work, where the individual's output is subject to technological control." It is clear that for a merit system to work, it needs to be accompanied by a performance-appraisal system that is understandable and in which people have confidence. This would seem to be the case at the company discussed earlier that uses a system through its maturity curves that combines merit with seniority.

If merit pay is to be effective, in addition to having the above conditions and an adequate merit pool, it would seem to be a wise practice to grant a merit increase on the employee's anniversary date or birthday, as opposed to the practice of granting all employees a merit increase based on their performance at the same time of year. This way, it would seem more like individual treatment rather than a general increase; the other way is too much like general increases being given in disguised merit form. Moreover, if the increase involves an opportunity for employee–supervisor communication, spreading the individual increases throughout the year will fit a supervisor's schedule better than bunching them all together at the same time.

A step system with fixed increments of some percentage or so many cents per hour also assumes a merit increase budget set at the beginning of the year. Otherwise, there would be complaints of inequities if, for example, some employees received larger merit increases in March than other employees (whose work performance was comparable) received in September, simply because of the economic conditions of the company at two different times of the year. While in favor of spreading increases throughout the year, it is one senior personnel manager's view that it would be a mistake to give increases on an employee's anniversary date or birthdate, believing that this practice would lock a company into an annual expectation on the part of employees, which can be avoided by individual timing guidelines based upon appraisal and position within a job's salary range—the practice of his company. If salary administration is separated from performance appraisal, and if there are clear guidelines with which the supervisor feels comfortable, perhaps this company's practice is more consistent with individual treatment and does offer some real advantages. Although appraisals would be on a regular cycle, salary reviews would not. The important question, of course, relates to the supervisors' ability to implement this approach without generating employee feelings of inequities through favoritism or discrimination.

Effective appraisals also depend upon the supervisor-to-employee ratio. If it is one-to-ten, the chances of good appraisals are much better than if there is one supervisor for every fifty employees. Effective appraisals also depend on systematic and useful supervisor training programs, which spend much time on how to conduct performance-evaluation interviews.

Another wise practice is to separate performance appraisal for improvement and career development purposes from performance appraisal for salary administration purposes in time. Many of the companies studied have done this, and personnel executives and supervisors have commented upon this practice in favorable terms. However, such separation can be difficult. It is difficult to get some supervisors to do an appraisal if it is not needed to obtain an increase for their people. One personnel manager said: "We tell managers to separate the appraisal rating from the pay increase, but some do not."

How merit plans *actually* work is important, not only for academic reasons but for practical ones as well. One reason is that there is a school of thought that holds that marginal workers are the easiest target for a union organizer attempting to get a foothold in a company. If this school of thought is correct, it becomes very important to have good performance appraisals or to treat everyone, even the marginal worker, the same. In fact, most of the companies studied do have regular performance-appraisal reviews for their hourly workers. A few companies are at different stages in implementation of management-by-objectives systems at the hourly level.

It has to be recognized and emphasized that it is difficult to measure performance with some jobs, and even when it is not, supervisors are reluctant to give honest feedback to employees for a variety of reasons, particularly if the feedback is negative. (For instance, many white supervisors find it difficult to give negative feedback to minority employees.) Also, as Meyer and others have written, most employees consider themselves "above average."

Therefore, perhaps it is understandable as well as inevitable that supervisors not only want specific guidelines but also tend to give automatic increases relating much more to seniority than to performance. Such systems are easy to administer and are, in a sense, "fair." Equal treatment, then, replaces individual treatment —it is "fair" to treat everyone the same, or at least about the same. Thus, it is quite understandable why many of the companies that claim they are merit pay organizations are not "full of merit." Moreover, this is probably a good thing in terms of employee relations.

While this view may be too extreme, perhaps a merit pay system is largely a popular myth in many companies. Even though a merit pay system is difficult (or all but impossible) to administer, it is a nice thing in which to believe. Also, if the company does not actually administer it as intended, a merit pay system will not cause any real trouble. Managers may like to believe that theirs is a merit company—like motherhood, apple pie, and ice cream, who can be against the merit principle? What member of top management wants to admit publicly that theirs is not a merit company?

While some employees undoubtedly interpret their merit increases as cost-of-living or longevity increases, perhaps others, particularly those interested in promotion, prefer to think of their increases as a result of good personal performance, even though their co-workers may have gotten the same increase. If they compare the size of their increase with the size of their co-workers' increases, perhaps all they really want to know is that they were treated the same: no better or no worse.

If even the minimal performer (the marginal or inefficient worker) in a company committed to keeping unions out receives an average increase, perhaps it will help keep him or her from turning to an outside organizer, without destroying the morale of the high performer at the same time. The high performer perhaps receives recognition in other ways: through praise from the supervisor, interesting assignments, and possibly through promotional opportunities that are not always so directly tied to seniority as they might be at a unionized company. The real payoffs with respect to motivation in these companies must lie in the nonfinancial area and in the area of promotional opportunities.

However, for some jobs in some companies it is also difficult to make and/or explain promotion decisions on an ability basis. As has been noted in Chapter 7, the merit principle with respect to promotions seems to have eroded in some companies, because more weight is being given to seniority and, in some cases, to the principles of affirmative action.

In sum, while the merit principle may indeed be only a myth, it may be an important myth, having symbolic significance for management and nonmanagement of nonunion companies.

CHAPTER TEN

The Salaried Method
of Payment

Approximately half of the companies studied do not have hourly employees. Blue-collar workers at these companies are salaried. In addition, two other companies have one or two experimental all-salaried plants. Some of the companies that do not have salary plans do have policies regarding payment for illness that are almost as protective as, as good as, or sometimes even superior to, the policies of some of the salary companies. However, like merit pay, salary plans mean different things to different companies. Moreover, they are administered in different ways.

The practice of giving salary status to blue-collar workers represents an attempt to get away from the "we–they" distinction between management and labor and between office and plant employees. Giving everyone salary status is consistent with the principle of equal treatment. Salary plans not only give added income security to the employee, but can also give the employee psychological or status advantages because they generally differentiate a company from other companies in its industry or community.

Though many executives label their companies as salaried companies, the term is used rather loosely. The salaried method of payment at one company may be very different from the salaried method of another. For example, salary status at one company may mean that the employee is entitled to five days of sick pay, at another company it may mean that ten days are given, or at other companies there may be no such limits. In short, some plans are more restrictive than others.

Another variable is that the limits in some companies are more generous in practice than by policy. Also, when some managers say that their employees are salaried, they mean that at their company there no longer is a time clock for blue collar employees, while other salary companies have retained the time clock for record-keeping purposes.

Although they vary, the salary plans and some other comparable programs at many of the companies studied offer employees significant additional income and psychological security. Moreover, most salary plans are consistent with the philosophy of individual respect and dignity and with the principle of equal treatment or no double standards. At these companies today it is not considered right to treat nonexempt employees differently from exempt employees.

However, salary protection or continuation plans are a relatively recent development in the history of the companies studied. No plan is more than twenty-five years old. These plans began to appear in the mid- to late-1950s. This chapter will not only examine the different salary plans as well as some of the approaches of the nonsalary plan companies, it will also discuss their functions and the companies' experiences with them.

MORE RESTRICTIVE PLANS

Although the salary companies pay their employees "salaries" rather than "wages," investigation of these pay plans reveals major differences in their provisions. Some of the plans pay for a few days of absence; however, they are sometimes administered more liberally than the policy states.

Attendance Bonus Plan

One company, for example, states in its employee handbook that "all employees . . . are paid on a salary basis." Yet, in the same handbook under the subject heading "Attendance Bonus Plan," it states:

> Office, clerical, technical, production, and maintenance employees are eligible for up to five days of paid time off for absence due to personal illness or personal business under the Attendance Bonus Plan. However, perfect attendance is encouraged by providing cash payment for each unused portion of the employee's leave allowance at the end of each year. At the employee's option, the unused portion may be carried over and saved in a "Bank" for use in the next or following years.

One not only notes the fact that absence for personal business as well as for illness is covered, but also the principle of equal treatment: Office and plant employees are treated alike. However, it should also be noted that this company's short-term disability plan provides that if an employee is totally disabled, is unable to perform all of the duties of his or her occupation due to accidental injury or sickness, and is under the care of a physician, an employee who has been with the company for one year or longer will receive 75 percent of his or her basic salary up to a maximum of thirteen weeks. If an employee has been with the company for less than one year, he or she will receive 50 percent of his or her basic salary. In the case of disability caused by sickness, the benefits begin on the eighth day, or on the day following the last day of compensable absence under the company's paid absence plan, whichever is later.

Paid Absence Allowance

Another salary company has a similar plan. Its policy statement reads:

Paid absence allowance is granted by the Company to compensate you for time lost due to the following circumstances:

Your illness
Illness of a member of your immediate family which requires your presence at home
Other personal reasons

During the calendar year of your hire, you will be allowed Paid Absence Allowance in accordance with the following table:

Length of Service		Paid Allowance Absence
At Least	Less Than	
0 month	3 months	0
3 months	5 months	1 day
5 months	7 months	2 days
7 months	9 months	3 days
9 months	11 months	4 days
11 months		5 days

A Paid Absence Allowance of five days will be granted to you at the beginning of your second and each subsequent calendar year of employment.

At the beginning of the following year you will be paid by check for any Paid Absence Allowance which you have not used by December 31st.

At the discretion of your Foreman or Supervisor, you may be paid for absences beyond your allotted Paid Absence Allowance.

Lateness, absence during the shift, and early departure may be charged to your Paid Absence Allowance.

Whether you are using your Paid Absence Allowance or not, if you are unable to report for work, you are required to notify your Department at your earliest opportunity, but not later than one hour after the start of your regular shift. Absences due to reasons other than illness require advance approval.

In the past at this company it was extremely rare to pay a person who was sick anything more than the five days the policy provided; new people are frequently paid beyond the five days, not only for sickness but for personal days as well. A project manager who had been with this company for ten years said: "Sick pay is administered with compassion. A lot of employees get more than five days." This manager also talked about the company's fine medical department, and cited the case of an employee the company had sent to the Mayo Clinic for an examination, at no cost to the employee. This, too, was above and beyond the terms of the company's benefit plan. In addition, this company also has short- and long-term disability income plans for when the employee is unable to work due to a nonoccupational accident or illness. Of the company's 25,000 employees, less than 6,000 still use a time clock to punch in and out each day. The majority fill out their own time cards.

At another company, which has been gradually extending its salary plan to all of its plants as it gains experience and solves the problems it encounters, employees who are paid weekly salaries are permitted a maximum of ten day's paid absence during a year for acceptable reasons, such as sickness and personal emergency. The removal of time clocks accompanied the introduction of this company's salary plan. Supervisors have the responsibility of determining whether or not an absence should be paid. For example, a decision must be made whether a late arrival is to be counted as a half-day absence, or recorded as paid or unpaid lateness. Much supervisory training in making these decisions has been associated with the introduction of the plan. This company's absence rate for sickness only was 1.5 percent before the introduction of the salary plan. While it increased to 2.3 percent immediately after the plan had been adopted, it subsequently declined to 2 percent.

Another company's salary program provides each employee who has been with the company a year or more with ten days for illness. Unlike the practice of some of the other companies, these days cannot be accumulated from year to year. This program is tied into the company's salary continuation program, which provides two-thirds of an employee's base pay for the first six months of illness, and one-half of his or her pay thereafter. With respect to the ten days of paid absence allowance, the company's personnel director believed there is very little abuse of the company's program. The average number of days per year that employees in the company are absent had been running at approximately 6.5 days.

MORE LIBERAL PLANS

At the other end of the spectrum is the company whose policy is:

Beginning with the first regular weekday of reported absence, this Plan
[the company's sickness and accident plan] will provide you with your regular

salary for each day absent to a maximum of fifty-two weeks in a period of twenty-four consecutive months. After these Sickness and Accident Income payments cease, each case is considered individually.

This very liberal plan covers regular employees starting on the first day of employment. In order to receive benefits, an employee absent for more than three consecutive workdays must, upon request, submit a certificate of disability from his or her physician to be eligible for any further benefits for that particular absence. If the employee is convalescing at home from a period of sickness or accident, he or she must report to the company in person, by telephone, or by letter, at least once a week during this convalescence. If the convalescence is away from his or her place of residence, the employee must furnish the company with a physician's statement telling the company why such an absence is necessary. The company, in deciding whether the employee is entitled to benefits, may require an examination by a physician of the company's choice.

The policy of another company is similar to that of the previous one, but for the fact that the maximums are only half as good. It states that:

Full-time and part-time permanent employees are covered from date of hire. The plan provides payment of regular base salary for each day absent up to 26 weeks (or 182 consecutive days) in any 12 consecutive months. An employee is eligible to receive payments for illness or injury which results in absence. Time off for any other reasons will not be reimbursed under this plan. The Company, at its option, may require confirmation that the employee was absent because of sickness or accident.

Thus this company, from day one, provides sick pay for legitimate illness of up to 26 weeks or 182 consecutive days, whereas the other company's plan will pay to a maximum of 52 weeks in a period of 24 months.

In between the plans of these two companies and the ones discussed earlier is the very different policy of still another company. What appears in one of its six employee handbooks, entitled "Your Pay" is:

If a regular employee or part-time employee scheduled to work twenty or more hours a week is absent because of illness or injury, he or she will, with department head approval, receive full pay (base salary, cost of living, shift differential bonus, and extended consecutive workday bonus) according to the following table.

Provisional employees, with department head approval, may receive full pay (as defined earlier) for up to one week and 65% of full pay for the next three months of absence.

Your department head may ask that your illness be verified by your personal physician before illness pay is authorized.

When an absence exceeds a week for provisional employees or a month for regular employees and eligible part-time employees, illness pay forms will

Years of Service	Number of Months at Full Pay	Number of Months at 65% of Full Pay
0-1	1	3
1-2	3	3
2-3	3	4
3-4	3	5
4-5	3	6
5-6	3	7
6-7	3	8
7-8	3	9
8-9	3	10
9-10	3	11
10 or more	3	12

be mailed to you. One is to be filled out by you; and another, by your personal or family physician. Both forms should then be returned to the pay operations department. Also, another illness pay form will be mailed to your physician each succeeding month of your absence.

A group leader who has been with the company for twenty-seven years said that: "The company's approach can't be beat. No one could offer you any more. You get three months' pay when you are sick, then insurance."

The salary plan of another company, adopted in 1955, is quite liberal. The company policy states that "Continuance of salary payment is provided to protect employees against loss of pay because of absence due to illness or injury." This company's disability plan is its salary plan. The absent employee's weekly salary will continue as long as management, at its discretion only, considers that "there is a reasonable prospect of the employee returning to his former job." At this company, employees absent for extended periods of time even participate in the company's general-increase program.

Again, while the plan states that there must be a reasonable prospect of the employee returning to his or her former job, the evidence suggests that the word "reasonable" is interpreted liberally. If there is *not* a reasonable prospect, under this plan, the employee will receive half of his or her salary until age 65.

However, the salary plan does have a qualification, which is that payments to the employee cannot go on any longer than the amount of time the employee has been with the company. For example, an employee who has been with the company for only five months could not receive more than five months' pay, even if he or she was legitimately ill for eight months.

To minimize employee abuse of the plan, company guidelines establish a twelve-day annual standard for absence control. The purpose of the guidelines was to help supervisors decide whether an employee should be paid for personal absence, or whether remedial action should be taken if someone appears to be abusing the salary program. The twelve days are divided into shorter periods, and the employee's supervisor reviews the records to determine when an employee's absence rate is running ahead of standard. Both the number of absences and the number of days of absence are reviewed.

When the manager of metal finishing was asked about the way the plan works, the reply was that:

> *Some people take advantage of the salary system. They abuse it. There is a regular attendance chart. One manager foolishly posts it on his wall so that his employees know when the warnings will come. I keep my attendance book locked up. Absenteeism generally runs about four and-a-half percent.*

Another manager, asked about the guidelines, said:

> *The attendance guidelines give you the equitables. There are three-month, six-month, and one-year guidelines. It is strictly numbers. If you are out four days on two separate occasions, you are outside the guidelines. The employee gets a verbal contact. If, however, you are out two times, three days each, you're not outside the guidelines. The attendance guidelines relate to the number of days and the frequency.*

Still another manager, when asked the same question, said:

> *The employee does not know the precise guidelines. But it takes six months to go from one disciplinary step to the next. For temporary employees, however, the discipline procedure is different. There you can go from a verbal directly to a final.*
>
> *But we bend over backward before discharging anyone. There are exceptions. For example, take the case of a 20-year man with an honest back injury. In that case, we do not rigorously follow the attendance guidelines.*

Two researchers investigating the administration of this company's plan found that:

> *The twelve-day limit is an informal one, but understandably, the guidelines do not apply to a long absence for sickness. Payments for absence beyond the guidelines continue, provided valid reasons are forthcoming. However, excessive absences may become the basis for managerial action— for example, a warning meeting, counseling, or dismissal.*

Commenting on the history of the plan and the company's experience with it, the researchers wrote:

> *The idea of an all-salaried work force rose directly from a review in 1955 of sick leave benefits. At the time of review, the absence rate of 4.6*

percent among production employees compared with one of 3.5 percent for salaried personnel.

[ ] initial increase in the total rate of absenteeism to 5 percent, a figure management believed to be reasonable for a change expected to have a beneficial effect on worker attitudes. Actually, absenteeism among production workers did not increase significantly immediately after the introduction of the new plan and has since settled at 4.7 percent, only marginally above the original rate.

Although they seem to make the job of the supervisor more difficult, liberal salary plans seem to have very positive employee-relations consequences, and they can visibly distinguish the company from others. One of the supervisors interviewed at the above company believed that the company's salary plan was the keystone of the company's benefits, commenting that:

> *A woman who has been with us for thirty-two years has terminal cancer. She has been absent for one and-a-half years. Yet, she is still receiving her salary. Employees hired from other companies cannot believe that you get paid when you are sick here. A rubber company closed its plant and we hired many of the men laid off. One said that the rubber company's plant was filthy, the rest rooms were dirty, and you had a brown-bag lunch. He said to me that he couldn't believe that here there is a cafeteria where you can get a hot lunch, there are good working conditions, and you get paid when you are sick.*

This supervisor said that a small group of employees do abuse the system, but that the annual perfect-attendance dinners the company gives are very crowded. If the employee has perfect attendance for a year, he or she receives a $50 savings bond and is invited to the company dinner. A manager of electrical and air conditioning maintenance, when questioned about the perfect-attendance dinners, said:

> *There is a $50 bond and a dinner for the employee who has perfect attendance for a year. The guy also gets the day of the dinner off. But some employees objected to the fact that on their day off they had to come to the plant for the dinner. Now, therefore, the dinner is optional. The company now lets you take any day off instead of only the day of the dinner.*

Yet another company's salary approach is different still, providing up to thirteen weeks of full and partial pay, according to service. Supervisors must use their discretion in deciding whether to pay for absences. While there are guidelines, when emergencies such as death, critical illness, or family emergencies or obligations overweigh the employee's obligation to the job, it is the company's policy to pay for the time taken to deal with them. Moreover, even in the case of unauthorized absences, dealt with through the company's disciplinary procedures, pay is not withheld for disciplinary reasons except in the case of a formal suspension. In the early days of this company's salary program, supervisors were hesitant to make these decisions. Investigating also the operation of this plan, the researchers who investigated the previous company found that:

> . . . [the supervisors] generally took the easy way out, when in doubt, by paying for time off. . . . six weeks after the program, a heavy . . . snow prevented many employees from getting to work. The program guidelines did not explain how to handle this type of crisis situation clearly enough for the supervisors and, consequently, a number of problems developed.
>
> Before the program, an employee was paid for the day if he made it to work in spite of the snow but was then sent home. Those who failed to get in at all were not paid. Under the program, some supervisors were not sure whether to pay those who stayed home, and inconsistencies developed (all should have been paid). To prevent recurrences of this kind, management developed additional, specific training materials to help supervisors make payment decisions, and in this way they alleviated a principal problem.
>
> After the company worked out the initial problems, [the company's] supervisors liked the change. One aspect of the new program that they particularly appreciated was their increased authority to grant requests for paid personal time off. Before the program, supervisors could grant only a half-day absence for the most serious emergency. They now have the authority to authorize time off when they believe it is really needed.

While this point will be made later, the discretion that salary plans give to supervisors is by no means insignificant. While some supervisors resent the loss of control associated with the removal of time clocks, they like the additional authority that accompanies the salary plan.

Yet another salary company, one without time clocks, gives its employees five days of paid sick leave every six months. This time may be accumulated. The employee handbook states:

> Sick leave is not an earned benefit, but one which is granted by the company to assure you of income during periods when you are unable to work due to illness or injury. Following each six months' active full-time service, you are eligible for five days of sick leave. Unused sick leave may be accumulated up to a maximum of ninety days. Remember, sick leave is to be used only during periods of illness and is not taken solely because it is provided.

In 1975, this company changed its policy so that there is no limit on the amount of sick leave the employee may accumulate. Moreover, the policy provides that one-half of the unused balance is payable to the employee at age 65. While employees like the fact that sick leave may be accumulated without limit, some of them, according to one employee interviewed, think it is unfair that only half of the accrued days are payable to the employee at age 65. They believe the payment should be for the total amount.

At a plant of this company, it was said that absenteeism and turnover were very low. This company also has flexible working hours for all of its employees. When asked if there particularly were misunderstood, the personnel manager said:

> There is some abuse, particularly at the lower levels. But we do not want to design policies for everyone based on the 5 percent who abuse the freedom our people have.

One worker, asked about these policies, said:

> The company is very fair. It has been good to me. I had my physical the other day. I was paid for the hour it took—it was put on sick leave. The company checks the employee's record, and gives time off with pay to the good employees. The company takes the view that if you are involved in civic affairs, the company pays you. I am a volunteer fireman in town, and I've always been paid.
> Flexible hours are great. There is, however, some cheating. I would say about 1 percent. What happens then is that the man's co-workers do not only put a lot of pressure on him, but also go to the boss and tell him.

A different company's salary plan commenced after an employee had been with the company for three months, at which time the employee, after seven days of illness, was eligible for a small weekly payment from the company's Mutual Benefit Association and for supplemental payments up to full salary from the company disability plan. The Mutual Benefit Association, it should be added, had a board of government of its own. Representatives were elected; this became "a great outlet for people with leadership qualities," stated the company's vice-president of personnel. To an extent this association provided an outlet for the informal leaders who might otherwise become union leaders. "The work," commented the vice-president, "has to be real work which is challenging—it can't be make-work. Our people take their work very seriously." The income sources of the Mutual Benefit Association were employee dues, assessments, and the profits from most of the vending machines in company plants.

Long ago, this company also established a plant disability board consisting of two company officials and three elected employees. This board interpreted company policies on the disability plan, could hear employee appeals, and was considered very powerful. An employee was free to bring his or her doctor or lawyer to the meetings. The composition of this board demonstrates much trust in employees on the part of top management, and power and responsibility are being shared.

The company's disability plan specifies that an employee with more than ten years of service would receive full pay for one year; one with more than five years of service would receive three-quarters of his or her pay for a year; while an employee with less than five years of service would receive full pay for thirteen weeks, and half pay for thirty-nine weeks. In addition, an absence plan provides for the first five days of illness at the discretion of department heads.

Illustrating the role of the supervisors, the policies that guide them, and the great differences among company salary plans, yet another company's policies divide absences into three categories: (1) personal emergencies, (2) borderline cases, and (3) absence for the convenience of the employee. With respect to absences for personal emergencies, the supervisor is allowed to authorize payment for the lost time if the employee has been meeting company attendance standards and the absence occurs for a sufficiently pressing reason over which the employee actually has no control. With respect to borderline cases such as absences for reasons such as an appointment to handle a mortgage closing, to obtain a driver's license, to attend a child's graduation, or to take a family member to the hospital other than in an emergency, the employee may or may not be paid, at the discretion of the supervisor. Supervisors are told that: "The determining factors, in addition to the reason for the absence, should be the employee's overall performance and regularity of attendance as well as the frequency with which absences for personal reasons occur." While permission for personal absences that are purely for the convenience of the employee may be granted, such absences are without pay. Finally, company policy states that payment for personal reasons should normally not exceed two days per calendar year. However, the policy also states that in certain cases "the length of paid absence may be predicated on the individual circumstances, taking into account the employee's overall record." The supervisor is also told that he or she:

> . . . should make every effort to see that his [or her] decisions covering payment or nonpayment are made on the basis of an impartial, fair, and carefully considered judgment in each case. It is also the supervisor's responsibility to see that each employee understands he is "on his honor" where explanations of absence are concerned and that this privilege is not to be abused.

While this company's absenteeism goal is 5 percent, in 1976 absenteeism was unexpectedly averaging about 3.6 percent.

NONSALARY PLAN COMPANIES

One company that does not consider itself a salary company has a plan under which benefits are, for many of its employees, equivalent to those provided by many salary companies. Once an employee has been with the company for six months, he or she is eligible for five sick days. After two years, the employee receives ten sick days and this gradually builds up, based on length of service, so that an employee with ten years' service is eligible for fifty-five sick days. Then, like some of the other companies previously discussed, upon expiration of his or her sick days the employee is subsequently eligible for short-term disability benefits—and then, if needed, long-term disability benefits.

The top personnel officer at one company mentioned that their company was working toward the implementation of a salary concept:

> Now the benefits are really the same between the hourly and the salaried groups except for the fact that there are unequal vacations. Hourly people also have a sickness allowance plan. But hourly people do have to use time clocks which are an irritant to the individual. We will eventually remove the time clocks.

This person seemed to equate the presence of time clocks with the absence of a salary plan.

Another company's accident-and-illness plan provides that employees who are paid biweekly, and who are unable to work because of illness or off-the-job accidents for periods under six months, are eligible for paid absence benefits if they have more than three months of full-time service. While the waiting periods are waived if the employee is hospitalized, the paid absence allowances are:

Length of Employment	Paid Absence for Each Year
4 months to 1 year	5 days (after 2-day waiting period)
1 year to 2 years	10 days (after 1-day waiting period)
2 years to 5 years	10 days each year
5 years to 10 years	20 days each year
10 years and over	65 days each year

One-half of the unused time each year is accumulated and added to the total time for which payments will be made. However, the total of current and accumulated time cannot exceed six months, at which time the employee begins to receive payments under the company's long-term accident-and-illness plan. This company also has the benefits that the so-called salary companies offer.

One nonsalary company that is keeping its new plants nonunion has a weekly sick-pay plan, which provides that an employee, on the first day of the month after he or she is employed, is eligible for eighty percent of his or her base straight-time weekly pay up to $65 per week. This benefit is payable for a maximum of twenty-six weeks, beginning on the fourth day of an off-the-job illness or injury, provided that the employee is under the care of a licensed doctor.

The sickness-and-accident insurance plan of a different nonsalary company provides that an employee who has completed six months of continuous service, and who is absent due to an illness or injury, will receive an amount that depends on his or her annual base pay rate, reduced by any amount of money he or she may be eligible for under any law providing compulsory occupational or nonoccupational disability benefits, including social security.

The most an individual employee can collect is for twenty-six weeks; sickness benefits begin from the eighth day of disability, or after pay stops, if later. However, this company also has a sickness-and-personal-leave plan that provides pay for up to five full days of excused absence, with an attendance bonus providing pay for unused days. This company, then, has everything some of the "salary" companies have.

Another nonsalary company's disability income plan reads:

> *For nonwork-connected illness and injury requiring days off from work, the Plan provides for salary continuation of from two weeks at full pay to twelve weeks at full pay, and forty weeks at half pay, depending on years of service from one to ten years. Exempt employees are eligible for benefits from date of hire, nonexempt salaried employees are eligible after thirteen weeks of employment, and nonexempt hourly employees are eligible after one year of employment.*

Note not only the eligibility period in this company's plan, but also how different the eligibility is depending upon employee classification.

Another nonsalary company's plan provides that if an employee is sick and unable to work, he or she may receive full pay up to six months, and under certain conditions, the period may be extended. Although there is no waiting period before one can start collecting, the new employee has to work for the company for a year before this policy applies.

As this discussion has indicated, these nonsalary companies have sickness and illness benefits that are equivalent to the benefits provided by the salary companies in many cases. However, they do not necessarily pay for personal time off, nor do they provide the psychological benefits associated with the absence of a time clock. Moreover, in some cases factory workers and office staff are treated differently.

ADDITIONAL CONSIDERATIONS

No Layoff Benefits

The discussion to this point has primarily concentrated on the sick-leave and absence policies of different "salaried" and "nonsalaried" companies. Nothing has been said about salaries or benefits during periods of layoff, for this study discovered not one plan providing such benefits. At the salary companies that have experienced layoffs, the salary status of production workers does not prevent them from either being laid off, nor does it prevent the associated loss of income. In this sense, at these companies the production workers, even with their salary status, are not necessarily the equivalent of management or of office workers. Indeed, many of the full-employment companies are salaried companies, where the issue of a reduction in the work force has not arisen. However, in cases where salaried companies have had layoffs, the employees so affected have not received any benefits from the company, although sometimes the company has continued to pay the employee's sickness-and-accident insurance for some set period of time.

Morale and Administrative Problems

Perhaps too much has been focused on sickness and accident benefits. While sickness, absence, and personal leave are associated with salary plans, perhaps what is more important is the demise of the time clock, and the fact that the employee is not docked if he or she is late for work or is absent for a good reason. These privileges and the feeling of equal treatment can undoubtedly go a long way toward creating a climate of trust and confidence.

Many executives claim that the significance of an all-salaried work force is not the method of payment but the philosophy of managing all the employees the same way. However, it was reported that better trained and stronger supervisors will be needed if the company makes a commitment to an all-salaried work force. As one executive said:

> With an all-salaried concept the company is constantly putting supervisors into situations of conflict that they were not exposed to before. For example, do away with time clocks and now the supervisor is subjected to at least four times a day a potential conflict with the employee if he is not on the job as he should be. The time clock, you must remember, takes away the question of judgment and conflict in ninety percent of the situations.

The fact that all employees are paid by the same method is not the critical variable—rather, what is important is the climate of respect, trust, and confidence. In discussing the company's experimental all-salaried plant, the vice-president of personnel of a predominantly nonunion company made the point well:

> The salary plan itself is not what makes the difference. It really demands almost an entirely different philosophy on the part of the plant managers and the supervisors if it is to be successful. This means that you have to select very carefully the management of the plant and provide them with the necessary training to assure that they have a good insight into the method of management which is supportive of an all-salaried concept.

Perhaps the comments of some of the supervisors interviewed well reveal some of the psychological dimensions of putting employees on salary status. When asked about one company's salary plan, a press operator manager, who started his career with the company after World War II as a press operator, said:

> The salary plan is the greatest thing that ever happened. It is a full-salary plan. It pays you when you are absent and you are not docked when you are late.

About the company's adoption of its salary plan, this manager said: "It came after the union drive." About the administration of the plan in general, and about discipline for attendance problems in particular, he said:

> *If you are out more than a year you participate in the increases. There are guidelines on attendance. You get a verbal, a written, and a final. But you have to let these stages go for six months.*

Another supervisor at this company, who had also been an hourly worker, talked about the company's history, the salary plan, and the union drives:

> *In the 1940s, the company would shut down departments for some months and you got transferred to other departments if you were lucky. Back in those days there was no seniority policy. If you were a good worker, it kept you. Back in those days there was no performance review. If the boss liked you, you got a nickel raise.*
>
> *The union people walked up and down the street. Every time they did so things got better. The company offered the salary plan and the union people said, "See, as soon as you talk union you get something." But now you can get the advantages of a union by not paying dues. We act as if there is a union here. There is no favoritism.*

Speaking specifically about the salary plan, the same supervisor said:

> *It is great. In the old days, only foremen and up were on the salary plan. The company made the workers here just as equal as the managers. They have the same benefits as the managers. Workers get a week's pay at Christmas. In the old days, managers used to get more. People have done well as far as the salary plan goes. . . . The benefits here are also excellent.*

Most of the salary-plan companies do not have time clocks, which have been replaced by time cards. (However, some salary companies have retained the time clock because management finds it helpful in record keeping. It is useful for accounting purposes, and it also helps supervisors control lateness and absenteeism.) Elimination of the time clock serves to blur, lessen, or eradicate the distinction between management and the workers, and between blue-collar workers and white-collar workers, because everyone is treated the same. As one company president put it:

> *The dignity and worth of the individual is a very important part of [our] way. With this in mind, many years ago we did away with time clocks, and more recently we introduced the flexible work hours program. Flexible, or gliding, time was originated within the company at our plant in Germany. Later, it was tried for six months or so at [one] division, and this year made available throughout much of the company. Again, this is meant to be an*

expression of trust and confidence in [company] people, as well as providing them with an opportunity to adjust their work schedules to their personal lives.

Interestingly, at one company with an employee-representation plan, when management was about to eliminate the time clocks, the employees protested. The employees did not want the time clocks withdrawn, saying that when there was a question about the hours worked and whether or not one was present, the time clocks constitute proof. Consequently, management retained the time clocks. (Perhaps these employees' concerns also say something about the climate of this company.)

Supervisors at another company talked about "the good old days" when the company had time clocks. Without them, they said, their jobs had become much more difficult. One supervisor commented:

> *There is a tendency for individuals to take advantage of [no time clocks]. Most people are in three locations. So the real situation is not two ten-minute breaks but breaks of twenty to thirty minutes. Lunch is supposed to be thirty minutes, but it is more like forty-five to sixty minutes. And people leave at 3 o' clock when they are supposed to stay until 3:30, although some of that could be considered shift relief.*

Regarding the company's time card system, another supervisor said, "The employee supposedly signs it each day but in fact an employee may sign it for three days at a time."

In admitting much abuse of the system, one supervisor did say that "no time clocks go with the philosophy of the company, which is liberal." This company unified the way hourly and salaried employees were treated in the mid-1960s, when the absence rate for workers affected by the plan was 5 percent. After the plan the absence rate advanced to 6 percent, where it remained for several years. In 1976, the company's absenteeism goal was 3.5 percent, although actual absenteeism was averaging 7 percent.

An industrial engineer at a company that has had a salary plan for almost twenty years, when asked about absenteeism, said: "Our target is 4 percent—sometimes, however, it is as high as 8 percent or 9 percent." A tool room manager, a person with a high school education who started with this company in 1951 as a burr-bench operator on a milling machine, offered this comment about absenteeism and the company's salary plan:

> *Most people who get fired get fired for absenteeism. The goal is 3 percent or 4 percent but if you have a five-man department and one man has a heart attack you have trouble.*
>
> *The company didn't always pay for the first three days. Now it pays from the first day's absence and this has caused some short-term abuse. In addition, the manager has the discretion to grant the employee up to five days*

off with pay for personal business. At any funeral in this area, four out of six
pallbearers will be from this company. This is because our people get paid.

When an employee does not have to punch a time clock, and is paid when ill or at a co-worker's funeral, he or she is being treated as a mature adult, as well as being treated the same way as the executives. To the extent that this is not offered by other companies in the community, it may be especially appreciated.

The way this latter company administers its policy also illustrates the latitude and discretion given to the supervisor. While the supervisor has guidelines to follow, he or she is permitted to grant days off for personal matters without checking with anyone in higher management or in the personnel department. This authority gives the supervisor added credibility, and surely makes him or her more than a "straw boss" in the eyes of the employees.

However, as has been indicated, I did hear of attendance problems and abuses of the salary plan at a number of companies. A company physician at one division that has had a salary plan for over twenty years, said that absenteeism has recently been averaging about 5.6 percent. It used to average about 2.2 percent. This doctor said that a member of top management asked if the work force is more sickness-prone today than in years past. The doctor replied: "They are not more sick. It is both the change in attitudes and the composition of the labor force which is responsible for the higher rate."

The vice-president of personnel at a salary company where absenteeism is running approximately 5 percent admits that there is some abuse:

> *It is like when you give employees free sandwiches for lunch. A few*
> *employees will stuff extra sandwiches in their pockets.*

However, overall this person does believe that the company gains from its salary plan. If a company adopts a full-salary plan, however, it must expect that there will be some employees who will abuse it.

A skilled trades supervisor at another company told of his problems administering the company's policies with respect to absence:

> *A "PI" day is a personal illness day. You are paid without any*
> *questions asked as long as the absence is under three-and-a-half percent.*
> *When the employee calls in and you make a big deal, the employee says, "Are*
> *you trying to tell me I'm not sick?"*
> *In many cases, I feel that the hourly people run the company . . . I've*
> *worked in a union shop. There you are told what to do. It is suspension, then*
> *discharge. With a union, it is all cut and dried. Here, it is harder. Here, the*
> *employee has a better deal than with the union.*

While few supervisors interviewed did not complain of attendance problems they felt were complicated by their company's salary plan, the managements of the companies studied do not think that their absence experience is out of line with respect to industry in general. In fact, the managements of these companies think their experience with attendance is generally better than the experience of their competitors and of the other large companies in their communities.

The possibility of abuse does cause a dilemma for management. On the one hand, if too many rules and procedures are issued to check up on absent employees, they could not only create ill will but also violate the spirit of the plan. But on the other hand, if there is excessive abuse and some employees are allowed to get away with it, this lack of equity could upset those employees who do not abuse the plan. Clearly, there is a need for some guidelines with respect to both the frequency and the duration of absences, so that whatever abuse does occur is at a tolerable level.

CONCLUDING ANALYSIS AND COMMENTS

A company wanting to have all of its employees on salaried status can choose one of three approaches: (1) It can have a liberal salary plan—no time clocks, and payment for time not worked for legitimate reasons; (2) it can have a salary plan with tight sickness and accident controls; or (3) it can have a short-term and long-term sickness-and-accident plan, and a personal-leave plan.

Although it can not be proven, and while there are administrative problems and some abuse, higher morale appears to go with the first approach—a liberal salary plan. Workers have a status advantage over workers in most other companies, and are perhaps better able to identify with the goals of the organization. Moreover, management is making a broad commitment to them. The plans and the ways they are administered demonstrate that management has faith in the workers and is treating them equally, and as responsible adults. Having no time clocks, not being docked for being late, and having the freedom to take time off for personal reasons, gives much responsibility to the individual. These plans, which are consistent with a desire to avoid the traditional we–they adversary relationship, can be a psychological and morale-building device. Flexible work hours, on top of a salary plan, give even greater freedom to the worker.

However, such plans do make life more difficult for many first-level supervisors. While liberal plans may be associated with higher employee morale, they may also carry an additional cost of lower supervisory morale. Much selling and training are required so that these plans are administered as intended. In addition to issuing attendance guidelines to supervisors, some companies have adopted perfect-attendance dinners, awards, extra cash, and days off to encourage perfect attendance. However, some supervisors think that such programs are not needed for the conscientious person, and that they do not do any good with respect to the problem employee.

While there is some abuse, the companies by and large report that they have had good experience with their salary plans. Undoubtedly, more could be said about the diversity of the salary plans discovered, the problems of implementing and administering them, and the salary-type features of the approaches used by some of the nonsalary companies. But the important issue, at least for this study, is the function these plans fulfill from an employee-relations point of view. Depending on the nature of the plan and the way it is administered, it can contribute to the development of a positive attitude, which will benefit the individual and the company.

As has been said, salary plans by themselves may not be all that important. However, because so many of the companies studied have them, they cannot be ignored. While salary plans have some very real costs, which depend on their design, they also have some benefits. And as part of a philosophy or a consistent program, they can be both significant and symbolic. As one executive put it:

> [*Adoption of a salary plan for blue-collar workers is indicative of*] *a philosophical change . . . developing employee relations practices to accommodate the 98 percent of our people who aren't going to abuse it and handling abuses on an individual basis.*
>
> *In years past, I believe, we created rules and policies based on our concern about the other 2 percent—and the 98 percent had to live with it. Today, we treat employees as mature adults and explain what our expectations are. And we've found the response is really no different among production and maintenance employees than it is among professional employees.*

As a symbol of a philosophy or of a philosophical change—and if they are seen as consistent with other policies, practices, and programs—salary plans, like the principle of equal benefits and the minimization of status symbols, can certainly play an important role. The plans, and the ways in which they are administered, can help build a climate that fosters confidence and trust in management. They can enhance the credibility of management and they can clearly differentiate the company's approach from what prevails in unionized environments.

CHAPTER ELEVEN

Benefit Policies
and Their Costs

This chapter covers benefit policies and plans—the supplements to pay. The reader will recall that part of the analytical framework was related to a comprehensive package of personnel policies and programs. The protection offered by many of the benefit programs to be discussed helps to satisfy the security needs of employees. These programs show management well-performing the traditional union role with respect to benefits and security, and in the process frequently enhancing its credibility with employees in tangible ways. This chapter begins by examining company objectives in the area of benefits, and then goes on to discuss the ways in which these plans are administered and communicated. Their costs, which are not insignificant, will also be considered.

BENEFITS AND COMPANY OBJECTIVES

The companies studied described their benefits in either "leadership" or "competitiveness" terms. Leadership objectives seem more closely associated with the philosophy-laden company; being competitive seems more closely associated with the doctrinaire company. For a variety of reasons, many companies are finding it increasingly difficult to maintain their traditional leadership posture with respect to benefits. In addition to pursuing either leadership or competitive objectives, the companies also emphasize security goals through the design and administration of their benefit plans. Moreover, many companies use benefits as one vehicle to highlight their "no-double standards" philosophy, doing so by providing equal benefits to all, whether a person is an assembly-line worker or the chief executive officer.

Leadership

A number of managers interviewed reported "firsts" and "leadership" in the benefits area. Many top managements seem to take pride in being first with a new benefit and in being perceived as a leader, or at least as an industry leader. A benefits manager at a company that devotes an amount equal to 44 percent of its payroll to benefits put it this way:

> We have been first with everything in the industry. We were first with medical insurance, first with a retirement plan, first with profit sharing, and first with long-term disability. Top management never says it costs too much but rather asks if the change is best at this particular time.

When asked if the company had a dental plan, a benefit found in several other companies, this manager said, "We're working on a Health Maintenance Organization Plan—it is the best and cheapest vehicle to go after dental."

In explaining the history of his company's leadership position, one vice-president commented as follows:

> Years ago [we] had a welfare plan. You were paid if you were sick but the decision was based on the judgment of a supervisor. This led to unequal treatment and the company developed a sickness benefit plan which was equitable. Wisconsin was the first unemployment compensation state and our plan was adopted several years before this or the law in New York State. Historically, our company leads government and unions by four or five years. But it is getting harder to do so because benefits are now over 50 percent of pay.

A personnel manager at another company explained the philosophy of its founder with respect to benefits:

> With respect to pay and benefits, the . . . family was always generous. [The founder], for example, always wanted to have more holidays than other companies in this city. The cafeteria was subsidized. Much was spent toward the upkeep of the facilities. The brass was polished. It is all a sense of pride. We are a humanistic organization by the culture.

Another company, in its employee magazine, compared its ten benefits with those of ten other large companies. The article included:

> *As a result of improvements, [the company] is now:*
>
> *Ahead of all ten on retirement. Previously, the company was ahead of nine and equal to one.*
> *Ahead of all ten on survivor benefits. Previously, the company was ahead of eight and behind two.*
> *Ahead of all ten on dental. Nine do not have dental plans.*

The ten companies, representing a cross section of American industry, include such diverse industries as motors, steels, chemicals, office products, electronics, and computers. The ten benefits compared were sickness and accident, total and permanent disability, holidays and vacations, medical, life insurance and survivors' income, retirement, tuition refund, military, employee stock purchase, and dental. The company analysis further revealed that the company was behind only one or two companies in holidays and vacations, medical, tuition refund, and employee stock purchase, and it was equal to two to four others in holidays and vacations, medical, and tuition refund.

This company obviously seeks to be a leader, and so has a unique "Special Care for Children Assistance Plan" and an "Adoption Assistance Plan." The first plan will provide reimbursement for a portion of the required charges for the care of a mentally, emotionally, or physically handicapped child up to a maximum of $25,000 per individual child. The second plan will provide financial assistance toward expenses incurred in the adoption of children. It reimburses the employee 80 percent of eligible charges, up to a maximum benefit of $1,000 for each adoption per family. In addition to a regular tuition refund program and pre-retirement counseling, this company also helps older employees pursue pre-retirement educational interests. The company's recently introduced retirement-education-assistance plan pays up to $500 a year, for a maximum of $2,500, to employees aged fifty-two and older to study anything they choose at an accredited educational institution.

As the above examples indicate, leadership consists of much more than good survey work. In discussing the issues of comparison with other companies and leadership, the benefits manager said:

> *In addition to our ten-company sampling, we continually observe and assess benefit patterns in other companies and industries. The methodology has become quite refined over the years.*
>
> *Of course, measurement with other companies is just one factor in determining the need for and timing of a plan improvement. Employee attitudes and needs are equally important. There must be a balance between statistics and human factors. If [the company] were only concerned with comparisons with other companies, for example, we would not have a "Special Care for Children Assistance Plan" or an "Adoption Assistance Plan."*

The point about balancing statistics and human factors is an important one. In commenting on this company's approach, a vice-president said: "We capture leadership by announcing the inevitable,'' also saying that the company wanted to be a distinguished corporation and that leading in the benefits area was one way of attracting and retaining outstanding people. An active personnel research unit, the results of employee-attitude surveys, imagination, and considerable financial resources all help this company in the achievement of its objectives.

Indicating the rivalry among some nonunion companies seeking to maintain their leadership status, a benefits administrator at another company claimed that they would have been first with special care for children and adoption assistance plans but for two factors. The first factor was that one member of their executive committee had a bias against adoption, and his views kept the executive committee from approving it. The second factor was that representatives from the company that did adopt it first had visited this company and had examined the proposal, shortly thereafter instituting their own adoption assistance plan.

Being Competitive

Some companies cannot afford the costs of an outstanding benefit package. Those that cannot afford to pay benefits better than the prevailing practices have nevertheless attempted to maintain the easily comparable and observable elements of the benefits package at an average or competitive level. One company's vice-president of personnel said that they followed this approach ''with the hope of generating an attitude among employees that the total package must be competitive.'' The company then cuts back in the expensive areas where it is difficult, even for an experienced professional personnel union official, to compare the plans or the costs.'' Another company's tactic, which will be discussed later, is to ''lead in pay and lag in benefits.'' This company believes its employees prefer top wages, which are more visible, to top benefits, which are less visible.

Some doctrinaire companies seem to follow competitive objectives, or sometimes even the objective of *appearing* to be competitive. The vice-president of one such firm said that if such tactics are to be successful, the company must not simply copy prevailing practices, lowering the level of benefits. Rather, they should develop a plan completely different from prevailing practices in order to disguise the discrepancy. When asked for an example, this vice-president said:

> Let's assume that the competitive practice in location X is to have a $9 pension plan. Then I think it is a terrible strategy for the company who cannot afford it to develop a comparable plan but only at the $7 or $8 level. Then it's too damn obvious that their plan is not as good as prevailing rates. On the other hand, if they take the equivalent costs and develop a totally different kind of pension plan, I'm not really sure that anybody would be able to tell for sure how that plan would compare to competitive practices.

Benefit work at another doctrinaire company also illustrates the above point with respect to benefit costs versus benefit values. At this retailing company there was an employee discount plan on merchandise that entitled employees to twenty-five percent off on apparel and twenty percent off on other merchandise. When the company received word that a unionized competitor was planning to offer its employees a plan more generous than its own, it immediately instituted a more liberal plan. Commenting on this benefit and its costs, a vice-president said:

> *This benefit change in fact generates bottom line profits. As long as the gross margin is over 40 percent it is okay for us to be discounting. Employee sales as a percentage of total sales are 4 percent. But the employees see this change as a great benefit improvement.*

This company also provides each employee with free life insurance in the amount of $2,000, which is converted to $1,000 after retirement. In regard to a life insurance change the company was planning, this vice-president said:

> *We have figured out a way to offer more insurance. But the way we'll do it, however, is that in effect the employee will pay for most of the additional insurance. We'll announce it in such a way, however, that the employees will perceive it as something very good that the company is doing for them.*
>
> *The main motivation in the treatment of employees is to avoid unionization. We try to get the biggest benefit buck for our people, for we're a very cost conscious company. Some benefits cost you little or nothing, but you can still get a lot of mileage out of them.*

Although neither these views nor the company's approach are typical, these comments indicate how benefit design and implementation fit into a company's union-avoidance strategy.

Security Goals

In addition to interests in leading or in being competitive that were evident in a number of companies, there was also much concern and thinking about the individual employee and his or her problems. This goal might be termed the "peace of mind" or security aspect of benefits. As the vice-president of personnel, now retired, of one company said:

> *Our benefits were outstanding. The company had a concept of protection from loss of income due to age, illness, or death. There was a sick-pay plan and a disability plan. Early on there was a mutual beneficial association which, as I recall, paid a sick employee $10 per week. The company was the first in the industry, in 1945, to develop a retirement plan. The pension plan vested after fifteen years and provided an option for a lump-sum distribution, which fit well with the employee needs of our business. This is because our work is very heavy and many employees cannot take it in their later years. Therefore, the lump-sum distribution was available and often used to enable*

these employees to go into some small business for themselves upon early
retirement.

An indication of this type of thinking is another company's decision to offer its employees a personal insurance program through payroll deduction. Personal insurance coverage is available for automobiles, homes, boats, personal articles, and so on. This program combines the advantages of low-premium rates and convenient payroll deductions (normally available only through group insurance) with the options offered by individual insurance. A different company's credit union offers similar programs.

The founders of yet another company are very concerned about the long-service employee and his or her welfare after retirement. Their benefit and retirement plans are accordingly designed to accomplish their security goals. Explaining how the philosophy works, a benefits administrator commented as follows:

> *Our benefits are geared toward the longer-service employee. For example, hourly people do not get any paid time off for either sickness or personal business during their first year. And while the company pays the full amount for group insurance after the employee's first year, it pays half after six months and one-quarter after three months. After five years, the company pays one-half of its cost for the employee's dependents.*
>
> *As for retirement, an operator making $7,500 per year would retire at 142 percent of final five years' pay. This includes the pension, social security, and profit sharing, with profit sharing accounting for 55 percent. A technician earning $12,000 would retire at 115 percent of final five years' pay.*

The amount for retirement income from profit sharing at this company depends on the profitability of the company and on the performance of its stock. This is because at this company, all the company's profit-sharing contribution is invested in the company's stock for participants' accounts. An employee automatically joins the plan after two years of service, and after five years of participation becomes fully vested.

Should an employee have a critical financial need, he or she is permitted to borrow up to 50 percent of his or her vested interest, with the stock in the account serving as security for the loan and the loan repayments made through payroll deduction. Also, under certain conditions an employee may make withdrawals from company stock. An employee is eligible to do so when he or she is 50 percent vested. The amount is limited to 50 percent of the company's contribution through the third prior year. There is a penalty of 3 percent of the number of shares withdrawn.

Although many employees would prefer to have the cash immediately, the founders' concern for the retirement security of their employees probably well explains the nature of the plan.

Equal Treatment

Equality, or equal treatment, is a principle for a number of the companies. As does an all-salaried work force, this philosophy demands that the same set of benefit plans apply equally to everyone in the company, from janitor to president. The practice of providing different levels of benefits for different groups of employees is looked upon with disfavor in these companies.

One company with the same benefit package for all employees has been accused of being too wage-oriented in the design of its benefits package by some of its executives. For example, the company's savings plan provided (before it was modified) that the maximum an employee may save is $37.50 per week. That figure was decided on for two reasons: (1) management felt that $37.50 is the most that the hourly employee could afford to save, and (2) $37.50 is the price of a government bond. While this maximum makes sense for the hourly person, it does not make sense for well-paid managers, many of whom expressed a wish to save more. It should be noted that the savings plans of the other companies studied relate savings to a percentage of salary, with every employee having the right to save up to, for example, 10 percent of his or her salary.

A manifestation of this equal treatment philosophy at a different company is the fact that all of the company's employees, managers and hourly workers alike, receive the same amount of free life insurance—$4,000. However, it should be added that many of the managers said they did not like this aspect of the company's benefit plans. The company's sick-pay provisions and $4,000 of free life insurance may be fine for the employee who earns $7,500 per year, but they are not as good for the $35,000-a-year manager.

It should be added that many other management practices at several of these companies are consistent with this philosophy of equal treatment. These practices help make the philosophy something other than "nice words." For example, several of the companies studied are "first-name" organizations. I was told at one company that when someone calls the president "Mr. [his surname]," he'll reply, "You must mean my father."

Several of the companies do not have executive dining rooms. Managers and other employees share the same cafeterias. While most of the executives at one company eat in a dining room, with waitress service, all other employees are also welcome there. In fact, many employees entertain their families in this dining room on special occasions. One should not ignore the significance of managers and regular employees sharing the same cafeteria, for many managers in other companies would not care for such an arrangement. Managers who work in such places must not place too much value on the superficial privileges of management. While these practices may be difficult to adjust to for some managers recruited and hired from the outside, this is undoubtedly not the case for managers who have been promoted from within and are in tune with their company's philosophy.

This lack of status symbols is also evident in the fact that at several of the companies visited there are no reserved parking spaces for top management. In these companies, parking, like the cafeteria, is on a first-come, first-served basis. Moreover, executive offices at some of the companies studied are modest, and many of them lack doors.

Two of the companies provide their employees with free coffee and doughnuts. The coffee-break areas are strategically located throughout the facilities of one of these companies. The coffee breaks are timed so that interdepartmental and intradepartmental communication is fostered. Members of top management go to coffee breaks regularly, since they consider their presence important. As one of them said: "The ethic here has to do with informality, dignity, and lots of open spaces."

The executives of one company do not even have offices. Commenting on this, the vice-president of personnel said:

> The company has always fought against offices. Now only the president, the chairman, and I have offices. I have one because I do some interviewing. We feel that without offices there are better communications. You know if people are at their desk; you don't have to look in their office to see if they are on the phone. This way of life, though it takes some getting used to, is simply much easier for a growth company.

Though a plant of this company was over 2,000 miles from corporate headquarters, the physical arrangements and internal climate seemed the same at this location as that found at headquarters. The division manager was right in the center of a large open space. Only the personnel manager had his own office, due to the confidential nature of some conversations that take place there.

Another indicator of the principle of equality or equal treatment is the fact that many of these companies do not have separate management bonus plans. Instead, there may be some form of profit sharing or a company-supported thrift plan in which all eligible employees participate. Also, in some companies the salaries of the top people are quite low in relation to the salaries paid to chief executive officers of other companies of comparable size, or in relation to the salaries of employees and managers. Elaborating on these points, a company vice-president and general manager said:

> One has to remember the kind of company we are and want to be. People who can manage within the context of the [company] ethic end up with profit-center management responsibilities. Our compensation policies are in a narrow range because success does depend on the contributions of all. [The founders] just don't see themselves earning $500,000 per year. It is only recently that they have paid themselves over $100,000 each per year. Engineering supervisors make $30,000 to $35,000 in this company and department managers make $40,000 to $50,000.
> Moreover, stock options are given to some nonsupervisory engineers

who make good contributions. The fact that there is no bonus for short-term results gives us a long-term emphasis, I believe.

At another company, some of the executives viewed the relatively low salary of the president as a problem, for it put a ceiling on how high their salaries could go. Another possible reason for the comparatively low salaries of some of the chief executive officers of the nonunion companies studied may be the fact that their own founders' stock had made them millionaires many times over. With an estate of several million dollars in stock and sizeable regular dividends, there is little reason for a high salary.

As one quickly realizes, in many companies there is much concern about the atmosphere and climate. The lack or minimization of status symbols is an extraordinarily important aspect of several of the companies. Whether one is discussing equal benefits, no time clocks, unreserved parking spaces, the lack of executive dining rooms, or equal bonus plans, one has to recognize that it takes a special kind of manager to stay on and to operate in such an environment. Many managers would seek the status symbols, privileges, and short-term rewards, which several of these companies do not offer, elsewhere.

Like so many of the other personnel policies and practices discussed, equal treatment may not seem too important. However, as a part of a philosophy or strategy, it can be both significant and visible. Many years ago, an organizational behaviorist visited one of the companies studied, where the principle of equal benefits is maintained, and wrote a report to management entitled "Some Impressions Regarding the Social Organization of [the Company]."

> *Looking at [the company], my first impression is that it is against the code of management to maintain authority by any mechanism which would tend to emphasize the social distance between management and the employees, or, to put it another way, to express the social distance between themselves and employees in any way other than would be found in a family. Management and employees eat lunch together; they drink "cokes" together; they bowl together; they share the same hours of work and the same toilet facilities. Many of the social distinctions between "office" and "shop" which are found in some manufacturing organizations are not present.*
>
> *Again, the patterns of behavior are more like those in a family, where, of course, parents are differentiated from children, husband from wife, sons from daughters, older children from younger children, but where these differentiations are the expression of a well understood and customary "way of life" more than a logic of efficiency or logic of formal organization.*
>
> *It may be a problem of the future, however, as the company continues to expand and, as a result, becomes more formalized, to find ways of maintaining a morale as high as that obtained under the familial orientation.*

While it is only one of many subtle processes, the principle of equal benefits, as do some of the other practices described here, attempts to minimize the "we–they" feeling that so often describes the relationship between the management and the hourly employees in large companies.

OTHER BENEFITS

While it is not possible to list them all, it should be noted that many of these companies provide their employees with excellent additional benefits. There were pleasant working conditions in a number of companies, and in several of them there was evidence of excellent medical facilities and services, as well as established safety and occupational health programs. Clean, subsidized cafeterias are common, as are recreation facilities and employee lounges.

One manufacturer of consumer products provides its employees with its merchandise free of charge. Another company, which manufactures equipment used in the home, either loans its products to employees for brief periods of time or lets them purchase them at a substantial discount. This is the case in a number of other companies whose products could be used by the employees of the company. One such company also sends its retirees a free box of its products at Christmas.

There are many examples of company blood banks, picnics, travel clubs, service awards, credit unions, college scholarships for employees' children, tuition assistance, suggestion systems with cash awards, and other such benefits. One vice-president of personnel termed some of these benefits the "fun-and-games part of personnel," personally disliking this aspect of personnel but nevertheless thinking it an important part of the total benefits program.

BENEFITS COMMUNICATIONS

A principal finding of this study is not only that the companies examined reported that they generally have outstanding or very good benefits, both in an absolute and a relative sense, but also that they spend a lot of time communicating their benefits to employees. The communication programs predate the Employee Retirement Income Security Act of 1974 (ERISA), a law that requires all companies to do a better job in the area of communications. Benefits communication is especially emphasized when the threat of unionization seems real.

Information Media

The companies studied use a variety of ways to communicate their benefits programs to employees. These include specific benefit booklets, articles in company magazines and plant publications, audio-visual aids, company letters, contests, and other means of communication. Let us look more closely at these various communication techniques.

COMPANY PUBLICATIONS

To begin with, attractive benefit booklets in easy-to-understand language are quite common. Each employee receives a copy of such informative material. In addition, company magazines donate much space to the subject of benefits. Concerning this, one benefits manager said:

> Six times per year there will be articles on the subjects of benefits, profit sharing, claims processing, etc. This is in addition to the articles which appear in the plant publications and the annual statement which the employee receives at home.

The feature article of one issue of one company's publication was entitled "How Your Compensation Pie is Cut." The winter issue of another company magazine contained an article saying: "Benefits move dramatically ahead: a dental plan, higher early retirement and survivors income, and child adoption aid reinforce [our] forefront national position in benefits. Here's perspective on the new benefits, and where the program stands competitively."

MANAGEMENT LETTERS

In addition to booklets and articles in company publications, several companies send an annual statement concerning his or her benefits to each employee's home. Consider this quote from the covering letter, signed by both the chairman and the president, which accompanied one annual statement of one company:

> [This company's] benefit programs are carefully planned and have been changed over the years to meet the changing needs of our employees. You can see that the three sections describe your security today as an active employee, your security after retirement, and the value of these benefits. Remember, as you grow with the company and your pay and service increase, so will many of your benefits.
>
> If you are a new employee and have not received a personal statement before, you will find your "Benefacts" report to be of considerable interest. If you have received a statement before, compare previous years' statements to this new report. This comparison will show you the improvement—the increased value—of your benefits over the last two years.
>
> Of necessity, this report only includes those benefits upon which a dollar value can be placed. Other less tangible benefits include steady employment, excellent working conditions and facilities, and the opportunity for advancement and personal development.

This company's statement details several items, including retirement. After listing what the employee may expect to receive after retirement, the statement even itemizes in total what the employee would have had to save at normal retirement in order to provide the same monthly benefit the company will provide. The statement also says: "Additional valuable benefits for which the cost has not been computed in your statement include: educational assistance plan, employee stock purchase plan, employee discounts, pay for other time not worked, and recreational activities."

When asked about disclosing benefit cost information to employees, the benefits manager of the company whose policy is to "lead in pay and lag in benefits" said:

> While I think employees should be told the cost of their benefits, I do not think this should be pushed too much. This is because there can be a backlash as employees today view benefits not as privileges but rather as rights.

The annual statement is sent to the employee's home, and a copy of it is also sent to the employee's supervisor. The supervisor goes over it with the employee: "This gives an excuse for the supervisor and the employee to talk," explained this company's administrative vice-president.

VISUAL PRESENTATIONS

Slide shows, films, and other types of visual aids are also used by companies to communicate their benefits. As one benefits administrator explained:

> What is important is how a benefit is perceived. I think we have done extremely well in communicating benefits. For example, when we adopted the new pension plan, there was a slide presentation and every employee was put through it. We always make presentations when we change things, be it the pension plan, the medical plan, or the new long-term disability plan. While I go to the plants when the presentations are made, local management runs the presentation.

Another company, the only nonunion one in its industry, puts on a slide show every twelve to eighteen months. This is part of this company's regular communications meetings. When pay and benefits are discussed, this company's management describes its own benefits and compares them with those of its competitors. An average of thirty to forty employees view each presentation.

In another company, the policy is to provide a benefits presentation to employees every eighteen months or so. In 1975, the benefits communications staff prepared a visual aid entitled "Employee Benefit Plans in Time of Need," which was designed for supervisors to use with their employees. The supervisor showed the employees the front of the chart while reading what had been written on the back. For example, one chart labeled "Multiple Medical Plan" contained the following:

Covered Charges	Multi Med Pays
Hospital	100%
Surgery	80%
Other	80% after deductible

While showing the chart, the supervisor was to say:

> Your Multiple Medical Insurance Plan has been designed to pay most of your medical bills. Multi Med pays covered hospital charges at 100%. Multi Med pays covered surgical charges at 80%. And Multi Med pays other covered charges at 80% after satisfaction of the deductible.

Commenting on approach, the manager of benefits said:

> The supervisor generally runs these presentations with four or five employees at a time, though it has been done with as many as thirty-five employees. The supervisor is trained, and our material shows where the company stands relative to competitors, especially in the area of retirement. During union campaigns, we put out all of our benefit plans relative to competitors. We lead in such areas as long-term disability and employee stock purchase.

Some of the practices described also illustrate the involvement of line management in employees communications programs. While it would be easier to have benefits experts conduct the meetings, having the line managers do so keeps them involved with personnel matters, adds to their credibility with employees, and gives them another opportunity to communicate with their employees.

CONTENTS

Another way this company has sought to communicate its benefits to employees is through contests. For example, the benefits staff put out a benefits booklet that contained a crossword puzzle. Completion of the crossword puzzle required the employee to look at every page of the company's employee benefits handbook in order to be able to ascertain the correct answers. Wives and children were also encouraged to enter the contest. The company employs 13,000 people, and amazingly, 10,000 people entered the contest. Commenting on this, a staff member said:

> The head of the benefits staff has a great imagination. The company's policy is to provide each employee with free life insurance at twice your pay up

to $300,000. Wives of company employees, because of the contest, would say, "I didn't realize my husband got that much life insurance." The prizes for the contest only cost about $2,500.

(This company also "gets its benefit message across" by using "message" drinking cups at coffee machines.)

These are all imaginative approaches toward accomplishing management's goal of making employees more aware of their benefits. These programs also help keep managers and supervisors close to the employees.

CARTOONS

An even more innovative approach has been taken by another extremely large company. An analysis of its written employee communications material uncovered the fact that although managers were reading the material, employees for the most part were not. Management came to recognize that its material really spoke only to managers in the language of managers. It also recognized that virtually everyone in the company read cartoons.

On the recommendation of some of the personnel people, top management changed its approach, and began communicating much of its views through cartoons. The change is regarded as successful, and readership surveys show that the cartoon material is usually read and is enjoyed.

EXCEPTIONAL APPROACHES TO BENEFITS

In addition to helping employees understand their benefits, several companies assist their employees with benefits in other ways as well. The benefits manager at one company put it this way: "We make sure that the employee gets a fair shake from the insurance company. We'll go to bat for him if there is any particular trouble." There is no doubt that such help, particularly in times of trouble, is appreciated. Since the average employee has few contacts with the benefits office, a favorable contact undoubtedly generates much good will. As an assistant vice-president at one company said: "Individual consideration is possible. And it does happen above and beyond the benefit plan." For example, this company was paying the nursing home costs of one employee's mother in order to ease the financial and emotional stress the employee was experiencing; this is a benefit not usually offered by the company. In addition, at the time of a commercial airliner crash, the company did much to help the families and relatives of employees who had been killed. Within hours of the crash, this company's president and the vice-president of personnel were at the scene, asking the families of employees how the company might help. Commenting on this, the vice-president of personnel said:

We maintain sufficient flexibility to treat the exceptional situation— that rare case of disaster or tragedy where [the company] can help alleviate

*great employee anguish or distress, even though no formal benefit plan
applies.*

In another company, a flood destroyed the homes of many employees. The
company made substantial sums of money available very quickly, and the vice-
president of personnel said: "I can think of no better use for this money." Also
after a flood, a different company permitted its employees to borrow, interest free,
up to 25 percent of their yearly salary. Every cent of this money was repaid. After
an extension, even the loan of an employee who was subsequently laid off was
repaid. This was the only company in its area to devise such a plan, and, given its
success, it was repeated after a second flood occurred.

While these examples apply as much to benefit administration as they do to
benefits communication, it would be foolish to think that the word of such actions
does not get around. This must result in much employee loyalty and good will.

BENEFIT COSTS

Although cost data are frequently hard to come by and there are
comparability problems, personnel officers said their benefits packages ranged
from eighteen percent to fifty-two percent of payroll.

The company that reported the figure of eighteen percent of payroll for
contribution toward benefits is in a very competitive, labor-intensive industry, and
did not include its profit-sharing percentage in that figure. New or part-time
employees are not eligible for profit sharing at this company. With profit sharing
included, the percentage is 24 percent.

The company that reported 52 percent of payroll to benefits included the
amount of its annual employee bonus in that figure. The bonus is considered a
benefit rather than part of salary. In recent years, the bonus has been averaging
about seventeen percent of an employee's pay.

Table 11-1 illustrates the way one company analyzed its 1974 fringe benefits. As the reader will note, this company calculated its benefits-to-payroll ratio
at slightly more than 37 percent. Such ratios are even more impressive when we
recall that these companies generally pay high salaries to begin with.

To get around the comparability problem, I sent a confidential list of large,
nonunion companies to the Economic Analysis and Study Section of the Chamber
of Commerce of the United States. The Chamber does a regular survey of
employee benefits. Its survey involves several hundred companies. Understandably, the Chamber was unwilling to release data to me by name with respect to
individual companies. However, it did review my list of companies and sent the
following information:

*Eleven of the nonunion companies in your list submitted data in our
1973 survey of employee benefits. All were manufacturing firms.*

TABLE 11-1   Analysis of Company's 1974 Fringe Benefits (Domestic)

	$ (Millions)	%
1. Base Payroll	241,914	100.00
2. Included Benefits:		
a. Shift differentials	1,555	0.64
b. Overtime, Weekend, Holiday premiums	2,251	0.93
c. Vacations	10,352	4.28
d. Holidays	9,169	3.79
e. Sick leave	4,343	1.80
f. Other leave	1,391	0.58
g. Other: (1) cash profit sharing	17,160	7.09
(2) stock purchase	4,573	1.89
(3) stock bonus	464	0.19
3. Qualified Benefits:		
a. Life insurance, sickness-and-accident benefits, and other group insurance	8,226	3.40
b. Annuity or funded pensions	10,899	4.51
c. Other: (1) travel insurance	20	0.01
(2) coffee, doughnuts, cafeteria, picnic, and other recreation	2,614	1.08
(3) educational assistance	492	0.20
(4) dues, subscriptions, and registration fees	881	0.36
4. Legally Required Benefits:		
a. FICA, SUI and FUTA[1]	14,797	6.12
b. Workmen's compensation	865	0.36
Total benefits (2, 3, & 4)	90,052	
Benefits + base payroll		37.23

[1]Abbreviations stand for Federal Insurance Contributions Act, State Unemployment Insurance, and Federal Unemployment Tax Act.

Average employee benefits for these eleven companies were 39.5 percent of payroll, 180.5¢ per payroll hour, and $3,821 annual benefits for each full-time employee. This compares with the all-manufacturing industry averages of 32.0 percent, 146.2¢ and $3,111. Eight of the eleven firms had percentage benefits higher than the average for their industry group, and three had benefits lower than the industry averages.

Of the eleven companies, four reported profit-sharing payments; of those four, two reported current cash payments (6.7 percent and 1.3 percent of payroll, respectively), one reported that its payment was to a deferred profit-sharing trust (4.7 percent of payroll), and one reported it made both cash and deferred payments (1.5 percent and 0.1 percent, respectively).

The Chamber's 39.5 percent average benefits figure does not include earned-incentive or production bonuses. Three companies, according to the Chamber, reported a bonus figure for that item, which averaged 2.2 percent of payroll; the percentages for the individual companies were 1.3 percent, 3.2 percent, and 2.1 percent. For the eleven companies, this figure averages 0.6 percent of payroll.

While the foregoing cost information is helpful and by no means insignificant, it raises at least three problems or issues:

First, it may not be meaningful to compare the eleven-company average of 39.5 percent with the all-industry average of 32 percent. The 32 percent is an unweighted average of 437 manufacturing companies. Large companies tend to pay larger benefits than do smaller ones. The nonunion companies studied are large, and they really ought to be compared with similar-sized unionized companies. However, a company may have a high benefits-to-payroll ratio because its pay scale is low. Banks and insurance companies, for example, frequently have high ratios not as a result of better benefits but because of lower pay scales. Generally, the large, nonunion companies studied do pay very well.

Second, the ratio figures may not be too meaningful, because some companies may buy benefits more cheaply than others. For example, Company A may more efficiently provide a certain level of benefits than does Company B. In other words, Company B may be providing the same level of benefits as Company A at a higher cost. Consequently, we should not necessarily give the company that reports a benefits-to-payroll ratio of thirty-six percent more credit than the company that reports its to be thirty-four percent without examining each benefit package. The benefits may be more, less, or the same, depending both on the demographic profile of the employee population and on the way they are purchased. For instance, the costs to the company of some benefits for a young work force are much less than for a company with an older work force. Moreover, some companies self-insure. Another complicating factor, of course, is the way in which different companies calculate their pension costs.

Third, the cost of benefits is one thing, the value of those benefits to the employee is another and different matter. What is important is *how* the employee values or perceives the company's benefits. This may have very little, or at least less, to do with their costs than with other factors. Employees do not usually know the cost involved. Sometimes, they may actually prefer low-cost benefits to high-cost benefits. Thus, the company that provides some attractive low-cost benefits on top of some basics may be better off than the company that provides more benefits in an absolute dollar sense.

While the majority of the benefit plans of the companies studied are not contributory, a few of them are. The vice-president of personnel at one of the companies whose benefits are contributory stated that:

> *We believe an employee should participate in his benefit programs. He*
> *will understand them better and pay more attention to them when part of their*

cost is deducted from his pay check. So, we have an employee contribution not only to offset the company's cost, but also to accomplish these other objectives.

Excluding profit sharing, this company estimates that its benefit contribution, as a percent of payroll, is 18 percent. The company mentioned earlier is able to implement its "lead in pay and lag in benefits" policy, yet still provide very good benefits by having employee contributions.

At another company, employees contribute 2 percent of their pay to the pension plans and, according to a personnel administrator, "it doesn't seem to bother anyone." At yet another company, employees pay part of the cost of the company's medical plans.

While contributory benefit programs may make the employee more aware of the company's benefits and also help keep company costs down, this feature is expensive for the employee, given the fact that his or her contribution is from after-tax dollars.

CONCLUDING ANALYSIS AND COMMENTS

This chapter has been concerned with the subject of benefit policies, their administration, and their communication. The policies, and the ways they are carried out, receive much corporate attention because they relate in an important way to the values and goals of top management, which are leading or being competitive, and providing employees with maximum security. Some benefit programs may represent vestiges of paternalism. Nevertheless, there are strong benefit packages and strong benefit communications programs, frequently involving the supervisors. Priorities are assessed and attempts are made to tailor benefit packages to the needs of the employees. The principle of equal treatment in benefits is also an essential part of the philosophy of several of the companies. In addition to getting the most "bang for the buck," the creativity and innovativeness of the companies can be seen in their adoption of attractive-image building benefits, as well as in specially-designed benefits to take care of special risks.

For a variety of reasons (including costs, government legislation, and the gains won by organized labor), it will be harder for these companies to continue to maintain their leadership posture in the future. As one vice-president of personnel put it: "Government legislation is the great equalizer." With respect to the international situation, this vice-president said: "Ninety-four percent of our benefit costs in Italy are legally required—how can we be a leader there?" While these legislated changes may be favorable from a social point of view, it makes it more difficult for a company to distinguish itself in this area. Similarly, the gains won by organized labor make it much more difficult for the nonunion company to use benefits as a way of differentiating itself from the unionized companies. At a minimum, this method of differentiation is rapidly fading for a number of companies.

The companies studied also exhibit a basic pragmatism toward benefits. At two companies with well-defined benefit philosophies, dental plans were clearly inconsistent with their philosophy. However, at one company in order to achieve settlement without a strike at its unionized facilities, the company had to agree to institute a dental plan during the second year of the contract. Having done so, the company immediately instituted a dental plan for its nonunion employees, thereby giving it to them a year ahead of their unionized employees. A dental plan was granted at the second company because other companies were doing it, and the trend seemed clear even though it was inconsistent with the company's benefit philosophy. At a third company, which was one of the first to treat pregnancy like other disabilities, did so because a respected manager told a key personnel manager that she would take a grievance on this issue to the company's president unless the company's policy was changed. Significantly, this change, for which the company can claim leadership, did not cost this company as much as it would cost many other companies. This is because, unlike some of the companies studied where over half the work force is female, in this company fewer than eighteen percent of its employees are female.

The majority of the companies studied have benefit plans that are noncontributory. While there are major data collection and comparability problems, the benefit packages, as a percentage of payroll, are expensive. This cost factor is especially significant given the fact that the pay scales of these companies are also high.

The excellent benefits provided by the companies relates to the analytical framework consideration concerned with a comprehensive package of personnel policies and programs. The benefit programs offered are comprehensive, and offer added security to the employee. Although the liberalness of company plans varies, the employees know that they will be taken care of adequately when they and members of their families are sick, and when they retire.

The benefit programs of the companies studied also fulfill the service role performed by a union. They are generally competitive with, or superior to, those of comparable unionized companies in the industries in which they compete. Moreover, good benefit survey work insures that this is the case. If these companies become unionized, it is extremely unlikely that it will be because of inadequate benefit programs.

Furthermore, the benefit communications programs enhance the credibility of management with the employees. In some cases, employees are not only told about their own benefits, but also how they compare with the benefits of other companies. Employees know that they are working for leading or competitive companies and that, in general, they would not receive superior benefits at unionized competitors.

CHAPTER TWELVE

Retirement, Cash Bonus, and Investment Plans

No chapter title adequately captures the diversity of financial benefit plans now in use in large, nonunion companies. A significant finding of this study is that a diversity of benefit plans are not only common in these large nonunion companies; but in most cases, they accompany traditional, defined-benefit retirement plans. Table 12-1 makes clear how abundant these plans are in the companies studied. Even in those cases where a deferred profit-sharing plan has been the exclusive source of retirement income (other than Social Security), other programs are being increasingly added to supplement retirement incomes. In general, the retirement plans and the cash bonus plans have been in existence for many years, whereas the investment plans have been adopted more recently.

This chapter describes the different characteristics of the programs that supplement traditional, defined-benefit retirement income plans. Then, it discusses their purposes, which fall into the following four classes: (1) to demonstrate the management's philosophy, (2) to encourage employee identification with company goals, (3) to aid employee motivation and communications, and (4) to respond to employee security needs, primarily with respect to retirement, but also for possible earlier needs.

RETIREMENT PLANS

It is not the principal purpose of this chapter to review traditional defined benefit pension plans; it is to examine the additional programs many of the

TABLE 12-1 Summary of Retirement, Cash Profit-Sharing or Other Bonus Plans, and Savings/Stock Purchase Bonuses Plans—1976, and Special

Company	Retirement Plans		Cash Bonus Plans		Investment Plans	
	Defined-Benefit Retirement-Income Plan	Deferred Profit Sharing	Cash Profit Sharing	Earnings-Based Bonuses	Savings and Thrift Plans	Stock-Purchase Plans
A	X		X		X	
B	X	X				X
C	X				X	X
D	X			X		X
E	X		X	X	X	
F	X		X		X	X
G	X				X	
H	X				X	
I	X	X			X	
J	X				X	
K		X			X	X
L		X*	X		X	
M	X		X			X
N		X			X	
O	X					X
P	X	X	X			X
Q			X		X	
R	X				X	X
S		X	X			
T	X		X		X	
U	X		X		X	
V	X		X	X		
W		X	X		X	
X	X				X	
Y	X*	X	X			
Z	X				X	

*Company also has a supplementary Contributory Retirement Plan.

X Withdrawn prior to 1976.

Note: By 1978 both companies listed with supplementary contributory retirement plans had dropped them. Company L began in 1978 a new noncontributory pension plan while still maintaining its deferred profit-sharing plan, to which an employee must contribute up to two percent of his or her pay to a maximum of $1,200. Company S combined its two plans and now has one contributory pension plan. The employee's contribution is two percent of his or her pay up to $14,700 and four percent of his or her pay over that base figure. For a production worker, the benefits this plan provides roughly work out to about two percent per year of service, including Social Security. That is to say, a production worker who retires after thirty years of service would receive sixty percent of his or her salary in pension benefits.

companies have implemented. These additional programs seem to stand by themselves and distinguish the large, nonunion company. However, before proceeding to a discussion of them let us discuss the more traditional retirement-income programs of six of the companies with such plans.

Defined-Benefit Retirement-Income Plans

Over the years, the trend has been toward the adoption of defined benefit retirement-income plans, so that by the time of this study, twenty companies had such plans. With defined-benefit plans (as opposed to defined contribution plans), the retirement income an employee will receive is set by a formula that is related to earnings and to years of service. So that the reader may better understand the nature of these plans, let us briefly review the approaches of six companies.

COMPANY A

The monthly retirement income of company A is figured in three ways—formula, points, and service—with the calculation that results in the largest amount being the one used for determining each employee's monthly retirement benefit. The *formula* method generally produces the highest benefits, providing 1 percent of an employee's average monthly earnings for the highest five of the last ten calendar years, multiplied by that employee's years of service. Earnings include all compensation (including the company's generous bonus plan). The *points* method multiplies the employee's accumulated number of points (age plus years of service) by a fixed amount. The *service* method provides a flat monthly sum for every year of service, to a maximum of twenty years. In this company in 1973, an employee who retired at age 65 with thirty-five years of service, with final average earnings of $650 per month, would receive $227.50 per month in addition to Social Security. Participation in this company's generously matched savings plan can add substantially to retirement income.

COMPANY D

In company D, the normal annual retirement benefit is calculated by adding 1 percent of an employee's final earnings—the highest earnings in sixty consecutive calendar months during the employee's last 120 months prior to retirement—to three-fourths percent of final average earnings in excess of $4,800, and multiplying the sum by the number of years of service. This company's formula works out so that an employee with thirty years of service can retire at 55 percent of his or her final year's salary—although unlike almost all of the other plans studied, it is contributory. For employees at this company to join the retirement program, they must contribute 3 percent of their annual pay, including any shift differential, through payroll deductions. This aspect of the retirement plan, according to the company's administrative vice-president, helps the company implement its "lead in pay, lag in benefits" philosophy. Social Security benefits are in addition to this company's retirement program.

COMPANY *I*

The retirement plan of company *I* pays an annual lifetime income equal to 1 percent of total earnings prior to retirement, with earnings for service prior to 1957 computed at the rate of total earnings for 1956. In addition, the company adds a special credit for all employees whose continuous service began in 1953 or earlier. It should be noted that this company's retirement plan is supplemented by a deferred profit-sharing plan, by thrift plan funds, and, of course, by Social Security.

COMPANY *M*

In company *M* the normal retirement allowance in 1974 was computed by adding one and one-fourths percent of the first $7,800 of average final compensation (determined from the five consecutive highest-pay years during the ten-year period before retirement) to one and one-half percent of the portion in excess of $7,800 of average final compensation, then multiplying by the number of years of credited service (to a maximum of forty). Thus, in this company an employee 65 years old with forty years of service whose average final compensation is $8,000 would receive a retirement allowance of $4,020, or approximately fifty percent of his or her former income.

COMPANY *O*

Company *O* offers two ways to calculate monthly retirement income—a service computation, and a service and earnings computation. Employees who retire on their normal retirement date will receive a monthly income equal to the greater of the amounts determined by the following computations: the service computation is $11.00 times the number of years of service; the service and earnings computation is one-twelfth of 1 percent of each year's compensation paid to and including $4,800, plus one-twelfth of 1.5 percent of such compensation over $4,800.

For the employee who retires at age 65 with thirty-five years of service, the company's plan provides a monthly retirement income of 66 percent, 52 percent, and 54 percent at assumed average earnings of $8,000, $12,000, and $16,000 respectively. This company's plan also makes adjustments in retiree's pensions for changes in the cost of living.

COMPANY *U*

In company *U*, retirement income is calculated as follows:

Step 1 1.2 percent of the final average salary, up to and including the average Social
Security wage base.

plus (+)

Step 2 1.4 percent of the final average salary above the average Social Security wage base,

times (×)

Step 3 Service completed before retirement date, up to and including thirty-five years of
service,

plus (+)

Step 4 An amount equal to 1 percent of the amount determined in Steps 1, 2, and 3,
multiplied by service over thirty-five years.

In this company, the final average salary is the average of an employee's
highest three consecutive annual salary rates in effect during his or her last ten
years prior to retirement. For example, if an employee retires at age 65 with a final
average salary of $12,500 (assume the average Social Security base is $11,000) he
or she will receive pension benefits from the company of $5,622.75. His or her
Social Security benefits, as well as those of the spouse (at age 65), will result in a
total annual retirement income of $11,109.75. The employee would also undoubt-
edly receive monthly payments from the company's liberal savings and investment
plan, as well as from a savings account with the company's savings and loan
association. For the employee who retires at age 65 with thirty-five years of
service, the company's plan provides a yearly retirement income of approximately
42 percent, 45 percent, 44 percent, and 45 percent at assumed final average
salaries of $10,000, $12,000, $15,000, and $20,000, respectively.

OTHER COMPANIES

In addition to the variations among the plans reviewed, there are other
differences in the provisions for early retirement, dependents' option, permanent
and total disability, death benefits, and vesting. Comparisons of company pension
plans are difficult because there are so many factors, including supplements, to
consider. In addition, some retirement income plans make adjustments for the
rising cost of living while others do not.

Let us now turn to the second retirement plan in use among the companies
studied, the deferred profit-sharing plan.

Deferred Profit-Sharing Plans

Of the two major types of profit-sharing, one type only—deferred profit-
sharing—is intended primarily to provide retirement income. The other type of
profit-sharing—cash profit-sharing—represents a current reward geared to the
performance of the enterprise. We will discuss cash profit-sharing in more detail
when we take up cash bonus plans.

At the time of this study, six companies had deferred profit-sharing plans;

four had cash profit-sharing plans (with payments related to company profits); and two had both deferred and cash profit-sharing plans. (If the study had been conducted several years ago, three more companies would have been included as companies with cash profit sharing plans.) In addition, two companies have other cash bonus plans that may pay approximately the same amount as is paid under cash profit-sharing plans, although not related to company profitability. Significantly, none of the predominantly nonunion companies have any type of profit-sharing or bonus plan. Such programs seem to be a unique feature of the large, entirely nonunion company. It is understandable that predominantly nonunion companies do not have these bonus plans, as they are difficult to administer, and could create too much pressure to install them in the unionized plants.

The purpose of a profit-sharing plan is to help provide for retirement, to ensure equity, to encourage greater identification with and interest in the organization, and to stimulate better performance.

Of the deferred profit-sharing retirement plans, one was started in the late 1940s, to replace a cash bonus system established in the 1920s when company *L* was founded. Company *M* started a deferred profit-sharing plan in the mid-1950s, but abandoned it in the late 1960s when management noted that most of the employees were exercising their new option of taking the money in immediate cash rather than deferring it to supplement the company's retirement plan. Consequently, the company folded the amount that it normally paid out in cash under the profit-sharing plan into the pay rates. With respect to this action a company *M* benefits administrator said:

> *We killed it because we felt we were not getting any mileage out of this "candy on the shelf" approach. The problem is that the money was supposed to be deferred to supplement our pension plan (which pays 65 percent of average annual pay) but the 25-year old today doesn't want to know that he will have $250,000 when he reaches retirement age.*

In the eight companies that currently have deferred profit-sharing plans, in no case is the plan the exclusive source of retirement income. Profit sharing is often supplemented with defined benefit retirement income plans, contributory retirement income plans, savings and thrift plans, or stock-purchase plans. Profit sharing was generally started very early in the history of these companies, and as they grew, management supplemented it.

Company *S*, for example, has a deferred profit-sharing retirement plan, a cash profit-sharing plan, and an employee stock-purchase program. Under the cash profit-sharing plan, payments are normally disbursed twice a year, in June and December. The total payment has been averaging 6 percent to 7 percent of each participant's eligible earnings. When the payments are made, local newspapers in the towns where this company's plants are located generally publicize the event. One such article read:

> *More than 1,100 employees of [the company] received checks averag-*
> *ing more than $400 last week as their share of the company's profit-sharing*
> *plan. Nationwide, the company distributed more than $10 million of its profits*
> *for the first half of the year to some 25,000 employees.*

This company's stock purchase plan permits employees to buy its company's stock at 75 percent of market price. Employees may elect to have up to 10 percent of their earnings deducted from their paychecks for this purpose. Approximately three-quarters of the company's eligible employees participate in this stock-purchase program, a percentage that has remained fairly constant since the program started. Due to a slowing of its growth rate and a decline in its stock price, as well as to the 1977 stock market decline, in 1977 company S made a large supplementary contribution to its profit-sharing plan so that pensions would be higher than they otherwise would be under the company's deferred profit-sharing plan. This was because the company had modified its deferred profit-sharing plan, so that now there is a guaranteed minimum pension of 45 percent of final pay.

Company B refers to its program as ''success sharing,'' which includes a pension, social security, profit sharing, and an employee stock-purchase option plan. This program is described in an employee publication:

> *Success Sharing is a new way to look at your work in [the company]*
> *throughout your career. Through this program, your personal goals for*
> *financial security when you begin work, during your career, and after you*
> *retire can be directly related to [the company's] goals for growth, production,*
> *and profitability.*

Given the company's assumptions, under this plan it is expected that a production worker earning $7,500 would retire with 142 percent of the average of his or her five years' pay. A technician making $12,000 per year would retire at 115 percent of salary; a manager earning $24,000 per year would retire at 99 percent of salary; and a manager making $50,000 would retire at 72 percent of salary. One worker with twenty-four years of service with the company recently retired with 168 percent of the average of her final five years' salary. The company's pension plan is career average, with a periodic update. The calculations assume a career progression of 5 percent per year. (As noted, this benefit package includes the pension, social security, and profit sharing, with 55 percent from profit sharing.) This calculation does not include whatever benefits an employee may receive from voluntary participation in the company's stock-purchase option plan, which enables eligible employees to purchase company stock, at the option price, through payroll deduction up to an amount equal to 10 percent of annual earnings.

These calculations do make some important assumptions about the company's continued profitability and the continued growth of the company's stock price. These are particularly important assumptions—not only because the company's contribution depends on the company's profitability, but also because the company contribution is invested in the company's stock. If the company's projections come true, this plan will yield a retirement income to the average employee that is greatly in excess of what the defined benefit retirement income plans (reviewed earlier) will produce.

At the end of 1974, as a result of this program 58 percent of company *B*'s employees owned stock in the company, either directly or through their profit-sharing accounts. The figure would be much higher, but the company has been unable to find a way to include its non-U.S. employees in its profit-sharing plan. The total amount of stock held by employees, not including that of the founders and their families, had increased from 8.2 percent in 1973 to 9.3 percent at year-end 1974. It is top management's intention for its employees to own approximately 25 percent of the company's stock by the 1990s.

The deferred profit-sharing retirement plans in the companies studied are quite different in many respects. Three are contributory on the part of the employee; the rest are not. Most provide for employee eligibility after a certain minimum period of service. Each plan has different company contribution formulas, vesting schedules, and provisions with respect to early retirement and to how the funds are distributed at the time of retirement.

Company *K* has put an unusual limit on the amount of money that may build up in an employee's profit-sharing retirement account—the cap is $1 million. Due to the success of the company and the rapid growth of its stock, this cap policy, as well as forfeitures, have made the profit-sharing plan self-financing for the past few years. Consequently, unlike its competitors, it has a no-cost retirement income plan that allegedly also has great motivational value.

To illustrate the differences in approach, it is instructive to examine in some detail the profit-sharing practices at two companies where employees must contribute a share. The terms of company *Q*'s plan include:

Employees are eligible after three years

Participation is optional

Employees may contribute 5 to 10 percent of base salary

The company contributes 8 percent of profits before taxes and bonuses

Early retirement yields full vestment

According to the employee handbook, ''an employee entering this plan today with $10,000 annual salary could expect to have $167,000 in twenty years, of which he would have contributed about $16,800. If he worked another ten years, that would grow to $939,000.''

With its three-year waiting period and optional participation, this plan is atypical. Employees who do not join make it better for those who do, for there are fewer employees to divide up the pie. Unfortunately, however, the company's projections have not been realized because of the steep decline of its stock in recent years.

Also requiring employee contribution, company L's plan restricts the contribution to a $200 maximum. The following terms exist:

Employees may borrow from their accounts for special needs, such as home loans, accident or illness, and education.

Participation begins following the completion of one full year of continuous service.

The employee contributes 2 percent, 3 percent, 4 percent, or 5 percent of his or her pay; maximum contribution is $200 in any one fiscal year.

The company contributes to the profit-sharing fund each year approximately 20 percent of net profit before taxes, after deducting a sum equal to a 5 percent after-tax return on the company's net worth. In accordance with Internal Revenue Service regulations, the maximum company contribution is an amount equal to 15 percent of the payroll of all profit-sharing participants combined.

Profit sharers who contribute the maximum $200 per year receive equal maximum shares of the company's contribution. If the employee's contribution is less than $200 in any year, his or her account is credited with a prorated, smaller share of company profit for that year. For example, if an employee contributed only $100, his or her share of profit would be half the maximum share.

Central to this company's plan is an advisory committee and a profit sharing council. The council is made up of employees from all across the United States, elected by employees from each plant for two-year terms.

The advisory committee, composed of the company's chairman, two members appointed by management, and two members elected by the employees, is responsible for the administration and the operation of the plan.

The profit sharing council meets with the advisory committee to review loan application policies. Management feels that employee participation strengthens "two-way communications" within the company.

The effectiveness of this profit-sharing plan is viewed differently by the personnel executives within the company. One person who had recently been recruited from another company, felt that the "new employee" wants money now, and is not interested in deferred profit sharing.

Another personnel executive disagreed about the role of profit sharing, saying:

> It is true that the young people today do not see profit sharing as a nest egg for retirement. But where else after one year can you put in $200 and get a 200 percent return? The young employee today sees profit sharing as a way to help buy something big, whether it is help with down payment of a home, furniture, or a college education for the children.
> Where else can you work for ten years and have a nest egg of $15,000? How else can someone who makes $7,000 or $8,000 per year be able to save that kind of money?

This executive thinks it very important to remember that more than half of the employees of this company are women, many of them second-wage earners, who particularly like this opportunity to build up a nest egg. This company recently amended its plan, to make it easier for employees to borrow funds for educational purposes.

In 1974, almost half of the profit-sharing fund was invested in common stocks, with the value of the company's stock equal to approximately one-third of the value of all common stock in the fund. In that year, the company contributed $2.37 for each dollar of the $200 contributed by an employee. This represents an immediate return of 237 percent. A further return of 26 cents for each dollar of contribution resulted from forfeitures. (The portion of an individual's profit-sharing that is not vested, if employment with the company is terminated, is relinquished [forfeited] and divided among the accounts of the remaining profit sharers.)

Since the late 1950s, company L has also offered a supplementary contributory retirement plan (SCRP) to employees earning in excess of $7,500 per year. Eligible employees contributed 5 percent of their annual earnings in excess of the $7,500. The effect of this is that the $10,000-per-year employee will retire with 150 percent of his or her annual income (with just over 10 percent of it from SCRP), while the $40,000-a-year middle-manager will retire with 90 percent of his or her salary (with over half coming from SCRP). At this company, profit sharing, together with Social Security, do quite well for the worker. However, SCRP is essential for the manager to attain a comfortable retirement income. In other words, for the $40,000-per-year manager to have a retirement income of more than $14,281 (with only $5,839 from profit sharing) he or she has to finance it by contributing 5 percent of his or her annual earnings each year. This is because under the design of this company's plan, whether an employee made $10,000 per year or $40,000 per year, the amount he received from profit sharing was the same: $5,839. It would seem that this company's deferred profit-sharing plan carries the principle of equal benefits to an extreme.

In late 1977, company L froze SCRP and adopted a noncontributory pension plan. The company maintains its deferred profit-sharing plan, but under the new approach the target is that employees with thirty-five years of service will retire at anywhere from 60 percent to 100 percent of their final salary. Retirement income will come from three sources: the noncontributory pension plan (which is integrated with Social Security), profit sharing, and Social Security. The new plan's objective is for those employees whose final salary is below $20,000 to retire at 100 percent of their pay. Corporate officers, however, will retire at only 60 percent of their final salary. It is clear that this change will provide a more adequate company-financed retirement income for higher-income people. At the same time the company adopted this pension plan, it also modified its deferred profit-sharing plan in several important ways. The changes were designed to not only provide all employees with a "fair and reasonable level of retirement income," but to also put even greater emphasis on the role of profit sharing at the company for savings and retirement. Employee contribution levels were revised. A new way of allocating profit sharing was developed, and higher levels of profits were to be contributed by the company to profit sharing.

The employee contribution to each plan changed as follows:

	Old Plan	*Revised Plan*
Profit sharing	2% to 5% of pay, up to $200 per year maximum	$200; or 1% or 2% of pay up to $1,200 per year maximum (optional contribution of 1% to 5% does not share in company contribution but does share in fund growth)
Pension plan	5% of pay over $7,500	Noncontributory

As of 1978, both contributions and service are counted in allocations. An employee is credited with one profit-sharing point for each dollar he or she deposits in the plan during the year, and also receives two points for each year as a plan member. For example, an employee who deposited $240 to the plan during the year would have 240 profit sharing points. If this employee had eleven years of service, he or she would have 22 service-related profit-sharing points, for a total of 262 profit sharing points. At the end of the year each employee's points are totalled along with the points of all other participants, and the total number of points are divided into the company's profit-sharing contribution for the year.

To pay for the higher level of benefits that will be available through the profit-sharing plan, company *L* changed the formula for determining how much of the company's profits will be shared among plan participants. While the company used to contribute 20 percent of profits (after first setting aside a reserve amount equal to a 5 percent return on the company's net worth), it now contributes 24 percent of profits (after the 5 percent is set aside).

As this description makes clear, company *L*'s costs will be much higher as a result of these changes. The company not only increases its contribution to profit sharing, it also assumes all of the costs of the defined benefit pension plan. The company's new plan, called "Profit Sharing Plus," is clearly much better than its old profit-sharing and SCRP plans, especially for the higher-paid people.

CASH BONUS PLANS

Half of the companies studied have or have had some type of cash bonus plan. Nine companies currently have such plans. Of the three companies that have abandoned their plans, two did so because they felt their plans were no longer effective. Both companies instead introduced employee stock-purchase programs. The third company dropped its cash bonus plans at the insistence of the federal government, one of its large customers. The company subsequently built the amount of the usual bonus into the salaries of its employees. The company does, however, offer an employee a savings and thrift plan, whereby it matches 50 percent to 100 percent of the employee's contribution. (Savings and thrift and company stock-purchase plans will be discussed later.)

Broadly speaking, there are only two types of bonus plans. The first and most prevalent type of plan is a bonus that is dependent on the profitability of the company. These we shall classify as cash profit-sharing (see Table 12-1). The second type of plan is a bonus of a fixed amount of cash related only to an employee's earnings rather than company profits. These we call earnings-based bonuses. Both types of bonus plans are similar in that the payment to employees is made at the same designated time (or times) each year.

Earnings-Based Bonus Plans

To illustrate the earnings-based bonus plan first, we will examine the two companies that have such plans.

COMPANY D

For several decades, this company has given its employees 4 percent of their pay as a bonus each year at Thanksgiving. The employees generally consider this shopping money for Christmas. In 1968, however, management eliminated all bonus plans for managers and salespeople. Although it did not eliminate the 4 percent bonus for production and maintenance employees at old plants, it has not established it in its plants that have been built since 1968.

Management considers this 4 percent bonus expensive, but fears the employee-relations consequences of eliminating it. Workers like it, and one said that if they ever voted for the union, management would eliminate the bonus. Therefore, in this employee's view, this was one of the two reasons why the employees had never voted for a union. (The other reason was the company's full-employment practices.)

COMPANY V

This company disburses both a vacation bonus of one week's pay and a Christmas bonus of one and one-half weeks' pay. This practice was initiated many years ago by the president at the time, a person described as "people-oriented," who forged the company's employee relations philosophy. The current vice-president of personnel believes that the former president started this practice when the company was very profitable, believing that some of those profits ought to be shared with the employees. This practice has continued through the years.

As has been noted, the size of the bonuses paid in the above two companies is directly related to the amount an employee earns. It is unrelated to the economic performance of the enterprise. It is not clear, however, whether the employee interprets these bonuses differently than do the employees of a cash profit sharing company, where the pay-out generally works out to be 4 or 5 percent of salary. From an employee's point of view, the difference between the programs is in the probability of receiving a bonus. Management must incur a known cost under the fixed bonus system, regardless of how well the company is doing, without receiving any of the alleged motivation and communications benefits which are said to be associated with cash profit sharing.

Cash Profit-Sharing Plans

The second type of bonus plan, though not always referred to as such, is really a cash profit-sharing plan, because the amount of company contributions is related to the profitability of the company. Two companies calculate and pay their employees bonuses quarterly. A third company pays its bonuses semiannually. However, in most companies the payment is an annual one.

Company U calls the payment it makes every March a "Wage Dividend." The company describes it in an employee publication:

> The Wage Dividend is another important way of recognizing the contribution made by all [company] people to the company's success. Payment of a Wage Dividend is dependent upon the cash dividends declared on the company's common stock and upon special action by the Board of Directors. It has been paid every year except once since 1912. The annual lump-sum payment, usually made in March, is based on the declared Wage Dividend rate multiplied by the individual earnings over the past five calendar years.

In 1975 the wage dividend amounted to 17 percent of pay, and all company people, from assembler to vice-president, received the same percentage.

Company A calls its bonus "Variable Pay." The amount, based on profitability, ranges from 0 percent to 25 percent of an employee's annual total pay. Like the company just cited, it also pays the same percentage to all employees regardless of salary, title, or position. Commenting on this, the company's vice-president of personnel said: "In 1975 the figure was 15 percent, and my secretary and I each received the same percentage of our salaries as variable pay." However, it is only recently that this statement has been true. In the past, nonmanagement personnel at company A had the bonus percentage applied to only half of their pay. It still takes nonmanagement personnel four years longer than it does management personnel to become eligible to receive the full bonus.

An enthusiastic company department manager offered this comment about the bonuses as well as its effects:

> *It is a wonderful thing. It used to be that just certain job levels participated fully, but now everyone participates. We see tremendous results. We're more a part of this company. We cut costs and work efficiently and with flexibility. The employees are more receptive to change as a result of it and more willing to discuss things.*

A group leader, when asked about the bonus, said:

> *The production workers used to be upset. They used to get the bonus on only half of their salary while managers got the bonus on all of their salary. The effect was the little guy got only 12 percent of his salary as a bonus while the big guy got 24 percent. It really didn't seem fair. Personnel heard the gripes. People were complaining.*

While not referring to its program as a bonus plan, the "Christmas Gift" program of company Y is not unlike the bonus plans of other companies. For many years, it has been the practice of this company to distribute to its employees at Christmas time a cash and a merchandise gift.

The amount of the cash gift, determined annually, has varied over the years, from a minimum of four days' pay to a maximum of eight days' pay. The check is distributed in early December, separately from the regular paycheck. The merchandise gift program is communicated to the employees through a catalog containing over 100 items and individual selection cards that are sent to them in the fall. The broad range of gifts includes items for personal use such as hair dryers and luggage, household items (such as electrical appliances and cookware), sporting goods (such as golf bags and fishing gear), and tools (such as drills and wrenches). The gifts are generally distributed by the employees' supervisors prior to Christmas.

At company T the cash profit-sharing plan, which usually amounts to 4 percent or 5 percent of pay, makes payments quarterly. However, along with one other company (company Y) listed in Table 12-1, there is not a thrift plan or a stock-purchase plan at this company. When asked about this, the personnel director of company T said:

> *A few years ago we suggested a thrift plan in place of profit sharing. The employees, however, did not want a thrift plan if it was to be a replacement for profit sharing. We are now considering the idea of a thrift plan again. We may introduce it in the future.*

In 1977 company T was considering adopting a savings and thrift plan in addition to its profit-sharing plan. The company planned to help pay for its cost by taking a small amount of money from its own profit-sharing contributions.

INVESTMENT PLANS

Two types of benefit programs can be classified as Investment Plans (see Table 12-1). The first type includes savings and thrift plans. The second type consists of stock-purchase plans.

According to the Bankers Trust Company's *1977 Study of Employee Savings and Thrift Plans,* sixty-one of the top 100 industrial corporations (as ranked by 1975 sales) have savings and thrift plans. Five of these companies started their programs during the 1972 to 1976 period.[1] While 65 percent of these plans cover all or substantially all employees, 35 percent of the plans limit participation to salaried or nonbargaining unit employees. Of the companies in my sample, 24 out of 26, or 92 percent, have either savings and thrift plans or stock-purchase plans. Although some of the plans are of recent vintage, the companies with such plans offer them to all employees, exempt and nonexempt. This is also true for both the predominantly nonunion and the entirely nonunion companies. Employee savings and thrift plans or stock-purchase plans that are open to all seem to be one distinguishing feature of the large, nonunion company. The widespread presence of these plans is additional evidence of the leadership policies the companies studied pursue in the area of benefits.

Fourteen nonunion companies have savings and thrift plans, nine have company stock-purchase plans, and one has both. The savings and thrift plans of several companies give employees the opportunity to invest a certain percentage of their payroll deductions in the company's own stock. All or part of the company's contribution may also be in company stock.

Company savings and stock-purchase plans are similar in some respects in both their objectives and the vehicles to accomplish them. The objectives of one employee's savings plan are: (1) to encourage long-term systematic savings, (2) to afford the opportunity to acquire a stock interest in the company, and (3) to provide extra funds for retirement or possible earlier needs.

With stock-purchase programs, an employee generally purchases company stock through payroll deductions at a discount from the then-market price. The discounts range from nothing to significant. With savings and thrift plans, the company generally matches a part—frequently 50 percent—of each employee's contribution. However, there is much diversity with respect to the design of these plans.

At one extreme is company *H*, which permits the employee to allocate up to 10 percent of his or her pay, through payroll deductions, to purchase its stock. The employee receives no discount from the market price, and even has to pay the brokerage commissions. However, this company has also recently implemented a savings plan, to which the company contributes. This company simply makes it

---

[1]Bankers Trust Company, *1977 Study of Employee Savings and Thrift Plans* (New York: Bankers Trust Company, 1977), p. 9.

more convenient for the employee to buy common stock. It is easier to do so through payroll deductions than by going through a broker. Another company's plan is also close to this extreme but for the fact that it allows its employees the convenience of purchasing company stock at the market price through payroll without paying any commissions. Significantly, this company limits an employee's participation not to a percentage of his or her salary, but to $100 per month. This feature, according to a benefits administrator, makes sure the program is for the benefit of the "little guy" and not for the benefit of the highly-paid executive who might like to save commissions on purchases of company stock. Another company is also at this extreme of the spectrum with respect to savings and thrift plans, permitting its employees to save up to 8 percent of their pay through payroll deductions. The employee must then select which fund in which he or she wishes to invest. Started in 1976, this program has no company-matched funds. Yet, 30 percent of the eligible employees participate. The company plans to begin matching some percent of the employees' contributions in the future.

At the other extreme are the companies that offer employees a substantial discount from the market price of the company's stock and/or match a very high percentage of what an employee chooses to save. What is particularly attractive about savings plans is that, while the company's contribution is a deductible business expense for tax purposes, employees pay no tax on company contributions or on earnings from their own and company contributions until a distribution is made. Moreover, if the distribution includes company stock, no tax is paid on the unrealized appreciation until the stock is sold.[2] However, with company stock purchase programs the discount employees receive on the price of the stock is treated as taxable income. Stock purchase plans, however, are of negligible cost to a company. Judged by participation rates, the plans studied appear to be popular employee benefits. This is understandable, for they generally represent a convenient way to earn high interest and a way to acquire company stock at attractive prices. Some illustrations are in order.

Savings and Thrift Plans

In one company employees who have been employed more than one year are allowed to contribute from 1 percent to 10 percent of their pay. The company contributes an amount as follows for each ordinary contribution: 40 percent of the first 1 percent, 30 percent of the next 1 percent, plus 15 percent of the third and fourth 1 percent contributed. The company does not match any contribution over 4 percent. All of the company's contribution, and any portion of the employee's contribution he or she chooses, is invested in the company's stock. The remainder of the employee's contribution is invested in an equity fund or in a fixed-income

[2]Bankers Trust Company, *1977 Study*, p. 10.

fund, depending upon the employee's choice. The purpose of this plan, according to the employee handbook, is that:

> *The plan is intended to promote thrift on the part of employees, enable them to supplement their pensions with additional funds at retirement, and give them an opportunity to acquire a personal interest in company stock, and thus become more interested in the company's affairs.*

In another company, company A, the employee may save from 1 percent to 6 percent of his or her monthly base salary. This company guarantees the addition of at least 50 cents (and more if profits are good) for every \$1 the employee allots. The company's contribution is in the form of company stock.

Four funds provide different types of investment opportunities from which participants may choose. "Fund A" is government securities, "Fund B" is diversified common stock, "Fund C" consists of shares of company stock, and "Fund D" provides a guaranteed fixed income. When savings dollars are invested in more than one fund, the allocation to any fund cannot be less than 10 percent of the participant's total monthly allotment. The company's contribution is used to purchase the common stock for the participant's "Fund C" account. At this company an employee is not permitted to designate that his or her salary deductions be invested in the company's stock. While some companies encourage employee ownership by offering company stock as one investment alternative or by offering a company stock-purchase program, this company does neither. However, since the company's contribution is so substantial relative to the employee's contribution, and because the company's contribution is in its own stock, a large percentage of the employee's account consists of company stock.

Although management and exempt employees always participate more than do nonexempt personnel, the rate of nonexempt participation seems to be higher in companies that match a greater percentage of the employee's contribution. In this company's generously matched plan, for example, 90 percent of eligible employees participate.

The thrift plan of another company, which has both a pension plan and a cash profit-sharing plan, provides that the company will contribute 20 percent annually of the amount saved by the employee. The employee is permitted to save up to 5 percent of his or her annual salary. While this plan is not as generous as some of the plans of the other companies studied, the results are nevertheless far superior to what an employee could do on his or her own with a bank savings account. In fact, a national magazine said that this company has "perhaps the country's most liberal employee-benefit and profit-sharing plan."

When one of the predominantly nonunion companies introduced a savings plan, initially matching 25 percent of the employee's contribution, it voluntarily offered the same plan to its union plants. When the union leaders said they liked the plan but favored 50 percent matching, management said they could take the plan as is or bargain for 50 percent during the next negotiations. The union accepted the plan. Subsequently the company increased its matching provision to 50 percent. While 84 percent of the eligible salaried employees and 64 percent of the eligible wage employees participate in the savings plan, the difference between union and nonunion employees is not significant: 44 percent of eligible nonunion employees and 61 percent of eligible union employees participate.

The savings investment plan of one company is quite different from any discussed. At this company, while the employee may contribute from 1 percent to 5 percent of his or her gross monthly base salary, the senior employee benefits more than does the junior employee, because the company's contribution depends not on the company's profitability but on each employee's years of service. If an employee has 1 to 2 years of service, the company matches 50 percent of his or her contribution. If an employee has 2 to 4 years of service, then the company matches 75 percent of his or her contribution. For 4 or more years, the company matches 100 percent. Like some of the other plans discussed, this program also offers the employees several investment choices.

The requirements for vesting of the company's contribution vary by company. In one company it is immediate. In another company 20 percent is vested after the first year, plus 20 percent for each additional year's service. At yet another company, for employees earning less than $25,000 per year, as to each year's contribution, it is 100 percent two years after the end of such year (for employees earning $25,000 or more it is 100 percent four years after the end of such year).

Company Stock-Purchase Plans

Most of the stock-purchase plans permit the employee to acquire the stock at a discount from the market.

Company O's program had a unique feature until the company amended its plan in 1976. According to the old system, in a given year employees could purchase the company's stock at 85 percent of the July 1 price or 85 percent of the current market price, whichever was lower. For example, if the July 1 market price were $100, an employee could purchase stock at $85 per share. If the employee's deductions had accumulated enough for one share on September 1 and the price of the stock had declined to $80, the employee could then purchase his or her share for $68. However, if the market price on September 1 had gone up to $120, the employee could then purchase his or her share for $85, thereby realizing a profit of $35, or approximately 40 percent. Moreover, if the employee wanted to sell his or her shares on the open market immediately, this was possible.

In the town where this company was founded, it was interesting to see three small stores that were open for a couple of hours during each of the company's shifts. These independent stores, which were in no way related to the company, would accept up to ten shares of the company's stock at the market price for cash. However, if an employee desired cash but did not want to sell his or her stock, he or she could deposit the shares at the credit union at the company and borrow against them. The credit union (an employee organization) made it easy for the employee to get cash.

This company's plan could function for some employees as a cash bonus plan. It was especially good during periods of rapidly rising stock prices. As has been stated, this company amended its employees' stock-purchase plan in 1976. Now the price at which the stock is bought is 85 percent of the average market price on the last day of the pay period in which the employee has enough money in his or her account to purchase a share. Eligible employees, however, can still purchase stock one share at a time through payroll deductions up to 10 percent of compensation. Although still good, the present plan is not as attractive as the old plan, but the company has never considered this program to be one of its major employee benefit plans.

One company without a stock-purchase program is this way because the chairman and founder of the company did not think employees should be subject to market risks by having a lot of their money "in one basket," that is, in the company's stock. Therefore, while this company has a savings and investment plan it does not have a company stock-purchase plan.

Similarly, the chairman and founder of another company rejected sponsored stock-ownership programs, not wanting employees to become hurt in their savings. However, the company did give employees an option to purchase 50 shares of the company's stock at $15 just prior to the company's going public at $16.25 in the mid-1950s. Many employees, it was reported, did exercise this option.

As has been shown, savings and thrift plans and company stock-purchase plans are extremely common in the companies studied. They are a tangible and highly-visible benefit that seems to distinguish the large, nonunion company from many unionized companies. Even if the unionized company has such a program, its plan may not include participation by hourly employees. While the cost of these plans depends on the design of the plan and on participation rates, frequently the cost is only 1 or 2 percent of payroll—much less than the cost of a bonus program. Participation rates, in turn, depend on the design of the plan. Through the individual's choice and/or through the company's matching contributions, many of the plans (like the stock-purchase plan) make employees owners of the business, which can make employees more interested in the company and its prospects.

While savings and stock-purchase plans, especially those savings plans that are involved with company stock, share some common features, they also have some very important differences. With a stock-purchase plan, employees may withdraw their shares and do with them as they please. For instance, they may sell them immediately, give them to children or grandchildren, or keep them to sell later or for retirement. This decision will be influenced by the outlook for the stock market as well as for their company's stock. However, in some companies an employee may not rejoin the plan the same year he or she has withdrawn from the plan. Savings plans have vesting schedules with respect to the company's contribution and various rules regarding voluntary withdrawals, but they are more flexible because of the variety of choice and because they are more long-term in nature. They may tend to tie an employee to a company more than might a stock purchase plan. Savings plans, much more than stock-purchase plans, do provide additional security to employees for their retirement years, as well as a reserve fund for major financial needs that may occur during employment. While employee participation rates are, not surprisingly, lower, stock-purchase plans nevertheless appear to be well-suited for growth companies.

PURPOSES OF PLANS

Now that the various retirement, cash bonus, and investment plans these companies have have been outlined and discussed, let us assess their significance. Why are these plans offered? What are their purposes? How well do they achieve their objectives? This section tries to deal with these questions, and suggests that these plans have as many as four different but closely related purposes.

Demonstration of Philosophy

Perhaps it should first be stated that these bonus and investment plans can serve as a visible sign that management is sincere in its philosophy. The plans can demonstrate fairness and economic equity. As the president of one company put it:

> *There are a number of corollaries [to this philosophy]. One is that employees should be in a position to benefit directly from the success of the organization. This led to the early introduction of a profit-sharing plan, and eventually to the stock-purchase plan.*

At several other companies it was said that the founders had believed in the basic concept of profit sharing. There was an almost religious conviction that employees should share in the profits they helped create by doing their jobs. However, in some companies the profit-sharing plan, at least initially, was a deferred one, and consequently the only retirement income plan.

The fact that so many of these companies have no separate bonus plan for management also demonstrates the philosophy of equity. Executives and janitors alike are in the same plan; each receives the same percentage of pay as a bonus. As the vice-president of one company said:

> *It is important to and consistent with our philosophy that we have no class system in the benefit package. You get the same pension or medical plan regardless of whether you are the sweeper or president.*

As has been noted previously, eliminating double standards is a theme that runs through the experience of several companies.

A bonus, a generously matched savings and thrift plan, or a good stock-purchase plan is highly visible. It can demonstrate in a tangible way that the company is different from many other companies, especially those that are unionized. These plans also seem uniquely well-suited to growth companies, which have traditionally had steadily increasing profits and rising stock prices.

Identification With Goals

Another closely-related reason why these plans are adopted is to enable the employee to identify more clearly with the goals of the company by having a stake in the company's future. Stock ownership, through a deferred profit-sharing plan, a company stock-purchase plan, or employees' or companies' matching contributions to a savings and thrift plan, makes each employee an owner of the company. As a result, employees may be more company-oriented, and may work harder to increase production and efficiency. When asked about the rationale of the cash profit-sharing plan, the employee-relations vice-president at one company said:

> Profit sharing has a sound philosophical base here. It is a general incentive. It is also a heck of a device for teaching employees the economics of the business.

The chairman of another company agreed with this point:

> The employees come to understand that the arithmetic does make sense. They realize that they have ten shares and maybe one of their top bosses has 10,000 shares and that they are all riding on the same thing—the performance of the company in the market.

A leading behavioral scientist at one of the companies expounded on this aspect of profit sharing:

> Through this system more people come to understand criteria of organizational effectiveness and the interdependence of individual and organizational goals. When all members of the group benefit from profit sharing, group involvement in increasing profits is encouraged. Profit sharing constitutes a lesson in economics, supporting the free-enterprise system.

Profit sharing does not always earn the unqualified approval of employees, however. Many supervisors were interviewed on this subject, and their comments revealed that some are more enthusiastic than others about profit sharing. One foreman with a high school education, who joined a company thirty years ago as a Grade 1 worker, became a supervisor eighteen years later, and who now supervises fifty-nine workers, said, "Profit sharing is fantastic. Where else would I have $50,000? I have more stock than some of the directors." When asked about profit sharing, another supervisor at the same plant, who had been with the company for seven years, expressed a different view:

> *No one understands it. It is not a big thing. It is mostly looked on as being a joke. It is generally 1 percent, 2 percent, or 3 percent of your pay. I could do just as well without it.*

A foreman with ten years of experience at the company commented about profit sharing:

> *Some years it is so low it is not worth talking about. If it is above 5 percent there are good comments. At 1 percent and 2 percent it is laughable. Now you can't take it in cash any more, which upsets some people. In the past people could take a percentage in cash although the percent that you could take was less than half.*

At this company the company's profit-sharing contribution is used to purchase company stock for the employee's account. The fact that this company's profit-sharing plan is a deferred one (on top of the company's retirement income plan) is significant. A cash plan might produce more positive comments. Higher company profits, no doubt, would also produce more positive comments.

At company *S*, a production worker interviewed pulled a calendar out of his pocket. On one page he had written down the amount of the bonus for each year. He liked the company's cash profit-sharing plan, but not its deferred profit-sharing plan. This company has both a cash bonus profit-sharing plan, paid twice a year, and a deferred profit-sharing retirement trust. Concerning the latter, this worker said:

> *The weakest point now is this company's pension plan. It is lousy. It is tied to the stock market. Most of us have lost. I lost $2,000 this past year. I had $8,000; now I have $6,000. It is peanuts when you have worked for a company for 18 years. Some unionized companies have better plans. In those companies, you get a certain amount of benefit related to years of service or final earnings. It is not tied to the stock market.*

Since the time of this interview, the company has modified its deferred profit-sharing plan, so that now there is a guaranteed minimum. The company now makes any necessary supplemental contributions to the fund so that employees will retire with 45 percent of their final pay.

At company *T*, where in 1975 the cash profit-sharing payment was 5 percent of each employee's salary, one employee representative, asked for her views regarding profit sharing, said:

Employees love profit sharing. They can't wait to get their checks. In
good years it is very good. And in bad years, it is still better than nothing.

One supervisor talked about employees who tease other employees who are
goofing off or are wasting material by saying, "You are killing the bonus."
Another employment representative said: "The company just doesn't realize that
profit sharing doesn't mean much any more." His reasons primarily concerned the
changed nature of the work force, with a very high percentage of young, part-time,
and short-service employees. Since everything is deferred, this company's profit-
sharing plan, which has a mandatory employee-contribution feature, is really the
company's retirement plan. In fact, it is the only source of retirement income other
than Social Security. However, the company does have a stock-purchase program.

Sometimes one hears of employees who purchase company stock through
the company's program and sell it immediately. Other times one learns of high
employee attendance at company annual meetings and real employee interest in
the company and its products. At many companies, managers reported that the
employees take enormous pride in the statement they receive each year from the
company, which informs them of how much money they have in their profit-
sharing accounts. Undoubtedly, this is more true during periods of rising stock
prices than during periods of decline.

Some of the supervisory interviews raised questions about how well profit-
sharing and stock-ownership plans accomplish their company identification goals.
How well these plans work surely depends on the nature of the plan, the size of the
company, the communications programs that are or are not part of the plan, as well
as the profitability of the company.

Motivation and Communications

How employees' stock ownership and profit sharing contribute to employees' motivation undoubtedly depends on the way these tools are used, as well as
the size of the company. Some companies reported that they viewed their profit
sharing as especially significant when they were smaller, but that as they grew
larger employees tended to take profit sharing for granted. It is not only harder for
employees to identify with a larger organization, it is also more difficult for them
to see the way their jobs fit into the larger picture in the big organization.

At a company that for many years has paid a large cash bonus, the director of
personnel said: "The bonus is taken for granted by the employees. The company
doesn't get five letters from employees thanking it for this money."

How these plans are to be kept meaningful is a difficult question. If incentive
results are to be achieved from profit sharing, communications must be tailored to
fit the situation. The communications media and their contents must change and
adapt to the growing size of a company; if this is done effectively, a company can
obtain some additional mileage out of its plan.

Some managers believe that profit-sharing and employee stock-purchase plans improve communications within a company. Management of company *L*, the company whose deferred profit-sharing plan provides for elected employee representatives, claimed that the elected employees discuss matters other than profit sharing at their meetings. As they bring feelings and attitudes from the factory floor to the boardroom, so do they take back to the plant new information and top management's concerns about the problems and the state of the business.

The president of a large company with over 70,000 employees considered profit sharing a key communication tool:

> *If you get your story across to the whole company, and we do this frequently through profit-sharing meetings, you are successful in staying nonunion.*
>
> *It is true that the employees are not sophisticated enough the first time to understand the numbers, but once they have been around five or six years they begin to believe and understand them. So consequently, the veteran employees are interested in the stock market quotations and think the arithmetic does make sense.*
>
> *The principal problem we have is that it is hard to reach the new employee. You just hope that the new employee gets carried along and gets sort of imbibed with the philosophy.*

The communications significance of the fact that large numbers of employees are stockholders has been noted in an organizational way in another company. At this company, shareholder communication is a part of the personnel department. As the vice-president of personnel said: "About 30 percent of our employees are stockholders, and we take this into account when we write the annual report." At another company, 100 percent of the employees are stockholders, and are expected to attend the annual meeting; if they do not attend, they must work.

The fact that two of the companies voluntarily abandoned cash profit-sharing plans certainly raises questions about the alleged motivation and communications benefits of these plans. The trend away from deferred profit-sharing trusts as the exclusive source of retirement income is also interesting. Profit sharing in large companies may not have the same motivation and communication benefits it was once thought to have.

Expectation of Security

In addition to demonstration, identification, and motivation and communications, profit-sharing retirement plans and company-supported savings plans, like defined benefit pension plans, undoubtedly also help improve the security of individuals. Although this may not be an important consideration to younger workers, it certainly is to older employees.

On the one hand, for employees to know that they can expect to retire at 100 percent or more of salary must give them a very secure feeling. That is not an unrealistic expectation in some of these nonunion companies where benefits from deferred profit-sharing plans, employee savings plans, and Social Security add up. On the other hand, whether or not it is prudent to have too much of an individual's future dependent upon the performance of the company's common stock is another matter. Given the uncertainties of the stock market this would seem unwise, in spite of the fact that one occasionally hears of the hourly person, who never earned a lot of money, retiring with $500,000 or $1 million in his or her deferred profit-sharing account. This can only occur if a high percentage of funds had been invested in the company stock and if the stock had done well. In this highly unusual set of circumstances, the employee retires with much more than he or she would ever have collected from a defined benefit pension plan.

Deferred profit-sharing plans can be risky. The performance of company stock depends on many factors other than the efforts of employees or even the company's record. In addition, the past experience of some companies will hardly apply to the recently-hired employee. The potential growth of $1-billion companies today simply cannot match the possible growth rates of $50- to $100-million threshold companies. A company can only grow at 30 to 50 percent per year for so long. Even if the company's stock is not a large percentage of the portfolio, deferred profit-sharing plans used as the exclusive source of retirement income (other than Social Security) can jeopardize employees' retirement security, especially if a significant part of the portfolio consists of common stocks.

Accordingly, many companies in recent years have come to question the wisdom of their profit-sharing plans and their investment policies. Some have become more conservative. Other companies that invested heavily in their own stock now supplement their plan with a defined benefit pension plan, or change the nature of the profit-sharing plan to minimize or remove the risk of losses in participant accounts. A guaranteed minimum is one such approach. With defined benefit pension plans protected by insurance, employees do not care about investment performance. But with profit-sharing plans they care a great deal.

As for savings and thrift plans, while the company's matching contribution may be in company stock, employees are generally given a wide choice as to how their funds are to be invested. For instance, they may be offered a choice among a common-stock fund, a savings fund with a guaranteed return, a balanced equity and fixed income fund, or the company's stock. Given these arrangements, eligible employees become more responsible for their own financial well-being and destiny. Similarly, with company stock-purchase plans, the employees are free to sell the shares they have purchased through payroll deductions at any time.

Management's reappraisal of investment strategy for profit-sharing plans is not only a result of the dismal performance of the stock market in 1973 and 1974, but also a result of lawsuits filed by disillusioned beneficiaries of company profit-sharing plans. The suits charged that the companies failed in their fiduciary responsibilities by investing too much in their own stocks. When its stock performed well, a company that invested heavily in its own stock was considered wise. However, when its stock fell dramatically, it was claimed that the company violated the "prudent man" rule.

Fear Factor

Unlike the positive reasons mentioned, there is another function fulfilled by some of these cash bonus and savings plans. Although data in support of this point are quite limited, some employees seem to fear that management would withdraw these generous benefits should they ever vote in favor of a union. Consequently, this fear factor can help management achieve its goal of remaining nonunion.

Charles A. Myers wrote that "nonunion firms may have gone further in providing more generous employee benefits such as profit sharing, partly to avoid unionization."[3] This study corroborates this statement, and also verifies that such companies are skillful at communicating their benefits to employees. Consequently, employees receive good benefits and they know it. It is not illogical to assume that they are aware of the benefits they receive compared to friends and neighbors who may work in unionized companies. Employees know that they receive a cash bonus once or twice a year, but that their friends and neighbors do not. They also know that their company offers its hourly workers a savings or stock-purchase plan and the nonunion ones do not. Thus, employees may reason that if they voted for a union, they might lose this benefit. Management may influence this thinking in subtle or in not-so-subtle ways during union organizational drives, and at other times.

CONCLUDING ANALYSIS AND COMMENTS

This chapter has shown that deferred and cash profit-sharing (or other bonus), savings plans and stock-purchase plans are quite prevalent in the benefit packages of the companies studied. These plans have been developed to accomplish different purposes. Four different but closely related purposes have been suggested:

1. These plans are consistent with the philosophy and goals of the founders; they demonstrate equity and fairness.
2. These plans help the employee identify with the purpose of the organization and give him a stake in the success of the enterprise.
3. These plans enhance employee motivation and management–employee coop-

---

[3]Charles A. Myers, "Management and the Employee," in *Social Responsibility and the Business Predicament,* ed. James W. McKie (Washington, D.C.: The Brookings Institution, 1974), p. 317.

eration by trying to align company and individual goals. They represent ways to improve management-to-employee and employee-to-management communications and understanding. To the extent that the supervisors are educated on the problems of the business through the way they are trained to conduct profit-sharing meetings, they in turn educate employees. Management also has an opportunity to be responsive to employee questions and concerns through such communication sessions.

4. Profit-sharing retirement plans, savings plans, and possibly stock-purchase plans (like defined pension plans) also serve an important security function. Employees know that when they reach retirement age, they may expect to be taken care of adequately. The programs of some of the companies add up to a super security package. Moreover, the programs of many companies make it attractive for the employee to save toward a down payment on a house or toward the expenses of a college education.

An additional factor may be that some of these plans help keep a company nonunion. The benefit is clearly superior to what the unionized company may offer, and the employee, well aware of this, may fear that management might withdraw it should a union be voted in.

As evidence from interviews indicates, the extent to which management is able to accomplish these objectives is unclear. The experience of the companies studied is uneven. Factors influencing this experience are the size of the company, the nature of the work force, the economic health of the company and the economy in general, the nature of the plans, and the ways in which management does or does not use them. A work force largely composed of young people seems to view deferred profit-sharing plans differently from older employees. Cash-payment profit-sharing plans obviously mean more when the company is financially healthy.

From the company's point of view, a deferred profit-sharing retirement plan is attractive. The company's contribution is not fixed; its amount depends on how much money the company earns. The company's contribution is only fixed as a percentage of profits. Since the pension reform law of 1974, the Employee Retirement Income Security Act (ERISA), profit-sharing plans are extremely attractive to management. Profit sharing is a known cost factor, not an uncertain liability over a period of years, with the company contribution depending on inflationary wage experience and investment performance.

As one company official said: "If the company were successful, we felt we could build greater retirement benefits for our people than we could commit ourselves to under a pension plan." In other words, the benefits to the employee could be greater than those a defined benefit pension plan would provide.

However, from the employees' viewpoint, a defined benefit pension program has some advantages over a traditional profit-sharing plan. There is a security in the employees' knowing that when they retire they will go with 50 percent or 60 percent of their final year's pay. Some of the companies in the sample make adjustments in pensions based on cost of living increases, but if the employees' pensions depend on the profitability of the company and the performance of the stock market, there is less security. With profit sharing, some security does flow from earlier eligibility, faster vesting, full funding, individual accounts, pre-severance withdrawals for home, education and illness, and no offset for Social Security.

In today's labor market it is difficult to see how a profit-sharing plan in which everything is deferred to retirement can be a source of motivation. With nothing passed out each year, the communications purpose of the plan would also seem more difficult to accomplish. A deferred profit-sharing plan might have made a company a trend-setter thirty years ago, but it does not do so today. Consequently, it is easy to understand why most deferred profit-sharing plans today not only provide cash-deferred options, partial withdrawals, and/or loans, but also are supplemented with other programs.

Ideally, it would seem that a company should have a defined benefit pension plan, or a deferred profit-sharing plan with a "floor" of benefits, or at least a guarantee of a minimum annual contribution. It should be recognized that historically a profit-sharing plan is not a "weak sister" of a defined benefit pension plan. Whether or not this will remain so for the future is doubtful. Another possibility is, of course, what some of the companies in the sample have: a defined benefit pension plan, and above this basic minimum, a profit-sharing plan. Or on top of the defined benefit pension plan could be a cash bonus and/or a savings and thrift plan, with individual employee choice about how either his or her funds or the company's contributions are invested. A cash profit-sharing plan might accomplish some of management's objectives better than one that is simply the standard one-or-two-weeks' pay variety. While either the full amount or some partial amount of the bonus could be deferred, it would seem best to leave this choice to the discretion of the employee.

In addition, if a company offers a savings plan, it would seem prudent to offer employees several choices, and permit them to decide how the funds should be invested. Of course, this is what the companies studied are doing. This approach is responsive to and consistent with the requirements of the Employee Retirement Income Security Act (ERISA) of 1974. If there is a company stock-purchase plan or a savings and thrift plan in which some of either the employee's or the company's contribution is in company stock, then management may better achieve its identification and motivation and communication objectives as well as its philosophy demonstration and security goals. Companies with only defined benefit pension plans, and no programs such as company-subsidized stock plans or matching-investment plans (with the company's contribution in its own stock), do not have any financial way for their employees to directly participate in the success of the enterprise other than through job security and satisfaction, raises, and promotion, which are by no means insignificant.

Although the ideal situation from an employee-relations point of view might be a defined benefit pension plan (or a profit-sharing plan with a set minimum) in combination with a cash profit-sharing plan and a company-matched employee savings account and/or stock-purchase program, the question of the costs of such programs must be taken into account. Pension plans generally cost 6 percent to 10 percent of payroll. A cash bonus or deferred profit-sharing plan, to be significant, could cost another 5 percent to 15 percent. A savings plan would cost yet another 1 percent or 2 percent to payroll costs. How are such plans to be financed?

Unlike a bonus plan related to weeks of pay, the amount from a profit-sharing plan would depend on the company's profitability. Theoretically, the extra effort and better communications associated with the existence of profit sharing would provide more than enough extra money to finance the bonus payments. This would be a double-win situation.

Managers of nonunion companies talked about the higher productivity and greater flexibility which they enjoy. Perhaps the costs of the bonus and/or savings plans are the price of increased flexibility. It will be recalled that members of top management spoke freely about the benefits of being nonunion. When asked about the costs of being nonunion, they saw few. They felt that even with higher wages and benefits it cost less to operate on a nonunion basis. Perhaps bonus and/or company-matched savings plans are one of the real costs of being nonunion to some companies. If so, they are costs that several companies have been willing to pay. If the experiences of these companies is relevant, it would be the view of the top managements of these companies that the benefits to-date appear to have greatly exceeded the costs.

As we have seen, profit-sharing plans and other employee ownership plans are frequently reasons for periodic communications with employees about the state of the company, its plans, and its problems. Meetings can make the communication of a two-way nature, and can be a useful feedback mechanism for top management.

Because the topic of upward and downward communications is so important, the next three chapters are concerned with formal communications programs feedback mechanisms. These formal communications programs are generally also important feedback devices for top management. Chapter 13 concerns attitude surveys, Chapter 14 focuses on other communications techniques or programs, and Chapter 15 discusses formal complaint procedures. Let us now turn to the subject of attitude surveys.

PART FOUR

Feedback Mechanisms and Communications Programs

CHAPTER THIRTEEN

Communications Programs: Attitude Surveys

Feedback mechanisms are a key variable of the analytical framework introduced in the first chapter. The top managements of the companies studied have devised and implemented a variety of feedback mechanisms or techniques to gain direct, nonhierarchical information about employees' views of company policies and practices, the way these policies are being administered, and the climate of the organization. While these mechanisms have other purposes as well, including downward communication, feedback is a principal objective. Although many of these programs are classified under the umbrella term *feedback mechanisms* here, the companies generally refer to these programs as *communications programs*.

A word frequently mentioned in the companies visited was "communication." Executives talked about keeping the lines of communication open. They talked about upward communication. They talked about keeping employees informed of the progress and problems of the business, and about being responsive to employee suggestions, complaints, and ideas. They talked about creating and maintaining a climate of openness and trust.

A vice-president of personnel interviewed, someone who had previously been director of labor relations in a unionized company, said that the principal key to remaining nonunion is to maintain an open communications system by which people believe they are treated as individuals rather than as members of a group, and by which they have a genuine opportunity to be heard.

There is no substitute for a good relationship and good communication between an employee and his or her supervisor, which builds and maintains an attitude of confidence and trust. The employee has to believe in the credibility of his or her supervisor and of top management. Put another way, the supervisor and top management must establish their credibility in the eyes of the employee. Among the ways top managements of the companies studied showed their concern about these issues was in its supervisory selection, training, and development. In order to combat the tendency to select the best worker to be a supervisor, some of the companies have assessment centers so that they can get a better idea of people's supervisory abilities before making promotion decisions. In addition, many of the companies direct substantial resources toward training and development, and hold introductory classes for new supervisors, as well as advanced classes for their continuing education.

However, most of the companies studied have gone beyond an exclusive reliance on good supervisor–employee relationships. These companies have introduced a variety of formal feedback mechanisms and communication programs that supplement as well as audit the supervisor–employee relationship. Furthermore, these programs serve as stimulation for the supervisor–employee relationship to work as effectively as possible. The main purpose of this chapter (and of Chapters 14 and 15) is to explore and analyze the steps that a substantial number of the companies have taken with feedback mechanisms and communications programs—and there are a wide variety of them—that are in addition to, or even above and beyond those concerned with supervisor–employee relationships. These communications programs are also in addition to company newspapers, bulletin boards, recreational programs, and—in some cases—dinners.

The basic function of the communications programs and feedback mechanisms examined here is to build employees' trust and confidence in management. There are at least six subpurposes of these programs.

First, these programs represent devices to learn of and to respond constructively to employee problems. It is unrealistic in a nonunion environment to expect many employees to voluntarily come forward with their problems. Therefore, it is necessary to have a variety of techniques to uncover and respond to individual employee problems before they become too serious.

Second, the programs seek to create a climate of openness in which the employees do not fear directing their complaints and suggestions to the attention of top management. Management gains information on how policies are working and on the climate of the organization, and then has a chance to respond. The opportunities for surprises are minimized.

Third, the programs (particularly attitude surveys and speak-out programs) attempt to meet the filter problem of lower-level management reporting only what it thinks top-level management wants to hear—presumably, good news.

Fourth, the programs communicate facts and information about the business downward. Some managements, to various degrees, open up to employees and supervisors—or to employees through supervisors—about the company, its progress, and its problems.

Fifth, because these programs seem to both supplement and check the supervisor–employee relationship, some programs seem designed to keep supervisors on their toes regarding the human-relations aspects of their jobs. The programs very clearly communicate to lower-level management that top management is interested in the work force and its morale. Many of these programs are an extension of the auditing role of personnel, because they operate around, rather than through, the supervisor. As such, these formal programs serve as an incentive to make informal approaches work more effectively.

Sixth, some of these programs are designed to help employees with personal as well as job-related problems, not only because it is thought a good thing to do, but also because such problems are frequently retardants of high productivity.

A particularly interesting finding of this study is not only the variety of techniques that have been developed to accomplish the same purpose, but also that many companies will use several of these techniques simultaneously. Except for employee-representation schemes, which will be discussed, the differences among the company approaches are interesting and significant to the companies but for the most part they are not fundamental. The important point is that the companies have strong communications programs (that, at least in part, represent top managements' feedback mechanisms), and that top management obtains feedback. How the feedback is obtained is less significant. Among the approaches to be examined are attitude surveys, counseling programs for personal and/or job related problems, employee representative systems, employee meetings, executive interviews with employees, person to person programs, question boxes and formal complaint procedures.

However, for the purpose of this chapter, discussion will be confined to attitude surveys. Then, in Chapter 14, we will examine the other kinds of communications devices used by companies—either with or instead of attitude surveys—as well as the rationale for doing so. Chapter 15 will be concerned with formal complaint procedures.

ATTITUDE SURVEYS: FORM AND SUBSTANCE

Approximately half of the companies studied use some form of an attitude survey, and four of the five largest companies in the sample conduct regular surveys. One company conducts attitude surveys on a biannual basis. This company's president, discussing a recently negotiated acquisition in the company's 1974 report, wrote:

> *We consider our employees the key ingredient to success. One of the*
> *first steps by [our] management was to take an attitude survey of our person-*

nel. Each employee's likes, dislikes, and ambitions were reviewed carefully.
Based on these findings, plans were formulated to further enrich their jobs. A
new pension plan already has been put into effect.

A representative of another company said that the organization uses various "sensing devices," with attitude surveys being one of them. The surveys are conducted periodically, and comparisons and trends are examined.

One company, which calls its survey its "people effectiveness" survey, states on the questionnaire that employees are asked to complete that: "Opinion surveys are used regularly throughout [the company] to help us understand how [our employees] feel about our effectiveness with people." This survey, used worldwide, is given in eight languages other than English.

In a different company, which hires an outside firm to do its annual survey, prior to the development and administration of the questionnaire the outside consultants interview a random selection of employees to help determine which subject areas should be included in the questionnaire. In yet another company, managers are told that the opinion survey is a valuable tool, not only to assess and improve employee satisfaction, but also to maintain efficiency and productivity.

Obviously, the form and substance of attitude surveys in use differ considerably. In one company, the survey is a regional personnel administrator visiting different plants and asking employees two different questions: "What do you like about the company?" and, "What would you like to see changed?" The personnel director of this company thinks it is a mistake to ask employees what they do *not* like, arguing that there will always be a lot of things not liked, many of which cannot be changed. However, by asking employees what they would like to see changed, one is undoubtedly also ascertaining what they do not like.

The written (or "paper-and-pencil") opinion survey helps top-level management gain a better understanding of employee attitudes, as well as of the attitudes of supervisory and other exempt personnel. This is because questionnaires are generally coded by division, location, department, and occupation, and are completed by several groups of employees. One company asks four groups of employees—production and maintenance, administrative, technical, and exempt—to identify themselves by job grade. Another company goes even further, for its check-off boxes are as precise as (for example) "machinery maintenance—first shift."

In addition to having many questions where the responses may range from "very good" to "very poor," or from "strongly agree" to "strongly disagree," the questionnaires also contain many open-ended questions that require a longer response. Examples of such questions from two companies are:

Company A:

> *I think . . . people effectiveness could be improved if . . .*

Company B:

Describe the two or three things you like most about your job or the company,

Now, describe two or three things that bother you the most about your job or the company.

How do you feel about the products manufactured by the company?

List any improvements or additions you'd like to see in the above benefits.

Annual Survey Approaches

At a service company, one of the three vice-presidents of personnel stated:

The survey helps identify problems and it keeps management on top of things. Management is convinced the survey is an effective tool of remaining nonunion. It allows us to keep our finger on the pulse, and we don't have to justify the budget request for the survey.

This survey, which costs approximately $60,000 per year, asks employees to rate the company with respect to the following factors: (1) fair treatment, (2) recognition and appreciation, (3) supervision, (4) pay, (5) working conditions, (6) job demands, (7) job security, (8) employee benefits, (9) adequacy of communications, and (10) reaction to the survey. The survey is computerized, and a positive index is calculated, which management can compare with the findings of the prior year as well as with those of individual units. (Although the survey format that had been used at this company for the past five years was in the process of being revised at the time this study was being done, the interview information and subsequent detailed feedback to line management appeared valuable.)

To administer this survey, a team of three corporate employee-relations people visit a company facility for two to three days; however, in many cases the survey is conducted by one or two employee-relations representatives. (The number of representatives involved and the duration of the survey vary according to the number of employees to be surveyed.) They interview as many employees as possible, and while the ideal goal is 100 percent, the coverage is usually 60 percent to 80 percent. Employees in small groups enter an interview room, fill out the questionnaire, and state their concerns.

The problem, of course, is survey follow-up. While much depends on regional and local management, employees are free to (and do) call headquarters collect to talk to a member of the employee-relations team about their problems. The employee-relations team spends about 60 percent of its time on the road, and they do one survey per year in each of the company's large units.

The president of this service company thinks the annual survey of rank-and-file opinion is one of the most effective communications systems, and wrote:

These surveys are our first line of defense against the buildup of unfavorable attitudes—our "early warning system" . . .

Many times the surveys bring to light small but potentially serious situations that can get out of hand if ignored. One recent survey, for example, revealed that employees resented not being provided with a safe place to store their valuables while they worked; they were troubled by occasional petty theft from their lockers. When this sentiment was brought to light, a safe storage place was made available for employee use, and a cause of ill will was eliminated.

In reviewing this company's survey results, it is clear that the personal interviews and the written employee comments are useful. The quantitative indexes, of course, also have their place. The first page of a report for one operating unit illustrated the process:

Employee Opinion Survey Summary

There seems to be a definite improvement in the attitude of the employees. This was evident by the large number of comments indicating that "things are much better this year than they were last year."

Many of the employees stated that since last year, they have seen an improvement in the attitude of managers toward employees. This was also reflected in the total overall positive index of 72 percent versus last year's 63 percent.

Of major concern to the employees were the following:

1. Many of the employees stated the need for a dental plan. However, many of them realize this will not be a reality any time soon.

2. Employees in the night shift indicated that supervision is weak during this shift and that some employees are doing as they please.

3. It was mentioned that some employees receive special treatment from managers because of their personal relationship outside the plant.

4. Employees stated that the quality of the food in the cafeteria needs to be improved, also, that more variation of meals is needed.

5. It was expressed that the plant is understaffed for the amount of work required. Sections mentioned the most were: the Store Room, Sanitation, and the Clerical Office.

Periodic Survey Approaches

The chairman of one company that administers an attitude survey periodically believes it is important to be clear on the purpose of the survey and to be mindful of its timing:

The original attitude survey was done here in 1950. It never occurred to anyone, including myself, to think about the way in which the surveys would be used. It was clear that some people doing the surveys were only interested in gaining knowledge. You have got to be committed in advance to making changes and improving the situation. Otherwise, you are not doing anything for people. I for one quite honestly think of an early survey as crap.

Periodically, it is good to do a survey, but you have to take into account the attitudes at a particular time. Sometimes when you're busy on a whole bunch of important projects or the company is experiencing problems and you know you won't have time to act, it would be a mistake to take the survey then. If we took a survey right now, the employees would be unusually negative. At other times, they are unusually positive, and you have to take this into account when you give the survey.

This company has developed an elaborate mechanism for administering and following up on its surveys. Its computer processing leads to rapid feedback, and randomly selected volunteer employee task forces analyze the results and make recommendations to management, with their reports going several levels above their immediate supervisor. Concerning this, a supervisor at this company said:

The workers feel that [the survey] doesn't count for anything until one of them is selected for the committee. Because only 5 percent of the people are involved, the other 95 percent feel it is so much hokum. You hear a lot of cynical remarks. Employees say, "What the hell good will this do—nothing really happened last year."

A former member of the company's personnel research staff had this to say about attitude surveys:

They can help improve management credibility. They can also raise a manager's level of understanding about how people really feel, if employees are given a sincere opportunity to address management in a candid fashion. Without upward communication bypassing the chain of command, there is no way for management to know exactly how people feel. *[Emphasis added.]*

Illustrating this point with respect to a union organizational drive, the researcher said:

. . . one attitude survey predicted a great deal of employee unrest and interest in forming a labor union. The survey was not believed by top management because, in interrogating midmanagement and supervision, few problems were uncovered. Follow-up interviews with employees and supervisors also showed very little employee discontent and dissatisfaction. However, a few months later, a labor union filed a petition for recognition and over 30 percent of the employees had signed union cards. Evidently, a significant gap and distortion occurred as information was passed up the line.

Hierarchy has a tendency to filter bad news on the way up and bring forward only that information lower-level management believes most accept-

able to top management. Some of this distortion is inadvertent; some is blatant self-serving filtering. Some personnel organizations, in accommodating the desires of top management, tend to discredit or discount evidence of poor morale. In some organizations, significant employee dissatisfaction has been hidden from the view of top management with the hope that it will either go away on its own or that, with a delay, the problems may be resolved and eliminated before key executives have to get involved. . . . Attitude surveys are increasingly utilized by nonunion companies that wish to remain that way.

As for what employee opinions should be surveyed, the researcher said:

[The questionnaire] should be broad enough to capture the key areas that are important to employee morale, motivation, and productivity. Obviously, sampling opinions on pay and benefits in terms of their favorableness of perceptions by employees is essential. For organizations that wish to remain in a nonunion status, the area of supervisor favoritism and fairness, and the perceptions the people have vis-à-vis management are also critical. It is also possible to survey attitudes regarding unions and employee interest in unionization. The favorableness of opinions regarding rules, procedures, and policies is also open for attitude measurement.

This same researcher also recommended that special safeguards be taken to preserve confidentiality, and that questions should not be asked about subjects that management does not intend to or cannot afford to change:

Cafeterias and parking lots are examples. These perennial areas of dissatisfaction rarely get improvement. They simply create the idea in the minds of employees that if they give the cafeteria and parking lot a strongly unfavorable score significant improvement will follow. Rarely does this occur, and this tends to discredit the other areas of attitude measurement in which improvement can and will be made.

While there always seem to be problems with cafeterias and parking lots, it would seem that if a company too much laundered the questions it asked, it would risk losing the confidence of its employees. Just as a company could lose credibility by violating (or even appearing to violate) anonymity and confidentiality, or by failing to follow through on survey results, it could also lose the confidence of its employees by using a questionnaire its employees perceived as not being meaningful.

Another company's questionnaire contains certain sets of questions, which ask the employee to rate the importance of a list of objectives. In different sets of questions, the employees are asked to rate their degree of satisfaction in achieving these objectives. Although in this company the survey results go to the supervisor, the write-in comments the questionnaire has room for are seen only by higher levels of management. This is to preserve anonymity, as certain comments might identify an employee to his or her supervisor. This company also asks employees and managers to rate the usefulness of the attitude survey. Presumably, at this company if many employees thought the survey was "hokum" and did not "count for anything," this feeling would be revealed in the survey results, because both employees and managers are asked how satisfied they were with the previous survey feedback meeting.

Because trend lines are useful to management, it is important that at least some of the questions asked each year be kept the same. However, one executive reported that it is a mistake to keep asking all the exact same questions each year, for if this is done, then some employees may play games with the survey. It would seem that this could be especially true if a company used a 100 percent sample each year.

PERSONNEL AUDITS

Attitude surveys are an integral part of the plant personnel audits that another large, predominantly nonunion company conducts. The surveys serve as a guide and catalyst for plant management to uncover and to act on existing or potential trouble areas. They are also used as a barometer for how a particular plant compares to other plants. The audits of individual plants by the company's corporate personnel department are conducted in a manner similar to an accounting audit. If a plant has recently had or is having employee-relations problems, an audit is conducted each year. If the plant is viewed as relatively "trouble-free," an audit is done every third or fourth year. The corporate director of employee relations, when asked about these audits, said:

> The audit results are for the use of the plants. They are not used by corporate to beat the plants over the head. The only use corporate makes of the audit results is for developing overall company policies.

The audit covers the entire area of employee relations from the employment situation in the geographic area to in-plant safety. The various subjects listed in the company's nonunion personnel guidebook, and reviewed by corporate representatives during plant visits, cover: employment, orientation and training, employee relations policy, how employee dissatisfactions are handled, safety, the employee booklet, absence control, overtime administration, Equal Employment Opportunity, area wage and fringe benefits survey, morale, employee activities and recreation, community relations, service facilities, and contractor operations. Although dozens of specific questions are asked in the audit about each of these topics, the questions particularly noteworthy for the purposes of this study are:

> What are the last three times and items that employees heard from plant supervision as to unions or as to staying nonunion? List.
> Is there a formal grievance procedure? Describe.

Are there upward communication devices such as request forms, "speak up" forms, call-in and record questions, shift meetings, personnel man available, personnel surveys/questionnaires, employee booklet review meetings, foreman/supervisor available?

What are the three main complaints that employees currently have?

What are the main strengths in employee complaint handling?

What are the main points needing improvement?

How is the employee manual revised? Are hourly employees able to suggest changes? Are foremen able to suggest changes?

How are changes, or new booklets, explained to employees?

Who reviews proposed changes and decides? How are these decisions communicated to suggestor?

What kind of seniority system is there? Is it well understood?

What kind of promotion policy and procedures are there?

How does an employee make known his desires to change jobs or departments? How often are transfers affected? Does a job opening ever go to a less senior candidate? Explain.

Is there a procedure for applying for promotion or transfer to the salaried payroll? Is it known to hourly employees?

Number and type of contractor employees in plant for last year? Union or nonunion?

Is contractor employee gate adequate and approved by legal authority? Is it used regularly?

Do contractor employees have separate eating facilities? Washroom facilities?

What degree of contact is there between contractor employees and plant employees?

Are there adequate and legally cleared "no trespassing" signs?

These are significant questions, ones which an uncommitted local management would find difficult to answer. The company's employee relations director, when asked about the reaction of employees and supervisors to the audits, said:

Reaction to the audits from wage employees is positive. We are complimented that corporate is interested enough to visit the plant, to interview them, and to solicit their opinions, advice, and complaints. Reaction of the foremen is ambivalent. They are unsure of what corporate intends to do with the results.

This director also said that the local managers are frequently resistant to the corporate attitude surveys. They feel that negatives will be heard and discussed, and that this will hurt their own careers. This concern demonstrates the importance that top management attaches to the management of human resources, as well as the need for top management's attitudes to be understood.

This same employee relations director felt that the company faces the challenge to develop better methods of measuring morale and satisfaction in the future, in order for it to continue to be successful at maintaining its nonunion status, and cited five pieces of evidence to support this view: (1) People's wants and needs are becoming more complex and at times conflicting, and it is difficult to decipher the conflicting signals. (2) With the unionization of white-collar groups, particularly teachers, students are leaving school with pro-union attitudes. (3) As industrial plants increase in number and size, it is becoming more difficult to maintain an emphasis on the individual employee. (4) With the increasing number of blacks in the work force, this company faces new problems. This director's experience had been that blacks as a group are more difficult to assess as to their needs and wants, and that they are more susceptible to group action, chiefly due to the success of the civil rights movement through group action. (5) Various segments of the work force have different needs and priorities, and it is becoming more difficult to balance those different demands.

A question can be raised as to whether or not there are substantial differences between audits and attitude surveys. An attitude survey can sometimes be viewed as one form of an audit; however, an attitude survey can also be viewed as less formal. With an attitude survey, there is possibly less commitment on the part of management to follow-up. Yet, audits and attitude surveys can also be quite similar. What is important is whether or not the results are taken seriously, and what is done because of them.

One large international company that had administered annual attitude surveys for almost twenty years now conducts them every six months. The company's director of personnel research commented that:

> At the start of the 1969–1970 recession, a decision was made to have more timely readings of morale, with some people wanting the survey done quarterly. Opinion surveys are a part of our management system, as opposed to being a research tool.

This company's attitude surveys are conducted worldwide; in the United States they are done on a fall (September to November) and a spring (March to June) cycle. The questionnaires are answered on company time, at the employee's work place or in the cafeteria. While a set of common questions is asked in all of the surveys, each questionnaire is tailored to fit the situation, with each division adding its own questions. The manager is responsible for giving feedback to his or her employees.

Of particular interest is the fact that this company has a huge data base. One study showed that training the manager how to give feedback improves the results of the survey; these findings resulted in the company increasing the amount of training it gives managers in this area. A division personnel director in this company said that some managers dread the opinion survey and that "this obviously indicates that they have something to hide."

SPECIAL SURVEYS

As indicated earlier, not all of the companies using attitude surveys do so on a regular basis. At least two companies have done special surveys at the time of layoffs. The corporate personnel group of one of these companies sent a telegram to each of its units with the following message:

> Per our communication, the following questions are to be asked of at least six survey applicants. Your assistance is appreciated.
>
> 1. What was the reaction in general to layoffs and do you feel that [the company] explored all alternatives before resorting to layoffs?
> 2. How would you rate the credibility of your boss, division management, corporate management?
> 3. How do you rate your confidence in [the company] and its management today as contrasted with one year ago when you joined the company?
> 4. What in your opinion has had the greatest impact upon your feelings toward [the company]?
> 5. How would you characterize the mood of your facility (e.g., friends, co-workers)?
> 6. How does [the company] compare with other companies in the treatment of its employees during these times of unusual economic pressures?
> 7. Do you feel that you have had an adequate explanation of the company's present economic circumstances?
> 8. What is your reaction to cost savings programs initiated at your department/facility to date?

As was referred to in Chapter 6, another company asked a member of its organization development staff to interview laid-off employees to ascertain their perceptions of how the company was treating them during that traumatic period.

LOWER MANAGEMENT REACTIONS

From interviews with supervisors and managers, it is clear that some are quite negative about attitude surveys. Their collective reaction to the use of attitude surveys indicated the attention lower-level management believes top-level management pays to the survey results. Supervisors question the usefulness of some of the questions, as well as the meanings attached to the responses. Supervisors also feel they are being "marked" or "graded" on areas beyond their control. For example, supervisors complained about particular questions. In one company, a supervisor said that at least 20 percent of his employees were not interested in advancement, therefore, the fact that his score was low on the opportunities for advancement question should not really mean anything. "If people do not want to advance, what does it matter how employees feel about opportunities for advancement?''

A supervisor at another company was frustrated with a similar question but for a different reason. The company's growth had slowed and there were just not the advancement opportunities that had once existed. What frustrated this supervisor was the fact that he had to write an action plan to improve his rating in this category. ''What am I supposed to do if the promotional opportunities simply aren't there?''

Supervisors also talked about the problem of ambiguous survey questions. ''The questions mean something different to every employee,'' said one supervisor. ''The worker who works in a T-shirt answers the question about working conditions different from the worker who works in a sweater.'' Supervisors also ask what the survey results mean to top management when the questionnaire is filled out by employees who do not speak English. Supervisors also spoke of the results being biased by the mood or attitude of the employee on the particular day the survey happens to be administered.

Supervisors reported that some employees view the survey as a joke; that some employees seem to feel that nothing will come of the survey. Some supervisors also felt that some employees will not respond to surveys truthfully. Supervisors seemed to sense a certain amount of gamesmanship on the part of the employees.

However, in general, supervisors seem to take attitude survey results seriously. This is not only because the results are seen by their bosses, but also because they must develop follow-up action plans that are monitored. One supervisor said: ''I'm a smidgen better than the site average—I've been lucky.'' Another said: ''The last survey was the worst one I have ever had. Several employees indicated they didn't understand their performance appraisal and this really hurt me.''

Commenting on his department's survey results, a department head said:

> There were few surprises. I was surprised, though, in that a couple of
> my managers didn't fare too well in terms of their effectiveness. Three out of
> twenty-three managers didn't fare too well; two of the three were a surprise.

When asked how he used the survey results, this department head gave an example relating to the company's salary plan. The survey revealed that 35 percent of the employees were favorable to the salary plan, 35 percent were neutral, and 30 percent were unfavorable: ''The problem is that the employees don't really understand the salary plan. What I learned, however, is that the managers don't really understand the salary plan either.'' He had assumed that the managers understood the plan. In response to this finding, he asked the plant's salary administrator to prepare a salary presentation for his use at a meeting with the managers. This illustration is but one example of how the survey can be an instrument used to improve communications among managers, as well as between management and employees.

It is probably unrealistic to expect that supervisors would view the use of attitude surveys with enthusiasm. Attitude surveys do stir up the employees. Even an outstanding supervisor cannot know in advance how the ratings will come out. Just as is the case with performance appraisal, improvement is always possible, but people prefer good news, or even no news, to negative feedback. Nevertheless, top management needs to be sensitive to the impact of attitude surveys on lower- and middle-level management so that the negatives can be minimized.

INTERPRETATIONS OF SURVEYS

How top-level and lower-level managements use the survey results is of critical importance. The numbers have to be interpreted with judgment. Supervisors need to know, from the perspective of top management, the purpose of attitude surveys, as well as their limitations and disadvantages, and they need to know that top management understands their problems. They also need to be trained and involved in the ways in which the survey results are used.

Surveys can reveal problems that might otherwise go unnoticed. One opinion survey administrator felt the surveys free people to look at problems:

> You either face problems or you sweep them under the rug. Without the survey, most managers would sweep them under the rug.

This interview also revealed that top management may have to pay special attention to the career needs of those responsible for the survey, as well as to interpret the numbers with judgment. Perhaps the messenger can get blamed for the bad news—as this young administrator said: "An attitude survey is not a popular thing to administer for a young manager in personnel." Top management had asked this manager to make five-year projections of employee attitudes. He projected that the percent favorable toward the company would advance from 59 percent to 65 percent, but top management insisted on a higher figure! Such projections seemed unrealistic and this manager agreed that he was engaged in an exercise that was somewhat ridiculous.

DISADVANTAGES AND/OR LIABILITIES

The companies that forgo the use of attitude surveys do so for a variety of reasons. Some believe that their disadvantages outweigh their advantages. Some feel that the risks or liabilities associated with attitude surveys are substantial. Some also think that the survey format is inconsistent with a company's objectives in the employee-relations area.

A personnel executive at a very large company commented:

> *We do not use attitude surveys with hourly people. An attitude survey implies that you want to deal with problems on a group basis. [The company] does not deal with groups. [The company] deals with the individual. And, by the way, we never say [company] employees. We always say [company] people.*

Yet, at another company where respect for the individual is one of its cornerstones, attitude surveys are viewed as an extremely helpful management tool. While it is nice to deal with the individual, some problems are departmentwide or companywide, and attitude surveys may help identify them.

The vice-president of personnel at one company, which does not use attitude surveys, said:

> *Attitude surveys are too general and not very helpful. We have better channels of communications through the personnel representative.*

Although a survey may not be very helpful if it is too general, this would, in part, seem a function of both its design and its administration. At this company, the personnel representatives, each serving 200 to 300 employees, get together once a month to discuss common problems. In addition, each personnel director and each personnel manager hold weekly staff meetings with the personnel representatives.

Whether or not these practices are as, or even more, effective than a periodic survey probably depends on the caliber of the personnel representatives and on their relationships with employees and supervisors, as well as on the climate in which they operate. At one company top management feels that the personnel people are close enough to those in the plant, making an attitude survey unnecessary.

An administrative vice-president at another company, which does not use attitude surveys, said that the company did not because "it means you are locked into doing something as a result of the survey and you can lose credibility." The counter to this view is that management has to be committed to acting on the results of the survey *prior* to doing it, and that if management does act, it would gain credibility with employees.

CONCLUDING ANALYSIS AND COMMENTS

Periodic attitude surveys accomplish a variety of purposes. They can be temperature-taking devices to see if employee attitudes are or are not "normal." They can give top management unfiltered information about the ways in which employees perceive a variety of matters. Top management can learn things it otherwise may not. Surveys give employees an opportunity to state their views on an anonymous basis. A guarantee of confidentiality is undoubtedly one of critical factors associated with effectiveness; another is a willingness on the part of management to act on the basis of the surveys' results. If no visible changes come from the surveys, employees may come to ridicule the process. If employee expectations are repeatedly raised and nothing happens, it may have been better not to have conducted the surveys at all.

Attitude surveys are capable of finding evidence of employee dissatisfaction. The larger the company, the more need there probably is for such surveys. Attitude surveys also lack the middle-management filtering process that can be associated with other information gathering approaches. The employees have a direct access to top management through the surveys.

If the surveys are conducted by outsiders, management may pay more attention to this "objective" information. Even if the surveys are done by the personnel department, as is the case in the great majority of companies studied, they produce "numbers and hard evidence." The results can provide an "early warning system" of potential problems. Discussion about morale and attitudes can sometimes be more productive if they are based on something other than "soft" data. Attitude surveys fill this void, for analyses of trends and comparative data can be made from them. When asked about the attitude survey data, a senior vice-president of personnel in a predominantly nonunion company that has several autonomous division heads said: "The survey results give me something to talk about with a division manager. It makes my visit more legitimate. It permits me to ask certain questions." As one of the managers interviewed said, with attitude surveys it is more difficult for line managers to sweep problems under the rug.

Whether the surveys are an effective feedback and communications tool depends on the way in which top-level and lower-level managements use the results. There has to be a commitment to investigate the problem areas and to take corrective action where appropriate. Insisting on action plans and periodic checkings of progress are essential. The comments of lower-level managers indicated the importance their top managements attach to the survey.

If top management is really concerned about employee attitudes, the surveys give them some "hard" data. Surveys permit top management to "keep its fingers on the pulse." If it is true that one cannot manage something until one can measure it, the surveys quantify something that, as has been said, is usually considered qualitative and "soft." Trends can be noted and comparisons can be made among departments, plants, and divisions. In addition, the numbers can be part of the performance appraisal of managers.

Given the competitive instincts of most managers, simply publishing the information can be useful. A manager does not want to look bad relative to his or her peers, especially if he or she believes top management takes the results seriously. Surveys, in addition, help personnel departments develop policies, programs, and training that are responsive to employee concerns and manager needs.

In sum, attitude surveys, depending upon their purpose and how they are administered, can be an effective feedback mechanism and an upward-communications tool. The companies that forgo the use of attitude surveys do so for a variety of reasons; mainly, they believe that the same objective can be better accomplished in other ways. It is to these other feedback mechanisms and communications programs that we now turn our attention.

CHAPTER FOURTEEN

Communications Programs:
Other Techniques

Chapter 13 discussed the principal purposes of the formal communications programs, mainly the attitude surveys, that many of the companies studied have adopted. The purpose of this chapter is to describe and to analyze other programs and techniques that various companies employ. Some of these programs have come about in response to problems identified through formal attitude surveys. The programs and techniques to be considered here include: counseling programs for personal and/or job-related problems, employee representative systems, employee meetings, executive interviews with employees, person-to-person programs, and question boxes. Although a number of the companies also have formal suggestions systems, examination of these programs was beyond the scope of this study. After discussing and analyzing these different approaches, there will be a brief summary discussion of their functions.

COUNSELING PROGRAMS

Counseling for Personal Problems

Several of the companies visited employ counselors to help their employees with personal problems. Sometimes this assignment is one of the jobs of the company's personnel representatives. Highlights of some of the different approaches currently being used are presented here.

One company with many female counselors refers to them as "house-mothers." A company publication describes their role as follows:

> You'll find them located with the minority of the production areas at larger manufacturing divisions, generally listening to or discussing the personal problems that people bring to them, or counseling new people. In this way, they serve as liaison between manufacturing and personnel departments.

A housemother interviewed in this publication said: "The goal is to get help as soon as possible, and to take people's minds off their personal problems so they can go back to work and not worry." One company manager noted that only the women, not the men, used the housemother. The personnel manager said that, although this division's housemother was in manufacturing as opposed to personnel, he thought she did more training and administrative work than counseling.

The company publication stated that housemothers dealt with all kinds of problems, ranging from baby-sitter difficulties to insurance complications to personality conflicts. In citing the importance of trust, the publication quoted a housemother:

> When they asked me to become a housemother, it took a while to gain the confidence of people on the line. In time, they learned that I wouldn't do anything without their approval or betray a confidence.

Another company, with a large number of young employees, also employs "housemothers," who are expected to guide the young people and to alert management to troublesome situations that may develop.

A supervisor in a different company, discussing the counselor's role, said:

> Sam [the counselor] keeps us honest. He is a good relief valve because some people are afraid to talk to their manager or supervisor. He always keeps things in confidence. Sometimes I'll try to find out from him who he is getting his story from but he'll never tell me. If Sam gets a whole series of complaints and it is clear there is a problem with a particular manager, Sam will talk to the manager. And he may go higher. Sam is not bashful and he has a good flow of information.

While this supervisor admits that many supervisors are not jubilant about their employees going to see the counselor, they think the counselor approach is important to preserve.

Whereas these companies have selected experienced employees or supervisors to be counselors, another company employs professionally-trained social workers to assist troubled employees. In another case, a company has two ministers as counselors, and it provides the employees with a chapel.

Personnel people who performed similar functions were found in other companies. A personnel representative at one company helped get the electricity turned back on in the home of an employee. Counseling employees to help them solve their personal problems can free them from worries that might otherwise interfere with their productivity at work.

While some employees with personal problems will go to their supervisor or to the personnel department, many will not do so. Consequently, one company was planning to introduce an employee assistance program, designed to enhance the handling of personal problems.

Counseling for Job-Related Problems

One personnel director, who said that "being nonunion you have to be particularly sensitive to employee complaints," related that he views the company's nurses as an adjunct to the personnel department:

> The nurses represent the personnel department and they probably hear what the personnel representative does not hear. The nurse has the ear of the employee and is a real aid to the lines of communications within the company.

How counselors, nurses, or personnel representatives use the feedback that comes *around* line management rather than *through* it is critical. Some of what they learn is confidential. If they reported everything to management and came to be regarded as spies for it, it is clear that they would lose the trust and confidence of the employees, thereby destroying their effectiveness. Although they are primarily a resource for employees, part of their job may be to counsel supervisors. Clearly, they could ruin their image of helpfulness if they used information foremen provided them against employees, or if they used information provided by employees about foremen in a dysfunctional way in discussions with members of management, including higher management. What information it is legitimate to provide management is a difficult question, as is the way it should be provided. As many of the people in these jobs said, they must walk a fine line between the management and the employees. In the judgment of some of the managers in these companies, counselors tip too much to the side of the employees. However, this seems understandable in the nonunion company, for if the employees do not feel comfortable discussing their problems with their supervisors or with a counselor or personnel representative, then perhaps they would turn to an outsider. What is clear is that people in these jobs, to be effective, have to handle carefully difficult issues, many of which involve issues of confidentiality, which requires good judgment and experience. The appropriate selection criteria for these jobs as well as proper orientation and training are important. Moreover, top management has to take steps which make them feel legitimate and comfortable in their sometimes very difficult and ambiguous roles.

One of the companies that conducted an attitude survey only once (in 1973) subsequently developed two different communications programs, including an in-plant counselor program.

This one attitude survey revealed a lack of good communications within the company, and: "The lack of response to problems equal[s] the seeds of unionization. While our plant counselor program, with worker representing worker, may have some legal problems, the risks of not doing everything were greater than the risks of doing what we did," commented the administrative vice-president. Management at this company selected a group of workers and identified them as *in-plant counselors (IPCs)* to management. They were given time off to assist with problems and to meet with management.

The IPCs assumed a liaison role between all levels of management and the worker. They are not representatives of the employees in an advocacy position, but instead act as human-relations funnels by directing problems to the proper authorities. IPCs make sure that grievances get handled, and they provide information to employees about company policies, personnel policies, or job-related problems. Frequently discussed issues include sick leave, wages, evaluations, vacations, seniority, and benefits. Much of what IPCs do is work normally done by supervisors.

Each IPC is selected by his or her supervisor and by the personnel department as an employee with supervisory potential. The criteria for selection to these positions, which rotate every two years, include: knowledge of the work area, an ability to get along with co-workers, experience with the company, trustworthiness, and an ability to be trained for this job.

Once chosen, each IPC is responsible for thirty to forty employees. If necessary, IPCs are paid overtime; however, most of their work is done during regular hours. IPCs spend two or three days in an initial training program where they learn about their duties, and about company policies and procedures. Throughout their term in office, IPCs meet monthly for on-going training.

In conjunction with the IPC program, the company has a staff of *employee coordinators (ECs)* who are assigned to different areas of the company, and who work with the manager of employee relations to help resolve employee complaints. These ECs spend half of their time in the plant talking to employees; the other half is spent in the office, where they interpret company policies and handle the personnel problems referred to them. Unlike the IPCs, the ECs have the authority to make decisions relating to grievances that are not specifically addressed in the policy guide.

A major reason for the effectiveness and frequent use of ECs by supervisors, IPCs, and employees is the selection process. ECs are hired from the work force in accordance with the company's open job-bidding system. Therefore, they are familiar with the company and the employees, and are able to listen, to empathize, and to direct employees to the proper authority for help with problems. Management intends to use this EC group more in the future to communicate ideas down to the rank and file, as well as to resolve individual problems and grievances.

The EC's are important contacts for the IPCs. The two groups meet monthly with the manager of employee relations to discuss policies and problems, as the ECs assist in developing the individual IPCs' skills in dealing with employees. Clearly, in this company the manager of employee relations has his own information system separate and apart from the foremen.

If an IPC cannot give an answer from the policy guide that will resolve an employee's problem, he or she will usually refer the employee to the direct supervisor, who will in turn try to handle the problem or grievance. One counselor said:

> I learned to keep my mouth shut until I heard the story from both sides. In most cases employees don't understand the policy and think they are being taken advantage of. Once the company policy is explained to them, they usually accept it.

However, if the employee feels that the supervisor's answer is unsatisfactory, or if he or she wants a response from a different source, the IPC will then refer the employee to an EC, who takes over. This has the obvious potential to pit the employee coordinator against the supervisor.

Executive Communications Helpers

One company established an *executive communications helper (ECH)* program in the mid-1960s for basically the same reasons that the above company introduced its IPC program. However, the ECH program has a history that is important to understand.

In the early 1900s, in order to know how people felt about the company's products during a period of rapid growth, the president of this company established sales councils. These councils were set up in each location, and the employees elected a president, a vice-president, and a secretary: the person with the most votes was the president, the person with the second most votes was the vice-president, and the one with the third most votes was the secretary.

As the company's retired vice-president of personnel put it: "With all of these people, discussions got well beyond sales problems. Many personnel issues were also discussed." When the company established a personnel department in the late 1930s, the personnel manager went to the sales council meetings, usually ending up as the secretary, for no one else wanted to do the paper work. The personnel manager's role was usually one of listening and interpreting.

In the 1950s, an international union that had made many attempts to organize the company, filed a charge with the National Labor Relations Board claiming that the local councils were an illegal employee organization. The charge was upheld, and so the company had to cease this practice. As the personnel vice-president put it:

> *Officially, at least, the council's agenda was reduced to sales problems, with other topics being ruled out. If personnel topics were raised, it would be said that this is not a topic we can discuss any more. But after the meetings, perhaps even in the wash rooms or in the hallways, some individuals would bring up personnel matters.*
>
> *There was a great deal of open communication. All this plus the commitment to being a leading company resulted in a level of pride and respect within and outside the organization. With the councils, the employees said, "Why do we need a union? We have one, our own."*

Given this history, it was easy for the company to recognize the need for a forum to discuss personnel problems. Consequently, the ECH program was devised. Company attitude surveys had also revealed a need for two-way feedback, and for finding a mechanism to generate grass-roots opinions and ideas unfiltered by management.

As with the IPCs, the ECHs serve as direct liaisons between the management and the employees, so that information need not be filtered through first-line supervisors. At each branch and for each shift, local management selects one person to be an ECH. (ECHs are not elected because legal counsel advised the company that it would be illegal to do so.) It is important to recognize that the ECH job is a second job that is done by the employee in addition to, and sometimes mostly, on hours apart from his or her regular job. The concept is that the employee, in this second job, is an assistant to the manager. The ECHs are paid separately at the rate of 5 percent of their pay for their regular jobs. Each ECH is responsible for twenty to seventy employees, and the criteria for selection is very similar to those for IPCs. One manager said: "You select people who might be elected by the employees if there were to be an election."

The ECH is available to employees to discuss problems and explain things. If an ECH discovers that many employees did not understand something, he or she will inform the manager. Similarly, if a manager is planning to change several shifts or to make other changes affecting the organization, he or she will check with the ECH in advance for feedback on how this may affect the employees. The hope is that this will add an important dimension to aid the manager in arriving at sound decisions. Once a month the ECHs meet as a group with the personnel manager and the vice-president of operations. Topics discussed may cover a wide range of matters, including such things as job bidding, vacation policies, seniority, operations plans, sales efforts, and communications needs.

Of course, some line managers are opposed to the ECH concept, which is a program proposed by the personnel department and supported by the vice-president of personnel and by the president. Line managers are particularly concerned about what might be said about their operations at these big meetings. Commenting on this, the personnel manager said:

> *This is what the local managers see as a bypass. In addition to discussing the state of the business, specific local problems are discussed at these meetings.*

When asked for an assessment of the program, the current personnel manager said:

> *It has helped us. The resistance of some line managers has helped us sell it to the employees, and now I am convinced that managers and supervisors view the program as less of a threat, and use the ECH as a communications link. For example, some local managers are urging their ECHs to argue at the big meetings for new equipment they can't get approved.*

Another personnel administrator, who considers the program a good one, nevertheless thinks that it could be better used. She also thinks that the managers do not talk as honestly to employees at the meetings as they should. As an example, she cited the minutes of each meeting, which contain an item about the need for a dental–optical program at the company. The minutes also always say "check corporate." This corporate personnel administrator said:

> *The reason we don't have a dental–optical plan is because we can't afford it, and it is inconsistent with our company's philosophy regarding benefits. Why didn't the managers tell them that! It has always been our philosophy to provide unusual protection against catastrophic illness—the illness the employee cannot afford, plan, or save for. Dental–optical is not in this category.*

The one unionized plant in one division of this company is the only location that does not have ECHs. When asked about this, two different explanations were offered. The division personnel manager believed that the lack of support of the ECH program at this plant is an indication of local management at the plant not wanting to communicate with its people. However, the retired vice-president of personnel said that the ECH program was not implemented at this plant during the period of the union drive because it could have been viewed as an unfair labor practice.

In analyzing the ECH program, one can see its value not only as a mechanism for helping the managers gain an added input prior to some of their decisions, but also as a way to resolve individual problems and to give employees some real influence. A plant manager would not ask an ECH to lobby for new equipment at a council meeting if the ECH organization did not have influence and power. Obviously, it is top management that gives it that power. The ECH organization is not a union, and lacks the formal power of one; nevertheless, this company organization does perform some of the functions of a union.

EMPLOYEE REPRESENTATIVE SYSTEMS

Two organizations, as well as the acquired company of another organization studied, have employee representative communications devices. These programs, which have been in use over a quarter of a century, are real representative systems. They go further than any of the counseling approaches discussed because in these companies the employee representatives are elected. These systems are quite close to unionism; moreover, they have some of the consequences of unionism.

One personnel director believes his company's employees' committee is very significant because top management listens to it and has great respect for it. However, he does admit that having elected employee representatives is of questionable legality, and that the company might be in trouble if it were challenged.

Because all three companies follow similar approaches, only one of them will be described in detail. The company selected is one in which the employee organization has been in existence for more than thirty years. An outsider who knows this company well has said that its approach is one of the least known but best communications programs in U.S. industry.

Council of Personnel Relations and the Main Council

The cornerstone of this company's communications programs is its *Council of Personnel Relations (CPR)*, along with its jobholders' meetings, and the question and request boxes located throughout the plants. The council is officially described as "an employee–management group whose purpose is to build a spirit of mutual confidence between employees and management, so that both may benefit from increased job satisfaction and organizational efficiency."

The CPR structure parallels the organization of the company, and consists of appointed management members with an equal number of elected members representing the employees in each section of the company. Meetings are held at various organizational levels, starting with section meetings attended by all employees in the section, and progressing through department or branch levels.

At corporate headquarters, there are also meetings held at division levels, and a *Main Council* whose meetings are attended by officers of the company and their elected employee counterparts. Meetings are held monthly, bimonthly, or quarterly, depending on location.

The Main Council serves as a permanent part of the company's organization. It participates by advising and counseling both management and employees on all matters concerning the operation of the company, including the well-being and fair treatment of all employees. Its objective and modus operandi, according to the company's employee handbook, are:

> To serve employees with increased job security and satisfaction in working conditions and earning opportunities. It seeks to serve management with a broad pooling of ideas and a means of informing all employees of the progress and problems of the business. It seeks to serve both groups through the development of a high degree of cooperation and commitment.

When asked about the cost of the CPR program, the company's chairman said:

> I have no idea. How would you measure it? You can't measure it. We have had this CPR philosophy for a long time. It is a way of life here and it is practical and pragmatic. An informed employee is a better employee, a more productive employee. We have no third party here. The employees feel they belong to a union.

When asked about personnel's role, the chairman replied:

> Beyond doing the mechanical things, personnel should monitor all personnel practices to make sure they are being carried out properly, and they should maintain and improve the openness of communication.

The employee-relations vice-president, in discussing the costs of the system, cited three. The first cost is all of the company time directed to meetings, since the company shuts down for meetings and that is nonproductive time. The second cost is the salaries paid to CPR members when they are attending meetings and serving employees. One Main Council co-chairman does that full time—he or she is elected, gets a salary, and does no other work. (The other Main Council co-chairman is the chairman of the company.) The third cost is that the CPR members at the Main Council are better informed about things than many members of middle- and lower-level management.

One employee Main Council member interviewed had this to say about what the council approach means:

> To me, being on the Main Council, a very big part of CPR is the understanding it gives us about the company and the industry we work in. Take competition. It's going to affect all of us. We're asking questions about it now and we'll be ready for it.
>
> It offers us a constructive way to work out problems. I think that word constructive should be emphasized.

CPR makes us all a part of the team. You feel that what you are doing is worthwhile. CPR is a two-way street for communications—it gives us a chance to understand each other.

An attitude survey conducted by an outside organization revealed that 70 percent of the company's shop workers, 78 percent of the office workers, and 89 percent of the supervisory force ranked the company "good" to "very good" in "letting employees know what is going on in the company." Furthermore, 67 percent of the shop workers, 78 percent of the office workers, and 93 percent of the supervisory force felt that "management tries to keep us fully informed."

A visit to the company revealed that this representative system, in addition to its formal role, also has an informal role. Namely, in the words of a personnel administrator, it serves as a "semi-informal grievance procedure." Interviews with the elected CPR members indicated that they saw their representation of employees as an important part of their job.

This company's representative system would appear to be a strong antiunion device, in that it provides an outlet for the employees who are the informal leaders. To the extent that the elected representatives have a strong role, there is no felt need for an outside organization to represent the employees.

Representatives, who are elected every two years, have to do a good job in the eyes of their constituents, which would suggest the usefulness of a certain degree of militancy. Then again, the visit to the company made it clear that a number of the elected representatives have a desire to enter management. The CPR work gives them much exposure to and contact with management. Thus, if CPR members acted irresponsibly, they would not further their goals of entering management. This company has a philosophy of promotion from within, and many members of the company's management are former employee representatives.

Although the CPR system has a long history, and is therefore ingrained in the fabric of the company, it does undergo periodic tests. One new division manager who was unfamiliar with the concept threw the CPR representative out of his office, and it was not until the vice-president of personnel intervened that the manager apologized for the incident. The vice-president of personnel, described by a subordinate as "the conscience of the organization," commented on this episode:

Because it is a new management, they do not know our system. The new guy in that division is a tiger who wants to do it all his own way. I have to test and intervene from time to time. If you have to fight, you have to fight.

It is difficult for new managers recruited from the outside to adapt to the company's approach. It takes about two years.

Another test of the system recently occurred. The company's usual approach to general wage increases and benefit changes is to have the personnel office present its recommendations to top management. The chairman of the company meets with the Main Council, and tells them on a confidential basis what the company is thinking of doing and asks for their reactions, showing them confidential salary surveys. This time, some council members did not approve of the company's salary and earnings survey of incentive workers, and they also objected to the size and distribution of the economic package. Subsequently, some of the confidential information was leaked by an employee member of the CPR before the final decision was made. According to a personnel representative, this angered the chairman. It was general knowledge internally that the chairman was quite unhappy with the Main Council, making this dissatisfaction clear to them. Over time, this has led to an improvement in the way the Main Council handles confidential information; however, in the short run management reacted by sharing less confidential information with the Main Council.

EMPLOYEE MEETINGS

Jobholders' Meetings

The same company whose CPR approach has just been described also conducts employee sessions called *jobholders' meetings*. These can be viewed as both downward and upward communications. Concerning these meetings, the company's chairman said:

> A basic tenet of our company philosophy is simply stated: When an individual or institution invests in our stock, he deserves a regular and complete accounting; the employee who invests his working life in our company deserves no less and conceivably more.

Once a year, at the time of the annual stockholders' meeting, the company holds jobholders' meetings that everyone (supervisors as well as employees) attends on company time. The purpose of the meetings is to review the progress and problems of the business during the year just ended and to discuss the year ahead. At company headquarters, the jobholders' meetings are conducted by a panel of company officers, and followed by a question-and-answer period led by the employee member of the CPR's Main Council. Jobholders' meetings in branch and district offices are conducted by the officers, other headquarters executives, and regional managers. The meetings are held after the jobholders' report has been issued, and the sessions may run as long as three hours. As the president put it:

> After a brief report on the company's financial health, employee wages and benefits, profit sharing, new facilities, and other topics of interest, a question-and-answer period follows.
> The only questions barred are those that relate to personalities. All

other topics are fair game and are answered spontaneously and as fully as possible.

Representative issues raised by employees during a typical jobholders' meeting are:

> Q.: *How does top management justify its present high incomes?*
>
> Q.: *Is there a plan to lay off employees in the face of a worsening recession?*
>
> Q.: *Why aren't mail-room staff allowed to wear blue jeans when they distribute mail in the dirty shop area?*
>
> Q.: *If the company's retirement fund is invested in stocks, wouldn't Treasury bills or other safer, high-yield vehicles be more productive?*

In a typical year the company holds over 100 meetings. Of the approximately twenty meetings held at company headquarters, the company's chairman will attend about half of them. For those meetings the chairman is unable to attend, other company officers are present. The company has more than 100 small branches throughout the United States, and at the branches it is planned that a corporate officer will attend every third year. However, the chairman will attend six or more of the jobholders' meetings that are held in the company's branches. Despite the time and expense of holding the meetings at headquarters and in the field, the chairman considers them "tremendously worthwhile."

> *Field employees want to see an officer of the company. They want to feel that they're not isolated, that they are part of the company, and that we understand their problems. They like to get information directly instead of through a long chain.*

The Main Council and these meetings are just two indications of the importance this company attaches to the management of human resources. Although these meetings take an enormous amount of top management's time, they undoubtedly add to its credibility. Top management considers the time spent worthwhile, and considers the company's turnover and absenteeism figures very low; productivity increases have been substantial. Despite the inflation factor, which must be considered, the company reported that in 1974 productivity increased 17.3 percent over 1973 as measured by revenues per employee. With regard to the same points, the company's vice-president of personnel said:

> *Generally speaking, and we've had this confirmed by independent observers, the pace here seems faster. There must be some causal relationship between the pace of work, productivity, and the sort of open communications that we try to maintain. We listen as well as talk and have many ways in which to do it . . . [Also,] employees will react better in a crisis if you have developed an atmosphere of mutual trust between workers and management.*

To present the whole story, however, it must be stated that this communications approach is not without its problems. Not surprisingly, some managers, especially foremen and some middle and top managers in the field, feel left out; they sometimes feel they are the last to know. About this problem, a senior personnel administrator commented:

> *The biggest flaw in our entire system is with respect to the first-line supervisor. He gets undermined and he is left in the dark. His decisions get overthrown, but this is only when he has done something the wrong way. We tell the foreman to use the CPR rather than letting the CPR use him.*

For years, this company has had a Foreman's Club and a Group Leader's Club, which meet monthly. The company pays for the costs of the breakfast meetings. The company's chairman addresses these groups once a year. The clubs also have other speakers, as well as a number of social affairs, including an annual dinner dance. However, with the advent of other communications devices, such as the CPR's Main Council and the jobholders' meetings, both the foremen and the group leaders have lost some clout. Therefore, in 1975 the company acted to fill this gap by establishing a management-level newsletter and a series of dinners initiated by the chairman. Key managers were invited in groups of ten to twelve to dine with the chairman with the ground rule being that no one will have dinner with the chairman in the same group as his or her boss.

A subsequent survey of the managers showed that, just as in the case of rank-and-file employees, they liked face-to-face meetings to express themselves, to learn what is going on, and to gain the sense of close participation in the company.

When evaluating the communications approaches of this company, one is struck by the commitment of the current and the previous chairman. One is also cognizant of the willingness of top management to change and to innovate as circumstances dictate.

Personnel Meetings

One company holds meetings of groups of employees that are considered critical to its communications program. These *personnel meetings,* as they are called, are viewed as an extension of the company's open-door policy. Normally, these meetings are held every twelve to eighteen months. (If there is a particular problem in a location, meetings will be held more frequently.) The purpose of the meetings is to let employees know the company's plans, problems, competitive position, and so forth.

The meetings are divided into two segments. First, corporate people present company programs, plans, benefits changes, and general problems. Specific reference is made to the company's competitors in terms of wages and benefits.

Top management not only wants to demonstrate that it has nothing to hide, but also that the company's pay and benefit levels are superior to those of its unionized competitors. Second, employees are encouraged to ask questions, voice complaints, offer suggestions, and discuss problems.

A personnel officer is responsible for coordinating these on-site meetings, and the department heads conduct them, with the division head or senior vice-president for that territory in attendance. Question-and-answer periods are held after the formal presentations, and these are "no-holds-barred sessions." Groups consist of employees who do similar work. While the groups can be no larger than sixty to seventy employees, the average size is thirty to forty employees. The sessions last three to four hours.

It is significant that local management is excluded from attending these personnel meetings, so that employees will feel free to speak openly. In addition to being downward communications devices, the meetings are also upward communications sessions. They are an important feedback mechanism for upper management; they also demonstrate top management's interest and concern in rank-and-file employees. Subsequent to each meeting, the local manager receives a copy of the minutes, as well as a list of the agenda items for his or her attention. Corporate personnel make sure that local management actually does follow up on the problems identified.

When a field location was visited to ascertain how this approach actually operates, I was surprised to learn from the plant manager that he conducts three meetings with his employees each year. Although this many meetings a year was not prescribed company policy (company policy calls for one meeting per year), this manager said that it is a practice followed in most of the company's large facilities. These meetings, which no supervisors attend, are to encourage better relations between employees and management. Although employees are compensated for attending these meetings, attendance is voluntary. Turnout generally runs 50 percent to 65 percent of the employees, which is considered good, because 15 percent to 20 percent of the employees, at any given time, are on vacation, absent, or not scheduled to work. The employees interviewed felt that management has firmly established its credibility with the responsive and cooperative attitude exhibited during the meetings.

It would seem that if the local plant manager regularly conducts these employee meetings, the risk of many local problems being aired by employees in front of top management at the yearly meeting is minimized. Consequently, if local management is doing its job well, it will not be embarrassed by what employees may say to various members of top management. If local management is on its toes, employees will be more likely to question company policies as opposed to local practices or problems once a year.

This particular plant manager has promoted the extension of management and employee meetings to all levels in his organization, and meets with all supervisors monthly. The department heads (who are individually responsible for eighty to 100 employees) also hold team meetings on a monthly basis with their employees and first-line supervisors, to further promote a unified effort within each department. Department heads meet formally with the plant manager weekly, as well as informally daily, for general briefings on specific problems.

Whether the success of its communications programs is due to these meetings, to a host of other policies, or to their combination—or simply due to the way this company is managed—does not matter. What does matter is that there seems to be considerable evidence of that success in both financial and human terms.

Some companies will invite employees to the annual stockholders' meeting. Many of these employees own stock directly, or indirectly through the company's profit-sharing plan. Like the jobholders' meetings described earlier, other companies hold meetings for employees shortly after the annual stockholders' meeting where, in addition to a top management presentation, there is a question-and-answer session for employees. In very large companies several meetings, sometimes at different locations, are held so that all of the company's employees may attend. I was unable to reach anyone I wanted to contact one day at one company, because everyone was at the annual meeting listening to and watching the company's chairman demonstrate new products. "It is a real performance. He puts on some show," said one manager. Another company follows up such meetings by sending to each employee a report that is a special edition of what is sent to the company's shareholders. In addition to reviewing the past year and presenting the outlook for the current year, the report asked each employee to complete a readership survey questionnaire contained in the back of the report. The questionnaire was to determine whether or not the report effectively communicated with the employees.

Other Forms of Meetings

Various other forms of meetings are used by a number of the surveyed companies besides those already described. *Service pin meetings, state-of-the-nation meetings,* and *Table Talk* are examples of discussions held on a regular basis between management and employees. One company holds monthly *cracker-barrel sessions* in which a randomly selected group of employees is invited to the plant manager's office to talk. This approach is similar to the *Skip Level* program one company uses. "Skip Level" means, as its name implies, that the vice-president of manufacturing meets regularly with groups of hourly employees. A personnel department representative said there were "high hopes" for this program:

> With Table Talk, all the foreman can do is say he'll check into it. The foreman does not have any real power. But with Skip Level, if the manufacturing vice-president says we'll take care of it, it will be done. He's got a lot of power.

The vice-president of personnel said that Table Talk and Skip Level are tools to help the company communicate during a period of rapid change. In contrast, a member of the personnel office staff said it is a way for the new vice-president of manufacturing "to lecture to the people," and sees it as a "meaningless gimmick" that the company culture, with its history of establishing traditions, will absorb.

The *problem-solving sessions* that one company conducts for its employees is seen as one of the principal reasons behind its nonunion status, according to the vice-president of personnel. Three consecutive meetings with employees at least yearly constitute the essence of this program. At the first meeting, run by the department manager who has been coached by a personnel representative, a regular work group of fifteen to twenty employees is asked: "What are the obstacles in the way of getting our jobs done better?" Responses are listed on the blackboard without any comment from management. Although the ideas are primarily in the operating area, employee opinions and complaints are not blocked. A personnel representative writes down the ideas and investigates them. At the second meeting, management provides feedback on the question and on the analysis of the group's ideas and suggestions. This part of the meeting is followed by dialogue between management and employees. At the third meeting, management informs the employees of the changes that will be made.

Interestingly, at the time of my visit the company was experiencing a union organizational drive, and this problem-solving practice was the subject of an unfair labor practice charge. The union claimed that under the Taft-Hartley Act employers cannot solicit grievances during an organizational drive. However, the company's position was that this was an established practice, and not something just begun during the organizational drive. Subsequent to my visit, the union lost the election by a two-to-one margin and withdrew the unfair labor practice charge.

In 1974 another company started a series of meetings it calls its *forums*. Held four times per year, the forums consist of a package presentation which lasts about forty-five minutes. Employees are invited to attend this meeting to discuss such topics as seniority and new benefits. Although the meetings are monitored by a personnel representative, they are conducted by line managers.

One vice-president described the company's practice of holding individual rather than group retirement parties as another way management keeps in touch with what is happening on the factory floor. Either a personnel representative or the industrial-relations vice-president always attends these parties, and expenses are provided so that several toasts can be raised for the retiree and his or her close friends. Commenting, the vice-president said:

> *Invariably, the parties are on Saturday night in the city. But [my assistant] or I go not only to honor the retiree but also to keep the lines of communications open with the other employees. This is a very good way of informally feeling out what is going on in the plant.*

In one company, an ombudsperson and employee-relations specialist has conducted conferences where she listens and six employees do the talking. She makes notes of the discussions and sends copies to the division president, to the vice-president of manufacturing, to the personnel director, and to various mem bers of lower-level management. Approximately one month later, she holds a repeat conference with the same employees. Both a personnel representative and a member of management attend (but not the employees' first-level supervisor). If the session involved job posting or insurance benefits, for example, then the appropriate expert would also attend. When asked how she viewed her role, this person said:

> *I have to walk a fine line. I see myself as representing the employee and sometimes I get whacked by management. I view myself as a middleman. Management has to be big enough to take the bitches and gripes as well as the ideas and suggestions. Frequently, employees are afraid to talk to their supervisors, and they will hold on to gripes they have held for years. The key to my job is building trust.*

Another company's technique, which its vice-president of personnel considers one of their most effective communications programs, is the lunches that the president and the executive vice-presidents have with twelve to fifteen employees in each division on a somewhat annual basis. The attendees are a cross section of employees: nonexempt and exempt workers, short- and long-term workers, minorities, and women. To the extent that they desire to do so, employees can submit individual questions or express areas of concern ahead of time. Instead, they can choose to ask such questions at a two-hour lunch session held off company premises, with just the president or an executive vice-president present. When asked about these luncheons, the company's vice-president of personnel said:

> *These luncheons have been well accepted. They have provided key top management both input on people's feelings and concerns as well as a chance for top executives to make general comments and personally meet with some of our people. These luncheons are one of the most effective communication programs we have.*

This technique, like some of the other approaches discussed and unlike an attitude survey, represents a direct and immediate feedback device for top management. Such meetings can give employees opportunities to voice their questions, suggestions, and complaints directly to a member or members of senior management. They can also serve as an audit on the quality of local management, as well as being a stimulus for local management to resolve what problems it can before they might be embarrassingly aired before senior management.

However, it should be added that some companies in the sample refrain from using group meetings of employees. These companies question the effectiveness of such meetings and/or think such meetings are in violation of the principles of management. The principles involved not only concern the sanctity of the employee-manager relationship, but the philosophy of individual as opposed to group treatment as well. Individual treatment in some companies may mean an aversion to groups of employees—these companies are so committed to their philosophies of individual treatment that, even for downward communications purposes, they will not meet with groups of employees. These companies accordingly deny themselves the benefits that can come from such downward communications and other employee participation programs.

EXECUTIVE INTERVIEWS WITH EMPLOYEES

Interviews with Individuals

The Skip Level program at one company is different from the one described earlier. Once a year every manager interviews each employee two levels below him. The written report of the interview is then sent to the personnel department. Evaluating the results in light of the time it takes to achieve them, the administrative vice-president said:

> *This is a safety valve of sorts, but some employees do not speak their minds because they are scared to do so.*
> *It doesn't, however, take much time because sometimes the supervisor just calls in someone and asks, "How's it going, Joe?"*

A similar program at another company seems stronger. Called the *executive interview* program, second- and third-level managers interview different employees at random. In explaining how this program works in one plant, a manufacturing superintendent said:

> *Each of us talks with one employee per week. We talk about the economy, the work load, the salary program, and other issues. I schedule each appointment three or four days in advance and I tell my secretary not to cancel it.*

The executive interviews are then written up on a form, and a copy is sent to the personnel department. In addition, quarterly meetings of managers are held. At these meetings, employee likes and dislikes are summarized and discussed. Concerning this program, one manager said:

> *With the executive interview program, the attitude survey yields few surprises. Moreover, if it is done well, as a consequence there will be few open-door complaints.*

Rather than having line managers conduct employee interviews, another company's personnel representatives must talk to every employee twice a year, and then complete interview cards. These cards are monitored by the corporate manager of employee relations. The guideline given to personnel representatives is that they should record anything that might have a bearing on employee relations. Comments concerning wages, work hours, benefits, and work conditions are to be noted. The interview cards are used as back-up information for the monthly reports prepared by personnel representatives; they are also reviewed if any significant problem arises in the plant or office. The company's personnel director regards this program as an invaluable tool for top management: "With the cards it is easy to pinpoint areas of concern and see patterns develop. We might find out, for example, that in a plant there are a lot of employees unhappy with vacation scheduling. This technique helps us keep our finger on the pulse."

PERSON-TO-PERSON PROGRAMS

Several companies use person-to-person communications programs, which are known by many different names. One company, whose approach has been copied by many others, calls its program "Speak Up!" Another company calls its program "Speak Out." Others label their programs "Confidential Interact," "Person to Person," or "Say It Here." These programs provide written or oral answers to employees' complaints, comments, and questions, which may or may not be published in a company newsletter. In most cases, employees' names are known only by the coordinator of the program and are kept confidential.

In one representative program, some 4 percent to 5 percent of the employees use the person-to-person program each year. Although the employee is instructed to sign his or her name and told it will be kept confidential, some employees will not sign their names. Management very carefully monitors the percentage of employees who use the program as well as the percentage of unsigned questions and complaints. These percentages are viewed as one indication of the climate of the organization: Too few questions would raise just as many concerns as would too many of them. If there were many unsigned complaints, management would be especially concerned, because anonymous complaints indicate a lack of confidence and trust in the company. If the employees do not trust management, they may seek assistance of a third party. The statistics are kept by business unit and location, so that top management is able to know where the actual or potential trouble spots are.

Although the instructions clearly state that "only one person should sign this form," group person-to-person forms, especially unsigned ones, are also monitored very closely. It is management's policy to deal only with individuals, not with groups of employees, but if a signed group "speak up" does occur, the members of the group, if appropriate, will be interviewed by an investigator individually.

Unlike some companies with such programs, in this particular company the program is not administered by the personnel department. However, approximately 70 percent of the person-to-person letters concern personnel or personnel-related matters. Consequently, they are forwarded to and answered by personnel officers, with corporate review of the answers for purposes of consistency and uniformity. The names of the employees who raise the issues are not known by either the preparer or the reviewer of the responses. Unless the investigation necessarily requires that the employee's name be revealed, which is done only with the permission of the employee, the identities of the employees with grievances or complaints are always kept confidential. At a site of nearly 10,000 employees, the personnel director discussed his role in the person-to-person program:

> So far, this year, there have been about 800 letters. I read each one as well as the answer which has been prepared, even if I have to read them at home at night. There will be such things as an open-door complaint, a request for a medical transfer to a warmer climate, or cases where an individual has been treated unfairly.

Person-to-person complaints, like the open-door complaints, are investigated thoroughly and promptly. On some issues, a corporate investigator will visit a plant and begin by interviewing the manager. On other issues, as in the case of an unsigned group person-to-person form or an employee who wishes to remain anonymous, the investigative process is obviously much more difficult. Sometimes a team of nonplant executives may be assigned to interview every employee in a department. Sometimes the result of an investigation is that the manager is removed.

When asked about the removal of managers, a senior personnel administrator said it was not at all uncommon for managers to be demoted for problems with employees, adding that midway through the year at his division, several managers had been fired. However, though they get "fired" as the manager, what generally happens is that they are either demoted to a nonmanagerial job or given a special assignment.

If person-to-person programs are to be effective, there has to be a top management commitment to provide objective answers on a timely basis. A high-level personnel administrator, who has either answered or reviewed hundreds of complaints over the years, said that in his fifteen years with the company he has never known the author of a person-to-person complaint unless as part of the investigation he had to interview the employee. He also considered it crucial that the program is administered outside the personnel department. As personnel policies and practices are frequently questioned, and as the personnel department is often a party of interest, this person felt it extremely important to avoid even the possible appearance of partiality.

Although the great majority of investigations end by backing management's initial determination, some decisions are modified or reversed. Furthermore, the employee has his or her "day in court," and a communications problem or a misunderstanding is frequently corrected.

The possibility of a person-to-person complaint keeps first-line managers more sensitive to employees. However, these programs also have the potential to undercut, demean, or demoralize the first-level manager. One supervisor interviewed gave two examples of this. The first example, which did not bother him, was a letter one of his employees wrote which stated that a light was out in the bathroom. The second example, which did bother him, concerned a job classification complaint: Employees felt a certain job should be upgraded, something this supervisor had been attempting to get done for over two years. (Only when the complaint finally reached the general manager was the job classification studied and changed.)

How complaints are responded to affects not only supervision but the employee as well. If confidentiality is ever compromised or if the answers appear to the employees as unresponsive or as whitewashes of management's actions written by lower-level managers, the employees will come to question the usefulness of the program. To avoid such an outcome, companies have not only instituted rigorous investigation and response procedures but have also involved senior personnel and line managers in the review and approval of written responses. Therefore, this review and approval mechanism has the advantage of being a feedback device that educates senior management about employee problems, and also insures that the responses prepared by lower levels of management will be done with more care and thought.

QUESTION BOXES

One company has a speak-out system in the form of a question box, into which employees are encouraged to put their ideas and suggestions. Commenting on this communications technique, a corporate personnel officer said:

> *With this approach you generally get a big response in the first six months to a year after introducing the box. Some 65 percent to 75 percent of the complaints have to do with production-oriented things. The employees really do want to do a better job but there are things standing in their way.*

Another company has a rumor box: Employees who hear rumors about anything can put their questions in it. The questions are then answered, with the answers being posted on the bulletin board. The company's personnel director sees the rumor box as "important but not a primary vent or safety-valve system."

CONCLUDING ANALYSIS AND COMMENTS

This analysis of the various feedback mechanisms and communications programs indicates that there are three different functions. *The first function is to involve employees in the problems of the business.* Employee participation is not a new concept, and several of the companies have adopted it to varying degrees. As the president of one of the companies put it:

> *We try to communicate to the employees the problems that we have in the company—the things that we need their help on.*

An administrative vice-president of another company looked at it this way:

> *If you don't inform employees, they will view the decisions as arbitrary. It is very important to communicate the state of the business. For example, recently during these difficult times we talked about the reasons for freezing the merit increases and the choices we had as to whether we should have a layoff or whether we should share the work.*

Some companies go much further than communications in their employee participation programs. *The second function is to give employees an opportunity to voice complaints, to offer opinions, and to make suggestions, and to give management an opportunity to uncover problems and to respond constructively to employees' problems.* To a degree, this is a substitute for the formal complaint procedures to be discussed in Chapter 15. Mechanisms are designed to bring problems to the surface and to resolve them. Attempts are made to take employee inputs seriously, and to act upon them. These mechanisms not only allow ideas to rise to the top of the organization—they also serve as a check on local, particularly first-level, management.

Efforts are made to let employees know that they have a voice which will be listened to by top management. Lower-level management knows that it should behave and treat people fairly; that if it does not, top management may hear about it, get upset, and take action. Therefore, lower-level management has an incentive to resolve problems informally before they become part of any formal procedure.

The third function is to create a climate in which it is legitimate for employees to request and receive help with personal problems, which supervisors or personnel representatives view as part of their jobs. As the director of personnel and manpower development of the company with in-plant counselors (IPCs) said: "A man who is worrying about how he will pay a big hospital bill cannot keep his mind on his work properly."

In recognition of the fact that in some cases an employee may not feel comfortable talking about his personal problems with his supervisor, companies make it legitimate for their employees to discuss them with another individual in the organization. As is true with the investigation of employee complaints, the rules that companies establish and maintain on the use of sensitive or confidential information have much to do with the effectiveness of a particular approach. Employees need to be able to trust individuals and programs. If employees know that confidences will not be violated, company people and programs can have credibility with them.

No one can fail to be impressed with the time and effort that top managements invest in their communications programs and with the variety of approaches. For personnel people, it may be that *how* one does whatever it is one is doing is more important than *what* one is doing. Consequently, some of the fundamental differences among companies are not that significant, although real employee representative schemes and those which come close to them, are quite different from the approaches of the other companies. These approaches are quite close to unionism, and have some of the problems of unionism, which seem to include a higher rate of grievances and the need to pay more attention to the political aspects of decisions in the area of employee relations.

In order to be effective, communications programs have to be real and sincere, they cannot be too mechanical, and there needs to be follow through. In thinking about this, it is useful to consider the story about the company president who liked to tour his company's plants and exchange pleasantries with the workers. When he routinely asked one worker, "How's the wife?," the response was "Still dead, sir."

With a climate of openness, trust, and confidence, in which the employees have faith in management, the programs described make sense. (In a low-trust environment, they would mean little—they would simply be gimmicks.) Their presence, backed by a committed top management, can help create the appropriate climate. In fact, one of their purposes is to help build and sustain the organization's climate.

One senior personnel executive stated the same themes very well:

> *You need to understand the degree of mutual trust and confidence which exists in our company between people, especially between management and employees. I feel that the elements of integrity and caring about the other fellow are a lot more important than the specifics of many practices and procedures. I would think that the lack of such feelings is the basic reason that unions exist.*

What seems particularly significant about communications programs and feedback mechanisms is that top management indicates to lower management and employees the importance it attaches to the goals of a specific program and to the climate of the organization through its words, and particularly through its actions.

CHAPTER FIFTEEN

Grievance Procedures

Although I do not wish to make the case here, one could argue that from an employee-relations point of view the differences today between the unionized and the nonunion large company are less than normally assumed. In fact, the gap between them has probably narrowed over time. One could even argue that over time, some nonunion companies have begun to look like unionized companies, at least in some respects. As an example, consider the extent to which some nonunion companies rely on seniority in promotion decisions as well as in layoffs, overtime allocation, shift preference, vacation scheduling, and so forth.

However, one clear distinction exists between the unionized and the nonunion employer: Although the unionized company generally has a formal grievance procedure with a final step that provides for binding arbitration of disputes, the nonunion company generally does not have this. For example, it is thought important in collective bargaining situations that the worker have the right to appeal his or her discharge to an outside arbitrator selected by the parties involved, to ensure that the worker has been discharged for ''just cause'' or that his or her contract rights were not violated. Management generally grants such a grievance procedure in exchange for a ''no strike'' clause.

Before continuing this line of discussion, let me point out that two of the nonunion companies studied do have formal procedures for arbitration of final-step grievances, with the company paying the arbitrator's fee. However, in these companies the arbitration step is used very infrequently. But this is not to say that it is not important. Two other companies have appeals boards to which employees can take their grievances. The membership of one of these boards includes hourly employees. This appeals board makes recommendations to the president of the company. The other appeals board, which consists of managers, is a decision making body. Neither board meets often.

While generally not called a grievance procedure, almost all of the other nonunion companies studied do have some formal mechanism for resolving complaints. In many companies this mechanism is called the *"open-door"* policy. This chapter describes these procedures, reviews the experiences of the companies that have them, and examines their functions. One interesting finding is that in most companies these formal procedures are either rarely or infrequently used.

OPEN-DOOR POLICIES

As the open-door approach is so common, for illustrative purposes let us begin by noting the exact wording of the open-door policies of four of the several companies that have one. Each statement is from the company's employee handbook.

The Open-Door Policy

The Open-Door Policy is deeply ingrained in [the company's] history. This policy is a reflection of our belief in respect for the individual. It is also based on the principle that every person has a right to appeal the actions of those who are immediately over him in authority. It provides a procedure for assuring fair and individual treatment for every employee.

Should you have a problem which you believe the company can help solve, discuss it with your immediate manager or your location's personnel manager or, in the field, with the manager of your location. You will find that a frank talk with your manager is usually the easiest and most effective way to deal with the problem.

Second, if the matter is still not resolved, or is of such a nature you prefer not to discuss it with your immediate manager or location personnel manager, you should go to your local general manager, regional manager, president or general manager of your division or subsidiary, whichever is appropriate.

Third, if you feel that you have not received a satisfactory answer, you may cover the matter by mail, or personally, with the Chairman of the Board.

Freedom of Discussion With Management

The company cannot emphasize too strongly its desire that all [company] people shall feel free to seek information or advice from members of management on any aspect of their relationships with the company, or to call attention to any condition which may appear to them to be operating to their disadvantage. Under the "Open-Door" policy, no individual need hesitate to do this, and his or her standing with the company will not thereby be prejudiced in any way. The management and supervisor or representative of the Industrial Relations Department ready to talk over any of these matters and to give assistance where possible.

The company believes that most matters will be satisfactorily resolved between the individual and the supervisor; but, if for any reason a person is not satisfied with such a resolution, he or she is completely at liberty to follow established company procedures to bring the matter to the attention of anyone in management. Procedures for getting assistance in handling personnel problems and complaints are available through the Industrial Relations Department to anyone who may wish to use them.

Open Door Policy/Management Review

You and your supervisor are encouraged to resolve any differences personally. However, [the company] has an "open-door" policy to help you resolve job-related problems or associated personnel matters. This is an informal method which allows you to consult your personnel administrator or higher management level when you can't work things out with your supervisor. If your problem is not resolved informally, there is a "Management Review" procedure for handling job-related problems. You may ask your personnel representative to help you record facts and arrange an interview with your department or division manager. You may then request review by successive managers up to your Group head if earlier reviews did not solve the problem.

You are encouraged to make use of these procedures if you and your supervisor alone cannot resolve a problem. Proper application of the "open-door" and "Management Review" procedures will usually result in a solution beneficial to both you and [the company].

Guarantee of Fair Treatment (Your Suggestion and Complaint Procedure)

[Company] policy provides that every employee, regardless of position, be treated with respect and in a fair and just manner at all times. In keeping with its long recognized policy, all persons will be considered for employment, promotion or training on the basis of qualifications without regard to race, color, creed, sex or national origin.

We recognize, that being human, mistakes may be made in spite of our best efforts. We want to correct such mistakes as soon as they happen. The only way we can do this is to know of your problems and complaints. NO MEMBER OF MANAGEMENT IS TOO BUSY TO HEAR PROBLEMS OR COMPLAINTS OF ANY EMPLOYEE.

If you have a problem or complaint, this is what you should do:

Step 1: Tell your immediate supervisor. During this discussion, feel *free to "lay your cards on the table." Your supervisor will listen in a friendly, courteous manner, because it is his desire to understand and aid in solving problems which arise in your work. Generally, you and your supervisor will be able to resolve your problem.*

    Step 2: *If you do not get your problems straightened out with your supervisor, see your manager or department head. He will obtain all the facts and endeavor to settle your problem in a fair and equitable manner. If you still are not satisfied, he will arrange for you to see your district manager or general manager.*

    Step 3: *Your district manager or general manager will confer with you, and all others involved, to carefully review the facts and circumstances. If, after a thorough discussion of the matter, you still feel the problem has not been resolved to your satisfaction, the entire matter will be referred to your Divisional Vice-President for his action.*

    Note: *Your problem may be such that you prefer to discuss it directly with your district manager or general manager, or a representative of the Employee Relations staff. Always feel free to do so. It is the policy of [the company] that all employee suggestions and complaints shall be given full consideration. There will be no discrimination or recrimination against any employee because he presents a complaint or problem.*

In each of these policy statements, the reader will note that although the employees are encouraged to first discuss the problem with their immediate supervisor, it is clear that these procedures make it possible as well as appropriate to elevate problems to a higher management level if they are not adequately resolved at the lower level. Unlike either arbitration or an appeal board, which includes hourly employees, these procedures ask higher-level management, rather than people outside the company hierarchy or fellow employees, to review the decisions of lower-level managers.

ACTUAL COMPANY EXPERIENCE

    This study does not permit one to make a definitive judgment on the effectiveness of these open-door policies, or on what these companies would be like if they did not have these procedures. Undoubtedly, the grievance procedures of some companies are more effective than others. While the evidence is scanty and uneven as to their effectiveness, it does shed some light. Some of the evidence runs counter to the views of those who feel that open-door policies are neither sound in principal nor workable in practice. Discussions with representatives of several large companies convinced me that open-door policies that are formal, and that are rigorous with respect to reviews and investigations, can be effective.

    The office of the chairman of the very large company whose open-door policy was the first one cited receives several hundred open-door complaints in a typical year. Investigators working out of the chairman's office follow up on these complaints under an exacting timetable. For example, one assistant vice-president, who had to fly to a southern plant of this company on New Year's Day to investigate one particular complaint, said: "Unless there is a procedure for grievances, a third party will be here."

Managers of this company are also free to use the open-door policy. Some managers in the company reported that it is legitimate for managers to use this procedure "only once"—therefore, the myth is that managers do not use it. However, according to company statistics, the reality is that managers use the open-door policy in the same proportion as their percentage of the employee population. With respect to this point, perhaps the words of John W. Gardner (and a Turkish proverb he cited) are relevant:

> *I would lay it down as a basic principle of human organization that the individuals who hold the reins of power in any enterprise cannot trust themselves to be adequately self-critical. For those in power the danger of self-deception is very great, the danger of failing to see the problems or refusing to see them is ever-present. And the only protection is to create an atmosphere in which anyone can speak up. The most enlightened top executives are well aware of this. But I don't need to tell those readers who are well below the loftiest level of management that even with enlightened executives a certain amount of prudence is useful. The Turks have a proverb that says, "The man who tells the truth should have one foot in the stirrup."* [1]

All open-door complaints in this company are given serious review and are answered on a timely basis. The open-door investigation starts with the assumption that the employee is correct. In the great majority of cases, the managers' decisions are supported. However, management's decisions are reversed or modified on occasion. Several years ago there were a number of myths within the company about the operation of the open-door policy. Four of them were: (1) only fools or "nuts" would use the policy, (2) the "open door" leads to the back door, (3) an employee who complains, even if his or her allegations are found to be correct, becomes a marked person in the company and will never advance, and (4) if a manager mishandles an employee relationship, necessitating the employee to complain, the manager's career is ruined—even if the manager's original action is sustained upon investigation, because he or she was not smart enough to keep the employee from complaining. In discussing these myths, the president of the company wrote in a company publication:

> . . . *an unhappy employee, who feels he is being treated unfairly, is guaranteed a fair hearing. . . .*
>
> *Although most problems should be settled in a frank discussion be-*

---

[1]John W. Gardner, *No Easy Victories* (New York: Harper & Row, Publishers, Inc., 1968), p. 43.

tween the employee and his manager, a man occasionally can gain satisfaction only by going to a higher level. For the employee's protection, each investigation is based on the initial assumption that his complaint is valid.

If the employee is found to have a good case, he will be upheld on his complaint . . .

If the employee's complaint is unfounded, he will usually gain a realistic view of the situation leading to it and return to the job with the air cleared. Regardless of whether he is upheld, an employee can continue to advance in the business.

Concerning managers, consequences are serious when we find evidence of mismanagement. One employee reported that a man who reviewed suggestions was offering to approve them if the suggester would "kick back" a portion of the award. When this was proven true, the man was dismissed from the company.

Managers who have handled Open-Door situations well have gained recognition which has contributed to their advancement. A dismissed employee complained that his manager had persecuted him by demanding that he perform a job that was impossible. Our investigation, however, proved that people in the area were doing similar tasks without difficulty. Also, the complainer had been carefully counseled over a six-month period prior to his dismissal. He was not reinstated and since then, the manager had made satisfactory progress in the company.

None of us likes being scrutinized in the way necessary to clarify the issues in Open-Door cases, but I feel the results of the Policy justify the anxiety which is generated. Perhaps some of you who read this have suggestions on how to improve our procedures and, if so, I would appreciate hearing from you.

In summary, I am convinced the Open-Door Policy is making a positive contribution to our people and I hope that future administration of the Policy will add to the health of the Company.

Top management's behavior toward internal complaints demonstrates to lower management and employees alike that they care about the way all employees are treated. When top management wants the decisions to be fair and is willing to investigate and review lower-level decisions, its credibility is enhanced to many employees.

Before analyzing the functions of these formal grievance procedures, the views of several people interviewed at various levels from each of the cooperating companies will be quoted. These comments illustrate the pervasiveness of these procedures, and/or the involvement of personnel people with employee problems. They are also the most effective way to give the reader a real feeling for the way these procedures actually work. In the real application of these procedures, and due to the importance of such topics as discipline and discharge, the reader will note that these subjects figure largely in several of the quotations. If these procedures are to have any meaning at all, they must certainly function effectively in these areas.

Company A

The open-door and the square-deal policy statements were written by our founder. They continue to exist today and they work. The employee can go anywhere in the organization. While there is a standard procedure for the employee who has a problem it is well known that the employee does not have to follow the standard procedure. Our president still leaves a certain amount of time weekly on his calendar for these problems.

personnel representative

I am not aware of any reversals through the open-door policy. Personnel, however, does become a review board. They ask: "Has the person been treated fairly?" "Is the documentation in order?" I am thankful they are there, for we sometimes tend to lose our objectivity. We go a long way before terminating an employee. Personnel remains objective. Sometimes, however, I think they are not in touch with the real world.

supervisor

The key factor in this company is the open-door policy. Some employees say that the door hits you in the butt when you go out. But I believe the policy has worked well. I would say that I spend half my time on the resolution of personal and personnel problems.

supervisor

One morning during an interview with the senior members of this company's personnel staff, the "Number Two" person in the department had to excuse himself from the group to meet with an employee who was demanding to see the company's president. This person, or someone else from the personnel department, frequently covers for the president. I learned later that the complaining employee was a deaf-mute who had been discharged. The personnel officer had spent the remainder of the morning with her, and said that he expected he would be spending some additional time with her.

Company B

Communication is very important. We have a real open-door policy in that our offices do not have doors. Accessibility and visibility are important. I go over to the coffee breaks frequently. I purposely move around to different coffee areas. There is also an employees' committee. I read the reports of their meetings. It is a way for the employees to be heard. They will talk about medical coverage, parking problems, and so on. The open-door policy and everything else we do isn't all that important. What is important is the first-line supervisor. If he identifies with the company's goals and believes that people are important, then everything else falls into place.

vice-president and general manager

The nonunion environment is an open one. There is an open-door policy and a grievance procedure. There are claims of favoritism and it isn't utopia. But as these complaints arise there are investigations and explanations.

supervisor

There is an open-door policy. You can complain. But some employees are nervous about it.

production worker

Company C

Our formal grievance procedure is spelled out in the employee handbook. It is not used that much. I try to grease it by advising foremen to encourage their employees to file grievances. I've tried to force foremen to put people through the procedure, for I think it could be a very good communications tool.

personnel manager

The open-door policy is very important. The employee feels his problems can be heard. He can sit down with anyone. A grievance can be pursued right up to the plant manager. We try to solve grievances on the lowest possible level.

There is one individual who has many grievances. This individual leads us to believe he is very interested in unions. We sit down with him on an almost weekly basis.

supervisor

Seldom do we have grievances from my department, thank God. There are a few employees who are always in personnel complaining that something is wrong. The open-door and the grievance procedure are important. My guys sometimes ask to see Bill [the personnel manager]. I ask if they want to see me first. If they don't, then I set up an appointment for them with Bill. Sometimes they go in to see Bill on their own.

I've sat in on some reviews conducted by the plant manager. He checks into matters. He asks very good questions and he gets to the facts.

supervisor

Company D

[The] counselor Fred [this is a company which employs a full-time counselor] is available when the employee feels he is not getting anywhere with either his supervisor or his manager.

The key at our company is that the middle managers consider their doors open all the time to people. Also, the production managers spend a lot of time on the floor. Most production managers are good listeners. They spend the time. They ▓▓▓▓▓▓▓▓▓▓▓▓▓▓▓▓▓▓▓▓▓▓▓▓▓▓▓▓ *then the employee should see Fred.*

The procedure is followed. But the employee is free to skip levels. About 85 percent of the time problems are resolved right at the first level where they should be.

Fred is very good. He keeps us honest. He cites some cases of bad judgment. He is a good relief valve because some people are afraid to talk to their manager or supervisor. Fred always keeps things in confidence.

In summary, what is important here is the credibility of management, the manager–employee relationship, the environment of friendliness, warmth, and caring, and the open-door policy through which problems get resolved.

manager

Company *E*

Any employee can call anyone anytime and get an answer. Employees are encouraged to go outside the line organization if necessary and personnel has a lot of visitors. The prime reason personnel is here is to talk to employees. Employees from all over the corporation come in.

We have an extensive review process with respect to the discharge of an employee. After the decision is made, the employee can appeal to anyone involved in the review process, including the president. This happens and decisions are reversed if the employee presents new information or evidence of extenuating circumstances of which the line managers were unaware.

assistant vice-president of personnel

Company *F*

There is an open-door policy. If the employee thinks he is being overlooked by the foreman or has personal or financial problems, or if he wants to get his paycheck a day early, there is no wall built up. Employees feel they can get to management. We remove the barriers.

The chairman has to approve all discharges of people who have been with the company more than ten years. We have a lot of blacks, some of whom have filed complaints of discrimination with outside agencies against the company. But no cases, following investigation, have been supported yet by the outside agencies. This is an indication of how fair the company is.

production manager

Company G

We believe in acting, not reacting. We're willing to admit we are wrong. We'll reinstate employees when we find they have been discharged unjustly.

personnel director

Company H

There are a variety of mechanisms to surface and deal with employee complaints. Plant managers receive gripes, for ours is a free and easy, open environment in which people are not uncomfortable talking. Employees will call or write our founder. At service pin meetings, we'll ask employees how things are going.

We talk openly about unions with the employees. I'll frequently say, "I'm your chief steward, what are your gripes?" Good communications is very important. If you don't inform employees, employees will view management decisions as arbitrary.

It is very important to communicate the state of the business. For example, we told the employees the reasons behind the decision to freeze all merit increases. We also talked about the possibility of closing down for a few weeks versus the idea of sharing the work.

vice-president of personnel

An employee with a gripe or complaint can go to the supervisor or the personnel office or a top operating officer.

Supervisors are told that sometimes they are going to be reversed. It is important to say, "Don't let the employee go over your head but rather put him over your head" so that supervisors realize they might be reversed and don't feel uncomfortable with the process.

Through our appeal procedure, some employees will be reinstated. We frequently make it somewhat easier for the supervisor because we will put the employee back to work someplace else rather than under his old supervisor. Our department has the reputation of bending over backward to save an employee.

director of personnel

Company I

We took a hard look at [another company's] formal grievance procedure, which provides for arbitration as its last step. We came close to adopting it. But it was not approved by the president. He is reported to have said, "The [other company's] system is not for us. We don't need a formalized system. There is not much frustration here. You haven't sold me." [This company has an open-door policy.]

vice-president of administration

Company J

Because there is no formal grievance procedure here the company feels it important to have a recognized, useful and effective problem-solving mechanism. There is an appeal procedure through the line manager but an employee can go to Employee Relations at any time. The final arbiter is the plant manager. The real test of the procedure's meaningfulness depends on the power relationship between the Employee Relations manager and the plant manager. Is he willing to stand up, be objective, and fix the problem? The fact that this procedure exists is more important than if it is used, for things actually get fixed before they get to the plant manager. I believe the process has credibility in the eyes of the employees. They see managers responsive to their complaints.

personnel representative

Company K

The company has the open-door policy. It is important. The employee feels that he can raise hell but he won't be fired. And that is very important.

There are grievance mechanisms in all of our plants. Management is told to assist employees in processing their grievances. This, however, is frequently difficult for sometimes the grievance involves the foreman whom management is telling to help the employee process his grievance.

director of labor relations

Company L

The company has the open-door policy. But I feel it is a myth. I don't think it works very well.

personnel director

Company M

The company had a formal grievance procedure for a number of years. A case could come before the personnel advisory committee, which consisted of key executives in personnel. It was only used once. To be honest, I'm not sure if a grievance procedure is still part of our policies. Most employees here are happy. There is a very positive sentiment. Most people that leave the company want to come back.

Our discharge procedures are carefully spelled out. Personnel really controls the termination process. It keeps the supervisors from doing something rash. There is a clear understanding that it takes three-to-six months to effectuate a discharge as well as good documentation of performance.

We have a "speak out" program where any employee can write a question or voice a complaint. Although our lawyers were fearful at the beginning, we also have an employees' committee. The minutes of the meetings are circulated to management. There is some concern that these meetings have become a forum for very specialized interests to complain and grumble but, on balance, the company's experience with it is quite positive.

vice-president of personnel

Company N

Although the grievance procedure is elaborately described in the employee handbook, in my twenty-seven years with the company I have not seen it used more than six times. We've never had a case go to the final step [the office of the president]. Most managers are very sensitive and if a problem could become a grievance and go to the president it is top priority.

I believe reasonable people are able to resolve their differences if there is enough time. The problem is that people take a stand and they are reluctant to back off. Therefore, you may have to elevate the matter a level or two. But people are not reluctant to say something is not right and admit a supervisor goofed.

director of personnel

Company O

The company has an open-door policy. More people than you would think use it.

Managers consult with personnel prior to taking disciplinary action. The Termination Review Board [whose membership includes employees] reviews all cases prior to termination. A terminated employee, moreover, can appeal to the employee Appeal Board, which consists of three managers: the director of Equal Employment Opportunity, the personal assistant to the president and chairman; and the manager of personnel relations.

personnel director

Company P

Human Resources can veto discharge decisions. The discharge procedure has all the classic steps.

A lot of employees use our open-door policy. The chairman receives many letters from employees. When he asks you to investigate a letter, this is something you do for him fast. He has a strong desire to treat people fairly and to deal directly with employees, although this is not possible now because of the company's size.

vice-president of human resources

Company Q

Employees are free to (and do) call headquarters collect and talk to one of the Employee Relations guy about their complaints. And the Employee Relations guy will follow through on it.

Our statement on fair treatment is posted on all company bulletin boards and is part of the new employee orientation program. It is a mechanism for resolving complaints. In addition, employees are able to see [the founder]. Many write him. A discharge has to be approved by two levels of management.

vice-president of personnel

Company R

Managers and supervisors know that they cannot fire anyone without obtaining prior approval from Personnel, since we believe terminating an employee is a very serious matter. Our disciplinary process is constructive and positive rather than punitive and negative in that it is more of a counseling approach to correct behavior and/or performance. It is only after working with an employee and not obtaining the required change in behavior or performance that we will consider a recommendation from operating management that an employee be terminated. We do not automatically withhold an employee's increase even though we may be involved in the disciplinary process with that employee; nor do we permit an employee to be given time off without pay as a penalty. Many times, we will try to place an employee in another job or department if we feel that it would help solve a problem.

personnel director

Company S

We have a four-step procedure to help our people get grievances resolved. A copy of it is given to each employee. We give each supervisor a copy of "A Grievance Is Your Opportunity." This brochure tells him how to prevent grievances and what to do about them. It concludes by saying, "Remember—you are judged not on absence of grievances but on what you do about them."

In the case of discharge, the employee may ask for the appointment of a fact-finding board, which will consist of three employees and two managers. This procedure is a tribute to the wisdom of our chairman. People are released from their assignments and they are given technical people on request as needed so they can get all the facts. They then make a judgment, and submit a report to the president.

This procedure has probably been used only five or six times in its history. No fact-finding review has ever not supported the discharge. I think this is so because much care is taken before a discharge. I also think that in some cases perhaps it is true that some discharges that ought to be made are not made.

                                        vice-president of personnel

Company *T*

Because I do not like to use terms from the unionized environment, we do not have a "grievance procedure." But our problem-solving policy is one of our most basic policies. We use it at the management level, too. We also use it to handle equal employment opportunity matters as well.

                                        vice-president of personnel

Company *U*

No one can unilaterally fire anyone here. There are several fail-safes. We see that the employee's case is developed and looked at in as favorable a light as possible. We have the mental frame of mind and the organizational position to understand and help the employee. Personnel is a spokesman. We take the employee's side. We see that the employee's position is given a chance, that it is not shoved back or put down. We give each a fair shake. Personnel is the advocate to the extent the employee's case has any merit. We get the viewpoint considered and weighed.

    Wise supervisors look upon personnel as a staff assistant so that they can utilize the company philosophy. Weak supervisors see us as offering a lot of interference. Autocrats see us as somebody to cope with. We tell the weak supervisors there is a better way to handle people. If, however, there is a real problem, we will go over their heads.

                                        plant personnel manager

A guy is innocent until proven guilty. From my point of view, personnel is on the side of the employee. Discipline takes a long time and is frustrating. For example, a person can be sick five days, come back a day, and be sick five days again.

    The open-door policy is used many times. In my eight years here, I have had three or four open doors. New employees are told about the policy. It is quite extensive.

                                              supervisor

Employees can use the dispute procedure, but not all employees know about it. I always inform personnel in advance and then personnel will set up the interviews. If it is an EEO [Equal Employment Opportunity] case, you should get personnel involved early.

                                              supervisor

Company V

Our Council of Personnel Relations [CPR] serves as a semiformal grievance procedure. If a guy is fired, he can call on his CPR representative to help him. The CPR representative can't always be on the side of the employee. For instance, he won't defend an employee with a really bad attendance record. But many CPRs are very political and they will defend an employee whether he is right or wrong. In my view, the whole system works pretty well. [This company has an employee representative system that was described in Chapter 14.]

personnel director

Company W

Our complaint procedure is identical to a grievance procedure. The employee can appeal. The first step is that the employee can go to the supervisor or the personnel representative. The second step is when the matter goes to the department manager who has to consult with a personnel person. The third step is the division level, the plant manager or the division director. A personnel person is part of this step, too. For the fourth step, the grievance goes to the corporate vice-president of personnel and the company head of the unit the employee is in. Although few in number, some cases do arise. You have to understand our way of life here. There is a lot of open-door communications.

director of employee relations

Company X

With respect to a discharge grievance, line managers must consult with personnel. If the employee has been with us for ten years or more, I have to approve the discharge unless it is for theft.

vice-president of personnel

Company Y

There are four or five written promotional grievances per year. Many grievances are never put in writing. This year there have been two over discharges and one involving a disciplinary suspension.

The grievance procedure is not heavily used. I believe this is because there are enough other safety valves. We do many things which make the filing of formal grievances unnecessary. There are a lot of oral complaints that never get put in writing. There is also a reluctance on the part of employees to stand up and be counted. There is employee fear. They do not want to be the one to complain.

But, in truth, I think grievances are handled very well. I'll receive two or three calls a week at home. There are also letters from employees. I think the personnel people here have good credibility. In four years, only two cases have gone to outside arbitration and the company has won both of them. [This company has outside arbitration as the final step of its grievance procedure. The arbitrator is selected by the Federal Mediation and Conciliation Service.]

personnel director

Company Z

People say no one is fired here. It is not so. Out of 10,000 employees we fired seventy-five last year.

For every 2,500 employees there are about fifty grievances per year. About half of lower management's decisions are reversed or modified in some way by higher management. Although the final step is arbitration, there haven't been more than two or three cases that have gone to arbitration. [This company has an employee representative system. The final step of its grievance procedure is outside arbitration.]

plant personnel manager

The employee rep has to take the case of an hourly employee who has a grievance, even if it is a nickel-and-dime matter and regardless of its merit. Therefore, the employee representative provides no legitimate counseling.

supervisor

As an example of a grievance, I had an employee who had good performance on everything but attendance. His 15-month average was 4 percent, whereas it is supposed to be 2 percent. Therefore, under the guidelines I did not recommend him for a raise. My boss supported me. But the employee representative [ER] said the employee was a great guy. The ER gave an untrue sob story about the guy to the building manager. And the building manager reversed my decision, leaving me hanging. This is when I began to turn off on supervision.

supervisor

EXAMINATION OF EMPLOYEE GRIEVANCE PROCEDURES

In analyzing the grievance procedures of the nonunion companies studied, we will attempt to answer two questions:

1. What is the purpose of the employee grievance procedures?
2. Why are they used so infrequently?

The Purpose of Employee Grievance Procedures

Although formal grievance procedures encourage employees to discuss their problems with their supervisors, it is clear that the existence of such formal procedures makes it possible for them to get around their immediate supervisors, permitting an employee with a problem to have a hearing at a higher level.

Grievance procedures provide a mechanism for individual dissatisfaction to be aired—and with additional people involved, more objective decisions are possible to attain. Employees have some protection from any arbitrary or hurried decision their boss might make. In addition, the procedures allow employees to challenge the appropriateness of a specific policy, or the way in which a particular department may be interpreting that policy.

To a limited extent, grievance procedures are also another feedback device for top management. By getting involved in individual cases, top management knows from firsthand experience something of what is happening on a day-to-day basis in the work force. If a particular department is having a large number of grievances, top management will know that something is probably wrong in that department.

While these grievance procedures are one avenue of communications, they seem to be less important as a communications vehicle or as a feedback mechanism than are other communications programs these companies have adopted. This is not only due to their relatively infrequent use; it is also because top management has put many other feedback mechanisms in place to ascertain what is going on down the line in the organization.

In addition to providing a formal channel for the airing of individual grievances and dissatisfactions, these grievance procedures also serve another important purpose: They help keep supervisors "on their toes" with respect to the human relations aspects of their jobs. Supervisors know it is not only possible, but also quite legitimate, for employees to challenge their decisions. Such a formal system discourages supervisors from ignoring employee problems and letting employee frustrations get bottled up. These grievance procedures encourage supervisors to do their homework, to do "what is right" by employees, and may also encourage the supervisors to be more lenient than they might believe is appropriate with employees.

Grievance procedures not only serve as a constraint or restraint on the behavior of lower-level managers; they also serve as a positive motivator to take the initiative with employee problems. Cognizant that top management and/or the personnel department may become involved, lower management has an incentive to follow the company's policies and practices, and to do its homework, to communicate, and to explain the reasons behind its decisions.

The Use of Employee Grievance Procedures

Although the grievance procedures of some companies are used more often than those of others, they seem to be used relatively infrequently. Moreover, it is rare indeed for a grievance to reach the final step of the company's procedure. For example, one company whose discharge policy—as a last step of the grievance procedure—provides for the appointment of a fact-finding board consisting of three employees and two managers to review and report to the president, has not used this last step more than five or six times in its entire history. In every case, the report to the president confirmed the facts on which the discharge was based.

In a company with an appeal board, each case has been reviewed by the company's termination review board prior to termination. This review board consists of approximately twelve people selected by the company's vice-president of personnel. Even though the management members outnumber the employee members, the board's composition does include managers *and* employees. Each major area of the company's business is represented. If the termination review board supports the termination, the discharged employee then has the right to appeal the decision if he or she feels unfairly treated by the company. The appeal is made to the employee-relations department, and in most cases it is anticipated that a satisfactory resolution of the grievance will be reached through the efforts of an employee-relations representative. However, if the employee still feels that a fair and equitable solution has not been reached, he or she may appeal to the employee appeal board, whose three members are the assistant to the president and chairman, the director of equal employment opportunity, and the manager of personnel relations.

In this company from 1970 through 1975, ninety-four employees have appeared before the employee appeal board. In four of the ninety-four cases, the board reversed supervisory decisions and the employees were reinstated. However, hundreds of employees have sought employee-relations counseling of one form or another: There were seven employees who were reinstated through the conciliation efforts of employee-relations representatives and supervisors—thereby, the appeal never reached the appeal board.

There are six possible explanations for the relatively infrequent use of these formal grievance procedures. First, it is possible that in these companies the working conditions and supervisors are so good, the employees have little to complain about. When the personnel director of a company with a decisional appeal board was asked for an explanation of why the full mechanism is used so infrequently, the reply was: "That is because our employees think the decisions management makes are right." It would be naïve to think that this reason could be the exclusive explanation; if there were many formal grievances, it might tend to imply much employee dissatisfaction, which the companies in this study try to avoid.

Second, a possible explanation for infrequent use of formal grievance procedures in some companies may relate to the environmental factors concerned with the size and location of company plants, as well as the nature of the work force. A large plant in an urban area employing more educated minorities and more "liberated" women may have more grievances, or at least more people ready and willing to complain, than will a small plant in a rural community employing white males and/or more traditional females. Although this explanation may indeed be true to some extent, it would seem that it is a partial explanation at best.

Third, it is possible that in some cases employees may not be aware of the formal grievance procedures, or if aware, they are fearful of using them. Employees may not have confidence in the program or in the way in which it is administered. If they think the system does not work, they would have little reason to use it. Moreover, in a nonunion company it may simply be unrealistic for management to expect employees to stand up and complain. If employees are fearful that management or their supervisor will retaliate or "get them" because they filed a complaint, they may be extremely reluctant to bypass their supervisor and use the formal procedure. Perhaps only the foolish or the very aggressive employee who is seriously aggrieved will feel comfortable in utilizing the formal complaint procedure. While this possible explanation may also be true to some extent, it would seem difficult to fully endorse this view on a long-term basis. If there are serious individual grievances and dissatisfactions, as there always are to some degree in any large work group, and if they cannot be dealt with through the system, they will appear in some other manner. Problems at the work place do not just go away.

Fourth, the supervisors of these companies may give their employees fewer reasons to complain due to the ways in which they themselves are selected, trained, and promoted. Also, if supervisors sense that those in their peer group who have too many people problems may be either demoted or not promoted, they may tolerate employee behavior that would seem to require disciplinary action under normal circumstances. There is interview evidence to support this explanation. A vice-president of personnel, in talking about the imbalances or possible abuses of one company's system, said: "Some discharges that ought to be made are discouraged. Personnel should be helpful to both sides but sometimes line managers perceive us as too much on the side of the employee."

The chairman of this same company said: "Labor trouble is always the result of a manager who gets itchy pants wanting to be a big shot and loses the personal touch. We have never fired an employee because he or she disagreed with the company. We have, however, fired a manager because he got into trouble with the people." Such actions may, understandably, make managers too hesitant to initiate the disciplinary actions that should be taken. Consequently, there is no management action taken that could give rise to a formal grievance.

Fifth, it may be that the effectiveness of the other feedback mechanisms and safety valves, such as the attitude surveys, speak-out programs, personnel representatives, and Skip-Level interviews, means that the formal grievance procedure will be used less frequently. Instead of waiting for grievances to surface, these companies are alert to possible problems and individual dissatisfactions, and they try to correct them before they become formal grievances.

Sixth and finally, the existence of the formal grievance procedure may create, stimulate, or even invigorate the pressures to resolve problems on an informal basis. Foremen may perceive negative connotations associated with the filing of formal grievances by their employees. Because foremen may not want to see the formal grievance procedure used by employees in their departments, they will try to keep close to their employees, and resolve their problems as best as they can. A foreman from one company that has an open-door policy said: "I spend half my time on the resolution of personal and personnel problems." While this may be an exaggeration, one may suspect that this company regards this as a very important part of a foreman's job. One might also suspect that a foreman would rather do this than have frequent investigations of open-door complaints arising from his or her department.

While I believe that each of the possible explanations has some validity, and that some reasons undoubtedly apply more to some companies than to others, it is my hunch that the last two reasons are generally the most important. The fact that the formal grievance procedures are not used very often usually means that the other feedback mechanisms and communications programs, and the more informal approaches of supervisors, are successful in resolving individual and group complaints before they reach the formal grievance procedure, or at least before its last step. Thus, while all the possible explanations have some plausibility, the last two are the most important. As A. H. Raskin so nicely put it: "The measure of a really effective grievance system is not how many cases go to arbitration, but how well it eradicates the atmosphere that spawns grievances."[2]

Some of the quotations cited earlier in this chapter say something about the internal climates of some of the companies studied. As someone who previewed the manuscript form of this book said:

> *The quotations from the personnel executives almost suggest a "familial feeling" or at least an attitude of "We want to do the right thing with respect to employees and we know our management wants us to do that."*
>
> *If I read these quotations correctly, the situations you are reporting sound quite different from some union situations one hears about, which seem to consider mutual distrust between employee and management as natural and inevitable. If this idea is once accepted, then nothing but an adversary*

[2]A. H. Raskin, "Arbitration in the Mines Has Created More Disputes," *New York Times,* December 4, 1977, Section IV, p. 5.

relationship between management and labor can ensue. Some writers seem
to think this is to be desired, but I doubt that distrust is likely to further
productivity.

The companies try to avoid an adversary relationship with their employees
and they provide many informal as well as formal outlets for employees to voice
suggestions and complaints. As one vice-president of personnel put it:

We have house organ reporters, safety committees, lots of contact
with management and numerous other informal outlets in addition to the
formal ones for employees to let off steam in a natural sense.

Furthermore, a variety of mechanisms will encourage supervisors and personnel
executives alike to be responsive to employee problems.

CONCLUDING ANALYSIS AND COMMENTS

Formal grievance mechanisms, although not widely used, are
nevertheless particularly important in today's environment, because employees
who feel discriminated against in a promotion decision because of their race, sex,
or age, or who think that their work area is unsafe, may take complaints to an
outside agency for investigation. Companies would no doubt prefer to respond to
individual or even group complaints through their own mechanisms and in their
own ways, rather than to have to comply with the requirements set during and
possibly after a government investigation.[3] A changed regulatory environment
increases the costs to the company of some types of employee dissatisfaction and
thereby encourages an organization to take the necessary steps to do a good job
internally.

The best grievance procedure may be the one that is rarely used; if, however,
it is not being used for the wrong reasons, it cannot be effective. If it is not being
used because employees fear retaliation, or because they think company investigations will be mere "whitewashes" to justify management's initial decisions, then
the formal grievance procedure is ineffective, becoming a "grievance procedure"
in name only. If the procedure is rarely used because supervisors make every effort
to resolve employees' problems immediately at the lowest possible level, fearing

---

[3]Professor Jack Stieber, director of the Michigan State University School of Labor and
Industrial Relations, has proposed that Congress enact legislation to protect nonunion employees from
unfair dismissal. Using the collective-bargaining process as a model, Stieber has proposed that
employees past their probationary periods, but not otherwise protected against unfair dismissal, be able
to appeal a discharge penalty to an arbitrator who is paid for by the employee, the employer, and the
government. *See* Jack Stieber, "Speak Up, Get Fired," *New York Times*, June 10, 1979. Section IV,
p. 19.

top management investigations and/or believing that such inquiries might reflect negatively on them, then the procedure may be working well. If one of the basic purposes of formal grievance procedures is to keep managers and supervisors "on their toes," then the procedures—even if infrequently used—serve a distinct and useful purpose if they stimulate managers and supervisors to avoid their use by making informal approaches effective. Although it would be difficult to judge how different the company environments might be without their open-door policies and/or formal grievance procedures, it must be remembered that what is important is *not* the number of cases at the last step; what matters is the low-level responses to the informal grievances that effective procedures may encourage.

If we analyze the different approaches, the grievance procedure with arbitration as the final step is quite close to unionism. It could create an adversary relationship between the management and the employees. However, if there is a reluctance to use this final step, as is true of the two companies in this study who do have this formal procedure, grievances can be resolved at lower levels in problem-solving discussions. It could also be argued that, by providing access to arbitration, a company might inspire or reinforce employee confidence in management's desire to be fair with its employees.

An appeal board with employee members can demonstrate management's credibility and trust in employees. A board that is advisory (as opposed to decisional) would seem preferable from management's point of view. With a decisional board, as with an outside arbitrator, there is the risk of a final decision that is unacceptable to management. Also, an appeal board, which resembles judicial review, could possibly have problems with the composition of the committee, and whether it is a standing or an ad hoc committee. The members of the board *must* have credibility; they cannot be viewed as proxies for management. Committees should not be set or "rigged." To choose such confidence-inspiring people in a credible way is not an easy task.

From the employees' viewpoint, an ad hoc committee partly chosen for its competence on a particular issue might be preferable to a standing committee. However, from an administrative viewpoint, a standing committee has advantages over an ad hoc committee. Moreover, although a committee containing employee members is advantageous from the employees' point of view, such committees— depending on their purpose and the ways in which they operate—can be suspect under the National Labor Relations Act. One very experienced vice-president of personnel, when asked about appeal boards, said:

> While I agree that appeal boards have some real advantages, I have some concerns about them. As long as that very fine line is treated appropriately, I believe they will serve a useful purpose. But there is a potential for problems. Sooner or later, if management and the board disagree too often, or there is a big emotional issue or a number of little issues which get to the emotions of a large number of that location's employees, employees may be encouraged to go the rest of the way by getting a union. And when they do,

they are really set up for a union to come in and say, "Well, you've got
everything except clout, why don't you join our union to get that too?" For
that reason, I think that one is playing with dynamite when one considers
having an appeal board.

With these and other potential problems, it is not surprising that the great majority of companies have chosen to have some form of the open-door policy. Although the personnel department is involved, such a policy is within the management hierarchy. Higher management reviews the challenged decisions of lower management. Procedures involving employees or outsiders that are too formal could also encourage a we–they adversary relationship, something the companies in the study wish to avoid.

If the open-door policy were used frequently, the procedure could become unmanageable. It would also be a signal that the informal approaches and the other feedback mechanisms had broken down. However, to be viable and have some meaningful effect an open-door policy does need some degree of use. Despite the fact that the mere threat of a formal grievance case creates pressures and incentives for informal problem solving, the reader should recognize the infrequent (as opposed to no) use of the procedure is significant and desirable.

If a grievance procedure is to have credibility, the employees must have confidence and trust in top management, and must also see the decisions of lower-level managers reversed or modified on occasion. Furthermore, the procedure must be publicized. As previously noted, employee handbooks, bulletin boards, special notices, and company magazines are places to help make it known. In addition, orientation and training programs for employees should communicate the purpose as well as the mechanics of grievance procedure.

Supervisors also need to be educated about grievance procedure: its purpose and the reasons for its existence as well as its mechanics. As one personnel executive said: "Supervisors are told that sometimes they are going to be reversed." Both the rationale and the mechanics of a company's open-door policy need to be part of supervisory orientation and training programs.

The topics or subjects about which it is appropriate to complain should be part of the descriptive literature. The procedures of most of the companies studied are quite broad as to what it is possible to discuss. This would certainly seem advantageous from an employee-relations point of view, where management is trying to maintain a climate of trust, openness, and confidence rather than a we–they dichotomy. If there is arbitration or an employee appeal board, the scope of appropriate topics is less broad.

Finally, it has to be clear that there is a guarantee of safe passage for the employee. The employee must be guaranteed a fair hearing. Whether the employee's complaint is denied or is found to have merit, the employee must be able to continue to advance in the business. As one company officer put it: "There is a strong feeling that there should be no recriminations with respect to any employee who complains. If we found a supervisor was giving a hard time to any employee who complained, he would be chewed out.'' Management must support and encourage the use of the system. It must also watch out for and protect those who do use it. There are all sorts of subtle retribution and retaliation possibilities to which top management must be alert.

For example, one company conducts follow-up studies of those who file complaints. Although it had been rumored within the organization that grievants suffered in terms of future pay increases, one follow-up study revealed, on the contrary, that grievants actually fared better in terms of pay increases than nongrievants.

Whether or not the mechanism should even be called a grievance procedure is another important question. Most of these nonunion companies wisely call their procedure for resolving grievances by another name. It might be a mistake to duplicate the union functions too closely, especially in this area. One reason this is done is to avoid a named procedure that is almost exclusively identified with arbitration by outside neutrals as the final step. A procedure called by the same name but that is so different from the model may be viewed as suspect by some employees. Management, therefore, is probably wise to call the procedure an open-door policy, a problem-solving discussion procedure, or an appeal or complaint procedure.

In conclusion, while it is my opinion that a formal complaint procedure is essential, especially in today's environment, it is also my view that what is even more important is (1) the way in which the existence of the formal procedure and the connotations associated with its use enhance the effectiveness of informal approaches, and (2) the ways in which the formal procedure is supplemented by other feedback and communications mechanisms. Management should not expect a formal grievance procedure to be used frequently, nor should it be relied on as a primary feedback device. However, in my view a nonunion company should not be without some kind of formal complaint procedure.

PART FIVE

The Conclusion

CHAPTER SIXTEEN

Conclusion

The basic purpose of this study has been to explore and compare the personnel policies and practices of a select group of large, nonunion companies. In reviewing these policies, several general conclusions present themselves. For one thing, the personnel policies of this select group of companies are attractive by any standard, and are in some cases widely recognized as outstanding. (Since these companies have stayed nonunion up to the present, it was presumed that their policies would be liberal.) It is also apparent that the policies of the companies in this study are similar to one another in fundamental ways.

Certainly, there was a consensus among the interviewed executives that the key to effective employee relations is the presence of trust and confidence between managements and employees. Such a climate is considered desirable for its own sake, and also because it fosters the efficient and effective long-run implementation of corporate strategy.

From the experiences of the companies studied there can be no doubt about the importance of the integrity of their managements and the climate of the organizations.[1] The critical question is not whether a climate of trust and confi-

---

[1] Professor Renato Taguiri has defined *organizational climate* as ''a relatively enduring quality of the internal environment of an organization that (a) is experienced by its members, (b) influences their behavior, and (c) can be described in terms of the values of a particular set of characteristics (or attributes) of the organization.'' See Renato Taguiri, ''The Concept of Organizational Climate,'' in Renato Taguiri and George Litwin, *Organizational Climate: Explorations of a Concept.* (Boston: Harvard University Graduate School of Business Administration, Division of Research, 1968), p. 27.

dence is important, but rather how such a climate is created and maintained. This field survey has shed much light on this important issue. It has suggested that the combination of certain top management attitudes, values, philosophies, and goals, and certain substantive policies—including the effective management of environmental factors and company characteristics; employment security; promotion from within; an influential and proactive personnel department; satisfactory compensation and benefits programs; effective feedback mechanisms, communications programs, and complaint procedures; and careful selection, development and evaluation of managers—will produce such a climate.

Figure 16-1 is a model or profile of the values, policies, and climate characterizing the sort of large corporation that will remain nonunion. It is derived from the basic and important similarities discovered in the companies studied. This model can be viewed either as the beginnings of a "theory of nonunionization" that is, in some ways, the reverse of a theory of union organization—or, more positively, as a theory of the effective management of human resources. I believe that this model represents a strategic alternative for top management. If top management wants to create a climate of cooperation rather than of conflict, then the combination of certain top management attitudes and values with certain substantive policies is likely to produce the desired climate. The desired climate will reinforce what produced it, and will contribute to productivity and profits in itself. In the following pages, we will review the components of the model in Figure 16-1.

TOP MANAGEMENT ATTITUDES, VALUES, PHILOSOPHIES, AND GOALS

The evidence clearly suggests that critical to understanding the nonunion status of the companies studied are the attitudes, values, philosophies, and goals of each top management with respect to the people in the organizations. As one very experienced vice-president of personnel put it:

> The real answer lies with the guy at the top and his philosophy and his top management team. This is terribly important, for there are many things that can get you off the track. In our company what we did was like a religion. Dedication was required and there had to be faith that what we did would pay off.

A vice-president of another company described the philosophy of the company's founder and said, "For this philosophy to work, the vast majority of management has to believe in it."

As has been seen throughout this study, the values and goals of top management are crucial to understanding the different (yet remarkably similar) basic approaches of the companies studied. The philosophies of the founders especially,

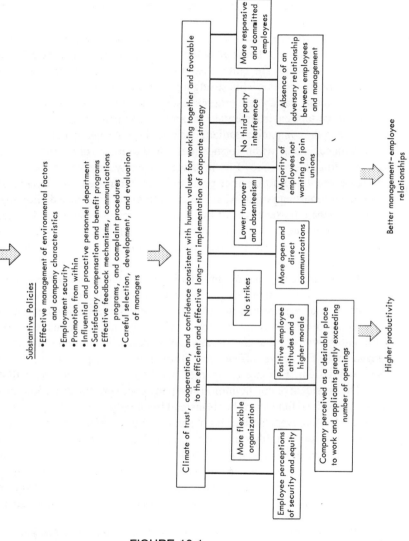

FIGURE 16-1

including the paternalistic attitudes of some, are an integral part of the present-day strategies of the companies. These founders had strong views about the ways in which people were to be treated in their companies. How their interest and concern for the employee became implemented and institutionalized in large companies while they were alive, and after their passing from the scene, is a central focus of this study.

In the doctrinaire companies (those committed to keeping their new plants nonunion) the goals and strategies of top management regarding the complex field of employee relations are quite clear to themselves and to the managers and supervisors down the line. This strong top management motivation is critical, not only with internal variables (certain substantive policies) but also with the management of certain environmental factors and company characteristics.

Among the companies studied, one can observe a number of general policies taken by management to transform values into the climate of confidence, cooperation, and trust they desire. For instance, in many companies the distinctions between exempt and nonexempt personnel are minimized. While necessary for government reporting purposes, such distinctions set up a false dichotomy that is anathema to the top executives of many of the companies studied. As a result, in some companies no one is referred to as an employee. Instead, everyone is a "company-name"-person. In other companies employees are referred to as "associates," or "members."

The principle of equal treatment and the avoidance of double standards are much in evidence at many of the companies studied. From vice-president to sweeper, all use the same parking area, receive the same medical benefits, and eat in the same cafeteria. Frequently these companies minimize many of the traditional status symbols that are usually associated with positions in higher-level management. Executive offices are frequently modest, spartan, or—in one case—nonexistent. In some companies people at all levels are on a first-name basis. The president of one nonunion company could presumably come to work in a chauffeur-driven limousine, but is instead frequently seen driving a "beat-up old Chevrolet." Moreover, the salaries of some of the top-level executives are modest in comparison to what other executives earn. Many of them do not have opportunities for bonuses, a substantial addition to the pay of senior managers at other businesses.* This means that in some of the companies, the differential between the lowest-paid full-time employee and the highest-paid manager is not as significant as the differentials that exist in other companies. These practices are consist-

---

*This sample did not include any companies whose chief executive officer earned the super high salaries the news media frequently highlight. So-called "perks" for top executives also seem to be minimal in many of the companies. (Perquisites or "perks" such as company cars, club memberships, elegant offices, *et al,* impart status and are not in keeping with the values of the top managements of many of the companies studied.)

ent with the principle of equal treatment.

By their *personal* example, the founders and the present top management of many of the companies studied demonstrate their interest in and concern about the employees of their companies. For instance, at one company management regularly appears at employee social gatherings in order to maintain close contact with the workers.

> *Management here mixes with the people. If the employees have problems, they know they can see someone.*

Often, the company history will include stories of heroic cooperation between employees and management in a concerted effort to get a job done.

At another company, two "old-timers" recalled the behavior and actions of the company's founder. Said one:

> *[The founder] was always concerned about the employees. He would talk to the elevator operator about her family. He'd always talk to the little employee. He always treated people with respect. The higher up you went in the company the more he expected you to take the heat.*

Recalling the founder's plant visits, another worker said:

> *[The founder] was great for overturning a firing. He also raised hell with the way the place looked. When they knew he was coming for a tour then they would spend a week cleaning up. If it wasn't good, he'd tell them to clean up and that he would be back. And he would come back. Therefore, they would paint machines and paint everything. The competition wasn't so great then and the company could afford to spend that kind of money.*

In describing the pattern of leadership by example, one personnel manager said that the company's policies "were based on trust, and if the policies were violated there would be action." This manager recalled a time when the founder of one of the companies studied, a company with which he had been associated, fired several people in the purchasing department when it was discovered that the company's policies were not being followed. Continuing, this manager said:

> The [founding] family's impact could be felt. There was humanism and
> morality. There was a loyalty which was nurtured, developed, and chal-
> lenged. The company had a unique process for selecting management. They
> got the right men for the jobs. The process was not political. [The founder]
> used to give employees his home telephone number and he would tell them to
> call him if there were any problems. But he would say to the management team
> that his home phone better never ring.
>
> The [founding] family at this company where I now work and the [other
> founding] family are similar. The morality we have here is the same as was
> there. But here you don't have the pressure from within which was there. Here
> we don't fire people and we don't ask a lot of them, either. The culture here is
> a nonmotivating paternalism.
>
> At [a unionized company where this man had also worked] the philoso-
> phy is threat and intimidation. There is no humanism [there]. Here . . . we
> try to link the dignity of a man to productivity. A man's faith and confidence in
> himself is terribly important.

At another company, the president and members of his staff had come by
company plane to visit a plant to personally investigate some serious allegations
made by employees in open-door complaints. This president has also inspected the
damage of floods and other disasters when company employees or members of
their families have been involved.

As this study has shown, this strong top management concern for employees
becomes institutionalized in these companies through various substantive policies.
The intangibles of leadership, personal examples, and the role and function of
symbols, however, cannot be ignored.

SUBSTANTIVE POLICIES

Given top management commitment, certain substantive policies
are crucial to the achievement of a company's objectives. These policies govern
the ways in which employees are treated. They increase the probabilities of
management's obtaining the kind of employee-relations climate that is desired.

Effective Management of Environmental Factors and Company Characteristics

Certain environmental factors and company characteristics, including
adequate profits, facilitate the approaches of the companies studied. While some
factors are fortuitous with regard to the company's goals, others are managed so as
to help achieve the company's objectives. Geographic location, the size of plants,
the nature of the work force, and how sensitive work and employee groups are
handled are, for instance, significant environmental factors over which manage-

ment has much control. A small plant in a rural location presents easier-to-handle employee-relations problems than does a large plant located in a big city. Also, one cannot ignore the importance of such factors as pleasant working conditions, company impact on the community, and company concern for the community and its offerings to family life in plant-location decisions.

Rapid growth and good profitability are also important variables to take into account, for they enhance many of the personnel policies and programs these companies offer. However, the rapid growth of some companies, providing many promotion opportunities, has also frustrated efforts to provide pleasant working conditions, for employees can experience cramped quarters as a company adds capacity.

Another company characteristic that is particularly important relates to ownership and continuity of management. As has been mentioned, two of the companies in the sample are privately owned. As a member of the personnel department at one of the privately-owned companies said:

> In understanding our company, one can't stress enough the effect of private ownership and the fact that people were answering only to [the founder].

A privately-owned company has, or at least may perceive that it has, more freedom than has a publicly-owned company. It does not have to worry about defending salary or profit-sharing policies at stockholders' meetings that may appear extremely liberal or generous to the casual observer.

Although all of the other companies are publicly owned, in some cases a sizeable amount of stock either was or still is held by key family members. A publicly-owned company whose chairman and major stockholder is either the founder or the son or grandson of the founder is different from a publicly-owned company that is operated by professional managers with insignificant stockholdings. The combination of position and ownership undoubtedly makes it easier for the people-oriented founder to implement his philosophy as to the ways in which people are to be treated in his organization.

If retired officers are counted as insiders, at approximately 70 percent of the companies studied either half or more of the boards of directors consist of insiders. Moreover, some of the outsiders on some of these boards have been closely connected to the enterprise, such as suppliers to the companies, lawyers, commercial bankers, and investment bankers. It may be easier to sell various personnel programs that appear expensive when so many members of the board are part of the company and have grown up in it. Although we are in an era of professional management, these companies nevertheless have a rich legacy and tradition that seems to affect the company's leaders, present managers, and employees—indeed the culture and climate itself—in profound ways.

The final company characteristic that is important to note relates to the degree of diversification of the companies studied. Although there are a few exceptions, the companies studied are relatively undiversified. Not all the entirely-nonunion companies are single-business companies, but there are not any conglomerates or even highly-diversified companies in the sample. Moreover, few of the companies studied have made many acquisitions. Expansion through growth rather than through purchase has been the general rule. This lack of diversification makes the relatively centralized standard and uniform approaches to personnel policy and administration matters more feasible. Such standardized approaches, whether they relate to pay, benefits, job posting, the implementation of full-employment practices, or even formal complaint procedures, would appear to be far more difficult in companies that are highly diversified. For example, promotion from within is easier to implement in a centralized, undiversified business. In turn, the managers of such companies are more likely to share certain beliefs and value systems consistent with those of the founder and other members of the top management about the way the organization is to be managed.

Employment Security

Due to either the company's full-employment practices and/or the traditional stability or growth of their company, workers at some companies know that they will not be laid off. In other companies, when a layoff becomes necessary, employees can expect it to be delayed as long as possible. Employees can also generally expect that seniority will be given much, if not exclusive, weight in the event of a layoff.

The companies studied utilize a remarkable number of techniques to provide full or nearly-full employment, or to delay layoffs as long as possible. Among the techniques used are: hiring freezes, reliance on attrition to reduce the work force, use of temporary or former employees for specified periods of time, inventory buildups, use and disuse of subcontractors, voluntary leaves of absence, vacation banking, special voluntary early-retirement programs, moving work to people, moving people to work, training, and work sharing.

Certain environmental factors and company characteristics were found to greatly facilitate the employment-security goals of top management. These include rapid growth, good profitability, and a high percentage of women in the work force, as well as management's ability and willingness to plan, forecast, and coordinate production to the market.

The significance of employment security can not be overestimated. Eliminating employees' feelings of job insecurity and fear of layoff can be an important cornerstone of a company's employee-relations program.

Promotion from Within

The policy of promotion from within—especially when accompanied by extensive training, educational, and career counselling opportunities, as well as job posting—is an important ingredient in the mix of substantive personnel policies that are offered by the companies studied. It is particularly significant when a company's growth rate makes a substantial number of promotional opportunities available each and every year. Through the combination of rapid growth and a commitment to promotion from within, many employees in these companies have had considerable opportunities for advancement, with the better pay, new challenges, personal growth, and learning that generally accompany a promotion. Moreover, companies that permit lateral moves give qualified employees opportunities to move into positions that they consider to be more desirable than their present jobs.

Such policies take real commitment, resources, and faith. To be sure, it is easier, certainly in the short run, to hire experienced people from the outside than to post jobs as training opportunities. Job posting also takes time. However, when outsiders are infrequently brought in to fill good jobs, such top management commitment to present personnel does not go unnoted by company employees. Up-from-the-ranks supervisors, who have benefited from a company's promotion-from-within policy, have reasons to be enthusiastic about the policy. Laboratory and office employees who started in plant jobs also have reasons to be pleased about promotion from within.

Promotion from within also helps a company to institutionalize and maintain its philosophy or approach as it grows larger. "Home-grown" managers know and respect the company's values and traditions. Unlike newcomers, they know many people and several different jobs and operations. They therefore serve as excellent role models and perhaps mentors for other employees in the company, who will follow in their tracks. The policy of promotion from within is facilitated by the recruitment and selection of very good people, by providing excellent development opportunities, and by being in a business that is not too diversified.

Influential and Proactive Personnel Department

Strong personnel departments play a key role in the development, implementation, maintenance, and monitoring of specific personnel policies and programs. Part of their job is to monitor and evaluate the climate of the organization. Given the values and goals of top management, the influential roles played by the personnel department with respect to top-, middle-, and lower-level management, as well as with respect to hourly employees, is not surprising.

The sources of personnel's power seem to be four: (1) closeness to top management, (2) the reward-and-punishment system for line management as it relates to personnel responsibilities, (3) specific delegated responsibilities, and (4) their own persuasive and administrative abilities and professional competencies.

Being close to and listened to by top management is important to a personnel department for several reasons. A high position in the management hierarchy will better insure that the personnel department's viewpoints receive adequate consideration in all strategy and policy deliberations. It is important that the personnel department's views be on an equal footing with the views of the finance, marketing, and manufacturing departments. It also makes it more likely that the personnel department's input will be better related to the problems and opportunities of the company. Being close to top management also makes personnel staff more confident and credible with line managers.

That the reward-and-punishment system for line managers in the companies studied stresses performance in the human areas also helps explain why personnel departments are able to exert influence. For instance, if a department manager is worried about a potential grievance or the results of the most recent attitude survey, he or she becomes receptive to expert advice. When effectiveness in dealing with employees is a measure of managerial competence, the potential for and influence of the personnel department increases significantly.

Specific delegated responsibilities during normal times (such as the right to veto discharge or promotion decisions), or during unusual times (such as "calling the shots" during a union-organizational drive), also increase the personnel department's influence.

Finally, good work presented in a convincing manner earns respect and influence. Capable personnel people who not only know the personnel business, but know the company business as well, are able to recommend and to "sell" wise courses of action. Line managers view their suggestions as helpful, or at least as necessary.

Personnel department voices that count not only help keep the company out of trouble, but more importantly, by recommending proactive, innovative policies and programs, they assist top management in achieving the goals of the business.

Personnel departments are also an important resource for employees, and can provide many kinds of information. They can be helpful if there are job-related or personal problems. They listen to employees' concerns. They represent a way around an employee's immediate supervisor. A personnel representative, with the support of the personnel department's chain of command, can be an advocate for an employee, thereby better assuring due process and fair treatment.

An active and influential personnel department is an important element in the pattern that emerged from this study. Such departments are key links between top management attitudes and values, and the achievement and maintenance of the desired organizational climate. They are the structural home of many influential activities.

Satisfactory Compensation and Benefits Programs

As the chapters on pay and benefit policies demonstrated, the companies in this sample lead, or are at least quite competitive, in the areas of compensation and benefits. For example, many of the companies offer employees salary status, profit-sharing and/or other bonus plans, and company-matched savings or stock-purchase programs.

The pay policies, generally geared to local labor markets, are designed to provide and to demonstrate equity. Steps are taken to make sure that pay rates compare favorably with those of comparable unionized companies. The great majority of the entirely-nonunion companies use pay for performance or merit pay plans, and these plans are frequently administered in a fairly automatic fashion, with much weight given to seniority rather than performance.

Salary status, when it is offered, is consistent with the principle of equal treatment. Salary plans are an attempt to get away from the we–they distinction between management and labor and between office and plant employees. Such plans, which give psychological advantages to the employees, can be a morale-boosting device, because they generally differentiate a company from other companies in its industry or community. Workers with salary status can feel that they are being treated in a special manner. When an employee does not have to punch a time clock and is paid for an occasional lateness or absence, he or she is being treated as a mature adult.

This study has emphasized the very attractive security packages that many of the companies offer. In addition to life insurance, employees know that their company's major medical benefits plan will reimburse them for most, if not all, of their expenses. Dental plans have also become common. Short- and long-term disability plans provide continuing income when an employee cannot work due to an illness or injury.

Pension plans and company-matched savings and thrift plans are designed to provide security at the time of retirement. Profit-sharing and stock-purchase plans are also a way to gain greater employee interest in and identification with the company and its goals. Such programs, by themselves, tend to facilitate communications and to also distinguish the large nonunion company from other comparable unionized firms.

Although of course not necessarily representative, the opinions of two workers at two different companies in the sample are of interest. Both employees interviewed were long-service employees. Their comments indicate that they view their companies' pay and benefit policies as fair and equitable. About the company's pay and benefit policies, one employee said:

> The company pays well. [Another company], which is nearby, goes on strike and we get the increase and have no strike. The benefits are very good.

> *Now they have a dental plan. I was in the hospital. The bill came to $1,300 and the company paid it all. I have four weeks of vacation and one week of sick days. It is very fair.*

The other employee commented about his company's approach:

> *People who pay union dues don't get the holidays we do or have the job security we have. My neighbor is a union member at [another company], and he's been laid off. Here it doesn't cost you money if your wife is in the hospital.*

Regular survey work on pay and benefits by a personnel department that is respected by top management assures that the company is able to achieve its pay and benefit objectives. These surveys not only facilitate management's equity goals, but also make the company's policies more credible to employees.

There can be no doubt about the importance of the pay and benefit policies of the companies studied. They are generally designed and communicated in such a way as to ensure that the company is not vulnerable to a union-organizational drive on the basis of pay or benefit issues.

However, many executives interviewed stressed that it is the accumulated effect of many small considerations rather than their pay and benefit policies that lead to a climate of trust. A person with over twenty years' experience in personnel work said:

> *Like the song "Little Things Mean a Lot," if you don't pay attention to the little things and the climate deteriorates and you lose your resiliency and trust with your employees, you find that you cannot buy people off with high wages and benefits. Too often we executives forget that the plant employee has just as much integrity and dignity as we ourselves have, and that they are not ready to prostitute themselves, degrade themselves, and lose their dignity by being bought off with higher wages. Surely, they'll push you for higher wages and benefits, but eventually you'll have to deal with the integrity issues, which in fact affect the employee relations climate.*

As one experienced personnel professional put it, "While it is fine to be concerned with the global policy issues, it is also important to make sure that the vending machines on the second shift work." A long-term production worker at another company expanded on this "little things mean a lot" theme, saying:

> *My department gave us a dinner last week. It was just to get the people together. How many companies would do that! They give cookouts with hot dogs and beer on company property at the end of the month when you work a lot of overtime. There is a lot of freedom here—you can go down for coffee when you want. Everyone calls the general manager by his first name. There are no ties. It is all very informal. It is the little things.*

This company also has excellent pay and benefit programs, including cash profit sharing, flexible working hours, and a company stock-purchase plan.

In summary, while the absence of competitive or leading compensation and benefit policies could be harmful for the organization, their presence is not given too much significance by company executives as a prime determinant of the desired organizational climate.

Effective Feedback Mechanisms, Communications Programs, and Complaint Procedures

Top management, through the personnel department, should establish effective feedback mechanisms and communications programs to monitor and evaluate the company's climate and to help ensure that their philosophies and objectives are actually being carried out. These mechanisms should be designed to supplement good employee–supervisor relationships, but they also serve as a check on the behavior of lower-level supervisors, who are critical to the effectiveness of the different approaches. An important purpose of these devices is to give supervisors an incentive to "do right" with respect to their employees.

In the companies studied, a variety of feedback mechanisms have been devised to gain direct, nonhierarchical information about employees' views of each company's policies and practices, the ways in which these policies are being administered, and the climate of the organization. In addition to trying to be responsive to employees' suggestions, complaints, and ideas, these programs also help keep employees informed of the progress and the problems of the business.

Attitude surveys "take the organization's temperature." Top management receives unfiltered information about areas of employee satisfaction and dissatisfaction. The "hard data" resulting from a survey can be an early warning system of potential problems. Trends can be noted and comparisons can be made regarding departments, plants, and divisions. Managers can be held responsible for attitudinal results and attitude-improvement programs. One company official considered their annual attitude survey to be a form of worker participation and industrial democracy, saying: "Workers are asked for their opinions and management responds as best it can so as to correct the problems identified."

Other feedback devices and communications programs attempt to involve employees in the problems of the business. They also give employees opportunities to voice complaints and suggestions. Management then has an opportunity to uncover and investigate problems and to respond constructively to employees' concerns. Programs that create a climate in which it is legitimate for employees to request and receive help with personal problems as well as with job-related ones can also be useful.

Formal complaint procedures, though used infrequently in most of these companies, are also important. If their presence encourages supervisors to make every effort to resolve employee problems at the lowest possible level, because they fear top management investigations and/or they believe such inquiries might reflect negatively on them, then the procedures are accomplishing one of their basic purposes. These procedures also permit the employee to get around his or her immediate supervisor, and to have a hearing at a higher level without fear of retaliation.

Careful Selection, Development, and Evaluation of Managers

Although the focus of the study was on the substantive personnel policies and practices with respect to production and maintenance employees, what became clear is that the careful selection, development, and evaluation of managers is also crucial.

An important way in which the organization's objectives with respect to employees are achieved is through the policies that govern the reward-and-punishment system, as they are perceived by line managers—from division general managers to plant managers to first-level supervisors. Line management needs to understand that its responsibility for human resources has high priority, and that effectiveness in dealing with employees is an important measure of managerial competence. With respect to middle- and senior-level managers, two points stand out.

First, as has been indicated, many of the companies studied have no separate management cash bonus plans to reward short-term performance. There may be stock options at some levels and other incentives associated with long-term company success, but in these companies the lack of short-term bonus plans seems to contribute to an absence of pressure, relatively speaking, for short-term results. Pressures for short-term production and profit objectives, so that managers can earn an incentive compensation that is a significant percentage of their annual salary, have the potential to create problems in the area of employee relations. Moreover, unions may arise as a counter to the pressures for the results managers may be bringing to bear on employees. Without cash bonuses based on bottom-line results, it becomes easier for top management to hold line managers accountable for the whole job, including their employee-relations responsibilities, as opposed to just the profit and return on investment goals at times of performance reviews. In addition to the philosophical inconsistency that such separate executive bonus plans would represent in some of these companies that are without such plans, it is probably also true that such plans are, or at least were, not needed in these companies for motivational reasons, because so many of the companies have been rapid-growth companies. With such growth, the combination of good pay and advancement, or the prospects for promotion, were probably sufficient-enough inducements to attract, retain, and motivate effective managers. Furthermore, the administration of individual executive bonus plans could be difficult for the organization under conditions of rapid growth, change, and frequent promotions.

Second, for those companies with separate management or executive incentive compensation bonus plans for key managers, it seems that much attention is given to employee-relations results in the criteria for deciding the amount of the bonus that a manager is to receive. In one entirely-nonunion doctrinaire company in the sample, the vice-president of human resources said that if one of the company's plants became unionized, neither he nor the plant manager would receive any bonus. This indicates the importance that top management attaches to its nonunion status and to its union-avoidance employee-relations programs.

Apart from the subject of bonuses, in many companies managers felt that there would be a stigma attached to their careers if their operation experienced a successful union-organizational drive, or even major personnel problems. In fact, some felt that such events would retard their advancement, or even end their career in the company. Promotion and job security are powerful management motivators, and with these perceptions it is not difficult to understand why line managers and personnel staffs keep their eyes focused on critical employee-relations issues. It also helps explain why personnel departments are listened to, and from whence they get their influence with line managers. This is obviously more true for some jobs than others, and it varies by company, but abilities in the employee-relations domain appear to be very important in managerial selection and promotion decisions in these companies. "People who demonstrate that they can manage well within the ethic of the organization are promoted," said a general manager of one company. "The absence of people problems is an important consideration in a manager's career advancement," said a vice-president at another company. At yet another company, performance is equally appraised in terms of "competence" and "relationships."

At the lower levels of the organization, similar forces appear to be at work with respect to the careers of supervisors. As a consequence, supervisory training and the development of the right attitudes of supervisors toward their people are given much attention. As one vice-president of personnel put it: "We spend a great deal of effort in the training area to assure minimum problems between supervisors and our people in interpreting and applying company policy." It is extremely important that the supervisor recognize and know how to deal with the little problem before it becomes a big problem.

One executive, in an analysis of the company's union organizational drives, reported, with respect to supervision, that:

> *Frequently, problem locations have one or more members of supervision, not necessarily restricted to first line, who are "public enemy number one"! Sometimes the involved individuals do not possess the qualities needed to be effective supervisors. However, many times the individuals have been given inadequate training for their job.*

In discussing both the selection and morale of supervisors in this company, this executive said:

Since supervisors, especially the first and second line, are the most important management representatives with employees, extreme care in the selection and training of this individual is essential. Poor selections are made; thus, individuals who have supervisory aspirations and capabilities which are overlooked or not recognized sometimes become frustrated to the point where frustrations are vented via efforts to organize the plant.

Exempt employees, up to and including plant management, can have morale problems resulting from concerns regarding their treatment or situations. Almost without exception, where we experience poor wage-roll morale, we have fundamental and serious problems within the ranks of supervisors. A supervisor who has an attitude problem cannot reasonably be expected to be effective in dealing with problems of subordinates.

Although it varies by company, considerable effort and time is devoted to supervisory development. Companies have prerequisite courses for the new supervisor and continuing supervisory education. The training programs of many of these companies are innovative and well designed.

In many situations described in these pages, the supervisor seems to have the most difficult role. In some of the companies, the preoccupations of the founder with the welfare and security of the hourly workers, many of whom are on salary, appear to have resulted in the depreciation of the role of the supervisors. The supervisors do not feel the security that they believe is felt by those they manage, in some cases. The employees' view of this may, of course, be different. The employees may not feel as secure as the supervisors think they do. However, if supervisors feel too insecure and experience too much anxiety, this could be detrimental to the long-run health of the organization.

Although the various substantive policies with respect to employment security, promotion, pay, and benefits are important from the employees' point of view, the glue that seems to hold things together is the careful attention and resources that are invested in the selection, development, and evaluation of the managers. This is because it is the managers or the supervisors whom the employees see on a day-to-day basis. At best, the employees have infrequent contact with top management, the personnel department, or a formal communications program. Well-trained supervisors who are sensitive to employees' problems and concerns, and who are working for managers up the line with similar concerns, are essential.

LABOR-RELATIONS CONSIDERATIONS

Although it was not the principal purpose of this study to compare and contrast the personnel policies and practices of the large, nonunion company with those of the large, unionized company, one would be remiss if nothing were said about the differences and similarities. Three points seem particularly noteworthy.

First, this study would seem to put to rest some of the myths and facile conclusions some people in unionized companies hold about nonunion companies. For those who believe that in large, nonunion companies workers are paid and promoted exclusively on the basis of performance and ability, and can be quickly dismissed if they do not perform satisfactorily, these findings will be a disappointment. Similarly, for those who believe that large, nonunion companies stay nonunion by simply paying more, this study suggests that although the pay and benefit policies are important, they are not necessarily the dominant part of the story.

Second, this study indicates the impact that the union movement and the institution of collective bargaining has had on the policies of large, nonunion companies. Especially with the apparent erosion of merit pay and of promotion based exclusively on ability, some of the large, nonunion companies studied have come to resemble the unionized company. The extent to which some of the companies knowingly or unknowingly tend to anticipate or to mirror some characteristics of the unionized environment is evident. The attention to competing with collective-bargaining settlements, as well as to such time-honored concepts as, for instance, seniority and call-in pay, is significant. The rules under which some large, nonunion companies operate encourage managers to act as if the company had a union.

Finally, it is significant that in some cases the companies studied not only duplicate much of union contracts, but also impose upon themselves policies that are more restrictive than those that may emerge or be imposed under union contractual arrangements. This is not only so with pay and benefit issues but, more importantly, with rules by which the plant is operated. Some of the companies deny themselves some of the flexibility that their nonunion status theoretically gives them. In doing so, they impose upon themselves some restrictions that are more severe than those found in the typical union contract. For example, while it is difficult to discharge employees in a unionized environment, managers do fire people in union companies. In spite of their greater liberty, some of the nonunion companies appear to err in the direction of not firing people. Some seem to lean so far over backwards to retain employees that it may hurt the organization.

With respect to promotion, some of the nonunion companies studied have adopted companywide, rather than plantwide or departmentwide, seniority. Moreover, the "promotion of the senior qualified person" is a phrase that does not exist in some union contracts. One would be hard-pressed to find many union contracts offering the employment security, the training and advancement opportunities, the bonuses, or the savings plans offered by so many of the companies in the study. While some executives of the companies studied have certain notions as to why unions are risky (managers cannot promote on the basis of ability, managers cannot fire people, and so forth), many of their companies go above and beyond anything that a union would be able to negotiate. These companies have assumed more obligations than exist in the typical union contract.

Notwithstanding any of these observations regarding similarity to union practices, I am not suggesting that these companies would be better off or even the same with a union. This is because these companies reported that they have better employee attitudes, more flexibility, and higher productivity; thereby they have lower costs, as well as some undefined intangibles that the unionized companies do not. These intangibles relate to morale, trust, confidence, spirit, good faith, an identification with management, and a consequent avoidance of the we–they adversary relationship that can so frequently characterize the union–management relationship. The fact that these companies have voluntarily adopted these policies and practices may also be significant in terms of the high morale and the climates of trust and confidence that they reported. The employees perhaps realize not only that they might not do as well with a union, but also that they might do worse. The approaches of some of these companies would seem to make the idea of unionism unnecessary or irrelevant for many employees. An international union vice-president, talking about one particular leading company in the sample, said: "I just wish we could get for our members what that company gives its employees."

FINAL CONCLUSIONS AND FUTURE CHALLENGES

It is my hope that this exploratory study not only makes a contribution toward a better understanding of personnel management in large, nonunion companies, but that it can also have a constructive influence on the entire field of personnel management in nonunion as well as unionized companies. Although there is a need for in-depth investigation at some companies, for empirical testing of some matters discussed in broad survey form, and for careful documentation and analysis of some of the patterns and practices that are common among many of the companies studied, the initial findings are not without major significance. This is particularly so because effectiveness in human-resources management, only partly as a result of increased government regulation, is increasingly being recognized by top managements as a key ingredient for competitive corporate success.

Future Challenges

If we look to the future, we can ask ourselves what, if anything, might change at the companies studied? For instance, what would it take for these companies to become unionized? More importantly, what are the significant lessons for effective personnel management? While there is no single or easy answer to these questions, this study does suggest some important considerations.

Although the degree of institutionalization varies by company, what some of the companies have achieved appears to be somewhat fragile. During the course of this study I saw some deterioration in the approaches of more than one of the companies in the sample. This deterioration seems to come about because of a change in top management, or because of a change in one or more of the company characteristics or environmental factors.

If one thinks that the companies studied have achieved the success they have not only because they have well performed the functions generally done by a union, but also because they have credibility with employees, then it becomes clear that there are a number of factors that could be responsible for significant changes.

For one thing, a change in the top management or in the top management's philosophy would predictably have a profound impact. For example, if a new president lacked some of the values of his predecessor, and/or failed to support the personnel department when it was appropriate to do so, this could have negative implications for employee relations. Similarly, if a breakdown occurred in certain substantive policies, say in either the feedback mechanisms or in management's generally constructive responses to employee problems, then we would anticipate difficulties. Several "unjust" discharges, for instance, could generate negative employee attitudes.

A prolonged and severe economic downturn within a company or an industry could create employee unrest. For example, if large-scale layoffs became necessary, and if, in the judgment of many employees, the layoffs were poorly handled, then employee interest in a third party (a union) to represent and protect them might quickly develop.

An area of growing concern to the executives of many companies is increasing government regulation, particularly as it affects the area of employee relations. Some companies believe that the government requirements under equal employment opportunity and affirmative action, the Employee Retirement Income Act of 1974, Occupational Safety and Health Act of 1970, and the like, tend to bring all companies to an equal level and to eliminate their opportunities to exercise leadership, to be creative, and to be flexible in personnel policies and practices. "The government becomes the great equalizer," is the way that one vice-president of personnel expressed it. Some feel that government regulations will force them to abandon traditional, successful policies of individual treatment in favor of new policies of equal treatment. Some also think that many minorities may prefer being treated as a group, and may not respond as favorably to management's traditional approaches. It is also felt that some of the "new breed" of employees, who have, for instance, been educated by teachers who were union members, may have attitudes more favorable to unions than those of their parents and grandparents. There can be no doubt that these are very real and genuine challenges to be faced. It will become increasingly difficult to be, and to be perceived as, a leader and an innovator. New kinds of employees may require different approaches.

Possible Responses

The companies studied have a history of leadership, innovation, and adaptation. If top managements stay committed, and the feedback mechanisms continue to be effective, the likelihood is high that creative solutions will be found by line and personnel managers working together cooperatively as a partnership.

Furthermore, what the companies studied have achieved cannot be easily bought or copied. The companies studied generally do an outstanding job. What has been done has taken time and hard work. It stems from the values and goals of top management, and depends on many intangibles, including leadership. Unless there is sincerity and the real essentials, copying the common practices of the companies studied will be to little avail.

If there is one main conclusion that stands out from this field study, it is that gimmicks and crash programs are not the answer. There is no single element of policy that distinguishes the group of companies studied. As one company officer wisely put it, "There is no Rosetta stone, but rather a kaleidoscope of things, and it is the actions as well as the philosophies which are important."

The companies in this sample have long traditions, deep commitments, and high consciousness on the parts of the founders and other members of their top managements of the overriding importance of the human element in an enterprise. Many personnel policies and programs—from job security and promotion from within, to pay and benefits to feedback mechanisms—flow from such commitment. If there is one piece of advice that might be offered, however, it would be for top management to question frequently, and to concern itself with content *and* process issues. This questioning and concern would range from the fairness of a particular discharge or the selection and training of supervisors to the nature of the health-care delivery system available to company employees or the adequacy of the company's retirement-income program. Although top management needs feedback devices, it also needs to remain personally involved in personnel management, and to constantly demonstrate to employees and managers alike its interest in and concern for employees.

Bibliography

ALFRED, THEODORE M., "Checkers or Choice in Manpower Management," *Harvard Business Review* (January–February, 1967).

To Amend the National Labor Relations Act, to Increase Effectiveness of Remedies. Hearings before the Special Subcommittee on Labor of the Committee on Education and Labor, House of Representatives, 90th Congress, First Session, to H. R. 11725. Hearings held in Washington, D.C., August 7, 10, 11, 14, 16, 17, 18, 24, 1967. Published in Washington, D.C.: U.S. Government Printing Office, 1968, p. 41.

ANDREWS, KENNETH R., *The Concept of Corporate Strategy.* Homewood, Ill.: Dow-Jones/Irwin, 1971.

Bankers Trust Company 1977 Study of Employee Savings and Thrift Plans. New York: Bankers Trust Company, 1977.

BAUER, RAYMOND A., "An Agenda for Research and Development on Corporate Responsiveness." In *Soziale Daten Unde Politische Planung,* ed. Meinoff Dierkes. Frankfurt/New York: Campus Publishers, 1975.

Behavioral Sciences Newsletter, book IV, vol. 9 (May 12, 1975).

BRADLEY, ALBERT, "Setting Up a Forecasting Problem," *Annual Convention Series,* American Management Association, No. 41 (March 1926), p. 3. Reprinted in Alfred D. Chandler, *Giant Enterprise: Ford, General Motors, and the Automobile Industry.* (New York: Harcourt, Brace, and World, Inc., 1964.)

BROWER, F. BEATRICE, *Sharing Profits with Employees,* Personnel Policy Study No. 162. New York: National Industrial Conference Board, Inc., 1957.

BRUCE, MICHAEL R., and DAVID W. HUNT, "Communications in Non-Union Companies," Masters thesis, Sloan School of Management, MIT, 1976.

CURTIN, EDWARD R., *White Collar Unionization* (a research report), Studies in Personnel Policy No. 220. New York: The National Industrial Conference Board, Inc., 1970.

DAHL, DAVE R., and PATRICK R. PINTO, "Job Posting: An Industry Survey," *Personnel Journal* (January 1977).

DAWIS, RENE V., and WILLIAM WEITZEL, "Worker Attitudes and Expectations." In *Motivation and Commitment, Volume II of American Society for Personnel Administration Handbook of Personnel and Industrial Relations*, eds. Dale Yoder and Herbert G. Henemann, Jr. Washington, D.C.: Bureau of National Affairs, 1975.

DROUGHT, NEAL E., "Grievances in the Non-Union Situation," *Personnel Journal* (June 1967).

DUNLOP, JOHN T., "The American Industrial Relations System in 1975." In *U.S. Industrial Relations: The Next Twenty Years*, ed. Jack Stieber. East Lansing, Michigan: Michigan State University Press, 1958.

DUNLOP, JOHN T., *Wage Determination Under Trade Unions*. New York: The Macmillan Company, 1944.

EISENMAN, CHARLES W., and CHARLES L. HUGHES, "Have Your People Talked to You Lately?," *The Personnel Administrator* (October 1975).

ELLIOTT, JOHN M., "Promotion from Within: Fact or Farce?," *Personnel*, Vol. 29, No. 3, November 1952, pp. 227–33.

EPSTEIN, R. L., "The Grievance Procedure in the Non-Union Setting: Caveat Employer," *Employee Relations Law Journal* (Summer 1975).

FOULKES, FRED K., "The Expanding Role of the Personnel Function," *Harvard Business Review* (March–April 1975).

GANNON, MARTIN J., "The Proper Use of the Questionnaire Survey," *Business Horizons* (October 1973).

GARDNER, JOHN W., *No Easy Victories*. New York: Harper & Row, Publishers, Inc., 1968.

GETMAN, JULIUS G., STEPHEN B. GOLDBERG, and JEANNE B. HERMAN, *Union Representation Elections: Law and Reality*. New York: Russell Sage Foundation, 1976.

GOODE, ROBERT V., "How to Get Better Results from Attitude Surveys," *Personnel Journal* (March 1973).

Guide to Modern Profit Sharing. Chicago, Ill.: Profit Sharing Council of America, 1973.

HARRIS, T. GEORGE, "Egghead in the Diesel Industry," *Fortune* (October 1957).

HEALY, JAMES J., "The Factor of Ability in Labor Relations," *Arbitration Today, Proceedings of the Eighth Annual Meeting of the National Academy of Arbitrators*. Washington, D.C., 1955.

HERZBERG, EILEEN, "Do Employee Attitude Surveys Pay Off?," *International Management* (August 1973).

HULME, ROBERT D. and RICHARD V. BEVAN, "The Blue-Collar Worker Goes on Salary," *Harvard Business Review* (March–April 1975).

HUGHES, CHARLES L., *Making Unions Unnecessary*. New York: Executive Enterprises Publications Co., Inc., 1976.

KAPONYA, PAUL G., "Salaries for *All* Workers," *Harvard Business Review* (May–June 1962).

KOTHE, CHARLES A., *Individual Freedom in the Non-Union Plant*. New York: National Association of Manufacturers, 1967.

LAWLER, EDWARD E. III, *Pay and Organizational Effectiveness: A Psychological View*. New York: McGraw-Hill Book Company, 1971.

LESTER, RICHARD A., *Company Wage Policies: A Survey of Patterns and Experience*. Princeton, N.J.: Princeton University, Industrial Relations Section, 1948.

LODGE, GEORGE C., and KAREN HENDERSON, "Changing Relationships Among Labor, Business and Government in the United States," a working paper prepared for the Trilateral Commission. July 1, 1977.

McCONKEY, DALE D., "Ability vs. Seniority in Promotion and Layoff," *Personnel* (May–June 1960).

McFARLAND, DALTON E., *Company Officers Assess the Personnel Function*, Research Study No. 79. New York: American Management Association, 1967.

METZGER, BERT L., *Profit Sharing in Perspective in American Medium-Sized and Small Business*. Profit Sharing Research Foundation, Evanston, Ill.: 1964.

METZGER, BERT L., and JEROME A. COLLETTI, *Does Profit Sharing Pay? A Comparative Study of the Financial Performance of Retailers with and without Profit Sharing Programs*. Evanston, Ill.: Profit Sharing Research Foundation, 1971.

MEYER, HERBERT H., "The Pay-for-Performance Dilemma," *Organizational Dynamics* (Winter 1975).

MEYER, MITCHELL, and HARLAND FOX, *Employee Stock Purchase Plans*, Personnel Policy Study No. 206. New York: National Industrial Conference Board, Inc., 1967.

MICHAEL, STEPHEN R., "Due Process in Nonunion Grievance Systems," *Employee Relations Law Journal* (Spring 1978).

MYERS, CHARLES A., and JOHN G. TURNBULL, "Line and Staff in Industrial Relations," *Harvard Business Review* (July–August 1956).

MYERS, CHARLES A., "Management and the Employee." *Social Responsibility and the Business Predicament*, ed. James W. McKie. Washington, D.C.: The Brookings Institution, 1974.

MYERS, M. SCOTT, and VINCENT S. FLOWERS, "A Framework for Measuring Human Assets," *California Management Review* (Summer 1974).

MYERS, M. SCOTT, "How Attitude Surveys Can Help You Manage: A Results-Oriented Plan for Texas Instruments," *Training and Development Journal* (October 1967).

MYERS, M. SCOTT, *Managing With Unions*. Reading, Mass.: Addison-Wesley Publishing Company, Inc., 1978.

Myers, M. Scott, *Managing Without Unions*. Reading, Mass.: Addison-Wesley Publishing Company, Inc., 1976.

NADLER, DAVID and others, "The Ongoing Feedback System: Experimenting with a New Managerial Tool," *Organizational Dynamics* (Spring 1976)

PEACH, DAVID A., and E. ROBERT LIVERNASH, *Grievance Initiation and Resolution: A Study in Basic Steel*. Boston: Harvard University Graduate School of Business Administration, 1974.

PENZER, WILLIAM, "Employee Attitudes Toward Attitude Surveys," *Personnel* (May–June 1973).

The Personnel Function: Changing Objectives and Organization. New York: The National Industrial Conference Board, Inc., 1977.

PIGORS, PAUL, and CHARLES A. MYERS, *Personnel Administration: A Point of View and a Method*. New York: McGraw-Hill Book Company, 1977.

PURCELL, THEODORE V., *Blue-Collar Man: Patterns of Dual Allegiance in Industry*. Cambridge, Mass.: Harvard University Press, 1960.

PURCELL, THEODORE V., *The Worker Speaks His Mind on Company and Union*. Cambridge, Mass.: Harvard University Press, 1954.

RASKIN, A. H., "Arbitration in the Mines Has Created More Disputes," *New York Times*, December 4, 1977.

ROSS, ARTHUR M., *Trade Union Wage Policy*. Berkeley, Calif.: University of California Press, 1948.

SCOTT, WILLIAM G., *The Management of Conflict*. Homewood, Ill.: Richard D. Irwin, Inc. and Dorsey Press, 1965.

SHAW, REID L., "A Grievance Procedure for Nonunionized Employees," *Personnel* (July–August 1959).

SIROTA, DAVID, "Why Managers Don't Use Attitude Survey Results," *Personnel* (January–February 1970).

SIROTA, DAVID, and ALAN D. WOLFSON, "Pragmatic Approach to People Problems," *Harvard Business Review* (January–February 1973).

SLICHTER, SUMNER H., JAMES J. HEALY, and E. ROBERT LIVERNASH, *The Impact of Collective Bargaining on Management*. Washington, D.C.: The Brookings Institution, 1960.

SPATES, THOMAS G., *Human Values Where People Work*. New York: Harper & Row, Publishers, Inc., 1960.

TAGUIRI, RENATO, and GEORGE H. LITWIN, *Organizational Climate: Explorations of a Concept*. Boston: Harvard University Graduate School of Business, Division of Research, 1968.

THOMPSON, DUANE E., and RICHARD P. BORGLUM, "A Case Study of Employee Attitudes and Labor Unrest," *Industrial and Labor Relations Review* (October 1973).

VOUGH, CLAIR F., and BERNARD ASBELL, *Tapping the Human Resource: A Strategy for Productivity*. New York: AMACOM, 1975.

YENNEY, SHARON L., "In Defense of the Grievance Procedure in a Nonunion Setting," *Employee Relations Law Journal* (Spring 1977).

Index